Contents

III. Ensuring Equity and Social Mobility

Cuban Economic and Social Development

Policy Reforms and Challenges in the 21st Century

Edited by Jorge I. Domínguez, Omar Everleny Pérez Villanueva,
Mayra Espina Prieto, and Lorena Barbería

Published by Harvard University David Rockefeller Center for Latin
American Studies

Distributed by Harvard University Press
Cambridge, Massachusetts
London, England
2012

Library of Congress Cataloging-in-Publication Data

Cuban economic and social development : policy reforms and challenges in the
  21st century / edited by Jorge I. Domínguez ... [et al.].

      p. ; cm. — (The David Rockefeller Center series on Latin American studies,
Harvard University)

  Includes bibliographical references.
  ISBN: 978-0-674-06243-6

  1. Cuba—Economic conditions—21st century. 2. Cuba—Social conditions—
21st century. 3. Cuba—Politics and government—21st century. I. Domínguez,
Jorge I., 1945– II. Series: David Rockefeller Center series on Latin American
studies, Harvard University.

HC152.5 .C82 2012
330.97291

Introduction

On the Brink of Change: Cuba's Economy and Society at the Start of the 2010s

Jorge I. Domínguez

Cuba may be on the brink of significant economic change, ready to make much more extensive use of market mechanisms, yet it may also be on the brink of significant economic trouble. The bulleted summary below highlights the worrisome story of Cuba's recent economic history. General volatility, stagnation, and bankruptcy afflict key sectors of its economy. A structural transformation has already begun toward an economy based on service exports. What will be the direction of Cuba's economic and social policy future? In this work, the authors diagnose the country's economic problems, suggest valuable approaches toward better outcomes, and also analyze the social challenges that are already part of its reality.

A Communist Party leadership contemplates change, in the face of:

- Widened inequalities between provinces and urban and rural areas;
- Widespread experience of downward social mobility;
- Volatility in economic growth rates;
- An economy propelled by the export of services;
- Stagnant agriculture and dependence on food imports;
- A bankrupt sugar industry; and
- Technologically obsolete manufacturing.

The Communist Party of Cuba held its Sixth Party Congress in April 2011 and limited its agenda to a discussion of economic topics and the selection of a new leadership. Although other issues in Cuban public life deserved attention, President Raúl Castro and his closest colleagues determined that the serious economic challenges required a focused and undivided attention at the Party Congress. The approval of the Communist Party's new economic program at the Congress also had political significance. It was an opportunity for the generation of the party's founding leaders, Fidel (born

1926) and Raúl Castro (born 1931), to assent publicly to a new path for the future of the Cuban economy—perhaps their last strategic decision after over a half century of governing Cuba. The Congress selected the new membership of the Communist Party's Central Committee and, in turn, the party's Political Bureau, and it convened a Communist Party Conference for January 2012 to address other issues, specifically the party's internal life.

This book is a successor to one published in 2004 by Harvard University's David Rockefeller Center for Latin American Studies and Harvard University Press. The introduction to that book featured an optimistic opening tone because it was written after a period of significant economic changes in Cuba that had rescued its economy from near collapse in the early 1990s and set it on a course for further change. The "bullet points" above sound a dour tone. Why is there such a difference? Alas, just as that book was published in 2004, Cuba's leaders shifted policies in response to an "external shock."

This "shock" was the willingness of Venezuela's President Hugo Chávez to supply petroleum to Cuba under a barter agreement whereby Cuba received oil products well below prevailing world market prices in exchange for Cuban health care and other services. Because Cuba's services were provided formally as expressions of "solidarity," they are not well represented in the export accounts, but a measure of the shock is evident in Cuba's account of imports from Venezuela, listed in Table 1. Cuba's imports from Venezuela (petroleum products, basically) doubled between 2004 and 2006 and doubled again between 2006 and 2008.

Table 1. Cuba's Imports from Venezuela

	2004	2005	2006	2007	2008	2009
Value, million pesos	1143	1864	2232	2243	4473	2605
Percentages of total imports	20	25	24	22	31	29

Source: Computed from Oficina Nacional de Estadísticas, *Anuario estadístico de Cuba* (Havana: 2010), Table 8.6.

The pressure on the Cuban government, felt acutely in the 1990s and early 2000s, to enact and implement significant economic policy changes, withered away. The government could seemingly afford to misallocate resources, subsidize bankrupt enterprises, and turn its back on efficiency and markets. Even well-recognized problems, unrelated to the choice of an economic model, remained unaddressed: for example, Cuba's population was aging rapidly, Cuba's pension law provided for women to retire at 55 and men at 60, and as a result the fiscal burden on the state to pay for pensions had become unsustainable, but no reform of the pension law was undertaken during the "Venezuelan bonanza" years. Venezuela's money freed Cuban leaders from having to think about changes that should have been adopted long ago. The feast ended when the worldwide financial crisis reduced Venezuelan resources sharply. In 2009, Cuba received a second but now adverse external shock: external resources seemingly vanished.

The external shock of 2009 focused Cuba's leadership on the need to enact changes. The crisis of 2009–2010 combined two distinct aspects, namely, the accumulated legacies of a malfunctioning economy whose structural problems had gone unaddressed for the bulk of the decade, along with a sharp and painful downswing—the world economy's great recession. One response was President Raúl Castro's decision to convene the Party Congress—the first since 1997.

The Diagnosis of the Cuban Economy's Problems

This book describes the severe challenges that the Cuban economy faces. During the twenty-first century's first decade, there was significant volatility in Cuba's economic growth rates and, during the decade's second half, there was a marked deceleration of economic growth rates. In fact, growth rates were low during most of the decade, except for a peak at mid-decade, which was assisted by a boom in service exports to Venezuela in barter exchange for Venezuelan petroleum sold below prevailing world market prices. By the end of the decade, the production of services accounted for three-quarters of gross domestic product.

More generally, in the 1990s Cuba's modest but important economic policy changes had attracted interest by investors from Canada, Spain, and other countries. Yet, in the 2000s, Cuba engaged insufficiently with various international partners to help it propel its economy; as a consequence, the number of international joint ventures fell steadily and dramatically following 2002 and for the balance of the decade.

On the eve of Raúl Castro's presidency, Cuba's economy suffered already from severe structural flaws. In 2008–2010, to be sure, the impact of the worldwide great recession also affected Cuba adversely, adding a destructive exogenous shock to a previously existing structural problem (see Chapters 1 and 7, by Omar Everleny Pérez Villanueva). Raúl Castro thus inherited a bad economy at a bad time.

The internal structure and behavior of the Cuban economy had also become severely distorted, to a large extent because of the Cuban government's policy of monetary duality. Two currencies circulate simultaneously, the *peso* and the *peso convertible* known commonly by its acronym CUC.

Some payments are made in pesos and others are in CUCs. The CUC is loosely based on the U.S. dollar; in recent times, the exchange rate between Cuba's two currencies has been approximately 24 pesos for 1 CUC. The Central Bank's commitment to retain fixed exchange rates for both Cuban currencies was a contributor to the Cuban banking crisis of 2009; Cuban banks froze accounts and stopped payments for many months.

More generally, monetary duality distorts all economic measurements, making it very difficult to calculate the economic performance or profitability of enterprises as well as Cuba's gross domestic product. Some enterprises appear more profitable than they really are, while others appear to be much less profitable than accurate measurement would show. Exporters are penalized through this system, and imports become easier, thereby contributing to Cuba's international trade deficit. State subsidies are triggered for enterprises that would not need them if there were accurate measurements. The economic divide between economic sectors in these two currencies also segments relations between Cuban enterprises—peso-based enterprises are separated from CUC-based enterprises as if they existed on different planets. And, because some activities have always remained in pesos, they suffer from underinvestment (see Chapters 2 and 5, by Pavel Vidal Alejandro).

No sector of Cuba's economy has been worse hit than agriculture. Agricultural production and agricultural exports fell significantly during the 1990s. While nearly all sectors of agriculture performed poorly during those years, none collapsed more dramatically than the sugar sector, which went *de facto* bankrupt at the start of the first decade of the twenty-first century. In the late 1980s, Cuba had produced over 8 million metric tons of milled sugar; by the start of the 2010s, annual production barely exceeded one million metric tons. Nearly three-quarters of Cuba's sugar mills have been shuttered. The collapse of the sugar sector was an outcome of seriously misguided Cuban government policies, in particular the misallocation of resources in the context of monetary duality.

Instead of reprogramming the old sugar lands to new purposes, the number of hectares of land that remained idle tripled from the start of the 1990s to the start of policy changes in 2007 under Raúl Castro's presidency. Productivity in agriculture remained poor throughout. During the twenty-first century's first decade, agricultural production recovered only in those products for which high prices were paid in free agricultural markets. As a result, Cuba became significantly dependent on goods imports to meet the population's nutritional requirements.

President Raúl Castro's government recognized several of these adverse trends and, starting in 2007, began to enact a number of modest changes in economic policies and organization. Prices paid to agricultural producers increased; they have begun to respond positively. Moreover, a key finding from ongoing research over many years has been that non-state farms are much more likely to make more effective use of the land available to them than do state farms. In order to stop and reverse the decline in agricultural production, the Raúl Castro government began to distribute state farm lands to agricultural producers who may work on these lands but not own them—they just had the right to use the land; many of these lands had been idle and thus the new tillers of the soil generated some improvements. But other post-2007 policy changes and bureaucratic reorganizations did not yield positive results (see Chapters 3 and 4 by Armando Nova González and Chapter 6, by Anicia García).

Several lessons may be drawn from this diagnosis:

- Good economic relations with Venezuela may be helpful but they also generated considerable volatility and created the illusion that economic policy changes could be postponed indefinitely. The Venezuelan state lacks competence; its most effective social policy has been the importation of Cuban health care and other service-sector workers. Economic relations with a less competent state vulnerable to dramatic volatility are not a reliable basis on which to organize the Cuban economy or set its government's longer-term economic strategy.
- The Cuban government's monetary duality policies seriously impair its ability to make effective economic decisions or allocate economic resources.
- Cuban agricultural production and productivity are most likely to increase if the government frees individual producers and cooperatives to access unfettered agricultural markets, set prices, and benefit from decision-making rights inherent in ownership (not just the rights to use the land, or *usufructo*).

A Different Path for Cuba's Economy: Some Reflections

Cuba's future economic strategy is likely to rest on a key premise, namely, whether it can harness the talents and skills of its people to advance the general welfare. Cuba's open economy has long been reliant on commodity exports, sugar above all. In the 1990s, Cuba re-opened its borders to welcome international tourists, but its principal tourism sector product is also a commodity—"beach tourism" accessible through inexpensive packages at enclave sites. At the same time, Cuba had invested spectacularly and successfully in education, but the economic returns on its half-century of investment in such human capital have been disappointing. Cuba now faces a key challenge of how to manage an open economy while mindful of its principal comparative advantage: its people's skills. Will the Cuban government permit and foster economic behavior to produce higher value-added products and services so the country may become at long last the Taiwan of the Caribbean—by transforming a small-island sugar economy in the tropics, next to a hostile neighbor, governed by a single party, home to a large military establishment, a nation that provides universal health care and mobilizes education at home and its diaspora abroad, to become one of the fastest-growing economies ever?

"Export substitution"—in Pedro Monreal González's apt formulation—accords a leading role to the state in designing an economic development strategy to move up a production chain, finding opportunities for successful international market specialization that would not simply depend on shifting from one low-priced commodity to another. The key to export substitution is not diversification among commodities that have equally poor developmental growth prospects but, rather, to add value through knowledge, skill, and technology—at last reaping the harvest of a half-century of investment in secondary and higher education.

Opportunities for change may exist as well to revive Cuba's agriculture. The sugar industry's bankruptcy could be reversed by emphasizing that its principal product is sugar cane, not merely sugar, thus looking to produce alternative sources of energy (more efficient than maize, for example), beverages including but not limited to rum, cardboard and paper, and other products, which Cuba has produced in times past even well before 1959. More importantly, in Chapter 6 Anicia García shows how agricultural production and exports could increase significantly if there were a shift toward a different mix of products than has hitherto characterized Cuban agriculture, with greater attention to harvest advances in technology and gains in human capital. Such a shift would make great sense independent of any change in future U.S.-Cuban relations.

These rosy futures are unlikely to arrive unless Cuba reestablishes macroeconomic equilibrium. The shift away from monetary duality is one component of this larger macroeconomic policy objective, but, in the near to medium term, it has become extremely difficult to accomplish in a low-growth economic environment and with rising inflationary pressures from imports and from domestic economic changes that the Cuban government has long charmingly called price "liberation." Yet, price changes, in turn, create incentives for producers to improve agricultural output, quality, and productivity and to foster high-quality work from the labor force. The Cuban government has a stake as well in restoring the international credibility of the Cuban banking system, which was a victim of the 2009 decision to stop payments to international creditors and trade partners. Such credibility would be enhanced if the Cuban Central Bank were authorized to allow the value of the CUC to vary or "float" (within boundaries set by the Central Bank) responding to market conditions, while still sustaining the value of the simple peso to protect the many Cubans whose income is predominantly in the latter (see Chapter 5 by Pavel Vidal Alejandro). The CUC had been conceived from the start as Cuba's monetary and exchange-rate policy response to engagement in international markets; the government and the central bank could restore such practices.

Cuba's best opportunity for an economic breakthrough under the current political regime would improve greatly if it were to learn from its East Asian peers—China and perhaps especially Vietnam. Vietnam fought a long and bitter war with the United States and it was subject to numerous U.S. sanctions, an experience incomparably worse than that of U.S.-Cuban relations. Vietnam has its own very large diaspora, which long harbored extreme animosity to the Communist Party and the political regime, but which in due course became one of the engines to finance Vietnam's economic growth. Both China and Vietnam transformed their economies. Each retained a fundamental role for the state's strategic indicative planning, providing and managing incentives and setting priorities, but market prices came to govern relations among enterprises and with individuals (see Chapter 7 by Omar Everleny Pérez Villanueva).

In any event, in both China and Vietnam agricultural reactivation played a key role in generating economic growth. Subsidized state enterprises were dismantled—a process that took a number of years—through closings, shifts to cooperatives or to joint ventures, or privatization. The law authorized various forms of property, including individual private property, as appropriate instruments for economic organization and production. International investment was welcome on a massive scale. Government institutions were reorganized, and the bases of the financial system changed. World Bank financing of enterprises was especially significant.

These prescriptions offer several conclusions:

- Cuba should substitute "brain" for "beach and brawn" exports. Cuba should harvest a half century of investment in human capital to emphasize high value-added economic activities in an open economy. Incentives policies must also be changed accordingly.

- Cuba retains a comparative advantage in aspects of agricultural production, and it should apply the skills of its people to new forms of management and applied technologies in agriculture.

- Cuba must regain macroeconomic equilibrium, restore the credibility of its banking system, and permit the bounded float of the convertible-currency peso.

- Cuba must learn from its more successful peers, Vietnam and China, to reinvent its economic model, confidently and boldly.

Social Challenges

Difficult as Cuba's economic challenges have become, the nation's social challenges are just as worrisome. The economic collapse of the 1990s, the limited Cuban market opening of the twenty years that followed the end of the relationship with the Soviet Union, and the expected and unexpected impact of government policies led to significant social mobility in Cuba. "Social mobility" implies that some individuals have been able to improve their life's circumstances appreciably, while for others conditions deteriorated markedly from what they had experienced in the 1980s. In general, state employment, employment in manufacturing and agriculture, and blue-collar jobs all declined. Non-state employment, employment in the service sector, and white-collar jobs all increased. Gender, race, and income gaps widened; men, whites, and those with access to CUCs via work in the tourism sector, international joint ventures, or with relatives who provide remittances did better. Because upward mobility was more marked in the private sector and the private sector remained small through the century's first decade, the results since the 1990s imply that downward social mobility was more prevalent. As inequality widened, perception of the gap became socially pervasive and problematic because most Cubans continued to value equality as a worthwhile societal objective. They also valued education greatly and would at times presume that an educated person's standing in society was higher notwithstanding lower CUC income (see Chapter 8 by Mayra Espina Prieto and Viviana Togores González).

In this new Cuba, the social structure has already been transformed. The state has become a less reliable agent to address people's microcircumstances. Households now shape social mobility pathways and acquire new economic significance. Cuba's social policy has not been well prepared to address these changes. It has provided the same subsidies to the well- and the poorly educated, the same rationing card for food and basic necessities to those with high and low income, and it has not targeted the needs of the poorest as the special object of national social policies because it continued to operate on the supposition that the condition of all Cubans was the same. Yet, the circumstances of ordinary Cubans render them unequal already, to a much greater extent than had been the case from the 1960s to the 1980s, when the Soviet Union paid for the cost of many Cuban social policies. Effective social policy in contemporary Cuba must target those who need support. Such a policy would be more effective in serving the poorest, and Cuba cannot now afford to subsidize those who are well-off.

Cuba's social challenges are evident as well across its territory. Today, as throughout most of its history, Cuba's eastern provinces show a much lower level of performance on the United Nations human development index and associated indicators. Cuba's territorial differences in social circumstances had narrowed appreciably starting in the 1960s, but they widened again since the crisis and associated changes begun in the 1990s. These widened inequities are evident between provinces and at times between municipalities in the same provinces. In the meantime, Cuba has become an overwhelmingly urban country across the length of its territory, but rural Cuba remains socially disadvantaged in important respects.

A related spatial dimension of social mobility discrepancies in contemporary Cuba is evident with regard to severe housing problems. During the closing decades of the twentieth century, Cuba succeeded impressively in providing potable water and access to the electric power grid to most housing units. Since 1990, the reliability of electric power supply across the country became uncertain, however. Yet, the most enduring and intractable problem has been the poor quality of housing as well as the deterioration that housing units suffered from the lack of maintenance. The accumulated housing deficit worsened during the 1990s and 2000s because both new construction projects and construction repairs declined. The quality of housing, too, became a new marker of social class differences and provided for spatial segmentation by social class (see Chapter 9, by Lucy Martín and Lilia Núñez).

The key findings are:

- Upward and especially downward social mobility characterized Cuba's experience since 1990 and reshaped the nation's social stratification.
- Women, darker-skinned Cubans, older people, those still in rural areas, and the eastern provinces have experienced the worst outcomes.
- Housing conditions have been and remain deplorable for the median Cuban.
- As a result, inequalities between individuals have increased; territorial inequalities have widened as well.

- Yet, Cubans continue to value equality and honor and believe in the power of education.

"Updating" the Cuban Government's Economic Policies

In September 2010, the Cuban Communist Party unveiled new economic proposals for discussion at the April 2011 Sixth Party Congress.[1] This new framework for economic policy is officially called an "updating" of the existing model, not a "reform" or a "transition." It calls for extensive opening to, and reliance on, "non-state" economic activities, but it shies away from employing the expression "private firms." It celebrates the possibility that cooperatives would take the lead in economic reactivation and that decentralization of operations and other activities to the local level would improve matters. Yet, cooperatives still operate under burdensome regulatory procedures and the mechanisms for decentralization remain opaque. The new economic program proposes to shut down economic enterprises that require government subsidies to survive. It widens the options for "self-employment," including the hiring of non-relatives, but stops short of embracing a model of "small and medium private enterprises." It commits the state to uphold and defend intellectual property rights in the economic realm. It is at times detailed enough even to recommend increased exports of shrimp and lobster, yet it remains eerily silent about the role of the U.S. government regarding the past or future of the Cuban economy.

The new economic program embraces many market principles, yet it also affirms the principled value of centrally set prices for many products and services. It does not fly the flag of equality; instead, it challenges citizens to recognize that "egalitarianism" is unsocialist and an impediment to better economic performance. It vows to eliminate the rationing card, dismiss government employees whose jobs are examples of featherbedding, and even suspend subsidies to workers' cafeterias. Economic rewards should go to each person according to the quality and quantity of the individual work effort.

In some important respects, Cuba's policy ambience at the time of the VI Party Congress was auspicious for the prospects of change. Market openings were authorized in the early 1990s, but at the time President Fidel Castro made it clear that he detested authorizing the changes that he felt compelled to authorize. In the past, Cuban officials have been dismissed under allegations of ineptitude or corruption, as during the so-called Rectification campaign of the mid-1980s, but such dismissals were part of a process of political re-centralization and market aversion. In the run up to the VI Party Congress, President Raúl Castro and his leadership team made it clear that they would dismiss the corrupt and the inept and also those who stood in the way of a market opening. This is the first time in a half-century when Cuba's top leadership seems ready to choose a market-related "updating" of its economic model.

There were other reasons to think that Cuba's leadership in 2011 meant to embark on this course. Raúl Castro's government has been decisive in several areas of economic and social policy. Consider some examples:

- Since becoming Cuba's president, Raúl Castro has replaced one by one, but systematically, nearly all members of the Council of Ministers inherited from his brother as well as many other key officials in party and government posts across the country.

- In late 2006, he stopped the mobilizational campaigns called the "Battle of Ideas," which had provided improvised and poorly thought-out responses to practical problems since 1999, and in 2008 he dismantled the ministerial organization responsible for such wasteful and ineffective campaigns.

- In December 2008, Cuba's National Assembly changed the pension law, raising the age of retirement by five years for men and women— a decision as difficult to enact there as any government faces across the world.

- The Raúl Castro government reversed a long-standing policy that had compelled secondary school students to enroll in boarding schools, arguing that it would save on resources. Cuba's youngsters may now live at home while attending secondary school.

- No "sacred cows" are protected if performance is unacceptable. Cuba is rightly proud of its health care system, but not everything works flawlessly. In 2011, Cuba's courts imposed severe sentences on the top management of the national psychiatric hospital for gross mismanagement and criminal behavior.[2]

And yet, not all signs pointed in the direction of useful change. Consider two examples of serious limitations in the process of economic updating. First, prospects for self-employment as a means to create non-state activities are quite limited. The Cuban government could have deregulated a wide domain of economic activities, except for some reserved areas, but that is not how it chose to proceed. Instead, it authorized only 178 self-employment activities, which it named explicitly. For example, it authorized self-employment for a "dance couple, Benny Moré style," and for the musical group "Los Mambises." In so authorizing, it made it clear that any other musical group had to request a distinct exception. Similarly, the government authorized self-employment for music and art teachers and for teachers of typing, short-hand, and languages. In so doing, it made it clear that other forms of non-state teaching remained prohibited. Likewise it authorized self-employment for tutors to go over school work, but did not allow it for teachers who were employed in schools.[3] This approach to deregulation greatly limited the scope for new non-state activities. It reinforced the long-evident perspective that the government would remain a micromanager even as it moved toward less direct state control of economic activity.

Second, the government's new approach to tax policy undermines its concurrent policy objective of job creation. At the December 2010 National Assembly convoked to explain the new economic program and legislative and regulatory changes already under way, Finance Minister Lina Pedraza explained that tax policy would be designed to "discourage as much as possible the hiring of workers."[4] The larger the *number* of workers employed in the non-state sector (a self-employed person may hire non-relatives), the higher the tax *rate*. Instead, a tax could have been levied on corporate profits, or on the income of the self-employed license holder; such a tax could have been progressive—the higher the profits or income, the higher the tax rate. The Cuban government's chosen approach to tax policy differed, however: the higher the number of workers employed (independent of revenues, income, or profits), the higher the tax rate, allegedly to discourage concentration of wealth. Yet, given that weeks earlier the government had announced its intention to dismiss 500,000 state employees over a six-month period, a tax policy that would punish job creation is bizarre.

Perhaps more worrisome is the insufficient attention afforded to social issues and social policies in the party's new program, which is also why in this introduction I have taken the liberty to call it just the "new economic program." The *Lineamientos*' full title, of course, refers equally to *la política económica y social*. Yet, the entire document allocates less than ten percent of its space to social policy, including under that rubric such important topics as education, health care, sports, culture, social security, and salaries and jobs. Belt-tightening and massive dismissals of state sector employees dominate these three pages. There is a remarkable absence of innovative thinking about the possible redesign of social policy. The word "poverty" does not appear in the document. Cuban leaders should not defer further a reconsideration of these issues.

The VI Party Congress

The Party Congress, not surprisingly, approved the *Lineamientos* as amended prior and during the Congress.[5] The Congress delegates, however, took their tasks seriously and successfully proposed an array of changes to the economic program, most of which were quite specific and did not change the thrust of the main policy shift.

First Party Secretary Raúl Castro delivered two long speeches at the Party Congress; one was his main report and the other was his concluding remarks.[6] In them, he highlighted many of the challenges that his government faces. In his main report, he felt compelled to give a spirited defense of the proposal for the gradual elimination of the rationing card, which for nearly a half century has sought to guarantee food and other items, at equally "laughably low prices" to the poor as to the well-off. He noted that this proposal had been the object of most debate prior to the Party Congress. He asserted that the state could not afford these subsidies, and that they provided opportunities for corruption and disincentives to work—all of which rendered them "noxious." He had to defend this proposal so strongly because the policy retained many supporters. His remarks were sufficiently emphatic that the Party Congress's third commission, to which the proposal was referred, gave it only perfunctory attention, assuming it will pass.[7]

Raúl Castro's main report refers at various times to the "bureaucratic obstacles" that some of the reforms authorized prior to the Party Congress had been facing. He lamented as well the "recent lack of understanding" that met attempts to change how some basic services were provided. In his closing remarks to the Party Congress, he noted that "thousands and thousands of hectares of agricultural land" remained idle notwithstanding Decree-Law 259, enacted in 2008, which had been supposed to unleash a wave of cultivators who would have use-rights to work such land. Bureaucratic slowdowns and at times blockage had undermined the effects of that Decree-Law. President Castro was accurate in calling attention to these various challenges, at least some of which are not mere obstacles or deficiencies but instances of bureaucratic insubordination from officials who resist change.

Notwithstanding these obstacles, his government persevered in enacting policy changes. He sought the endorsement of the Party Congress not just for the new economic policy framework but also for more specific initiatives, including changing Decree-Law 259 to make it easier to work agricultural land, authorizing the private sales of homes and cars, and instructing Cuba's state banks to provide loans to the newly self-employed and the population at large.

Similarly, although the agenda of the Party Congress was formally limited to economic topics, Raúl Castro's main report addressed the need to improve the demographic representativeness of party and state institutions in terms of race, gender, and age. The lag in facing up to this question, he said in his main report, was truly "shameful." The Party Conference called for January 2012 was tasked with discussing these matters.

In the same spirit of *de facto* widening the Party Congress agenda, toward the end of his main report Raúl Castro argued that religious faith and patriotism were not only mutually compatible but also rooted in "the very foundations of the nation." He referred to his decision in 2010 to free a number of those whom he called the "counterrevolutionary prisoners" and others called "political prisoners." He noted accurately that he made the decision but also that he had chosen to do so do "within the framework of a dialogue based on mutual respected, loyalty and transparency" with leading Roman Catholic bishops, naming Jaime Ortega and Dionisio García, respectively the Cardinal Archbishop of Havana and the President of the Bishops' Conference.

Raúl Castro's most salient non-economic political comment at the Party Congress came early in his main report. He described in some detail how many meetings there had been in advance of the Party Congress to discuss the new economic program, how many people had participated in them, how many suggestions had been made, which topics received the greatest attention, and how many specific items had been changed. In the midst of this recitation, he said, "there was no unanimity . . . and that was exactly what we needed, if we really wanted a serious and democratic consultation with the people." It may have been the first official praise of the absence of unanimity in a half-century of Cuban politics.

Alas, change is difficult even for Raúl Castro himself. Consider one of his better initiatives: the Communist Party of Cuba should not be in charge of administration or the direct implementation of government policy. Administration and implementation are the responsibility of government officials. The confusion in the roles of party and government has had the effect of preventing government officials from making decisions, implementing those decisions, and being held responsible for them.

Yet, one of Raúl Castro's equally praiseworthy instincts gets in the way of eradicating the confusion. He is building a team and meets with team members to communicate his ideas and listen to theirs. Thus every week he holds a joint meeting with the executive committee of the Party's Political Bureau and the executive committee of the Council of Ministers. Every month he meets with the Council of Ministers and, depending on the topic, invites the Party's Political Bureau and Secretariat, the Council of State, or others. The effect of holding such joint meetings gives confusing signals: there is no difference between party, government, or state institutions.

A second example of the difficulty of embracing change is the reluctance to "update" the generational composition of the party's leadership to match the "updating" of the party's economic program. At the end of the 1997 Fifth Party Congress, the median age of the 24 members of the Political Bureau was 54. At the end of the 2011 Sixth Party Congress, the median age of the 15 members of the Political Bureau was 70. The Political Bureau shrank its membership, disproportionately dismissing younger members, and adding only three new members. Raúl Castro himself turned 80 years old on 1 June 2011; his designated successor in both state and party functions, José Ramón Machado, is approximately a year older.

There are many reasons why a generational renewal of the leadership would be warranted, but in the context of this book consider just one: economic actors, be they Cubans contemplating the prospects of starting a small business under the legal guise of "self-employment" or foreign investors who may partner with a Cuban state enterprise in a joint venture, must make educated guesses about the likely future. Yet, how can one formulate rational economic expectations when the top leadership is in the last chapter of their lives? The inability of the Party Congress to couple generational updating with economic policy updating shortens the time horizons and necessarily increases uncertainty.

Conclusions

The chapters of this book were researched and written before the Cuban government announced its new economic program in the fall 2010. The inferences that I draw from those chapters to assess Cuba's circumstances on the eve of the Communist Party Congress and the responses of the government and the party to the nation's challenges are, therefore, mine alone, and all mistakes in interpretation are also mine alone. The great value of these chapters is that they describe, analyze, and frame effectively the key issues that face Cuba's economy and society while presenting a wealth of empirical research. The book invites readers to draw their own conclusions.

The book's authors describe challenges that Cuba's economy and society face that require economic and social policy responses well beyond what Cuban leaders have proposed and the Party Congress discussed and approved. Academic work has intellectual and practical value precisely because it lifts the time and scale horizons to think about problems and their possible solutions, thereby inviting all readers of this work to think beyond the specific issues of the day.

It is good news that the general direction of the economic policy proposals of the Cuban leadership, ratified by the Party Congress, draws its sustenance from evidence-based research, much of which is reflected in the chapters of this book that address economic topics. Let me emphasize that this is good news in two ways: first because the economic policy changes respond to evidence-based research, and second because these changes proceed in the direction that the research recommends.

There is less good news with regard to issues of social mobility, poverty, housing, territorial equity, and associated societal concerns. The research presented in the pertinent chapters of this book enables me to suggest the hypothesis that, under foreseeable circumstances, the proposed new policies will generate at first more downward than upward social mobility. This is likely for two different reasons. The first is the relative inattention of the new program to the issues raised in those chapters of this book. The second may be called the early results of the policy change as it bears on these societal issues.

Consider just one topic: jobs. The research reported in this book shows that upward mobility in Cuba over the past twenty years has sprung mainly from jobs in the non-state sectors. Non-state job creation should thus be a high priority. Raúl Castro's main report to the Party Congress indicated that somewhat over 200,000 people had applied for self-employment between October 2010 and April 2011. Good news, yet that was also the same time period for the proposed dismissal of 500,000 state workers, cited earlier in this chapter. In a country with a population of just over 11.2 million people in 2010,[8] this is a big change. (Many of the new licensed self-employed were probably simply legalizing their previous small businesses in the illegal or "black" market, thereby adding fewer net jobs). In late February 2011, on the eve of the Party Congress, Raúl Castro announced that the dismissals policy would proceed more slowly.[9]

The tension between the need for non-state job creation and the government's new proposed tax policies, addressed earlier in this introduction, was also the source of an important debate at one of the Party Congress's five commissions, which the Cuban press reported. Many delegates criticized the tax that requires the self-employed to pay the same set amount of money every month independent of their profits, no matter in which city they work. Congress delegates noted that profits were higher in Havana than elsewhere. Few people outside Havana had registered for self-employment because these excise taxes were too high. Thus too few non-state jobs were being created outside Havana, deepening the territorial inequalities that the research in this book also highlights.

Cuba needs non-state jobs now and, our research tells us, such jobs would spur upward social mobility. Tax policies could be designed to raise revenues without providing disincentives to job creation. Evidence-based research on societal topics, not just on economic topics, would improve the government's policies and serve Cubans more effectively.

The Cuban government will be compelled to update its updating of economic and social policies and, on this score, the news is good. The government engaged in intensive internal debate over the preparation of the *Lineamientos*, preparing two different economic forecasts, issuing five different versions of the instructions to be considered by eleven committees that worked on specific items in the economic program, and then generating four different versions of the new program itself.[10] Prior to and during the Party Congress, moreover, many additional specific changes were made to the new economic program. A government and Communist Party that are becoming accustomed to debate, disagreement, policy modification and reconsideration would be more likely to correct mistakes that emerge in the initial stages of updating.

Cuba is on the brink of change. Significant albeit still modest economic policy reforms are under way. Generational leadership replacement will occur in due course. Over the past two decades, the impact of intended and unintended changes on Cuba's society has already been dramatic, and there is every reason to expect that the consequences of upcoming changes, even if they remain modest in intention, will also be substantial. The collective hope of all the authors of this book is to encourage readers, and in particular Cubans everywhere, to think analytically, rely on evidence, and participate in discussions with others that expect, not unanimity, but respect and engagement with ideas and disagreements that will help open the paths of the future and shed light on the questions that will arise along the way.

In the torrent of change-oriented words that Cuban leaders have unleashed since late 2010, none is more encouraging than President Raúl Castro short comment to the December 2010 National Assembly in the midst of its formal plenary, "Why do we have to butt in on people's lives?" *Granma* recorded that the Assembly burst into applause—the only such interruption during the entire quite long meeting. May Cubans embrace this libertarian spirit. May it open the gateway to a better future.

Endnotes

1. VI Congreso del Partido Comunista de Cuba, *Proyecto de lineamientos de la política económica y social* (Havana, 2011).
2. *Granma*, 24 January 2011.
3. Ministerio de Justicia, *Gaceta oficial de la República de Cuba* 108/12 (8 October 2010), 119–127.
4. *Granma*, 16 December 2011.

5. *Granma*, 19 April 2011.
6. For the main report, *Granma*, 18 April 2011; for the concluding remarks, *Granma*, 20 April 2011.
7. *Granma*, 18 April 2011.
8. *Granma*, 29 April 2011.
9. *Granma*, 1 March 2011.
10. *Granma*, December 17, 2011.

PART

I

Igniting Domestic Economic Growth

1

The Cuban Economy:
An Evaluation and Proposals
for Necessary Policy Changes

Omar Everleny Pérez Villanueva

Politicians, social scientists, and general readers have noted in Cuban and international academic forums and periodicals that the well-being enjoyed by the Cuban people in the 1980s has been seriously compromised since the economic crisis of the 1990s. This worsening of conditions can be attributed not only to external factors such as the breakup of the international socialist system, the tightening of the U.S. blockade, and the worldwide economic crisis suffered by underdeveloped countries, but also to internal factors that have kept the country from taking full advantage of the human and material potential available on the island.

Although Cuba, in the middle of the first decade of this century, experienced an economic recovery from the collapse in GDP in the mid-1990s that followed the demise of the Socialist Bloc, it continues to maintain high import coefficients due to long-standing structural difficulties. The country is highly dependent on food imports as a result of a deficient agrarian policy. It imports energy to a significant extent, although less than in the past, and it still requires many intermediate inputs to the productive process. Cuban industry and agriculture continue to suffer from low levels of efficiency and productivity.

Institutional reforms in the mid-1990s allowed the population to diversify its sources of income. The growing role of market forces in the once state-dominated economy and the strategies being pursued by people for generating income have led to slow but growing social differentiation. This process continues, despite measures taken to counteract it through various programs related to the so-called Battle of Ideas (2000–2008).[1]

The duration of the Special Period[2] points to the difference between the length of time it takes to develop social processes and the length of time as experienced by real human beings. It should be a national priority to address the social inequalities unintentionally generated over the course of the Special Period as the country tried to implement profound and necessary economic changes with the least possible social cost.

To prepare for the challenges that Cuba will have to face in the future, I will analyze its economic situation using a set of indicators that will tell us about the current economic state of the country and about the social and economic well-being of the Cuban people in the present and recent past.

Macroeconomic Performance

The Cuban economy grew rapidly between 2001 and 2006. During this period the Gross Domestic Product (GDP) grew at an average 7.5% per year at constant prices of base year 1997. From 2001 to 2003, however, it grew at an annual rate of just 2.9%, while between 2004 and 2006 it grew at a yearly average of 9.3%. As Figure 1.1 shows, the Cuban economy has been growing at slower rates since 2007. The factors that explain this downturn in economic growth include the effect of several hurricanes, the continued, systematic decrease in the performance of several traditional productive sectors including sugar and agriculture, the lack of growth of service exports, decreases in efficiency, increases in the prices of imported goods, and external and internal financial deficits.

The share of GDP derived from agriculture, construction, and the transportation sectors has diminished. In contrast, the share of services has

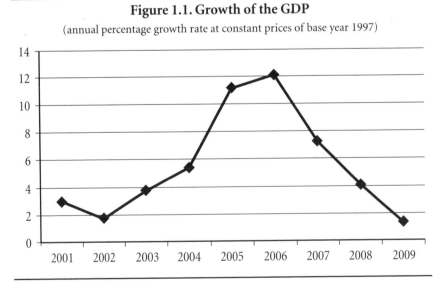

Figure 1.1. Growth of the GDP

(annual percentage growth rate at constant prices of base year 1997)

Source: Oficina Nacional de Estadística, *Anuarios Estadísticos de Cuba* (Havana: various years)

Figure 1.2. Structure of 2009 GDP in Percentages

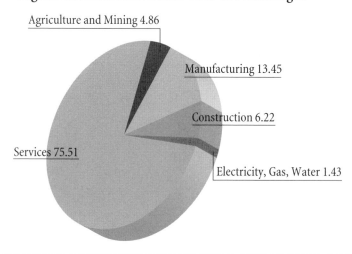

Agriculture and Mining 4.86

Manufacturing 13.45

Construction 6.22

Services 75.51

Electricity, Gas, Water 1.43

increased significantly. In 2009, the service sector represented 75.5% of the GDP.

The Cuban state's allocation of available resources reflects the priority that it has accorded to social programs within its overall development strategy. Nevertheless, while gross fixed capital formation was 60% greater in 2006 than in 2001, its share of total spending has decreased to less than 10% of GDP from over 30% in 1990.

The growth of the GDP has been accomplished without sacrificing macroeconomic equilibria reached since the middle of the 1990s. The fiscal deficit has been kept to a controllable size (about 3.2% of GDP). When the deficit increased at rates higher than expected in 2008 and 2009, significant budget cuts were undertaken. Monetary policy has succeeded in reaching a key target of achieving the stability of the CADECA's[3] exchange rate. At the same time, the monetary liquidity of the population reached extraordinary levels at over 26 billion pesos in 2009, equivalent to 40% of GDP.

The Cuban economy has had to develop in circumstances of adversity including serious droughts, violent hurricanes, difficulties generating electricity, and increased pressure from the United States that included further restrictions on travel by Cuban citizens to that country, stricter limitations on remittances to Cuba, and, most recently, attempts to seize Cuban assets held outside the country.

Cuba continues to suffer from structural problems in its economy, including a scarcity of hard currency earnings, distortions in its relative pricing system resulting from an overvalued official exchange rate, lack of convertibility between its currency and those of other countries, monetary duality, segmented markets, poor performance in the sugar industry and in agriculture, and inefficiency in public entities. President Raúl Castro has commented on these problems in numerous public statements.[4]

Positive results were reached in certain sectors such as petroleum and natural gas extraction. Oil production has increased six-fold since 1990. Gas production was negligible in 1990 and has now reached over a million cubic meters. These accomplishments have allowed Cuba to reduce its oil imports when prices on the international market increased rapidly. The petroleum agreement with the government of Venezuela also helps to mitigate the inflationary price spiral of the crude oil it imports.

In general, manufacturing production has decreased steadily. The sector contributed 13.45% to the GDP in 2009, but performance has varied dramatically among the various industries. Nickel, beverages, spirits, tobacco products, and some other manufactures increased, while sugar production plummeted with harvests less than 15% the size of those at the beginning of the 1990s.

Only 1,000,000 tons of sugarcane were harvested in 2009, due to the unavailability of necessary resources for even the basic needs of sugar-based agro-industry such as equipment and capital investment, a lack of work incentives to agricultural and other producers, and the low priority that the government accorded to the sector during the 1990s. A process of de-capitalization had unfavorable repercussions for crop yields and sugar production, leading to significant reductions of sugar exports and reduced flows of hard currency and financing that affected the national economy. The closing of half the sugar refineries in the country left 100,000 people out of work and required a difficult retraining process. The situation of the unemployed and underemployed former sugar workers has still not been definitively resolved. New sources of productive employment for these workers must be found in the near- to mid-term.

Agricultural production and the sale of products in agricultural markets are important to the population's consumption of food products and thus to its well-being. Agricultural production has continued to decrease in recent years. Its participation in the GDP was less than 4.86 % in 2009 due to the sharp decline in the growing of sugarcane, a continued decline in the number of livestock, and the stagnation of non-sugar agriculture. While the reality of tangible problems, including shortages of financial and material resources, must be acknowledged, there are also organizational and institutional problems in the Cuban economy that have had a significant negative impact on the economic performance in agricultural production.

Figure 1.3. Agricultural Production in Millions of Tons

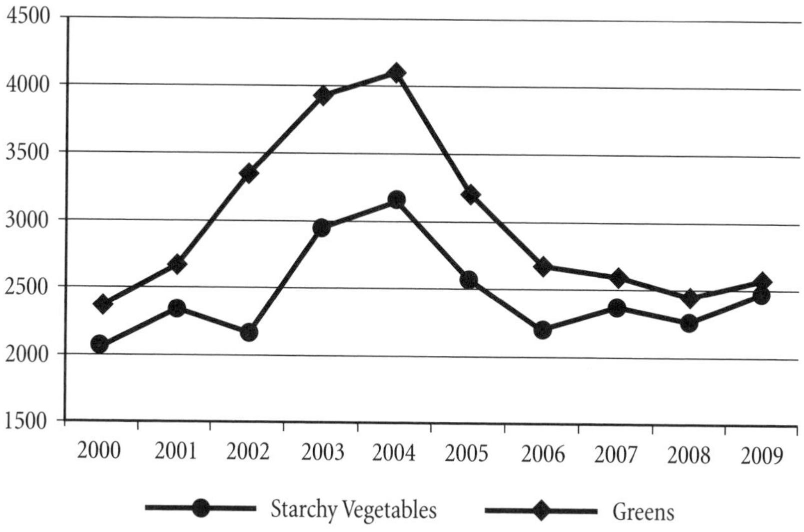

Source: Oficina Nacional de Estadística, *Anuarios Estadísticos de Cuba* (Havana: various years).

The economic reforms of the 1990s enabled some strictly regulated state agricultural enterprises to be grouped into somewhat more flexible Basic Units of Cooperative Production (UBPC), but the highly centralized environment in which they function discouraged producers and impeded any increase in yields or production. The availability of external supplies was inadequate, and the state procurement and distribution enterprise (*Acopio*) sets such low prices for agricultural products that they are sometimes below the cost of production.

Figure 1.3 illustrates that the production of *viandas* (starchy vegetables such as potatoes, sweet potatoes, yucca, cassava, plantain, and others) and of other vegetables (*hortalizas*) basic to the Cuban diet (greens such as tomatoes, cabbage, lettuce, onions, and others) decreased at a time when food prices were rising rapidly worldwide.

Cuba's agricultural markets experienced significant price decreases between 1994 and 1996, as the opening of these markets hampered the price speculation that had prevailed for agricultural goods in the black market. In addition, money began to grow scarce while production increased and then stabilized. In the last 10 years, however, there has been no tendency for prices to fall in keeping with the decreased purchasing power of the population, especially for those households dependent on salaries from the state-dominated sphere of the economy. In order to lower consumer prices, it has become necessary to seek alternative means of increasing agricultural production.

Activity has also decreased in the livestock sector, particularly regarding cattle. Decreased volumes of feed deriving from sugarcane led to an unfortunate dependence on imported animal feed. Droughts in the eastern provinces, inefficient herd management, and structural weaknesses in overall organization contributed to the shrinking of this sector.

The UBPCs oriented toward raising livestock have not demonstrated significantly improved results. New agricultural methods clearly call for new management methods and mechanisms. Existing mechanisms with a centralized and vertical orientation should be replaced by economic-financial instruments. The state should limit itself to outlining policies, establishing and implementing appropriate instruments to execute them, guarantee the availability of necessary scientific-technical services, and protect the natural environment, while leaving decision-making on management and production issues to the people directly involved.

Poor performance in the agricultural sector negatively affects the country's fiscal gap and trade deficit. For example, the amount of food that had to be imported in 2007 to reach a daily consumption level of 3,287 kilocalories and 89.9 grams of protein per person was greater than the amount imported in 1989.

Although Cuba overcame the crisis of the first half of the 1990s, the years leading up to 2009 were characterized by a deficit in the supply of available food for consumption and demand. While the overall nutritional state of the population has improved (with the exception of dietary fat intake, which is not a surprise given that oils are mostly imported and charged to consumers in convertible Cuban pesos), certain levels of malnutrition have also been found to be present in some households.

Low levels of agricultural production and the resulting increase of food imports in an environment of rising commodity prices mean that the country's agricultural strategy and policies should be reconsidered. A way must be found to stimulate development appropriate to the economic environment, and new ways must be found to unleash the potential of the labor force. Some modifications of agricultural policy were made in the first half of 2008. Among other measures, an incipient market for agricultural inputs has been established, land and livestock have been provided to private producers; and municipal enterprises have been strengthened, thereby reducing the verticality of decision-making.

Construction has increased enormously in recent years. Growth in the sector was 37.7% in 2006, concentrated in the areas of petroleum, electricity, and tourism infrastructure and in the areas prioritized by the government as part of what is known as the Battle of Ideas. These areas included housing, school, and hospital construction and the repair of existing schools and hospitals. By 2009, however, the value of new construction decreased by 9% as investment contracted due to a discrepancy between the resources allocated to projects and the capacity to carry them out.

Although substantial resources were invested in the 1970s and 1980s to expand the supply of housing, the housing deficit was still acknowledged to be a problem in 1989 and the crisis of the 1990s contributed to the further deterioration of existing housing stock. In 2001 and in subsequent years a sharp drop took place in housing construction, caused by the allocation of resources to rebuilding housing damaged by multiple hurricanes and to other priorities. It has been clearly demonstrated that the construction of new housing will not by itself resolve the housing question. Resources must also be allocated for the maintenance of the existing housing stock.

The state accorded increased priority to the construction of new housing in 2006 because of the deterioration of existing housing stock and the housing deficit that had accumulated over decades. A program was established for the construction of 100,000 housing units annually, emphasizing household construction versus state-led housing development. This program was found to have many deficiencies and in fact has since been reduced in scope.

Problems with public transportation have had a negative influence on the well-being of the Cuban population. Insufficient capital formation in the sector led to a rapid deterioration of equipment. A large-scale investment program outlined in 2007 permitted the importation of buses and other transportation equipment from the People's Republic of China.

To summarize, Cuba's GDP grew rapidly in the mid-2000s, but the growth rate has been smaller since then; the economic recovery process has not been rapid enough to regain the levels of economic well-being that existed prior to the crisis years in the early 1990s. New policies are needed to stimulate economic reactivation and increase productive dynamism while maintaining macroeconomic stability, in order to keep the advances in social equity and the provision of basic services that the Cuban government has provided across the last decade.

In 2008, there were signs that the government was willing to take steps to update Cuban socialism, including the elimination of certain prohibitions. These changes included the legalization of the sale of certain consumer items such as computers and DVD players, and the granting of public access to services such as cellular telephony that were previously reserved for enterprises, the diplomatic sector, and foreign citizens. The restriction on Cubans staying at hotels built to serve the needs of international tourism has also been lifted. In addition, Resolution 9 of the Ministry of Labor and Social Security introduced measures to allow for salaries and wages to be set with more flexible ceilings and caps. Decree-Law 260 of 2008, concerning the work and salaries of retired teachers and professors, provides incentives to draw them back to the classroom; Decree 259 allows idle land to be assigned in usufruct to private parties.

The Evolution of the External Sector

The characteristic current accounts deficit in Cuba's balance of payments was transformed into a current account surplus in 2004, but overall balances have continued to fluctuate. The factors that have driven this turnaround include the increased export of professional services, specifically those of health workers deployed in developing countries on medical missions, and the receipt of remittances widely estimated to be between US$900 million and US$1 billion. Indeed, the service sector was the greatest generator of export income starting in 2004. There were significant qualitative changes within this sector, as the value of knowledge-intensive services overtook the value of the tourist sector in generating income.

In contrast to sugar exports, nickel exports have increased significantly in the last three years, in view of both increased production and higher prices. In 2009 nickel was Cuba's most important goods export. Foreign sales of non-traditional high value-added products have also increased, including products in biotechnology, pharmaceuticals, and advanced medical and diagnostic equipment. New markets have been found for these products and about 200 of them have been licensed by health authorities in 52 countries. The current structure of export products indicates a significant transformation. Medicines constitute the second most important export subsector while the sugar subsector has become less important. Nonetheless, sugar remains one of the products for which Cuba has the most productive potential.

The recovery in the export sector is undeniable, but the value of exports in 2009 was still 31% less than in 1989. In 2009, most of the commercial trade in merchandise was with Venezuela, China, the United States (due to Cuba's food purchases), and some European countries. This was a structural change in the composition of trade by regions and countries compared to the early years of the 1990s.

In the mid 2000s, Cuba recovered its ability to pay for imports. The structure of these imports does not favor capital goods, however, with the exception of gasoline and diesel-powered electric generators and similar

Figure 1.4. Foreign Trade of Goods and Services in Billions of Pesos

Figure 1.4. Foreign Trade of Goods and Services in Billions of Pesos

Legend: ●——● Exports   ◆- - -◆ Imports

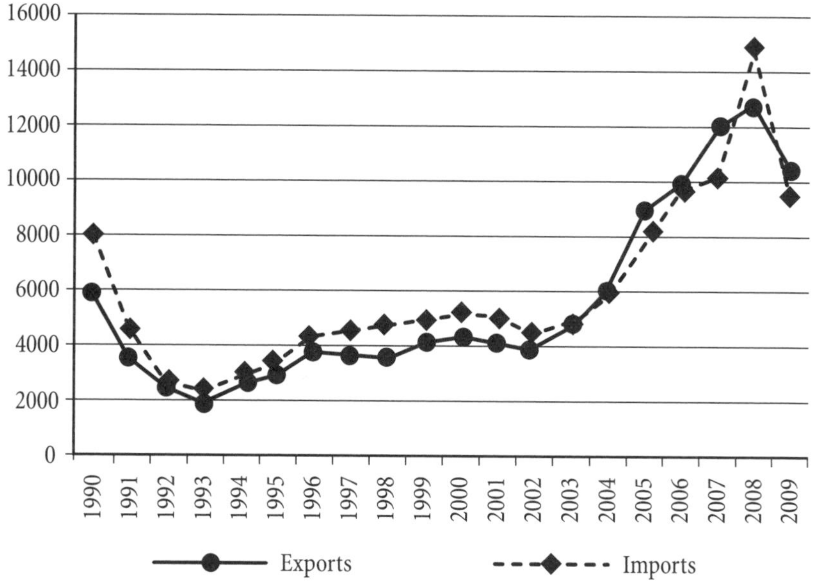

Source: Oficina Nacional de Estadística, *Anuarios Estadísticos de Cuba* (Havana: various years).

items. Instead, imports are concentrated in the food sector (including many products that could be produced domestically) and in intermediate goods. Food imports remain high due to the insufficient performance of the agricultural sector as discussed above, and imports of raw materials and industrial equipment have increased as a result of the economic recovery.

This imbalance has led to a merchandise trade deficit of about nine billion pesos equivalent to 11% of GDP. This high figure could be reduced by increasing domestic production of certain goods currently imported. To do so, the Cuban state should give maximum priority to increasing worker incentives, make some necessary institutional changes, and eliminate excessive centralization.

Gross revenue from tourism surpassed US$29.5 billion between 1990 and 2009, growing from US$243 million in 1990 to 2.1 billion convertible Cuban pesos (CUCs) in 2009. More than 7 billion CUCs were spent on tourist development during that period. Of this amount, more than 2.3 billion pesos were spent on tourist infrastructure, airport capacity, and new technology for tourist services and telecommunications. Some 28 million people visited the country, and the number of hotel rooms increased from 12,900 to 49,000, almost half of them administered by foreign hotel companies.

Tourism decreased in the late 2000s for domestic and international reasons. Internally, factors including high prices, management and maintenance difficulties at some hotels, the limited supply of services outside the hotel sector, and the 8% revaluation of the CUC are important reasons for a reduction in the growth rate of the total number of tourists entering Cuba. In addition, external factors such as global financial turbulence, slow economic growth in tourists' countries of origin, and high oil prices leading to increased transportation costs, especially for European tourists, have also had a significant negative impact.

Foreign investment has been concentrated in key sectors such as petroleum, nickel, telecommunications, and tourism. International investment by Cuba has appeared in incipient form, primarily in biotechnology in Asian markets such as China, India, and Malaysia. Venezuelan investment in the Cuban economy has increased in oil, nickel, petrochemicals and communications.

Cuba's credit capacity is still limited worldwide except with China and Venezuela, the latter within the framework of the Bolivarian Alternative for the Americas (ALBA). This is due not only to Cuba's limited credit-worthiness, but also to the pressure of the United States government, which continues to apply punitive economic measures against the country.

Prices, Income, and Employment

Following a deflationary episode in 1999–2001, inflation increased sharply after 2003. The spike in the consumer price index was driven by the increase in prices in non-regulated markets for essential consumer goods. These include higher prices for some products in the ration stores and farmers' markets, higher electric rates and gas prices, and higher prices of other products including household appliances and some food and personal hygiene items.

The population's income is an important variable because its availability for spending is a necessary precondition for demand and therefore consumption in all accessible markets. Nominal income continued to grow during the 2000s as a result of the increases in wages for state workers in the public and state enterprise sectors, the growth of some productive activities, the entry of remittances to the country, and other factors. The median monthly nominal salary, which is the most important component of the population's income, also continued to grow, reaching 427Cuban pesos in 2009, a significant increase from what it was in 1989. However, the increase in the nominal salary has not been enough to overcome the deterioration of real salaries given the even greater increases in the Consumer Price Index (CPI) over the period. This has created significant problems for the majority of households that depend on their salaries as the most important source of income. Real salaries remained far below those of 1989.

A salary reform was implemented in 2005 mandating that professional qualifications, education, and knowledge base be taken into account when setting workers' salaries. Raises were most common in state-financed sectors such as health and education. The social security (old age) pensions received by 1,468,641 citizens were subsequently raised at an annual cost of 1.035 billion pesos. In addition to these, 257,030 family units comprising 476,500 people began to receive 50 additional pesos in the form of social assistance. The minimum salary was raised from 100 pesos to 225 pesos. The total additional expenditure for these measures in 2005 was over 3,4655 billion pesos. These measures alleviated the economic situation of many households in state-financed sectors as well as that of retired workers and others receiving pensions. The increase in liquidity during the period led to new price increases for scarce agricultural and black-market goods because there was no adequate increase in the production or importation of consumer goods. As a result, personal income remains insufficient to cover the necessary purchases of Cuban families due to the elevated prices for food. A portion of the population continues to be unable to satisfy all of its basic needs, especially for food. The relationship between income and consumption is highly distorted.

For real salaries to increase, the Cuban marketplace needs a greater supply of products available in exchange for the currency in which salaries are paid, or there must be a revaluation of that currency. The policies implemented at this time, however, have not proven strong enough to stimulate the adequate development of productive forces, i.e., labor productivity.

What might be some of the causes of the current economic situation?

- As a result of its structure, the GDP growth rate still does not allow for greatly increased levels of consumption.
- Industrial and agricultural productivity and efficiency continue to be low.
- Because of the low profitability of enterprises, taxes on the sale and circulation of goods (particularly taxes on cigarettes and beverages) represent a larger proportion of state revenues than taxes on the profits of producers. As long as this situation persists, neither nominal salaries nor state spending can be increased in a sustained fashion without creating inflationary pressure.
- The liquidity of cash within the population is increasing, but it is ever more concentrated in the hands of a few and is often held in bank accounts.

The existing monetary duality and payment for consumption in a currency other than the Cuban peso (the proportion of total consumption of goods and services that is paid either by Cuban convertible pesos or hard currency) are excessive, in view of the overvalued official exchange rate. This situation has increased social inequality. A portion of the population's consumption is still derived from goods obtained in regulated and rationed markets where prices are quite low, subsidized, or distributed without payment. In light of the population's income level, the supply of these goods is limited.

The total volume of remittances may have decreased as a result of regulations enacted by the George W. Bush administration. However, although it is not possible to establish their volume with any precision due to the different means by which they are sent, the amounts have not decreased greatly if one measures them by the ongoing sales in "dollar stores" (*Tiendas de Recuperación de Divisas* - TRDs), which continued to increase.

The official unemployment rate has been low; in 2009, it was 1.8% compared to 7.9% in 1995. However, job creation in recent years has been based on the country's development strategy focused on the tertiary sector. From 2002 to 2008, job creation was concentrated in new social programs associated with the so-called Battle of Ideas. The fact that fewer people are working in Cuban industry is symptomatic of the continued paralysis of many activities, reductions in industrial investment, and the lack of hard currency needed to purchase industrial inputs and improve the utilization of existing capacity.

The state's employment policy itself has contributed to underemployment in many cases. A critical fact is that workers lack motivation on the job because they spend much time and resources to secure their basic needs. This quest significantly detracts from the creative energy that would under normal circumstances be available to them for their official profession. The difficulty is reflected in daily life. Many professionals working in the fields for which they were trained must have a second job to supplement their low salaries and ensure the fulfillment of daily needs. In other cases, individuals simply migrate to work in other sectors where their specialized education plays little role, but where they are able to secure greater economic security. In the worst of cases, individuals seek employment outside Cuba so they may send remittances to their families that remain on the island.

The state should continue to play a leading role in addressing and resolving these problems. While the public maintains confidence in the state's ability to meet these challenges, the state in its turn should put more faith in the potential contribution of family and individual capital to the country's development. This contribution can be realized if recognition of household assets is encouraged and conditions are created for these assets to be utilized productively within the framework of the law.[5]

Fiscal Policy

In general, the national budget is the principal source of financing for social policies. The share of fiscal resources for these policies is set in the national currency and its disbursement is structured in a decentralized fashion. The use of funds is determined in keeping with the necessities of each region.

The share of government spending allocated for expenditures in the scarcer hard currency is structured in a much more centralized fashion. A significant portion of financing for investments in infrastructure and its modernization is also supported by the state budget and to some extent from donations by international institutions. In practice, the degree of centralization of the allocation of resources in hard currency acts to counter the decentralization that is being sought in the financing of policies in national currency based on local disbursements.

The 1990s were characterized by a tendency toward increasing current spending despite the economic crisis that ignited the Special Period. Many of these budgetary outlays took place in the areas expected to have the greatest social impact. Cuban economic policy was directed toward meeting social needs, a goal that received particular emphasis in 2001 and the years that followed. The most important objectives of the national government were to provide free high-quality educational and health services, guarantee the solvency of the social security system, and meet the needs of senior citizens, the handicapped, and other groups and individuals that have been most affected by the rise in inequality within Cuban society. The government's so-called Battle of Ideas focused on improving the social policies that had the greatest impact on the quality of these educational and health indicators.

While the Cuban model has always sought to increase social equity, it has focused more on making services available for free than on providing opportunities for monetary income to citizens to ensure their access to these services. Consequently, universal access to services is a necessary pre-condition in social policy design. Spending on education has increased over time to improve the quality of services and to meet the needs imposed by demographic growth. Likewise, spending on public health has increased in recent years in order to improve levels of health care and service quality. Deteriorated facilities including polyclinics, hospitals, and pharmacies have been rehabilitated.

The infant mortality rate is an effective indicator for evaluating the performance of the health sector, especially primary care and infant and maternal care. Cuba's infant mortality rate has declined markedly since 1960. In the first decades after that year the decline was attributable to post-neonatal health care, principally the widespread campaigns for vaccination programs against immuno-preventable diseases. Children are now vaccinated against 13 diseases. The infant mortality rate in 2009 was 4.8 per 1,000 live births, confirming Cuba's leading place among Latin American countries and its position among the 30 countries in the world with the lowest probability of death after a live birth.

Demography

Demographic studies in Cuba in recent years have characterized the country as being in the advanced stage or culmination of one demographic transition or possibly in the early stages of a second transition. All studies recognize that the prediction for zero or negative population growth in the next ten to fifteen years has come to pass sooner than expected. In fact, the growth rate of the Cuban population has been negative since 2006. Both the reduction in the birth rate and the growth of the over-60 population has accelerated. Sustained emigration is another contributing factor.

The population grew at the very slow rate of .2 per thousand in 2005. It decreased by .4 per thousand in 2006, .2 per thousand in 2007, .1 % per thousand in 2008, and .3 % per thousand in 2009. The share of the population between 15 and 59 years of age as a proportion of the total population has grown in the last fifteen years. This group totaled over 7.7 million people in 2009. The proportion of the population between birth and 14 years of age has decreased given the low birth rate; the proportion of the population 60 years of age and older has increased. In 2009, about 2.1 million Cubans were between birth and 14 years old, and about 1.9 million were 60 years or older.

The key characteristic of the Cuban demographic transition is the aging of the population. The entire society and all its institutions must prepare to deal with this phenomenon, which began in the early 1970s. By the end of that decade the gross reproduction rate had fallen below replacement level, and the population of people 60 years and older had surpassed 12% of the total. In 2009 it reached 17.0%.

The country's rapid demographic change includes changes in the population's territorial mobility. Internal migration decreased in the 1990s. However, emigration increased to a rate of over 30,000 people per year for a total of over 200,000 people in the last five years. Population mobility (excluding forced and induced migration) has historically been motivated by a search for opportunities for better employment and improved goods or services, including services directly or indirectly associated with individual or family self-realization.

Principal Challenges and Future Actions

The Cuban economy faces many complex challenges in seeking to maintain its social and economic project and the well-being of the population. Social and economic distortions and disequilibria must be confronted, and time is short.

- Internal factors that continue to constrain economic growth must be overcome in the short to medium-term. Among them are financial restrictions on hard currency, which continue to be one of the direct causes of unsatisfied consumer needs.

- State enterprises are currently subject to an adverse environment related to problems of price formation, the official exchange rate, the exchange regime, the centralized authorization required for purchasing, and other planning, regulation, and control mechanisms. Enterprises must achieve a level of efficiency sufficient to be competitive on the international market.

- The so-called income-consumption model is still seriously distorted as evidenced by its effects on labor motivation. Labor compensation systems must be altered to resolve problems in satisfying the needs of workers through salaries, other forms of income, or redistributive channels. Other problems that must be addressed include a reduction in the degree of market segmentation and improvement in the availability and provision of goods and services.

- The restructuring of sugar agro-industry remains incomplete. The recovery of production in the industry has stalled, also affecting the production of food on land ceded to growers for this purpose by the Sugar Ministry (MINAZ).

- There has been no progress toward achieving food self-sufficiency through the improvement of the agricultural management model.

- Given the cumulative effects of deterioration, greater short-term priority should be placed on the maintenance of infrastructure and equipment.

- The productive specialization of the Cuban economy must be changed radically, from an economy based on the exploitation of natural resources to an economy based on the intensive use of knowledge. The existence of Cuba's strong potential in knowledge-intensive development does not by itself guarantee the achievement of positive outcomes.

- The strategic objective is to grow, as other necessary benefits derive from growth. However, new springboards must be found to increase production. Performance is declining in sectors and activities such as tourism that have been used to increase production in the past.

- More measures should be undertaken to recover previously attained levels of social equity. Despite progress in recent years with such decisions as the delivery of household appliances associated with the Energy Revolution,[6] the problem of insufficient family income has not been resolved satisfactorily for the majority of Cubans families. Part of the population is still unable to cover all their expenses with the formal income that they receive. As a result they have to seek income from alternative sources or do without many goods and/or services.

- While Cuba is advanced in terms of social indicators concerning health, education, culture, and other areas, access to certain goods and services such as recreation, travel, transportation, and communication is far below the world average for comparable countries.

- Cuba reaped substantial advantages from its relationship with Venezuela in the 2004–2007 period. Nevertheless, the relationship has additional untapped potential to develop reindustrialization programs that would complement and support newly dynamic sectors and allow for the recovery and expansion of sectors that are strategic in light of their impact on the quality of life of the population and on the external sector.

- Cuban state enterprises have not demonstrated a capacity for economic innovation as one of their basic functions. Not only does the economic system suffer from functional deficiencies, but it has reached a kind of dead end from which a new direction is required.[7]

- In conclusion, economic reform should be seen as the first of the structural changes that the country requires. Cuba's economic problem is that the current economic system cannot serve as a starting point for the country's development.[8]

Necessary Policy Changes

The Cuban economy is in urgent need of structural transformation and decentralization in agriculture, manufacturing, and services. The state must play the regulatory role that is appropriate in relation to these economic activities and must concentrate its efforts in the country's fundamentally strategic sectors.

Fifty years of Cuban socialism have demonstrated with some exceptions that centralization and distancing from the market have provoked recessions and other negative economic phenomena. This tells us that we should not necessarily follow this road in the future and that, without altering the socialist project to which many of the Cubans on the island have committed themselves, the state should study a future role for itself regulating enterprises rather than directly administering them.

Agriculture must be granted the autonomy that the new forms of production, especially the UBPCs, call for. Significant allotments of state land should be provided to those who are able to make it produce. Commodity prices paid by the state to small agricultural producers should continue to increase. The development of sugarcane-based energy agro-industry should be promoted to revitalize the sugar industry and expand the production of derivatives, especially alcohols.

Two steps should be taken as part of a process to eradicate monetary duality: devaluation of the official exchange rate, and setting up an exchange mechanism for use of the Cuban peso by institutions.[9]

The ration card should be replaced with a new system for subsidizing food that is more efficient and has better distributive effects. The number of ministries should be reduced and the functions and level of centralization in the public sector should probably be changed.

Policy changes currently taking place seem to have the following priorities: implementing import substitution (particularly in agriculture), stimulating a return of foreign investment, and diversifying international commercial and financial relations. These policies, when applied, will stimulate or motivate new practices within the Cuban system. All evidence is that changes in the Cuban economy are just getting started. The steps taken up to this time represent only a small proportion of the changes required in order to meet the stated objectives and increase the purchasing power of Cuban families.

Finally, new reforms to the Cuban economic system are needed in several key areas to enhance the role of the market; improve the quality of regulation of the forms of property; and adopt the organizational model of enterprises. In the words of Cuban economist Pedro Monreal, ". . . in the case of Cuba, a new economic reform is a necessary first precondition to the other structural changes that the country requires in order for its development to progress."[10]

Endnotes

1. The Battle of Ideas was a campaign launched in Cuba during the dispute with the United States over the custody of the boy Elián González. The campaign continued until about 2006, focusing on strengthening social programs in Cuba with a strong emphasis on Cuban youth.
2. This is a term that is employed in Cuba to denote the period of economic adjustment that was sparked by the collapse of trade with the Socialist Bloc. It is assumed to continue until the present-day.
3. CADECA is the official currency exchange agency.
4. Speeches by Raúl Castro on July 26, 2007, in the province of Camagüey and on February 24, 2008, at the National Assembly of the People's Power Assembly in Havana.
5. Angela Ferriol, Maribel Ramos, and Lía Añé, *Reforma económica y población en riesgo en Ciudad de la Habana, Research report for the Programa Efectos Sociales de las Medidas de Ajuste Económico sobre la Ciudad—Diagnósticos y Perspectivas* (Havana: INIE-CEPDE/ONE, 2004).
6. This is a program that encourages energy saving as a key principle guiding energy consumption. It has included the introduction of new electric domestic appliances and light bulbs that are more efficient in energy use. In addition, it features improvements in energy production based on the use of generators and gas, as well as renewable energy sources.
7. Pedro Monreal, "El problema económico de Cuba," *Espacio Laical, Suplemento Digital* 28 (2008).
8. Ibid.
9. Pavel A. Vidal, "La dualidad monetaria en Cuba," in *Boletín del Centro de Estudios de la Economía Cubana* (Havana: Centro de Estudios de la Economía Cubana, 2007).
10. Monreal, "El problema económico de Cuba."

2

Monetary Duality in Cuba: Initial Stages and Future Prospects

Pavel Vidal Alejandro

Introduction

The U.S. dollar was introduced as a legal currency for domestic transactions in the Cuban economy in the early 1990s. Dollarization was only partial, however. The Cuban or "national" *peso* continued to be used in many areas of the economy, such as for the payment of salaries and storing value. After about ten years of the dual circulation of these two currencies, the government took steps to de-dollarize the economy. As a first step, it targeted the bank accounts of state enterprises and transactions between them and, in a second stage, it took aim at sales at state retail stores and most of the population's savings accounts.

If the dollar had simply been replaced by the Cuban peso, that move would have eliminated monetary duality. But this did not occur. What happened was that the "convertible" Cuban peso, or CUC, another currency that had first been issued in 1994, began to replace the U.S. dollar in 2003 and 2004. The economy is no longer dollarized, but two Cuban currencies circulate simultaneously and monetary duality continues. Currency unification is now an explicit goal of the Cuban government, a move that seems to favor the Cuban peso; it is likely that at some point the convertible Cuban peso will be entirely eliminated.

When the dual monetary regime was instituted in the 1990s, a series of distortions were introduced into the currency exchange system. There were two different rates of exchange between the Cuban peso and the convertible Cuban peso, and the Cuban peso was made non-convertible in the enterprise sector. These problems will need to be resolved by the Central Bank in order to establish adequate exchange policies that are a prerequisite to eliminating the use of dual currencies.

Certain beliefs and expectations about the benefits of currency unification have arisen among the Cuban population that do not reflect the probable results. Most analyses that examine Cuban monetary duality tend to associate it with income inequality. However, income inequalities are due to structural factors rather than monetary policy. For this reason, another challenge faced by the government is to bring popular expectations on the benefits that can be derived from the elimination of a dual currency regime into line with the outcomes that can actually be achieved by doing so.

My analysis of the dual currency regime is presented in five sections. Following this introduction, section 2 describes the process of dollarization in the early 1990s. Section 3 discusses the reverse: the de-dollarization in the 2000s. Section 4 evaluates the current situation and the costs of the dual currency regime. The final section projects likely future scenarios describing the steps that must be undertaken to eliminate the dual currency regime. This scenario assumes that the Cuban peso will be the only means of payment, but most of the analysis is also applicable if the government decides to adopt the convertible peso as the sole domestic currency. This article does not analyze the additional monetary and financial complications that the global crisis generated in 2008–2009.[1] During this period, the economy suffered banking and currency crises associated with the convertible peso, which added new challenges to the dual currency regime.

Dollarization

An economic crisis was set off in Cuba in the 1990s by the disappearance of the European socialist bloc. The crisis was aggravated by the United States government's blockade and the inefficiency that characterizes Cuba's centralized and state-dominated economic system. Cuba's GDP contracted 34.8% in the four years following 1990. The state budget was reduced significantly, and the revenues of virtually all enterprises fell dramatically. Nevertheless, nominal spending on health and education was not reduced, and state subsidies to enterprises experiencing losses were increased in order to avoid massive unemployment. These budgetary decisions provoked a fiscal deficit averaging 24.9% of GDP from 1990 to 1993.

Dollarization was an aspect of the economic policy adopted to confront the crisis and its associated fiscal and monetary disequilibria. Since the country had limited access to international financial markets and inside Cuba there was no market for public debt, the state financed its fiscal deficit with a loan from the Central Bank. The monetization of the fiscal deficit produced excess liquidity and, at the same time, high inflation in informal markets. Prices are estimated to have increased more than 150% in 1991 and more than 200% in 1993. The black market exchange rate came to exceed 100 pesos to the dollar, while before the crisis it had been about five pesos to the dollar.

Initially there was a spontaneous process of partial dollarization in transactions among the population because of its loss of confidence in the Cuban peso. Subsequently, the government itself promoted the dollarization of certain sectors of the economy. It allowed people to keep bank accounts in U.S. dollars, some stores could make retail sales in dollars, and the number of enterprises that operated and paid taxes in dollars increased. In the following years more bank credit designated in this foreign currency became available.

The dollarization of part of the economy was necessary to provide a currency that was more stable than the Cuban peso to be used in the economic activities that would drive the recovery process. The U.S. dollar began to be used in tourism, foreign investment, remittances, and other emerging sectors. This was a way to isolate the development of those sectors from the disequilibria and instabilities that dominated the rest of the economy.

Dollarization and monetary duality could probably have been avoided with stricter control of inflation and state spending. Yet reduced social spending would have provoked high unemployment. Given the magnitude of the crisis, this would have led to severe suffering for thousands of families. Instead, the impact of the crisis was distributed among the majority of the population through an inflation tax.

Nominal salaries in Cuban pesos were frozen and real salaries dropped by more than 70% due to inflation. Inflation was a vehicle for the transfer of financial resources from salaried state employees to the state budget. In effect, state employees and state pensioners financed the fiscal deficit. Their sacrifices made it possible to avoid unemployment and maintain existing levels of spending on health and education.

At first, then, dollarization was the consequence of a fiscal policy that sought to avoid the asymmetrical ramifications of the crisis. As an unavoidable result, however, it generated inflation, diminished confidence in the Cuban peso, and detracted from the value of that currency as a means of payment and storing value.

Monetary duality outlasted the years of the immediate crisis and spread to other segments of the state enterprise economy as a mechanism for economic regulation. Dollarized enterprises increased their autonomy and relative decentralization, tied in part to a campaign for "enterprise optimization" (*perfeccionamiento empresarial*). This initiative was intended to bring change to Cuban state enterprises by transforming their internal operations, granting managers more decision-making authority, and providing workers with greater incentives for productivity. Centralization was never completely abandoned, however. Enterprise optimization bogged down and became bureaucratized.

A number of factors associated with monetary duality served as instruments and mechanisms for the regulation of economic functions and the assignment of resources. These included the power of the government to decide which enterprises would operate with Cuban pesos and which would use U.S. dollars; the centralized assignment of foreign exchange to enterprises that continued to function with Cuban pesos—in an environment where such enterprises could not acquire dollars in the currency market; dual exchange rates; and the segmentations that resulted among households and enterprises operating in different currencies.

Monetary duality and its financial and exchange ramifications are components of an economic policy environment characterized by overly discretionary decision-making with few general rules, excessive prohibitions, and disparate decisions producing an economic situation that is difficult to measure and understand, what has been called "a hand-crafted economy" (*economía hecha a mano*). Policy makers have now recognized that monetary duality causes more distortions than benefits; there is a consensus in government institutions that the time has come to bring about the transformations required for its elimination.

De-dollarization

Table 2.1 contains a summary of the actions taken by the Cuban Central Bank to bring about the de-dollarization of the economy. They are listed chronologically beginning in July 2003.

De-dollarization was not actually the goal of the measures but rather a means to obtain other objectives. The Central Bank's Resolution 65 of 2003 was intended to impose greater control on the financial resources held in U.S. dollars within Cuba. It was announced at a moment when the government was criticizing the process that had taken place in the 1990s of relative decentralization and greater management autonomy for Cuban enterprises. In hindsight, this policy measure was a turning point that marked a return to excessively centralized procedures.[2]

Resolution 80 of 2004 was a response to actions taken by the United States government to prevent Cuba from using its U.S. dollar holdings. Cuba was in danger of being unable to make international bank deposits with the U.S. dollars spent in the country by the population and by tourists. Several months earlier, the Union of Swiss Banks (UBS) had been fined US$100 million by the United States Department of the Treasury for accepting deposits of U.S. currency from Cuba and "other enemy countries."

As the domestic market for goods and services shifted from dollars to convertible Cuban pesos, the Cuban population and tourists were required

Table 2.1. De-dollarization Measures

Resolution 65/2003 of the Central Bank of Cuba

In July 2003, the convertible Cuban peso (CUC) became the sole means of payment used to denominate and realize transactions between Cuban entities, including the receipt of loans and credits. All accounts in U.S. dollars or other hard currency held by these entities were converted to convertible Cuban pesos at the exchange rate of one CUC to one U.S. dollar. In the future, banks would automatically exchange all U.S. dollars for CUCs upon deposit.

An exchange control regime was instituted to govern the exchange of CUCs for U.S. dollars and other hard currencies by the enterprise sector. Cuban enterprises that had accounts in CUCs had to seek authorization of the Cuban Central Bank to purchase hard currency required to make payments for commercial transactions or on outstanding debts. A Hard Currency Approval Committee (*Comité de Aprobación de Divisas* - CAD) was established for this purpose.

Resolution 80/2004 of the Central Bank of Cuba

On November 8, 2004, all entities that accepted U.S. dollars in the form of cash for payment in transactions within Cuban territory would henceforth accept only convertible Cuban pesos (CUC). The price of services provided to the population and to foreign visitors that had been previously been designated in U.S. dollars would henceforth be designated in convertible Cuban pesos. Price conversion would be based on the prevailing exchange rate of one CUC to one U.S. dollar.

On November 14, 2004, a 10% tax was levied on the purchase of CUC and Cuban pesos with U.S. dollars in the form of cash. However, the fee would not apply to the balances of bank accounts opened before November 13 so people had time to deposit the U.S. dollars that they had in their possession. From that day forward these bank accounts have not accepted U.S. dollar deposits in cash and customers have been able to withdraw CUCs or U.S. dollars without being subject to the 10% tax.

Agreement 13 of the Committee on Monetary Policy of the Central Bank of Cuba

On March 18, 2005, the exchange rate of the Cuban peso for the population was fixed at 24 Cuban pesos with respect to the U.S. dollar and 25 Cuban pesos with respect to the convertible Cuban peso at CADECA, the official currency exchange agency with branches throughout the country. This effectively increased the value of the Cuban peso by 7.5% as the previous rate of exchange was 26 Cuban pesos to the U.S. dollar. It was announced that "conditions have been established conducive to a progressive, gradual, and prudent revaluation of the Cuban peso."

Agreement 15 of the Committee on Monetary Policy of the Central Bank of Cuba

This announcement stipulated an 8% revaluation of the exchange rate of the convertible Cuban peso in relation to the U.S. dollar and other hard currencies by April 9, 2005. Bank accounts held in U.S. dollars were not affected and the population was offered a grace period within which to convert their monetary holdings in keeping with the new conditions.

Source: Texts of resolutions and agreements issued by the Cuban Central Bank as edited by the author (see www.bc.gov.cu).

to exchange dollars for one of the two national currencies to be able to spend these monies on consumption. They were additionally required to pay a tax of 10% when exchanging U.S. dollars. This created an incentive for people to receive transfers either by bank wire or in foreign currencies other than the U.S. dollar. Before this Resolution, 80% of foreign currency inflows were in the form of U.S. dollars, a proportion that was reduced to 30% one year later with the dollars being primarily replaced by euros.[3]

The possession of foreign currency was not legally punishable under Resolution 80. The population was able to maintain bank accounts in dollars and to possess other foreign currencies. This was probably critical in avoiding the inherent risks associated with measures to encourage currency substitution. The instrument used to discourage the entry of physical dollars into the country was not a prohibition, but a price increase in the form of a tax. A number of options were available to the Cuban citizens. They could act in keeping with their own preferences and perceptions of risk.

Four months after the promulgation of Resolution 80 and after over three years of a fixed exchange rate, Agreement 13 of the Committee on Monetary Policy revalued the Cuban peso at the CADECA currency exchange agency. For the first time, the direction of the targeted value of the Cuban peso was announced ahead of time, in this case an increase in its value. Agreement 15 then established a revaluation of the convertible Cuban peso. This agreement did not affect existing bank deposits and, because the changed value of the currency was announced in advance, people had time to adjust their monetary holdings. The fundamental goal of Agreements 13 and 15 was the reallocation of the population's wealth toward domestic currencies.

Thus the revaluation of the national currencies, and above all the particular characteristics of the agreements and the expectations that they generated, motivated a transfer of savings from U.S. dollars to the convertible Cuban peso and the Cuban peso, accelerating a transfer that had already begun, albeit to a lesser extent, with the proclamation of Resolution 80. In conclusion, de-dollarization altered the denomination of the currency in the population's bank accounts; the U.S. dollar was also replaced as a means of storing value.

In the 12-month period following these monetary measures, the population's bank balances in U.S. dollars decreased by 57% while accounts in convertible Cuban pesos grew by more than 300% and deposits in Cuban pesos grew by 35%.[4] A small share of the population's on-demand and timed bank deposits continued to be designated in U.S. dollars along with the bank accounts held by joint ventures and foreign enterprises (those with 100% ownership by foreign capital), foreign associations, and diplomatic, consular, and other representations, as these accounts were not changed to convertible Cuban pesos by Resolution 65.

The measures had another set of favorable consequences: the level of international reserves in Cuba's Central Bank grew, the measurement and control of the money supply improved, and the autonomy of monetary policy was generally enhanced.

Of the actions contributing to de-dollarization, the most costly seems to have been the revaluation of the convertible Cuban peso with respect to U.S. dollar. The 8% revaluation of the CUC contributed to a decrease in the tourism to Cuba as the volume of foreigners visiting the island fell in 2006 and 2007. Other weaknesses of moving away from the dollar manifested themselves years later. The lack of transparency and the absence of a monetary rule to control the issuance of convertible pesos became determinants of banking and currency crises in 2009, as described in Chapter 5.

The de-dollarization of the Cuban economy cannot be understood without analyzing the evolution of monetary stability. One of the greatest achievements of economic policy since 1994 is its having recovered and sustained fiscal and monetary equilibrium. This created the conditions for the government to propose the substitution of the convertible Cuban peso and to some extent the Cuban peso for the U.S. dollar. Monetary stability restored confidence in the Cuban peso and lent credence to the new currency, the convertible Cuban peso.

Table 2.2 illustrates that, since 1994, inflation has been brought under control and the fiscal deficit has been reduced, as has the inflation-inducing growth in the money supply (monetary aggregate M_{2A}).[5] The rate of exchange of the Cuban peso in CADECA money-changing agencies was revalued and then stabilized. The economic recession was brought to an end; the GDP saw positive growth, which accelerated in the mid 2000s. The growth of the GDP also benefited from monetary stability and provided a more favorable environment for the management of fiscal policy.

A currency board regime provided the convertible Cuban peso with important initial support and was vital to its successful adoption. For every convertible Cuban peso in circulation, there was one U.S. dollar on reserve in the Central Bank. The rate of exchange of the convertible Cuban peso with respect to U.S. dollar was fixed at 1 CUC = 1 USD until it was revalued by 8%.

The Cuban financial system also developed in the 1990s; government economic policy always respected bank account deposits. As already noted, Cuban monetary authorities did not seize existing bank account deposits as part of the measures that were implemented to de-dollarize the economy.

Table 2.2. Macroeconomic Data, 1990–2007

	Inflation	Fiscal Deficit /GDP	Variation in M_{2A}[1]	Exchange Rate[2]	Growth of Real GDP
	Percentage	Percentage	Percentage	Cuban pesos per 1 CUC	Percentage
1990	2.1*	10.0	19.8	7.0*	−2.9
1991	158.0*	23.2	31.6	20.0*	−10.7
1992	93.6*	32.7	27.4	45.0*	−11.6
1993	204.5*	33.5	32.1	100.0*	−14.9
1994	−10.1*	7.4	−10.0	40.0	0.7
1995	−11.5	3.5	−7.0	30.0	2.5
1996	−4.9	2.5	3.1	21.2	7.8
1997	1.9	2.0	−1.0	23.0	2.7
1998	2.9	2.4	2.8	21.6	0.2
1999	−2.9	2.3	2.0	21.4	6.3
2000	−2.3	2.4	5.9	21.5	6.1
2001	−1.4	2.3	17.6	26.5	3.2
2002	7.3	3.0	10.4	26.5	1.4
2003	−3.8	3.0	−0.9	26.5	3.8
2004	2.9	3.7	7.7	26.5	5.8
2005	3.7	4.6	35.5	24.5	11.2
2006	5.7	3.2	2.5	24.5	12.1
2007	2.8	3.2	8.4	24.5	7.3

Source: Oficina Nacional de Estadística – ONE, *Anuario Estadístico de Cuba*; Banco Central de Cuba, *Informe Económico.*

*CEPAL, "La economía cubana. Reformas estructurales y desempeño en los noventa" (México D.F.: Fondo de Cultura Económica, 1997).

[1] The monetary aggregate M_{2A} includes cash and bank accounts in Cuban pesos held by the population.

[2] Average of official exchange rates for purchase and sale by the population.

Within the financial system, since its inception in 1995 the CADECA continuously provided the population with unrestricted convertibility for the two national currencies to U.S. dollars and other foreign currencies.

The Current State of Monetary Duality

As noted, de-dollarization did not mean the elimination of monetary duality. The segmentation of the economy and different exchange rates have been maintained, making for a quite heterogeneous currency exchange policy. The present configuration of currency markets in Cuba is as follows:

- The rate of exchange for the **population** is 24 Cuban pesos for one convertible Cuban peso. Currencies can be bought and sold at this rate in the CADECA exchange facility. Individuals can engage in transaction in the market for goods and services using either Cuban pesos or convertible Cuban pesos. They are also allowed to have savings accounts denominated in either of these two currencies or U.S. dollars.[6]

  The Cuban peso operates under a fixed exchange rate regime set by the Central Bank's Committee on Monetary Policy. From 1995 until 2001, the Cuban peso at CADECA had what could be described as a managed floating regime.

  Convertible Cuban pesos are bought and sold at CADECA currency exchange agencies at a fixed rate of one CUC to 1.08 U.S. dollar. The rate of exchange of the convertible Cuban peso with respect to other foreign currencies depends on the value of the dollar on international currency markets. When Cubans or foreign tourists sell dollars at currency exchange agencies they pay a 10% tax.

  Enterprises and institutions are prohibited from converting their currency holdings at CADECA agencies.[7]

- For **Cuban enterprises and institutions**, the Cuban peso and the convertible Cuban peso are equal in value. Enterprises cannot use their income in Cuban pesos to buy convertible Cuban pesos or foreign currency. Thus the Cuban peso has no convertibility in the business sector. The exchange rate of the Cuban peso for enterprises (also commonly referred to as the official exchange rate) serves only for accounting and record-keeping purposes to produce balance sheets, reports, and statistics for institutions that operate using the two domestic currencies.

  Enterprises that operate in Cuban pesos require hard currency to pay for imports. A single, centralized hard currency account (*Cuenta Única de Ingresos en Divisas del Estado*) was established at the Central Bank for this purpose through Resolution 92 of 2005. The Ministry of the Economy and Planning and the Central Bank assign available hard currency at their discretion.

  Enterprises with bank accounts in convertible Cuban pesos can purchase foreign currency to pay for imports and make other international payments. In this case the same exchange rate applies as for the population: 1 CUC equals US1.08.

- **Foreign enterprises and institutions** operate their accounts in foreign currency. In some cases they have requested permission from the Central Bank to also undertake transactions using bank accounts in convertible Cuban pesos.

What are the principal costs attributable to the present monetary and currency exchange situation?

The official exchange rate of one Cuban peso to one convertible Cuban peso is greatly overvalued. This produces distortions in almost all economic measurements, from the accounting balances of individual enterprises to calculation of the GDP. The overvaluation of the Cuban peso makes some enterprises appear to be more profitable than they are and others appear deceptively unprofitable, while there is no real correspondence between their supposed profitability and their real efficiency.

The distortion particularly affects exporters, as less than one Cuban peso is recorded for every U.S. dollar brought into the country in exchange for exports. It also stimulates imports because the accounting balances do not reflect the real cost of imported products, and the cost of Cuban products stated in Cuban pesos appears too high when compared to the cost of similar products that are imported. The official exchange rate is an obstacle to evaluating the competitiveness of Cuban goods and services.

As a result, the state budget is distorted. Many of the subsidies currently assigned through the budget to domestic state enterprises experiencing losses would not apply were it not for the official exchange rate policy, and the budget does not capture the profitability rents of some enterprises because they are obscured by the official exchange rate. It is difficult to anticipate the net effect of the devaluation of the Cuban peso on the budget deficit, as it would have a multiplicity of impacts on the economy. For example, it would increase the subsidies of the imported food products that the state distributes to the population through the ration card.

Monetary duality has other negative consequences deriving from the non-convertibility of the Cuban peso in the state enterprise sector. This policy weakens the domestic market by creating segmentation and reducing the ties among Cuban enterprises and also their ties with foreign investment and the external sector.

A number of important domestic economic activities were never dollarized and have continued to be designated in Cuban pesos. The current exchange regime does not stimulate investment in these Cuban and foreign enterprises. Instead, the current system incentivizes enterprises to conduct activities that bring in convertible Cuban pesos, even though these activities are often not those most needed in the larger economy.

The disadvantages mentioned above are not ones most frequently mentioned in discussions of Cuban monetary duality, which is most often identified with income inequality. Since the 1990s, salaries in the least productive areas of the economy have continued to be paid in Cuban pesos while the most dynamic activities, such as tourism and foreign investment, were initially dollarized and then converted to CUCs. This created a gap between low-paid state workers—who indirectly financed state employment and social expenditures during the crisis—and households that were able to access income from these more dynamic sectors and from remittances or compensation via foreign contracts: people such as artists, athletes, and, most recently, medical doctors and other professionals who are deployed to developing countries. Another source of income other than state salaries has been the growing array of illegal activities that accounts for a large part of today's economy.

The gap between state salaries in Cuban pesos and those other sources of income in hard currency has given rise to the inaccurate perception that monetary duality is the main cause of inequality. However, inequality primarily stems from low state salaries, and these are the result of low productivity. Inequality is not a monetary problem. Basically, it is a reflection of structural weaknesses in a centralized state system of production that became visible during the crisis and the reforms that were adopted in the 1990s.

Monetary duality is not extensively debated in the Cuban media, and official discourse has at times associated income inequality with dollarization and the dual currency regime. This lack of understanding and analysis has led to popular demands for improved real household earnings, with the expectation that disparities can be reduced through the adoption of a unified currency. In 2008, the Communist Party of Cuba publicized a document in which the matter has been analyzed comprehensively for the first time and that attempts to correct popular misconceptions. The document explains that "the solution to the loss of purchasing power by salaries depends not on decisions whose impacts are fundamentally limited to monetary policy, but on those that increase production," and it points out that the elimination of monetary duality "is not a measure that would in itself create wealth."[8]

Future Prospects

The circulation of two currencies, the overvaluation of the official exchange rate, the duality of exchange rates, and the inconvertibility of the Cuban peso for enterprises are closely related issues that should be resolved with simultaneous policy measures. The establishment of a unified exchange regime is a condition for the elimination of monetary dualism.

Four fundamental actions must be undertaken in order to eliminate monetary dualism.

(a) Devalue the exchange rate for the Cuban peso in the state enterprise sector.

At the current official exchange rate of one Cuban peso to one convertible Cuban peso, it is not possible to open the exchange market for the Cuban peso to institutions. If this were attempted today, there would be insufficient revenue in hard currency or international reserves to satisfy the demand represented by the quantity of Cuban pesos in circulation. In order to reach an equilibrium, the official exchange rate (one Cuban peso to one CUC) must first be devalued. This would reduce the purchasing power relative to hard currency of bank accounts designated in Cuban pesos.

To achieve this goal, government authorities will have to implement either a gradual or an immediate devaluation. The first approach seems more sensible since the value of the Cuban peso has almost never changed, and enterprises would need time to adjust their activities. Time would also be required to adjust economic policy instruments: subsidies, taxes, monetary and credit policy, bank oversight, and the allocation of fiscal resources.

There are some foreseeable impacts from this measure. The state budget, relative prices, and financial results of enterprises, banks, and other institutions would change with the devaluation of the Cuban peso. In particular, the financial balance sheets of enterprises that are distorted by the current exchange regime would be the most negatively affected.

As the cost of inputs and capital expenditures in convertible Cuban pesos and U.S. dollars would increase due to the devaluation of the official exchange rate, state enterprises could pass these increased costs in the final prices of goods and services charged to consumers. Many of these goods and services are also inputs for other enterprises. The consequences of the adjustment of the exchange rate would be passed along to almost all of the country's institutions through inflation.

As a result of the financial interrelationships among enterprises and between these entities and banking institutions, a worsening of the financial situation for certain state enterprises would reduce their capacity to pay their debts and therefore adversely affect their creditors.

Economic authorities must avoid the surge of an inflationary spiral in order to preserve monetary stability and ensure that the devaluation of the nominal official exchange rate would translate into a devaluation of the real exchange rate. Authorities should identify enterprises that are most negatively affected and those that are beginning to suffer losses, and take appropriate action. The changes will cause difficulties for the state enterprise sector but will also provide it with opportunities.

Economic policy should guide and regulate the "misalignment" brought to the economy by the alteration of the real exchange rate. These impacts should be managed, not avoided. The "misalignment" stemming from this policy change is in fact its principal contribution, because it is a change of direction from the point at which the overvaluation of the Cuban peso began to distort almost every aspect of the process of measuring the assets, liabilities, revenues, and expenditures. It would improve the environment for transparency in making economic measurements and decisions.

(b) Unify the exchange regime available to enterprises with the exchange regime available to the population.
Authorities will have to determine how much to devalue the official exchange rate and at what point the official exchange rate will coincide with the exchange rate available to Cuban consumers at CADECA, i.e., establish an equilibrium between both rates. The exchange rate currently available at CADECA exchange agencies of 24 pesos per convertible Cuban peso is not in equilibrium because not all the supply and demand for hard currency within the economy participates in the CADECA system.

Although the entire economy could be converted to a single currency simultaneously and a single exchange rate between Cuban pesos and convertible Cuban pesos could be set as a prerequisite, the transition to currency unification could also occur gradually within certain economic spheres while maintaining different exchange rates.

(c) Convert state retail markets and individual bank accounts to Cuban pesos.
To eliminate monetary duality for Cuban households, prices in convertible Cuban pesos should be multiplied by the current rate of exchange and set in Cuban pesos at CADECA exchange agencies. Bank accounts can be converted into Cuban pesos or maintained in convertible Cuban pesos for a period of time.

In reality, eliminating the dual currency in markets directly tied to the population will not be difficult since the Cuban peso is already convertible through CADECA exchange agencies.

(d) Convert institutional bank accounts now designated in convertible Cuban pesos to Cuban pesos and make the Cuban peso convertible for the enterprise sector operating in Cuban pesos.
After the official exchange rate of the Cuban peso to the Cuban convertible peso is devalued, all institutional bank accounts can be converted to Cuban

pesos. Enterprises whose convertible Cuban pesos have been changed to Cuban pesos should be permitted in some way (with more or less restrictions to be determined) to acquire foreign currency for the purpose of importing goods.

Enterprises that currently operate in Cuban pesos would come to participate in this exchange market. The businesses that must wait for the centralized assignment of hard currency under the current system would greatly benefit. Under the current system, the assignment of hard currency operates independently of such an institution's efficient performance, while in the context of an exchange market (with either more or less restrictions to be determined), the access of an enterprise to hard currency would be more closely tied to its economic performance.

This chapter has summarized a scenario for the transition of the Cuban economy to a single currency. This transition could take place at a faster or slower pace and with the use of measures that are more market-oriented or measures that maintain greater control over the assignment of hard currency, exchange rate values, and prices. Clearly many aspects of the process have yet to be evaluated, above all after the first measures to unify the currency regime are introduced. The devaluation of the official rate of exchange between Cuban pesos and Cuban convertible pesos is the measure that would introduce the most strain on the economy. Nonetheless, the effect of this and other policy reforms linked to this process would provide real benefits. These benefits would probably not meet all the expectations of the Cuban population, but they would certainly have a net positive impact on the economy.

Endnotes

1. For a discussion of this crisis, the reader is referred to Chapter 5 in this volume.
2. Resolution 65 was followed in 2005 by Resolution 92, which established that all revenues in the form of U.S. dollars under the rubric of fees, taxes, levies, or any other name be deposited in an account at the Central Bank of Cuba called the "Unique Account for State Revenues in Foreign Currency" *(Cuenta Única de Ingresos en Divisas del Estado)* and that the assignment of these resources would be centrally controlled. It also established that the Foreign Currency Approval Committee *(Comité de Aprobación de Divisas,* CAD) would be responsible for authorizing transactions in convertible pesos to different institutions, reserving the right to veto any such transaction. The approval of such transactions would have to be carried out prior to the agreement of the contract, not at the time of payment. Cuban banks could not process any operation by a Cuban entity in convertible pesos or foreign currencies unless it had been previously authorized by Foreign Currency Approval Committee.

3. Francisco Soberón, "Statement at the Congress of the National Association of Cuban Economists (Asociación Nacional de Economistas de Cuba, ANEC)" (2005).
4. Ibid.
5. In 2005 a significant increase in the money supply occurred (35.5%) without inflationary effects because it resulted from monetary substitution from the U.S. dollar to the Cuban peso as part of the de-dollarization process.
6. At the beginning of 2008, the savings of the population were divided among different currencies in the following proportions: 58.9% in Cuban pesos, 35.9% in convertible Cuban pesos, and 5.2% in U.S. dollars. Partido Comunista de Cuba, "Material de Estudio, Abril–Junio" (2008).
7. There are very few openings for exchange rate arbitrage with respect to the Cuban peso. Not only are enterprises prohibited from exchanging currencies at CADECA, but the volume of currency exchanged at the agency and its restriction to cash-only transactions effectively preclude its use by enterprises and institutions.
8. Partido Comunista de Cuba, "Material de Estudio, Abril-Junio."

Commentary
The Importance of the Right Incentives

Dani Rodrik

For someone who has not worked on Cuba's economy, reading these first two chapters is a bit like returning back to the 1970s. In Cuba, the government has apparently still not made up its mind about whether it wants to have a market economy or not. Economic policy seems to be driven by a process of muddling through with no clear goal in mind. A "convertible" peso circulates along a "non-convertible" one. Reminiscent of the Soviet-type systems, state enterprises' profits are calculated in meaningless accounting units.

In such circumstances, Omar Everleny Pérez Villanueva is surely correct when he notes that Cuba is "in urgent need of a profound economic or structural transformation, with an emphasis on decentralization." The difficult question is how to undertake this transformation without generating macroeconomic instability and social tensions in the transition. The experience of the former Soviet Union and countries of Eastern Europe provides some warnings. Countries that had reasonably strong prospects of quick EU membership had the luxury of anchoring their institutional transformation on European models, which helped with both the economics and politics of reforms. Others were not as lucky, and the 1990s ended up being quite turbulent.

Meanwhile, China's experience stands as proof of concept for an alternative path—a gradualist, two-track, reforming-at-the-margins kind of strategy, which was able to generate rapid returns without unsettling prevailing distributional bargains.

It would be probably futile to import the Chinese—or for that matter the Vietnamese—model wholesale to Cuba. The specific reforms implemented by China—the household responsibility system, the township-and-village enterprises, special economic zones—were solutions designed to overcome local constraints and take advantage of local opportunities.

But there is one single overarching lesson from China that *can* be adopted wholesale, and that is because it is a universal one. Economic reform is all about getting incentives right. Getting incentives right, in turn, does not necessarily require wholesale, across-the-board reform. It simply requires ensuring that enterprises and firms obtain market-based incentives *at the margin*. For many years after 1978, China's central planning system operated alongside the market, with little cost to overall economic growth. That is because Chinese farmers and enterprises knew they were free to transact in markets (at free-market prices) once they fulfilled their obligations to the state.

So the critical question for an economy like Cuba is how to shift to market incentives at the margin. An obvious place to begin is to allow enterprises and household to transact at a more market-determined, realistic exchange rate.

One thing that we have learned from the 1970s is that nothing does more harm to an economy than an overvalued exchange rate. Keeping the local value of the dollar low discourages production for world markets, subsidizes imports, taxes import-substitution, and pushes the economy towards consumption rather than production. In order to sustain the level of the exchange rate, elaborate mechanisms of exchange controls and foreign-currency allocation have to be instituted. Before long, people are spending more time trying to evade the controls than thinking about how to be more productive and innovative.

Pavel Vidal Alejandro highlights these and other costs of the Cuban currency system and notes the high degree of overvaluation of the official peso. Without currency unification, it is very hard to see how a desirable pattern of structural change can be set into motion in Cuba.

There are the usual worries about currency unification. It can result in large redistributions of income—from those whose incomes derive from non-tradable services to those who earn or save foreign currency. It can also be inflationary if not managed well.

But there are ways around these problems. On the redistribution front, it is possible to take a page from the Chinese book and manage the transition by making the official peso convertible at the margin. Exporters, for example, could get the devalued, higher rate only for export earnings above what they earned, say, in the previous year. Similarly, importers would pay the higher rate for dollars only for allocations that exceeded their previous quota. This provides the appropriate incentives at the margin, but without eliminating the streams of rents and transfers implicit in the previous regime.

As for inflation, this too is often a misplaced concern. In the presence of an overvalued currency and administrative allocation of foreign currency, there is already lots of hidden inflation in the economy. The scarcity rents of imported goods and services get reflected in black-market prices that greatly exceed official prices. When the currency is devalued, the supply of tradeables increases and these scarcity rents disappear. As Anne Krueger, among others, showed (again in the 1970s), the consequence is, if anything, anti-inflationary. Of course, maintaining macroeconomic and fiscal discipline is important during this process.

But there is a broader issue that goes beyond the technicalities of currency unification. Pavel Vidal Alejandro describes Cuba as "an economic policy environment characterized by overly discretionary decision-making with few general rules, excessive prohibitions, and disparate decisions producing an economic situation that is difficult to measure and understand." In this sentence, we have the crux of the problem. If the private sector gets mixed signals about the direction of reform, no amount of policy tinkering will have much effect.

The government needs to make up its mind, and communicate its strategy clearly. Will it foster private markets and private entrepreneurship, or not?

Let me end on a note of optimism. No one can deny that the challenge of restructuring socialist economies is huge. There is much to do, and most of what needs to be done is politically difficult and economically uncertain. Yet lagging behind has its advantages. Cuba's human resources endow the economy with a significant catch-up potential. When so many things are wrong in the policy environment, one doesn't need to fix everything at once to get a significant boost in economic growth. Do a few things right—send the right signals to entrepreneurs and investors, allow incentives to operate at the margin—and you can get a huge response. A small number of reforms targeted at binding constraints may have a large and widespread impact. The rest of the reforms can be done along the way.

3

Cuban Agriculture in the "Special Period" and Necessary Transformations

Armando Nova González

Agriculture has a strategic and decisive effect on the Cuban economy because of its multiplier effect on other economic sectors, its potential to generate export income, contribute to food production, create employment, and generate gross national production. The historically high level of specialization in sugar exports has contributed to insufficient domestic food diversity and production, leading thus to a high dependency on food imports. Together, these factors contribute to Cuba's severe vulnerability to food security.[1]

Until the end of the 1990s, Cuban sugar exports represented a significant portion of the total value of goods produced and more than 75% of the value of the country's total exports. Before 1959, Cuba exported between 2.9 and 3.0 million tons of sugar to the United States each year, representing approximately 55% of the total volume of sugar exports. In 1960, which was the last year before the United States suspended its quota of Cuban sugar, sugar exports to the United States were 1.9 million tons. These exports then shifted to the former Soviet Union and former socialist countries in Eastern Europe, which together imported between four and five million tons relative to an annual average production of 7.5 to over 8.0 million tons between 1975 and 1990. Cuba's trade arrangements with these countries contributed to the persistence of an agricultural model based on mono-production and mono-exports with distortions for its economy.

By the late 1980s and the early 1990s, the multiplier effect of the sugar-cane industry on various economic sectors and branches of the economy continued to be significant. Sugar was the impetus for 14% of Cuba's mechanical production; it created demand for 20% of the country's steel and heavy industry, 13% of basic industry, and 8% of light industry. It also provided for 9% of gross electrical generation using the cane residue, bagasse. The sugar-based agro-industry also employed more than 400,000 workers, representing 12% of the employed labor force of the country. Between workers and their families, more than 2 million Cubans depended on different aspects of the industry. In addition, sugar represented a significant source of earnings for the economy as a whole.

The Cuban farm sector had achieved important levels of output in terms of both total volume and volume per capita by the early 1990s. These results were based on input-intensive industrial agriculture, with high levels of investment, inputs, and equipment per hectare, but low levels of efficiency, and significant external dependence.[2] In the 1980s, this agricultural model began to show signs of exhaustion, especially in the second half of the decade. The evidence appeared in the decline of a group of indicators of economic efficiency: output increases were achieved on the basis of low yields, increased investment spending per hectare, and rising inputs per unit of production, among other indices. The disappearance of the socialist bloc and with it Cuba's assured conditions of secure markets, preferential prices, and fair terms of trade—which had provided, among other things, a decisive underlying support for the economy and the farm sector—was the last straw. This shock on top of the existing trend in declining indicators of efficiency unleashed the economic crisis of the 1990s, especially in the farm sector.

Cuba responded to this crisis by instituting a series of transformations in agriculture. The most important of these measures were:

- The creation of Basic Units of Cooperative Production (UBPC; *Unidades Básicas de Producción Cooperativa*) in October 1993.
- Excessively large state farms were subdivided into several UBPCs each. From then on, the UBPCs would work the land as collective proprietors holding usufruct tenure for an unspecified period, and without paying rent.
- The reopening of retail Farmers' Markets in October 1994. This policy change made a substantial contribution to deflating the very high prices prevalent in the underground economy while broadening the opportunities for food supply to the population. The Farmers' Markets have been seen as a stimulus to production and to producers, because producers can sell at higher prices than those traditionally paid by the *Acopio* (the state wholesale purchasing agency).
- The granting of land to private individuals in usufruct tenure in 1994.

Thus, the year 1993 marked the beginning of an important process of transformation in Cuban agriculture. This process is ongoing, and difficulties have become evident in the operation of the UBPCs and to some degree also in the CPAs, CCSs, and private farms (which has limited to utilization of their productive potential). As I will argue, the lack of change in the operating environment helps to explain the problems that have been encountered to ignite production. The evidence will show that the early 1990s reforms have lacked the necessary continuity and depth and instead came to a halt and even went back toward more centralized forms of administration in both the macro- and micro-economies, causing renewed restriction of the development of the forces of production. The CCSs and private farms, which hold property rights, have provided the highest yields utilizing the smallest quantity of resources. Thus, these forms of property must be supported, along with other new modes such as usufruct rental distribution that gives the producer or producers the right to make all the appropriate decisions in pursuit of full realization of the property's potential.

In this chapter I will describe the agricultural reforms in the early 1900s and assess their impact in the period between 2004 and 2007. The chapter begins by reviewing the role of the agriculture sector in the Cuban economy to provide the necessary background for the discussion that follows, in which the agricultural reforms are first described and then evaluated. My focus is on the period between 2004 and 2007, which is a particularly critical period after the sector's significant contraction in 2003. In the concluding section, a set of proposals are presented to help increase the productivity of the agricultural sector in the Cuban economy.

The Role of Agriculture in the Cuban Economy

The agricultural sector plays a decisive role in the Cuban economy because of its direct and indirect participation in the Gross Domestic Product (GDP) as well as its multiplier effect. Considering only its current direct participation in GDP could lead to underestimating its importance. While at the end of 2007 it contributed only 3.8%, the sector had been directly responsible for between 7 to 8% of GDP before a significant drop in agricultural production in 2003 (see Table 3.1).

Production in a significant group of industries including sugar and its derivatives, food, tobacco, alcoholic and non-alcoholic beverages, leather, rope, timber, and others depends totally or partially on raw materials produced by the agricultural sector. These industries contribute 6.4% to GDP. Other activities such as the transportation and marketing of agricultural products or processed agricultural products are estimated to account for approximately 10% of GDP. Thus about 20.2% of GDP depends directly or indirectly on agricultural activity, even with the current depressed state of

Table 3.1. Gross Domestic Product by Economic Activity
(% at 1997 prices)

Sector	2003	2006	2007
Total	100.0	100.0	100.0
A. Goods	8.4	16.4	17.0
Agriculture	6.8	3.2	3.8
Fishing	–	0.3	0.3
Mining	1.6	0.7	0.6
Sugar industry	–	0.4	0.4
Manufacturing	16.5	11.8	11.9
B. Basic services	17.9	16.3	15.3
C. Other services	57.2	67.3	67.7
Other services by subsector:			
Commerce	–	19.7	18.1
Education	–	12.0	12.0
Public health		15.0	17.0
D. Culture and sports	–	3.9	4.1
E. Public administration and social assistance	–	3.3	3.3

Source: Oficina Nacional de Estadísticas (ONE). *Anuario Estadístico de Cuba* (Havana: ONE, various years).

agricultural and livestock production. It is thus easy to see why the recovery of the agricultural sector matters to the Cuban economy.

The multiplier effect of the agricultural sector is also illustrated by its production linkages, including its up and downstream spillover effects on the Cuban economy. When the agricultural sector fails to reach its expected production targets, the economy faces significant increases in costs to compensate for the sector's deficiencies. To some extent this is what has happened in recent years, stimulating an ever greater volume of food imports amounting to some US$1.7 billion in 2007, more than 18% of total imports. A significant portion of these imported foods could be produced competitively on the island, especially given today's high commodity prices in international markets. In 2008, Cuba spent over US$2 billion on food imports. These shortages have led to a more vulnerable economy in terms of food sufficiency and a greater dependency on international sources for food.

Table 3.2 illustrates the dependence on imported food from 1950 to 2005. By 2005, domestic production accounted for only 42% of total caloric consumption and only 38% of protein consumption. Domestic production accounted for 57% of total animal protein intake and only 29% of vegetable protein consumption.

Table 3.2. Percentage of Imported Macronutrients in Daily Food Consumption

Nutrient	1950	1975	1980	1985	2005
Calories	47	56	53	53	58
Protein	53	64	61	59	62
Animal protein	–	35	31	35	43
Plant protein	–	65	69	65	71

Source: Compiled from various sources including Marcos M. Fernández, "Algunos Aspectos de las Condiciones de Vida del Cubano, antes del Triunfo de la Revolución (1959)"; *Revista Demanda Interna* 2 (1987); Oficina Nacional de Estadísticas (ONE); *Anuario Estadístico de Cuba* (Havana: ONE, various years); and Armando Nova, *La Agricultura en Cuba: Evolución y Trayectoria (1959–2005)* (Havana: Editorial Ciencias Sociales, 2006).

Table 3.3 illustrates the change in the participation of the agricultural sector in generating export earnings. The share of export earnings derived from agriculture decreased from 83% in 1991 to just 17% in 2006. Sugar products had generated 77% of all exports earnings in 1992, but by 2006 this sector contributed only 8% of the total. In contrast, nickel exports reached 48% of export earnings in 2006, in large part due to high international market prices.

Table 3.3. Agricultural and Total Exports, 1991–2006

(US$ billions)

Year	Total Goods Exported	Agricultural Exports	Agriculture as Percent of Exports
1991	2.9795	2.4864	83
1992	1.7794	1.3657	77
1993	1.1566	.8603	74
1994	1.3308	.8717	66
1995	1.4916	.8612	58
1996	1.8655	1.1243	60
1997	1.8191	1.0533	58
1998	1.5122	.8497	56
1999	1.4958	.7109	48
2000	1.6753	.6596	39
2001	1.6219	.7979	49
2002	1.4217	.6183	43
2003	1.6716	.5455	33
2004	2.1880	.5211	24
2005	1.9946	.3901	20
2006	2.7594	.4727	17

Source: Oficina Nacional de Estadísticas (ONE); *Anuario Estadístico de Cuba* (Havana: ONE, various years).

Twenty-one percent of the economically active population works directly in the agricultural sector, but many more work in the numerous industries that rely on agriculture as a source of supply of raw materials. Almost four million Cuban households depend on the performance of the agricultural sector. This is another illustration of the significant multiplier effect of agriculture on the national economy.

The agro-industrial sector has positive spillover effects thanks to its ability to generate renewable and non-contaminating electrical energy, biofuels, and biogas through the use of sugarcane biomass, thereby producing significant economic, social, and geographic advantages. Sugarcane-based bioenergetic agro-industry is self-sustaining in terms of energy and it also produces energy surpluses and positive balances in the absorption and emission of gases. The cane plantations absorb carbon dioxide (the principal cause of the greenhouse effect and rising temperatures on the planet) from the air and, as a result of chemical reactions, they expel it in the form of oxygen. It is estimated that one hectare of sugarcane can absorb more than 60 tons of carbon dioxide and produce about 40 tons of pure oxygen per year, acting as a carbon sink and producing the same beneficial effects on the atmosphere as a growing forest.

The sector also acts as a stimulus to economic activity as it demands goods that areproduced by different industrial sectors of the national economy, such as machinery, tools, and other equipment, clothing and shoes, agro-chemicals, tires, batteries, and fuel.

Economic Changes in the 1990s

The establishment of the Basic Units of Cooperative Production (UBPCs) at the end of 1993 and in 1994 initiated a significant change in the agriculture sector. With the exception of land, the means of production held by overly large state enterprises were distributed to cooperative production units. The land itself was transferred to these units in usufruct for an undetermined period of time. A few months afterwards, the free agricultural market (*Mercado Libre Agropecuario*) was reopened in October 1994. The history and positive experiences of Agricultural Production Cooperatives (*Cooperativas de Producción Agropecuaria,* CPAs) over the course of more than 20 years served as a model for the establishment and operational mechanisms of the UBPCs. Along with the existing CPAs and the Credit and Services Cooperatives (*Cooperativas de Créditos y Servicios,* CCSs), the new UBPCs firmly established cooperative production as a framework for the development of agricultural and livestock production in Cuba. Table 3.4 shows the significant changes in land tenancy and use that stemmed from these policy changes.

Table 3.4. Land Use and Tenancy before Changes in Agricultural Production in the 1990s and in 2005 (thousands of hectares)

| | 1989 | | 2005 | | | | | |
| | Total | | Total | | Of the Total: Agriculture | | Of the Agricultural: Cultivated | |
	Area	%	Area	%	Area	%	Area	%
Total	11,016	100	10,988.6	100	6,597.1	100	3,222.7	100
State	9,065	82	6,391.8	58	2,658.6	40	909.4	28
Non-State	1,951	18	4,596.8	42	3,938.5	60	2,313.3	72
UBPC	–	–	2,551.2	24	2,177.2	33	1,182.3	37
Products:								
Sugarcane	–	–	1,335.8		–		810.1	
Coffee	–	–	134.7		–		29.8	
Plantain	–	–	105.5		–		26.2	
Citrus and fruit	–	–	168.2		–		51.7	
Rice	–	–	201.3		–		54.3	
Various crops	–	–	795.0		–		128.1	
Tobacco	–	–	66.4		–		2.2	
CPA	868	8	700.6	6	593.1	9	344.7	11
Sugarcane	235		–		–		201.9	
Non-sugarcane	633		–		–			
Coffee	–		–		–		18.6	
Plantain	–		–		–		12.0	
Citrus and fruit	–		–		–		12.5	
Rice	–		–		–		14.2	
Various crops	–		–		–		64.9	
Tobacco	–		–		–		8.8	
CCS	833	7	914.6	8	794.3	12	534.6	16
Private (*Campesinos;* farmers)	250	3	431.4	4	373.9	6	251.7	8

Source: Oficina Nacional de Estadísticas (ONE); "Principales Indicadores del Sector Agropecuario" (Havana: ONE, various years); and Oficina Nacional de Estadísticas (ONE), *Anuario Estadístico de Cuba* (Havana: ONE, various years).

It has been pointed out on more than one occasion that the UBPCs were established abruptly, and that agricultural workers were suddenly transformed into members of cooperatives and owners of collective property in an extremely difficult economic context and in the midst of a general economic crisis.[3] Having acquired the means of production, they were burdened with significant debt that had to be paid off within a specified period of time. In practice, the payback periods and rates were extended and, in some cases, cancelled. The UBPCs still face a number of problems that have plagued them since they were founded, of course, and new difficulties have arisen in the last fifteen years. Among them are the following:

- UBPCs must fulfill sales commitments to the *Acopio* (the state procurement and distribution office) that amount to more than 70% of their essential products; they are also committed to selling a proportion of their food products not classified as essential.[4] The prices paid by the state procurement agency are much lower than those in the free agricultural markets and generally do not cover costs.[5]

- UBPCs are told what items to produce, how much of each to produce, and to whom they should be distributed.

- Intermediary bureaucracies group UBPCs and centralize decision-making regarding what they should produce, to whom and at what price it should be sold, what inputs they will receive, what investments they should make, and other matters.

- The resources needed by UBPCs are centrally assigned. There is no market where producers can obtain inputs or equipment.

- Livestock and dairy UBPCs cannot market their products (milk and meat) at free agricultural markets, nor can rice-growing, citrus-growing, and potato-growing UBPCs.

- Internal accounting problems affect the economic condition and stability of cooperative members.

These problems add up to a lack of needed autonomy for UBPCs; many of these units are unprofitable. With no ability to distribute profits, they provide none of the needed economic stimulus.

The sales of food products at free agricultural markets have also faced significant problems. In general terms, the free market must compete in an oligopolistic economic sector. The state distributes the *Acopio* in markets operated by the Ministry of Domestic Commerce (*Ministerio de Comercio Interior,* MINCIN). State markets managed by the Ministry of Agriculture (*Ministerio de Agricultura,* MINAG) have also emerged; these state markets operate with price ceilings that are not very different from those in markets operated by MINCIN. However, MINAG markets are characterized by their limited supply and inferior quality of goods. This situation has persisted since each of these state-run markets began to operate independently.

In fact the sale of products in agricultural markets has become more monopolistic over time. The state provides increasing proportions of both meat and crops to markets operated by MINCIN and MINAG. The direct participation of UBPCs, CPAs, CCSs, and private producers in free agricultural markets is steadily decreasing. Given their large number of producers and consumers, the markets for food should function and clear through prices set as if under perfect competition. Because of the problems outlined above, however, food prices are set at levels equivalent to those set under quite imperfect competition.

Agricultural Production from 2004 to 2007

Agricultural production declined steadily from 2000 to 2006. In 2007, it grew slightly from its 2006 level, which had been the lowest since 2000 (see Table 3.5). With respect to livestock, particularly cattle, we see fewer head slaughtered. An increase in the average weight of the animals has not sufficed to prevent a decrease in the total production of meat (see Table 3.6). The total volume of milk increased, stimulated by an increase in the price of milk as well as a slight increase in the number of milking cows from 317.6 to 318.2 (600 cows).

In animal food production, all indicators for porcine livestock improved compared to the previous year, with the state sector being the largest producer, representing 86% of the total volume of pork. This general increase in supply made it possible for the state to increase its supply of products to the free markets (6,422.4 tons of pork cuts in 2007 compared to 3,349.6 tons of supply and sales in 2006).

Table 3.5. Production of Plant-based Foods, 2004–2007
(thousands of quintals) 1,000 quintals = 48.95 metric tons

Products	2004	2005	2006	2007	% change 2007 vs. 2006
Roots and tubers:	**31,738.4**	**26,559.0**	**23,817.5**	**24,283.5**	**1.96%**
Subcategories:					
Potatoes	7,113.5	6,738.2	6,143.9	2,967.5	−51.7 %
Sweet potatoes	10,567.8	7,168.1	–	–	
Malanga (taro)	5,304.5	3,940.9	–	–	
Plantains	18,023.3	12,657.0	14,339.5	18,083.2	26.1 %
Fruit	6,735.3	5,474.1	5,584.4	5,837.1	4.5 %
Viandas (root veg., tubers)	11,288.0	7,182.9	8,755.1	12,246.1	39.9 %
Vegetables	**53,677.3**	**42,926.2**	**37,963.0**	**36,729.7**	**−3.2 %**
Subcategories:					
Tomatoes	10,442.6	9,193.7	8,442.5	7,522.0	−10.9 %
Peppers	1,202.0	1,053.1	901.0	873.9	−3.0 %
Onions	1,902.3	1,850.5	1,623.7	1,580.4	−2.7 %
Garlic	712.6	682.5	487.1	484.8	−0.5 %
Rice (wet paddy)	**10,628.6**	**7,991.6**	**9,439.5**	**9,400.0**	
Maize	**6,537.8**	**5,344.5**	**5,085.4**	**5,774.1**	13.5 %
Dry beans	**1,722.7**	**1,295.3**	**974.0**	**1,191.3**	22.3 %
Citrus	**17,428.9**	**10,872.2**	**7,306.5**	**10,102.5**	38.3 %
Fruit	**10,659.0**	**8,683.5**	**8,488.0**	**8,715.5**	2.7 %

Source: Compiled by author based on Oficina Nacional de Estadísticas (ONE), "Principales Indicadores del Sector Agropecuario" (Havana: ONE, various years); and Oficina Nacional de Estadísticas (ONE), *Anuario Estadístico de Cuba* (Havana: ONE, various years).

Table 3.6. Livestock Production, 2000–2007

Category	Unit of measurement	2000	2001	2002	2003	2004	2005	2006	2007	% 2007 vs. 2006
Bovine										
Animals Slaughtered	Thousand head	491.6	478.3	460.7	371.8	388.6	466.2	360.6	339.6	-5.82%
Weight on hoof	One thousand metric tons	145.5	141.8	131.7	112.1	107.7	118.4	111.3	109.5	-1.62%
Average weight	Kilogram	296.1	296.5	285.8	301.6	277.2	254.0	308.5	322.3	4.47%
Milk production	One million liters	422.8	436.2	400.7	429.4	362.4	322.7	371.7	411.3	10.65%
Milking cows	Thousand head	368.4	369.8	364.6	360.3	325.2	274.2	317.6	318.2	0.19%
Liters/cow/day	Not available	3.14	3.23	3.01	3.26	3.05	3.22	3.20	3.5	9.37%
Existing population of bovine livestock	Thousand head	4110.2	4038.5	3973.7	4025.3	3942.6	3703.6	3737.1	3787.4	1.35%
Porcine										
Slaughtered	Thousand head	1100.9	985.8	963.5	1098.8	1097.7	1161.8	1463.8	2134.5	45.82%
Weight on hoof	One thousand metric tons	73.1	58.9	68.5	75.4	73.8	86.3	119.1	181.9	52.73%
Average weight	Kilogram	66.4	59.8	71.1	68.6	67.2	74.3	81.4	85.2	4.67%
Existing population of porcine livestock	Thousand head	1221.8	1307.2	1351.8	1335.6	1245.3	1293.3	1410.2	1502.1	6.52%
Poultry										
Total eggs produced	Billion units	1.3376	1.1776	1.3656	1.4644	1.4052	1.7271	1.9132	1.9837	3.68%
Subcategory: Eggs produced under modern industrial conditions	Billion units	1.1527	.9827	1.1572	1.2625	1.1863	1.4946	1.7188	1.7609	2.45%
Population of laying hens	Million head	5.1459	4.7903	4.1987	4.5865	4.4903	5.7117	7.0428	7.3159	3.88%
Eggs per laying hen	One	224	205.1	275.6	275.3	264.2	261.7	244.1	240.7	-1.39%
Feed/10 eggs	Kilogram	1.8	1.9	1.5	1.4	1.5	1.5	1.6	1.6	0.00%
Poultry meat	One thousand metric tons	27.2	26.5	12.9	9.5	10.1	8.6	9.3	12.0	29.03%
Ovine-Caprine										
Meat	One thousand metric tons	5.508	6.143	6.847	7.301	7.783	7.781	8.042	8.897	10.63%
Animals slaughtered	Thousand head	209.4	241.7	248.6	264.6	284.6	291.6	301.2	320.0	6.24%
Average weight	Kilogram	26.3	25.4	27.5	27.5	27.3	26.6	26.6	27.8	4.51%

Source: Compiled by author based on Oficina Nacional de Estadísticas (ONE), "Principales Indicadores del Sector Agropecuario" (Havana: ONE, various years).

There were production increases of eggs and meat in the poultry sub-sector, even though the number of eggs per laying hen decreased (this indicator declined consistently since 2005), and the consumption of feed per egg did not improve compared to 2006. The goal of producing two billion eggs was originally thought to be attainable in 2006 but was not met, nor was the goal of 2.3 billion eggs for 2007.

Problems in the agricultural sector have led to inefficiency in the use of land, with many uncultivated and unproductive agricultural land areas (see Appendix 1) and low agricultural yields (see Appendix 2).

Necessary Policy Measures

Initial steps have been taken to establish a market where producers can obtain inputs. The government is setting up stores where producers can purchase raw materials, with their buying capacity indexed to their productive performance. Timely steps are also being taken to empower municipalities and to give producers themselves their appropriate role in the decision-making process with respect to agricultural production. Municipal Agricultural Offices (*Delegaciones Agropecuarias Municipales*) are being set up for this purpose.

The agricultural sector is in urgent need of significant policy changes. The changes described above, begun in the 1990s, must continue, and new measures must be taken to stimulate the sector's productive forces. The following improvements should be considered:

- Reduce the number of institutions and simplify the structures both at the base and the superstructure so that production units or enterprises gain autonomy. Agencies responsible to four different ministries are currently involved in the production of food, and they have entirely homologous structures right down to the base level. These structures should be cut and simplified.

- Local people should have a key role in food production and in finding solutions to problems. From the national to the municipal level, there is a lack of horizontal relations between units in the current structure. Under the process of decentralization required by the agricultural sector to improve its functioning, the various agro-economic productive entities located in each municipality (the UBPCs, the CPAs, the CCSs, the private sector, and state enterprises) need to develop wide-ranging horizontal relations. These would help to solve specific economic, technological, financial, management, and other local problems without having to wait for decisions from on high.

- In order to increase their sense of ownership, the UBPCs, the CPAs, the CCS and other enterprises in the productive system of the agricultural sector need to be free to decide how to efficiently combine productive factors and obtain productive resources as well as make decisions about their products and how to manage them.

- Recognize the UBPCs as enterprises with rights to operate as any normal business operation and with the same obligations as well.

- Allow the inputs markets to purchase machinery, equipment, tools, irrigation systems, services and other goods. This would help to close the circle of the productive cycle and to promote development on an expanded scale.

- Support the role of the market as a tool to help producers by facilitating the process of distribution.

- Resolve the ambiguity over the term "usufruct," given that this causes uncertainty among individual and collective producers and compromises their sense of ownership and confidence in their rights. The solution to this problem requires the standardization of rental relationships to establish the rights and obligations of renters and tenants, by clarifying the terms "legal ownership" and "economic ownership" (which guarantees full property rights with regard to decision-making and its results). Together with the other policy measures indicated here, such changes will resolve the uncertainties surrounding ownership and stimulate the development of the sector's productive forces.

- Planning should play a regulatory role in the allocation of resources for the economy as a whole as well as at the local level, in order to help producers to succeed in closing their productive cycle.

- The state should participate in the market like other actors, but it should also act as regulator of prices and use appropriate economic mechanisms to balance supply and demand.

- Eliminate barriers to the sale of certain products and against certain producers in the markets.

- Sell most production in markets where the forces of supply and demand operate freely and stimulate producers to increase production. Sales commitments to the state through the mechanisms of *Acopio* should be limited to essential products.

- Promote direct market sales by individual and cooperative producers. The distribution chain should be simplified; taxes and other costs associated with sales should be reduced. If the share of value created by producers that stays with them ismaximized, it will act as an indispensable stimulus to increased production.

- Increase the participation of foreign investment in the different branches and sub-branches of the agricultural sector, beginning with those areas where production has declined the most and that are susceptible to a rapid process of recovery to produce food for the domestic market, replace imports, and generate renewable energy and export agriculture.

During the process of their implementation, these policy changes would themselves bring about or stimulate a series of new measures within the existing system. It would be a dynamic and dialectical process of constant and ongoing development of the productive forces of the Cuban economy.

Appendix 1

Balance of Land Availability and Land Use, 2005 (thousands of hectares)

Total Land Available	**10,988.6**	
Land with Agricultural Use Potential	6,597.1	100.0%
State	2,658.6	40.0
UBPC	2,177.2	33.0
CPA	593.1	9.0
CCS	799.6	12.0
Private	368.6	6.0
Land in Cultivation	**3,222.7**	**100.0%**
State	909.4	27.6
UBPC	1,182.3	37.0
CPA	344.7	11.0
CCS	531.9	16.6
Private	254.4	7.8
Not in Cultivation	**3,374.4**	
State	1,749.2	
UBPC	994.9	
CPA	248.4	
CCS	260.0	
Private	121.9	
Of this:		
Pasture	**2,268.5**	
State	1,072.4	
UBPC	681.6	
CPA	192.9	
CCS	218.7	
Private	102.9	
Idle	**1,105.9**	
State	676.8	
UBPC	313.3	
CPA	55.5	
CCS	41.0	
Private	19.3	
Non-Cultivable Land	**4,391.5**	

Source: Oficina Nacional de Estadísticas (ONE), *Anuario Estadístico de Cuba* (Havana: ONE, various years).

Appendix 2

Land Use by Province, 2008 (thousands of hectares)

		Total Land	Land Available for Agriculture	Cultivated Land	Cultivation Index (%)	Idle Land (%)*	Forestation Index (%)
	Cuba	10,988	6,619	2,998	45.1	18.6	26.4
1	Pinar del Río	1,090	506	265	52.4	14.0	42.9
2	La Habana	573	401	278	69.3	3.7	13.3
3	Ciudad de La Habana	72	32	21	66.3	5.9	4.1
4	Matanzas	1,180	531	221	41.8	17.6	35.5
5	Villa Clara	841	615	279	45.4	16.2	14.8
6	Cienfuegos	418	307	133	43.4	27.6	14.8
7	Sancti Spíritus	673	485	206	42.5	19.7	14.3
8	Ciego de Ávila	678	441	239	54.3	21.6	19.7
9	Camagüey	1,561	1,060	310	29.2	34.9	19.3
10	Las Tunas	658	504	194	38.5	31.3	13.8
11	Holguín	929	522	278	53.3	4.5	32.2
12	Granma	837	547	241	44.1	14.0	21.4
13	Santiago de Cuba	615	349	187	53.5	4.7	34
14	Guantánamo	616	245	118	48.2	6.0	49.9
15	Isla de la Juventud	241	68	12	18.5	25.4	55.9

*Excludes deforested land.

Endnotes

1. Although the sugar industry was downsized and restructured in 2002, the sector retains its significant multiplier effect on the domestic economy. Food imports have continued to increase in a sustained fashion, reaching economically unsustainable levels. In 2008, these imports rose to US$2.5 billion, which represents approximately 20% of the country's total imports and 5% of GDP in constant prices. The major food items imported include rice, beans, fats, soybeans, corn, wheat, powdered milk, among other items. This subject is described and analyzed in detail in Anicia Garcia's chapter in this volume.

2. Armando González Nova, *La agricultura en Cuba: evolución y trayectoria (1959–2005)* (Havana: Editorial Ciencias Sociales, 2006).

3. Armando Nova, "Las Nuevas Relaciones de Producción en la Agricultura." *CUBA: Investigación Económica INIE* 1 (1998).

4. Anicia García, "Mercado Agropecuario, Evolución Actual y Perspectiva." *CUBA: Investigación Económica INIE* 3 and 4 (1997): 116.

5. R Villegas. "Las UBPC como forma de realización de la propiedad social en la Agricultura Cubana" (Granma: Universidad de Granma, 1999).

4

Cuban Agriculture Reforms after 2007

Armando Nova González

As we saw in the preceding chapter, the agricultural reforms implemented in the early 1990s were insufficient to increase the food supply grown in Cuba. Because of the continued slowdown in the farm sector, as demonstrated by a decline in agricultural and livestock output (or, in the best of cases, in stagnation of output),[1] a series of changes were introduced beginning in 2007 to attempt to reactivate agriculture. Among the measures that were implemented are: higher prices paid for milk, beef, and agricultural products; a step toward decentralization that identifies the *municipio* (municipality) as the key level of decision-making for agricultural activity; and the simplification of ministerial structures and functions related to food production and processing. The purpose of this chapter is to describe these reforms in greater detail and to examine their impact on agricultural and livestock production.

Among the set of policy measures designed to boost productivity, the most important one has been to grant to individuals usufruct tenure in idle agricultural land (land not under cultivation), a move intended to lead toward a productive holding of land. This step, however, is a necessary but not a sufficient condition.

To illustrate this point, a review of recent agricultural performance is helpful, as it shows that the results obtained thus far are short of expectations. At the close of the third trimester of 2010, total farm production had dropped by 5.1% in comparison with the same period during the previous year.[2] Production of vegetables dropped (see Appendix 1) by 9.8%, while livestock grew by only 0.3%. There was a 5.1% increase in milk supply, 1.5% in egg production, and 24.3% more chicken (1.8 thousand metric tons live weight). Production of pork, beef, and sheep counted together with goats dropped by 1.1%, 6.0%, and 1.2% respectively. In the cane sector, sugar production in the recently concluded harvest (2009–10) also dropped, to extremely low levels. The preliminary figures for 2010 suggest that farm goods have contracted by 2.8%.[3] Indeed, production has dropped in twelve fundamental areas including rice, pork, eggs, vegetables, beans, root crops and plantains, and citrus.

The 2007 reforms have not yielded satisfactory results because they have not provided solutions to three fundamental issues: full ownership, the necessary recognition of the real, objective role of markets; and the absence of an organized, well-structured operating system (that is, the measures have been carried out on an *ad hoc* basis). In order for the guidelines advanced in preparation for the Sixth Congress of the Communist Party[4] to be fully implemented, all three issues must be addressed. The concluding section of this chapter attempts to offer some recommendations in this regard.

Agricultural and Livestock Production

Agricultural and livestock production has been showing signs of instability and, since 2004, decreases (see Figure 4.1). This tendency continued until the end of the third quarter of 2009 (in comparison to the same period in the previous year). By the end of 2009, agricultural and livestock production as a whole was 100.5% of the 2008 total, which indicates an almost completely flat trend. The production of food products of plant origin rose by 5.6% as a result of increased production of moist paddy rice, but this was offset by a decrease in livestock production, which fell 4.6% during the same period.

Total production of *viandas* (tubers, root vegetables, and plantain) decreased by 0.5%, of which the reduction in plantains was the largest contributing factor. Plantain production fell by 18.5% (110,900 tons less than the year before), while tuber and root vegetable production grew by 9.5%, including a 47.8% increase in potatoes and a 49.2% increase in sweet potatoes. The production of *malanga* (taro), *yuca* (cassava) and other tubers decreased by 19.0%, 26.7%, and 1.5% respectively.

During the 2000s, the volume of other vegetable produce increased by 11%. More specifically, tomato production rose by 43.3%, but this crop suffered significant losses during the harvest and post harvest interval due to transportation problems, a shortage of packaging materials, and inadequate industrial capacity harvest processing. Onion production increased by 2.6%, garlic by 25.8%, pumpkins by 6.1%, melons by 11.1%, and other produce by 3.3%. There was a decrease in cabbage production; pepper production fell 6.3% and cucumbers by 4%. Maize production decreased by 6.4%, while the harvest of moist paddy rice increased by more than 40% and dry beans by 37%. Citrus production increased slightly at a rate of 1%, while tropical fruit production fell by 3.2%.

Comparing the levels reached at the end of 2009 with figures from the third quarter of the same year (see Table 4.1), the significant increase in

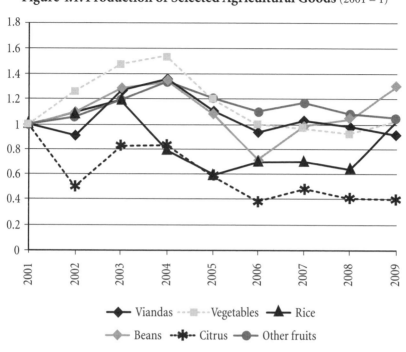

Figure 4.1. Production of Selected Agricultural Goods (2001 = 1)

Source: author's calculations using the principal indicators of the agricultural sector for 2001–2009 as detailed in the 2005–2008 Statistical Yearbooks of Cuba, Social Economic Panorama 2008 and 2009, all data from the National Office of Statistics, hereafter ONE.

sweet potatoes stands out. In the fourth quarter of 2009 alone, sweet potato production increased by 48%, which represented 77.2% of the total increase in tuber and root vegetable production for the quarter. Sweet potato production rose because of a significant increase in planting[5] and the extension of its harvest beyond its ideal time-span.[6] To the extent that sweet potatoes remain in the ground unharvested, yield per unit of area increases, but the crop becomes susceptible to infestation by the sweet potato weevil,[7] resulting in decreased quality for human consumption. In addition, the land used for sweet potato harvesting should generally alternate with a crop of regular potatoes so the extended time dedicated to sweet potatoes production may in fact undermine the production of potatoes in the same year. That is how high levels of sweet potato production contributed significantly to the 5.6% increase in agricultural production in the year 2009.

Table 4.1. Comparative Agricultural Production, 2008, and First, Second, and Third Quarters of 2009 vs. Fourth Quarter of 2009, and 2009 vs. 2008 (thousands of metric tons)

Product	Annual Production, 2008	1st, 2nd, and 3rd Quarter, 2009	Annual Production, 2009	Increase in 4th Quarter, 2009	% Increase in 4th Quarter	2009/ 2008
Total Tubers, Root Vegetables and Plantains	1,674.4	1,162.0	1,667.2	505.2	30.3	
Tubers and Root Vegetables, including:	1,074.6	845.1	1,177.3	332.2	28.2	1.09
Potatoes	192.0	283.8	283.8	–	–	1.47
Sweet potatoes	375.0	279.3*	535.9	256.6	48.0	1.43
Plantains	599.8	316.9	489.8	172.9	35.3	0.81
Vegetables, including:	1,582.4	1,362.6	1,689.6	327.0	19.7	1.06
Tomatoes	327.3	428.4	476.3	47.9	10.1	1.45
Peppers	38.8	32.3	36.5	4.2	11.5	0.94
Onions	73.2	66.7	75.0	8.3	11.1	1.02
Garlic	21.3	21.4	26.8	5.4	20.1	1.25
Cucumbers	85.4	54.7	73.5	18.8	25.6	0.86
Rice (moist paddy)	435.8	192.0	600.0	408.0	68.0	1.37
Maize	229.3	109.7	205.5	95.8	46.6	0.89
Beans (dry)	43.8	49.3	60.4	11.1	18.4	1.37
Citrus	366.8	242.9	391.1	148.2	37.9	1.06
Fruit	399.6	307.4	387.6	80.2	20.6	0.96
Total	4,732.1	3,425.9	5,001.4	1,575.5	31.5	1.056

*2008 production up to September was 195,100 metric tons.

Source: Produced by the author based on data published in *Principal Indicators of the Agricultural Sector and the Social Economic Panorama, Sept.–Dec. 2009*, National Office of Statistics, ONE.

Livestock production decreased in the fourth quarter of 2009 as it had throughout the year (see appendices 3 and 4) due to decreased hog production, breaking it down into decreased production of hoof animals, deliveries for slaughter, and lower average weight, as well as smaller overall porcine population. The reduction of the porcine population was mainly noted in the private sector (CCS—*Cooperativas de Crédito y Servicio*—and private farmers, which are the most stable supply sources for fresh meat in the free agricultural markets). Porcine production fell because of the unavailability of generally imported feedstock; this in turn resulted from a shortage of foreign exchange liquidity, which has limited the importation of raw materials. On the other hand, poultry production showed an increase of 115.5 million eggs, but its total was still less than in 2007. The number of laying hens decreased, but the number of eggs per laying hen increased, indicating improvement in the rate of feed consumption for every 10 eggs produced. Meat production fell for the second year in a row.

The production of bovine livestock showed improvement (see Figure 4.2). Meat production increased given increased delivery of animals for slaughter and slightly increased average weight (an increase of 0.6 kg per animal). The volume of milk acquired by the *Acopio* increased for the third consecutive year thanks to more milking cows and a slight increase in average output per cow (0.2 liters per cow). The increased price of milk in 2008–09 contributed to these results, which, however, remained below existing potential. The quantity of milk delivered directly to the population continued to increase. The bovine population also increased.

In sum, the data show that the productive forces in the agricultural sector are still constrained.[8] The negative tendency in food production for 2001–2008 has not turned around. Agricultural and livestock production in 2009 showed little change (100.5%) from the previous year; the first quarter of 2010 shows a decrease of 8.8% in crop and livestock production compared to the same period in 2009(see Appendixes 8 and 9).

Figure 4.2. Bovine Population and Milk and Meat Production, 1989–2009

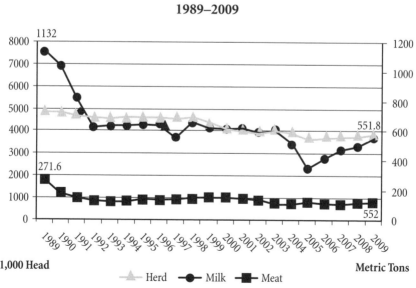

Source: Produced by the author based on data found in the Yearbook and *Principal Indicators of the Agricultural Sector*, ONE, 1989–2009.

Reforms in 2007–2010

Since 2007, a series of measures have been taken to stimulate food production, including the following.

1. Increased prices paid to agricultural producers

Increased price per liter paid to milk producers by the state and the payment of part of this amount in convertible Cuban pesos (CUC), thereby increasing the capacity of the producer to purchase inputs. Farmers are paid directly, and the funds are deposited in the bank branches in their municipalities.

The higher prices paid for milk increased production that had been directed to commercial purposes. Producers gained incentives to sell their products to the state agency responsible for procuring and distributing agricultural goods and to stores that resell such products directly to the population. This change generated some savings in fuel and other transportation costs related to the use of motor vehicles thanks to savings from delivering milk directly and in a timely manner to consumers. By end 2009, the price increase had been implemented in 89 of 168 municipalities (53 % of the total), 66 of which meet 100% of their own local needs. At the same time, these changes had collateral consequences such as reduced deliveries to related industries, reduced utilization of industrial capacity, and reduced production of related products including butter, whey, and others.

Table 4.2. Industrial Production (metric tons)

Product	2006	2007	2008	2009
Liquid milk	162.6	151.5	118.5	130.5

Source: Selected Statistics from Cuba, Social and Economic Panorama. National Office of Statistics, ONE, 2007.

Meat prices increased, but this did not stimulate production. The government made new attempts to do so with groups of producers in cooperatives (agricultural production cooperatives or CPAs, credit and service cooperatives or CCS and UBPCs), as well as with private producers[9] who are engaged in preliminary and final fattening of meat animals.[10] The CCSs have reported encouraging results, delivering animals weighing an average of 450–500 kg.[11]

The payment of meat in convertible Cuban pesos (CUCs) increased the purchasing power of producers, who can now use these funds to acquire inputs in new agricultural stores, which operate in 70 of the country's 168 municipalities to help make the production cycle less dependent on the centralized allocation of resources. Unfortunately, these stores generally have a limited variety of products in their inventory. About 64 products are distributed through these stores, but their availability is not consistent and prices are usually high.

Eighteen cents of a CUC are also paid to producers for each 100 pounds (45.5 kg)[12] of product sold in the state *Acopio* wholesale market, representing approximately 0.0018 CUC cents per pound, which translates into 4.5 cents of a Cuban peso based on the exchange rate of 25 pesos in Cuban pesos per CUC. This is an important stimulus for producers, although it is low relative to the retail prices earned.

The domestic retail market for food is divided into the free agricultural state markets (*Mercados Libres Agrícolas Estatales,* MAE), the free agricultural state markets with unregulated prices (*Mercados Libres Agropecuarios,* MLA), the regulated and rationed market (subsidized), and the markets that operate in Cuban convertible pesos, which are popularly known as "*Shopping.*" Table 4.3 compares the prices paid by the *Acopio* (the state agency that purchases, stores, and distributes agricultural products) for a group of products (including those placed under high-incentives prices) with retail prices received in the state agricultural markets (MAEs) and agricultural free markets (MLAs). This comparison reveals the difference between prices paid by consumers and prices received by producers, ranging from 25% to 65%. This profit margin accrues to commercial intermediaries at even higher rates

Table 4.3. Comparison of Wholesale and Retail Prices in Different Types of Markets (Cuban pesos)

Product	Price paid by Acopio* per quintal**	Price paid by Acopio per pound	Price paid by Acopio plus stimulus, per pound	Retail price at MAE (pesos/pound)	Retail price on free market (pesos/pound)	Free market price in relation to Acopio price	MAE price in relation to Acopio price
Black beans	450	4.50	4.545	6.00	10.00	2.20	1.32
Carrots	120	1.20	1.245		10.00–15.00		
Rice for consumption	290	2.90	2.945	3.50	4.00	1.36	1.20
Cassava	50	0.50	0.545	0.90	4.00	7.34	1.65
Burro plantain	60	0.60	0.645	1.10	3.75	5.81	1.70
Sweet potatoes	60	0.60	0.645	0.80	2.00	3.10	1.24
Garlic	1,000	10.00	10.045	10.00	25.00	2.49	–
Onion	320	3.20	3.245	4.00	10.00	3.08	1.23

Key: *Wholesale; ** One *quintal* = 45.36 Kg or 100 pounds.

Source: Compiled by author based on data distributed by Economic Directorate ANAP, February 8, 2010, and observations at state agricultural markets (MAEs) and free markets.

relative to the retail prices in the agricultural retail market, where differences remain despite price ceilings. Therefore, prices determined by markets where supply and demand are allowed to operate provide a greater stimulus to producers, while the official price stimulus remains insufficient. The state *Acopio* should pay a stimulus price that is equivalent to the prices obtained in unregulated agricultural markets and international market prices, especially for those products that substitute imports.

2. Distribution of uncultivated agricultural land (potentially productive)[13]

Among the measures enacted in 2008–09, the most important one in terms of increasing domestic food production has been the distribution of uncultivated agricultural (potentially productive) land, a step that should have been prioritized and implemented long ago, when the lack of cultivation of this land contributed to the ever-growing and sustained increase in food imports. It is paradoxical that the Cuban economy requires the importation of a significant volume of food products, many of which could be produced competitively on the island, given that Cuba has a significant quantity of idle land (1,758,962 hectares, which is equivalent to 27% of the total land available for cultivation), valuable human capital, numerous research and experimental stations that provide useful information, and the relevant technology. All of this leads one to ask why this production is not taking place, and what makes domestic food production difficult?

In July 2008, the government issued Decree-Law 259, and its operating procedures were established through Regulatory Legal Decree 282 in August 2008. Both were important steps leading to the distribution of idle lands. They clarified and codified important aspects of this change: for example, the period for which usufruct was established; likewise, the terms "economic property" and "legal property" were defined.[14] The measures introduced taxes (or rents as some scholars categorize them), recognizing the importance of the means of production (land) being delivered for use, which should be protected and improved.

Yet Decree-Law 259 fails to take certain factors into consideration. First, the duration of time for which land is given in usufruct to natural persons is set at 10 years (albeit renewable) with no distinction as to the nature of its intended agricultural use, although differing time spans are required for short-cycle crops, semi-permanent or permanent crops, or livestock. Second, the law fails to take into account that differing amounts of investment will be required, depending on the type of cultivation or livestock activity in a given territory. According to Article 15, payment for improvements made or acquired, with the exception of housing built by the beneficiary from the usufruct, will be made only when the period of usufruct is over. This may lead the usufruct holder to make only the minimum necessary investments; it is a significant obstacle to more permanent settlement by the agricultural producer, leading him to see his time on the usufruct as transitory. Cuban agricultural regions require repopulation. Without an agricultural population, there is no guarantee for stable or sustained agricultural production. Thirdly, the agricultural producer requires a certain level of infrastructure to store and protect tools, animals, seeds, inputs, equipment, etc. People engaged in agricultural activities cannot neglect the land or live far away; they must establish themselves and live on site. Agricultural and livestock activities require a permanent human presence. The law, however, does not stipulate how investments made in housing improvements should be factored into compensation for farmers.

Finally, subsection (c) of Article 14 states that one cause for the termination of the usufruct is "ongoing noncompliance with contractually agreed production as determined by specialists." While farmers are required to deliver a proportion of their end product for sale to the state procurement agency (*Acopio*) in order to guarantee that certain levels of output reach the intended social sector, the exact proportion of products sold to the state is not defined. Instead, Article 7 of the decree, subsection (a), requires only that the producer "fulfill contracts for the delivery of products." However, commitments to sell to the state reach and surpass 70% of total production, which has become a disincentive to producers.[15] In fact, the *Acopio* should function like any other buyer and pay market prices to stimulate production.

The approval of applications and the transfer of idle lands are subject to a prolonged bureaucratic process, a problem that only began to be addressed in 2009. In order to request the use of lands in usufruct, Decree 282 requires the applicant to file nine documents. If the initial application is denied and the applicant appeals or initiates a complaint, thirteen documents are required. Once an application is presented, the Municipal Director of the National Land Control Center has 30 days to respond in those cases where the property boundaries correspond to the graphic and text information submitted by the applicant, and up to 60 days if a land survey is required. Once the relevant document is issued, the Municipal Director of the National Land Control Center has three days to present it to the Municipal Delegate of Agriculture, and the Municipal Delegate of Agriculture has 30 days to issue approval for the allocation of the property in question. Thus, if the process proceeds smoothly and no land survey is required, 63 days must pass from the time the application is first filed for land in usufruct until its final approval, after which time the usufruct can be issued. Otherwise, the process may be extended for an additional 30 days, for a total of 93 days.

If the application is denied and the applicant appeals the decision, more time passes. Within ten days, the applicant-appellant must deliver his appeal addressed to the Provincial Delegate of Agriculture through the offices of the Municipal Delegate of Agriculture. Then the Municipal Delegate of Agriculture must deliver the appeal to the Provincial Delegate of Agriculture within five working days. The Provincial Delegate of Agriculture will issue a notice of approval or rejection within 15 days, and this notice will be delivered to the applicant-appellant within five days by Municipal Director of the National Land Control Center. Thus, 35 days would be added to the process in addition to the 63 or 93 original days, so if the request is initially denied and an appeals process is undertaken, the entire process of requesting land could last between 98 and 128 days.

By the end of 2009, 100,000 permits had been issued for approximately 920,000 hectares, which represent 52% of all idle lands.[16] It is estimated that 35% of the land delivered in usufruct is now planted. By January 18, 2010, 121,711 applications had been filed,[17] 88% by natural persons, of whom 79% did not own any land. The applications anticipated the following possible uses of land:

Table 4.4. Land Use by Type of Activity

Activity	%
Bovine livestock	42.0
Rice	6.0
Various crops	41.0
Tobacco	1.5
Coffee	1.6
Small livestock	7.7
Sugarcane	0.2
Total	**100.0**

Source: Compiled by the author from various sources, 2009.

Land is a necessary but not sufficient condition for an immediate increase in food production. Other systemic changes would include measures to consolidate a market for inputs, services, and capital assets to which the producer would have access by means of the purchasing power generated by his production. Producers should also be allowed to decide what to produce and where to sell the output, based on market behavior and social needs, and they should be allowed to freely contract the labor force required for their operations. Moreover, new financing and periodic technical assistance should be made available to farmers. All of these measures would allow for a successful realization of the property usufruct[18] in which the individual feels personally responsible for decisions and results, facilitating a systemic approach to a successful productive cycle.

3. Transferring Acopio and commercialization activities to the Ministry of Domestic Commerce

Beginning on August 1, 2009, in the City and Province of Havana, the *Acopio* activities of procurement and distribution of agricultural goods were transferred to the Ministry of Domestic Commerce (MINCIN). This reform had already been tried in 1976, but these activities were returned to the Ministry of Agriculture in 1986 without having solved the problems of low domestic production.[19] In reality the procurement and distribution of agricultural production today is characterized by a highly regulated market, the existence of a dual currency regime, and insufficient food supply, especially in the UBPCs, the CPAs, and state sectors. The state model (state property, *Acopio*, and commercialization) has dominated the distribution and exchange phase of agricultural production with mediocre results including post-harvest losses, delayed payments to producers, production disincentives, and other problems.

After a series of damaging hurricanes in October of 2008, the administration decreed price ceilings on agricultural food products sold in the free farmers' markets (MLAs). This and other measures were instituted to prevent a disproportionate rise in prices and hoarding by speculators. However, the price caps also contributed to decreasing supply; supply had already been decreasing before the damage caused by the hurricanes, because official prices were insufficient to cover the costs that accumulated along the entire chain of commercialization. Markets were almost completely emptied out, and state markets with price ceilings did not have the capacity to meet the demand that the free agricultural markets were no longer allowed to meet.

An additional series of requirements, authorizations, and other restrictive steps did not help to maintain a continuous flow of food supply in the MLAs. With the introduction of these obstacles, supply was diminished. At the same time, despite the establishment of price ceilings, sales mechanisms emerged in this market that in practice led to increased prices at certain moments, precisely the opposite of what was originally intended. The reduction of supply, particularly in the last quarter of 2008, also restricted the options available to consumers and increased the selling power of suppliers.

During this period, the familiar food supply stores in residential neighborhoods were closed, and agricultural fairs were canceled. Food stores began to reopen at the end of the year, but then closed again, with fewer options for consumers to obtain food. The food supply stores primarily supplied by cooperatives (CCSs and CPAs) had provided a more predictable supply and better quality and selection than state markets with price caps, albeit with slightly higher prices. They were also geographically closer to consumers and therefore more accessible.

Thus, the measures introduced to reorganize *Acopio* and the sale of agricultural products in different markets resulted in greater centralization and increased monopoly by the *Acopio* and in the commercialization of food. By focusing on price controls, restrictions on sales, closing supply posts, and limiting the transportation of agricultural goods between provinces, the reform reduced incentives for producers. Producers were given little margin to participate in the value chain generated during the commercialization phase of the production-distribution-exchange-consumption cycle. Because of the limitations introduced by these reforms, producers were not stimulated to produce more.

The evidence for a persistent negative trend in agricultural and livestock production from 2001 to 2009 and the inefficient use of land (the sector's fundamental means of production) shows up in the data depicting an ever-increasing amount of idle agricultural land and low agricultural yields. Thus, the productive forces in the agricultural and livestock sector remain constrained; the obstacles that constrain the development of these productive forces must be eliminated.

The relations of production must also be transformed. The economic relations of production depend upon the distribution of the means of production in society and the determination of the ownership of the means of production. The form of property determines the nature of the nexus, i.e., the connection between the producer and the means of production during the stage of material production and also with respect to the relations of distribution, exchange, and consumption. The distributional structure of a society and the income level of its members also depend on the form of property that is adopted. The modification of the relations of production requires an analysis of forms of property and how property issues are resolved along each step in the production-distribution-exchange-consumption cycle.

The question arises whether the conditions experienced by producers have given them a sense of ownership. From the central national level to the local level, repeated organizational and structural changes have at certain times disrupted the continuity of the productive-distributional agro-chain, distancing producers even more from the commercialization of their products. However, these changes have always taken place within the framework of the state's monopoly or near monopoly on *Acopio* and other commercialization, regardless of which ministry or central entity was tasked to coordinate these activities at any given time. The key to success of reforms is to ensure that producers gain a sense of ownership at every stage of the production-distribution-exchange-consumption cycle.

Producers are unlikely to stop working on the land in order to work directly on the commercialization of the product, yet it is possible to establish some continuity and social recognition of their work by extending their participation through second-level marketing cooperatives. These cooperatives respond to the interests of producers in commercializing their production to wholesalers and retailers, depending on the product (whether more or less perishable, having consistency and uniformity, quality, demand, and price). Individual producers may also participate in the commercialization of their own product depending on their material circumstances and their logistical capacity to manage a larger share of the distributional process within the authorized organizational forms. Under this framework, a significant portion of the value generated along the marketing chain would accrue to producers themselves, providing additional incentives. This approach would also begin to solve an old, important, and persistent problem regarding the role of intermediaries in the production-distribution-exchange-consumption cycle (before 1959, based on a strong personal profit motive, see Table 4.5; after 1959, based on providing for the social good; Table 4.6 illustrates the relationship between retail prices and prices paid by the *Acopio* in 1998). In general, intermediaries have appropriated the greatest share of the value generated in the production-distribution-exchange-consumption cycle. New conditions can be established so that producers receive most of the value that is generated, thereby stimulating food production at an accelerated pace.

Measures to stimulate producer participation would engender diversification and discourage monopolies in the commercialization process, helping individual producers and groups to share more directly in, and influence, the market. It would simplify the marketing chain and reduce losses and social costs. Diversity in the *Acopio* and commercialization process with the participation of individual producers, cooperative members, and the state *Acopio* could be presented as an alternative to traditional monopolistic forms and as an important aspect of the transformations necessary in the relations of production to eliminate the blockages or chokepoints that impede the development of productive forces.

Table 4.5. Prices of Agricultural Products in the 1950s

Product	Price received by producer in pesos	Wholesale price in pesos	Retail price in pesos	Retail price as a multiple of price paid to producer
Peppers	2.76	15.00	20.00	7.2
Pumpkins	0.61	3.50	5.00	8.1
Tomatoes	1.38	30.00	45.00	32.6
Pineapples	3.08	20.83	30.00	9.8
Avocados	1.01	9.00	15.00	14.8
Sweet oranges	0.91	2.73	4.00	4.4

Note: Source document does not specify the unit of product measurement.

Source: Report of the *Junta Nacional de Economía* [National Economic Board], 1953.

In order to calculate and project economic performance, methods based on scientific principles and effective techniques should be adopted, replacing overly schematic thinking and normative methods for calculating production estimates, projecting changes in demand on the part of the population, and determining the direction of industry and how to generate export income.

Table 4.6. Prices Paid to Producers and Prices in the Retail Market, 1998

(Cuban pesos per *quintal*; 1 *quintal* = 100 lbs.)

Product	Price paid by *Acopio*	Retail price (state market)	Retail price in state market as a multiple of the price paid by *Acopio*	Retail price in agricultural free market	Retail price in agricultural free market as a multiple of price paid by *Acopio*
Pumpkins	7.60	40.00	5.2	164.00	21.5
Cabbage	4.20	15.00	3.5	157.00	37.3
Tomatoes	19.00	45.00	2.3	205.00	10.7
Malanga	16.00	70.00	4.3	338.00	21.1
Mangos	9.00	40.00	4.4	400.00	44.4
Sweet potatoes	7.50	20.00	2.7	114.00	15.2
Cassava	8.00	15.00	1.9	127.00	15.8
Burro plantains	6.00	40.00	6.7	185.00	30.8
Garlic	143.00	250.00	1.7	500.00	3.5
Pineapples	6.90	45.00	6.5	500.00	72.4

Source: Compiled from data published in *Análisis de precio con relación al costo de los distintos cultivos*, August 1998, Ministry of Agriculture.

Elements that alienate producers from decision-making and from a sense of belonging, and implicitly deny or minimize the real existence of the market, should be identified and removed. It is a mistake to establish additional structures that may generate more bureaucracy, or to estimate demand based on a consumption pattern that had been historically constrained by limited supply and few options, instead of first consolidating and expanding the market for inputs, tools, and machinery. Other existing obstacles are regulations that prohibit direct producers' sales to enterprises other than the state *Acopio*.

One sometimes gets the impression that these mechanisms, structures and regulations are intended to supplant the market or deny its existence and the role it plays, when in fact the market is an objective reality. Ignoring the existence of the market also means ignoring its potential utility as a tool to facilitate a distribution process in which state institutions participate along with other forces, a process that includes market forces but where the state regulates prices and other market expressions, utilizing appropriate economic means to seek price equilibrium, balance between supply and demand, and concern for consumer interests.

When production of certain agricultural products (tomatoes, rice, and sweet potatoes) increased, primarily in the first quarter of 2009, it also became clear that there were problems with respect to *Acopio*, commercialization, transport, and processing of agricultural and animal products. This problem had already existed within the production-distribution-exchange-consumption cycle, and although it manifested itself as a crisis at a particular point in the cycle (*Acopio* and commercialization), the real problem is in the production stage. In other words, the root of the problem is limited supply, not circulation, even if there are also problems with the procurement and distribution chain that should be solved along with the system of which they form a part.

The processing and packaging industry for agricultural products (part of the *Acopio* and commercialization stage of the product cycle) is sorely deficient to nonexistent. In the case of fruits, vegetables, tubers, and grains, this deficit increases the possibility of losses. The processing industry suffers from insufficient capacity, technological obsolescence, and a shortage of containers. Thus, reformers must also analyze how to make preserved harvested foods last longer (warehousing and cold storage). A systemic approach must be adopted, and new practices applied at all stages of the Cuban agricultural cycle.

4. Decentralization of governmental functions and changes in organizational structures

The municipality is the key element in decision-making and policy implementation regarding the use of agricultural land. A Municipal Delegation

Figure 4.3. Municipalities Selected by the Ministry of Agriculture

Source: MINAG, *Resultados y Perspectivas*, October 2009.

of Agriculture has been constituted in each of Cuba's 168 municipalities. Thus far, the delegations have focused on turning idle land over to producers and overseeing livestock holdings. Three productive scenarios have been defined for each municipality: urban agriculture, suburban agriculture (within a radius of approximately 10 km. from city limits), and conventional productive zones. These scenarios were implemented in the province of Camagüey starting in 2009.

The Ministry of Agriculture (MINAG) has selected 17 municipalities (16 conventional municipalities and the special municipality of the Isle of Youth) as testing grounds for integrating these three scenarios (see Figure 4.3). All entities that produce food in the municipality participate in this experiment, whether or not they are directly overseen by the Ministry of Agriculture (cooperatives (UBPCs, CCSs, CPAs, state farms, etc.).

The Ministry of Economy and Planning (MEP) has selected an additional five municipalities to which it provides economic resources and assists with decentralized forms of economic management to foster import substitution, increase food production and employment, and generate export income (see Table 4.7). In addition, state structures are being simplified. The first step in this process was the merger of the Food Industry Ministry with the old Ministry of Fishing. Steps have also begun to merge the Ministry of Agriculture and the Ministry of Sugar. The final goal is to constitute a single Ministry of Food to oversee agriculture, fishing, and the food industry.

Table 4.7. Municipalities Selected for Economic Incentives Plan by the Ministry of Economics and Planning

Province	Municipality
Pinar del Río	La Palma
Matanzas	Martí
Sancti Spíritus	Yaguajay
Granma	Río Cauto
Guantánamo	El Salvador

Proyecto PADAM ACTAF, December 2009.

Whither the Agricultural Sector?

Cuba needs to know where it is headed and what it seeks to accomplish in the development of its agricultural sector. The measures adopted thus far to increase domestic food production are important, but they lack a systemic focus to address all the steps in the production-distribution-exchange-consumption cycle and the linkages between this cycle and other microeconomic and macroeconomic sectors.

Crucial questions that must still be addressed broadly and deeply include the resolution of how property relationships will be structured and the role markets will play in food distribution. The key challenge is to free the still-constrained productive forces in the agricultural sector to allow for increased production leading to an improved food supply that would exercise a downward pressure on prices. Other opportunities and forms of employment also need to become viable. Expanding cooperative, private, and family forms of agricultural and industrial production as well as the provision of services could multiply job opportunities, income, and purchasing power.

Although the measures adopted thus far are insufficiently systemic in their perspective and their effects, domestic food production is likely to grow in the short term. This will not be sufficient, however, to stem the need for high volumes of food imports to maintain the supply of food and the corresponding level of consumption. The current lack of liquidity in foreign exchange is a significant constraint. In fact, food imports declined in 2009 with respect to 2008 levels and this trend may have continued in 2010.

Several factors will determine whether the proposed goals of the reform strategy are met, among them,

- will the economic measures be applied deeply and broadly?
- will the approach be systemic?

- will the measures be conceived and implemented as part of a coherent strategy to reach desired objectives?

Figure 4.4 summarizes the advisable steps to reach this goal. Prior to undertaking any reforms, let us analyze and assess the situation of Cuban agriculture in the current economic environment. Weaknesses and deficiencies should be identified, including current and growing food insecurities, sources of insufficiency in domestic production, sources of inefficiency, and explanations for the deterioration of current technologies and infrastructure. The strengths should also be identified and reinforced: the availability of idle agricultural land, scientific and technical accomplishments, level of human capital, technological infrastructure, potential sources of energy, and others.

This strategic analysis should be conducted at each municipality, incorporating the interrelationship of different territories with the national context and their place within it. Most problems are situated and defined at the level of the municipality, and that is where they are best resolved, based on local capacities and the appropriate degree of decentralization with respect to decision-making and policy implementation. Clearly, a strategy is required to establish the policies and instruments that should be adopted to increase the food supply.

Figure 4.4. Where Are We Going?

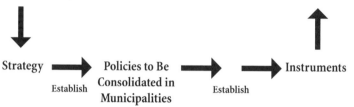

Current Situation

- High level of food imports
- High level of idle land
- Low level of goods exports
- High level of agro-industrial decapitalization and deindustrialization
- Deteriorated infrastructure
- Lack of liquidity in foreign exchange
- Scientific-technical development
- Human capital
- Energy problem

Desired Situation

- Maximize Food Security
  1. Greater availability of food
  2. Access to food by the population (nominal and real salary, budgeting income-expenses)
  3. Result (food quality)
- Increased goods exports
- Import substitution
- Cane-based bioenergy for agro-industry, use of other biomass sources and other renewable energy sources
- Industrial development

Strategy → **Policies to Be Consolidated in Municipalities** → **Instruments**

Establish　　　　　　　　　　　　　　　Establish

1. Productive use of agricultural land
2. Diversity and direct participation by producers in wholesale and market retail markets for agricultural products and livestock
3. Simplify organizations and functions
4. Decentralization
5. Soil improvement and consolidation; Forest development; integrated fight against pests and disease; utilization and protection of water resources
6. Foreign direct investment (FDI)
7. Energy program
8. Freedom to employ labor force

1. Distribution of idle land
2. Establish and consolidate a for inputs, services machinery, equipment, tools
3. Credits, microcredits, financing, agricultural insurance; projects structures for agro-producers
4. Eliminate barriers to access to market by producers and products
5. Establish producer associations
6. Greater autonomy
7. Access by all producers to FDI
8. Renewable energy source

Appendix 1. Agricultural Production, 2001–2009

(in thousands of *quintales*; one *quintal* = 100 lbs.)

Product	2001	2002	2003	2004	2005	2006	2007	2008	2009
Tubers and roots, including:	**23,910.1**	**22,616.9**	**28,347.3**	**31,738.4**	**26,559.0**	**23,817.5**	**24,283.5**	**23,361.8**	**25,596.6**
Potatoes	7,181.3	6,856.7	6,567.5	7,113.5	6,738.2	6,143.9	2,967.5	4,174.08	6,171.9
Sweet potatoes	5,290.4	5,073.9	7,709.6	10,567.8	7,168.1	–	–	8,152.5	11,652.6
Malanga	1,617.8	2,186.1	3,157.7	5,304.5	3,940.9	–	–	–	–
Plantain	14,754.7	11,429.3	16,895.9	18,023.3	12,657.0	14,339.5	18,083.2	13,039.65	10,650.4
Fruit	4,857.3	3,239.7	5,256.1	6,735.3	5,474.1	5,584.4	5,837.1	4,065.38	3,239.2
Vianda	9,897.4	8,189.6	11,639.8	11,288.0	7,182.9	8,755.1	12,246.1	8,974.2	7,411.1
Vegetables, including:	**33,241.5**	**37,882.7**	**48,088.4**	**53,677.3**	**42,926.2**	**37,963.0**	**36,729.7**	**34,401.3**	**36,907.9**
Tomatoes	5,433.4	6,781.8	7,865.8	10,442.6	9,193.7	8,442.5	7,522.0	7,217.6	10,356.9
Peppers	722.7	682.2	1,006.7	1,202.0	1,053.1	901.0	873.9	845.6	793.5
Onions	1,121.0	1,023.2	1,061.8	1,902.3	1,850.5	1,623.7	1,580.4	1,591.3	1,630.5
Garlic	492.7	348.5	465.9	712.6	682.5	487.1	484.8	463.0	582.6
Rice (moist paddy)	3,065.7	15,044.0	15,561.4	10,628.6	7,991.6	9,439.5	9,556.9	9,478.6	13,044.0
Maize	4,761.3	4,438.2	5,854.9	6,537.8	5,344.5	5,085.4	5,774.1	4,984.9	4,469.7
Beans (dry)	1,099.7	1,216.4	1,516.9	1,722.7	1,295.3	974.0	1,191.3	952.2	1,313.1
Citrus	20,807.3	10,385.2	17,233.2	17,428.9	10,872.2	7,306.5	10,102.5	7,974.2	8,503.9
Non-Citrus Fruit	7,269.4	7,331.3	9,198.7	10,659.0	8,683.5	8,488.0	8,715.5	8,689.4	8,411.3

Note: 21.74 *quintales* equal one metric ton.

Source: Compiled from data found in *Principales Indicadores del Sector Agropecuario*, National Office of Statistics ONE, 2001–2009; *Anuario Estadístico de Cuba* 2008;

Appendix 2. Agricultural Production, January–September 2009

Product	Total TMT	2009/2008 %	State TMT	Non-state TMT	UBPC TMT	CPA TMT	Private* TMT	Private % total
Tubers and roots, including:	**845.1**	**102.9**	**182.3**	**662.9**	**160.3**	**108.2**	**394.4**	**46.7**
Potatoes	283.8	150.3	97.0	186.8	116.3	55.5	15.0	5.3
Plantain	316.9	60.0	72.8	244.1	46.2	25.0	173.0	55.0
Vegetables, including:	**1362.6**	**106.6**	**396.2**	**966.4**	**83.8**	**77.3**	**805.2**	**60.0**
Tomatoes	428.4	144.2	80.2	348.2	24.8	32.2	291.2	34.0
Peppers	32.3	90.1	8.4	23.8	1.4	2.6	19.8	61.3
Onions	66.7	100.7	8.9	57.8	1.3	1.5	54.9	82.3
Garlic	21.4	112.2	2.1	9.4	0.2	0.4	18.7	87.4
Cucumbers	54.7	77.0	18.6	36.1	3.4	2.7	30.1	55.0
Rice (moist paddy)	**191.7**	**158.3**	**55.9**	**135.9**	**38.2**	**4.8**	**92.9**	**49.0**
Maize	**109.7**	**88.3**	**12.1**	**97.7**	**16.4**	**8.7**	**72.6**	**66.2**
Beans (dry)	**49.3**	**130.8**	**5.2**	**44.1**	**3.5**	**5.2**	**35.5**	**72.0**
Citrus	**242.9**	**112.5**	**175.7**	**67.2**	**34.0**	**4.1**	**29.1**	**12.0**
Non-Citrus Fruit	**307.4**	**86.8**	**58.8**	**248.6**	**25.0**	**16.2**	**207.5**	**67.5**

*Credit and Service Cooperatives (CCS) and private. TMT: Thousand metric tons.

Source: *Principales Indicadores del Sector Agropecuario* (3rd Quarter 2009), ONE, November 2009.

Appendix 3. Livestock Production and Indicators, 2002–2009

Bovine	Unit	2002	2003	2004	2005	2006	2007	2008	2009
Slaughtered	Thousand head	460.7	371.8	388.6	466.2	360.6	339.6	368.5	370.3
Weight on the hoof	Metric tons	131.7	112.1	107.7	118.4	111.3	109.5	120.7	121.5
Average weight	Kg	285.8	301.6	277.2	254.0	308.5	322.3	327.5	328.1
Milk production	Million liters	400.7	429.4	362.4	322.7	371.7	411.3	482.0	535.8
Milking cows	Thousand head	364.6	360.3	325.2	274.2	317.6	318.2	364.5	370.3
Liters/cow/day	–	3.01	3.26	3.05	3.22	3.20	3.5	3.8	4.0
Existing population bovine livestock	Thousand head	3,973.7	4,025.3	3,942.6	3,703.6	3,737.1	3,787.4	3,821.3	3,892.8
Porcine									
Slaughtered	Thousand head	963.5	1,098.8	1,097.7	1,161.8	1,463.8	2,134.5	2,280.5	2,107.8
Weight on the hoof	Metric tons	68.5	75.4	73.8	86.3	119.1	181.9	194.3	170.7
Average weight	Kg	71.1	68.6	67.2	74.3	81.4	85.2	85.2	81.5
Existing population porcine livestock	Thousand head	1,351.8	1,335.6	1,245.3	1,293.3	1,410.2	1,502.1	1,553.8	1,469.2
Poultry									
Total egg production	Million units	1,365.6	1,464.4	1,405.2	1,727.1	1,913.2	1,983.7	1,920.4	1,931.9
Eggs produced under modern industrial conditions	Million units	1,157.2	1,262.5	1,186.3	1,494.6	1,718.8	1,760.9	1,704.3	1,693.6
Population of laying hens	Thousand head	4,198.7	4,586.5	4,490.3	5,711.7	7,042.8	7,315.9	7,271.1	7,100.0
Egg/laying hen	One	275.6	275.3	264.2	261.7	244.1	240.7	234.4	239.0
Feed/10 eggs	Kg	1.5	1.4	1.5	1.5	1.6	1.6	1.7	1.6
Meat produced (peso pie)	Metric ton	12.9	9.5	10.1	8.6	9.3	12.0	11.1	10.6
Ovine-caprine									
Meat production	Metric ton	6,847	7,,301	7,783	7,781	8,042	8,897	10.3	10.5
Slaughtered	Thousand head	248.6	264.6	284.6	291.6	301.2	320.0	361.6	358.6
Average weight	Kg	27.5	27.5	27.3	26.6	26.6	27.8	28.0	29.0

Source: Compiled from data found in *Principales Indicadores del Sector Agropecuario,* National Office of Statistics, ONE, 2002–2009.

Appendix 4. Livestock Production and Indicators, January–September 2009

Livestock	Unit of measurement	Total	2009/08 %	Private/total as %	Livestock	Unit of measurement	Total	2009/08 in %	*Private/total as %
Bovine					**Poultry**				
Slaughtered	Thousand head	273.2	99.2	0.3	Eggs produced	Million units	1,446.3	97.1	1.6
Weight on the hoof	Metric tons	87.9	98.8	0.3	Eggs produced under modern industrial conditions	Million units	1,289.1	98.0	–
Average weight	Kg	321.7	99.5	–	Population of laying hens	Thousand head	7,103.3	97.0	–
Milk production	One million liters	384.6	108.3	60.0	Eggs per laying hen	One	181	100.6	–
Milking cows	Thousand head	374.2	108.2	58.5	Feed/10 eggs	Kg	1.6	100.0	–
Liters/cow/day	–	3.8	102.7	–	Meat production (weight on the hoof)	Metric tons	7.4	86.0	6.0
Existing population of bovine livestock	Thousand head	3,911.6	101.7	53.5	Average weight	Kg	1.4	107.7	–
Porcine					**Ovine-caprine**				
Slaughtered	Thousand head	1,401.9	82.6	12.1	Meat production	Metric tons	6.1	83.6	72.0
Weight on hoof	Metric tons	113.9	78.2	10.3	Animals slaughtered	Thousand head	212.7	83.9	70.0
Average weight	Kg	81.2	94.6	–	Average weight	Kg	28.2	102.5	–
Existing population of porcine livestock	Thousand head	1,563.0	99.5	53.3					

Key: *Private = CCS and private grouped together by ONE.

Source: Armando González Nova, "Alimentos agrícolas en el 1er trimestre 2009," *IPS* 22/11, June 15, 2009.

Appendix 5. Retail Prices at Various State Agricultural Markets from July 2009 to February 2010 (Cuban pesos per pound)

Product	Market 33 and 30 in Playa, Havana (July 10–12, 2009)	Market 33 and 30 in Playa, Havana (Jan. 22–23, 2010)	Market 19 and 48 in Playa, Havana (July 10–12, 2009)	Market 19 and 48 in Playa, Havana (Jan. 22–23, 2010)	Market 33 and 30 in Playa, Havana (Feb. 14, 2010)	Market 19 and 48 in Playa, Havana (Feb. 14, 2010)	Market 33 and 30 in Playa, Havana (Feb. 21, 2010)	Market 19 and 48 in Playa, Havana (Feb. 21, 2010)
Plantain	2.50	–	2.50	–	–	–	–	–
Banana	–	–	–	–	–	1.00	–	–
Sweet potato	0.90	0.80	0.90	0.80	–	–	–	–
Malanga (guagui)	2.50	–	2.50	–	–	–	–	–
Malanga isleña	1.10	1.10	–	–	1.10	–	–	–
String beans	5.00	–	–	–	–	–	–	–
Burro plantain	0.80	0.80	–	0.80	–	–	–	–
Maize in kernels	3.00	–	–	–	–	–	–	–
Pineapple	–	–	2.00	–	–	–	1.60	1.60
Pumpkin	0.60	–	0.60	–	–	–	–	–
Garlic	–	–	14.00**	8.00*	8.00*	8.00*	8.00*–10.00**	5.00***
Black beans	–	–	6.00	–	–	–	–	–
Red beans	–	–	–	6.50	–	–	–	–
Rice	–	–	3.50	3.50	3.50	3.50	3.50	–
Split peas	–	3.50	3.50	3.50	3.50	3.50	3.50	3.50
Cassava	–	0.90	0.90	0.90	–	–	–	–
Onions	–	–	4.00	4.00	6.50**	6.50**	6.50	4.00*–6.50**
Tomatoes	–	2.50	2.50	2.50	2.50	–	2.50	2.00
Cabbages	–	–	–	–	–	–	1.50	–

Key: **First quality. *Second quality. ***Third quality

Source: Gathered directly from the respective markets by the author in 2010.

Appendix 6. Comparative Retail Prices at Various Markets from January to February 2010 (Cuban pesos per pound)

Product	MAE* (Jan. 23, 2010)	Supply-demand (Market 19 and 42 in Playa, Havana Jan. 23, 2010)	MAE* (Jan. 31, 2010)	MAE (Feb. 14, 2010)	Supply-demand Market (19 and 42 Jan. 31, 2010)	Supply-demand Market (19 and 42 Feb. 14, 2010)
Sweet potatoes	0.80	2.00	0.80	–	2.00	2.00
Malanga (guagüí)	–	6.00	–	–	3.50	5.00–6.00
Malanga isleña	–	–	1.10	1.10	–	–
Cassava	0.90	4.00	–	–	4.00	4.00
Garlic	8.00**	25.00***	8.00–10.00	8.00	25.00	25.00
Onions	4.00+	10.00	4.00+	6.50	6.00–10.00	7.50–10.00
Carrots	–	15.00	–	–	15.00	10.00
Black beans	–	10.00	–	–	10.00	12.00
Tomatoes	2.50**	6.00–8.00	–	2.50	6.00–8.00	5.00–6.00–7.00
Pumpkin	–	2.00	0.70	–	2.00	3.00
Lettuce	–	6.00	–	–	7.00	7.00
Burro plantain	–	–	–	–	–	3.75
Peppers	–	–	–	–	10.00	10.00

Key: *Markets 33 and 30 and 19 and 48 in Playa. Havana. ** Third quality. *** First quality. + Includes tops

Source: Compiled by author based on direct observation in 2010.

Appendix 7. Prices in Free Supply-Demand Market from January to February 2010

Product	Supply-demand (market 19 and 42 in Playa, Havana Jan. 23, 2010)	Supply-demand (19 and 42 Jan. 31, 2010)	Supply-demand (19 and 42 Feb. 14, 2010)	Supply-demand (19 and 42 Feb. 21, 2010)
Sweet potatoes	2.00	2.00	2.00	2.00–3.00
Malanga (guagui)	6.00	3.50	5.00–6.00	6.00
Malanga isleña	–	–	–	
Cassava	4.00	4.00	4.00	4.00
Garlic	25.00*	25.00	25.00	
Onions	10.00	6.00–10.00	7.50–10.00	8.00
Carrots	15.00	15.00	10.00	10.00
Black beans	10.00	10.00	12.00	10.00
Red beans	12.00	12.00	12.00	12.00
Tomato	6.00–8.00	6.00–8.00	5.00–6.00–7.00	5.00
Pumpkin	2.00	2.00	3.00	3.00
Lettuce	6.00	7.00	7.00	
Burro plantain	–	–	3.75	
Peppers	–	10.00	10.00	10.00
Lemons	–	15.00	–	15.00

*First quality

Source: Compiled by author based on direct observation, 2010.

Appendix 8. Agricultural Production as of March 31, 2010

Products	Total TMT	% 10/09	Non-State TMT	Non-State % of Total	Non-State % Fulfillment(6)
Tubers and roots, including:	273.9	91.0	139.0	51.0	113.6
Potatoes	80.8	65.6	3.2	4.0	65.1
Plantain	100.6	174.9	57.0	57.0	194.6
Fruit	26.8	128.7	14.3	53.4	129.2
Vianda	73.8	201.1	42.7	58.0	234.1
Vegetables, including:	425.5	74.9	271.4	64.0	77.5
Tomatoes	170.5	65.1	123.4	72.4	68.7
Peppers	9.7	75.1	6.8	70.0	79.8
Onions	27.3	101.5	22.1	81.0	104.0
Garlic	8.8	82.7	7.3	83.0	105.4
Rice (moist paddy)	25.6	145.7	20.8	81.3	176.6
Maize	21.3	105.0	18.3	86.0	109.1
Beans (dry)	19.6	69.5	14.9	76.0	75.0
Citrus	131.7	78.4	26.5	20.1	119.2
Fruits	46.8	116.1	32.6	70.0	114.4

Source: Elaborated by the author based on data found in *Principales Indicadores del Sector Agropecuario,* ONE, 2010.

Appendix 9. Livestock Production as of March 31, 2010

	Measurement unit	Total	% 10/09	Non-state	Non-state % total	Non-state % fullfillment
Bovine						
Slaughtered	Thousand head	91.6	97.2	0.786	0.86	903.4
Weight on the hoof	Metric tons	30.7	97.0	0.298	0.97	692.6
Average weight	Kg	328.6	96.8	378.9	–	–
Milk production	Million liters	89 742.2	94.1	56 665.2	63.1	103.0
Milking cows	Thousand head	316 529	103	192 172	60.4	111.3
Liters/cow/day	–	3.1	88.6	3.27	–	–
Existing population bovine livestock	Thousand head	3 890.3	99.9	2 152.7	55.3	102.8
Porcine						
Slaughtered	Thousand head	458.6	104.0	64.0	14.0	159.9
Weight on the hoof	Metric tons	35.6	96.7	4.8	13.5	164.3
Average weight	Kg	77.6	93.0	78.5	–	–
Existing population porcine livestock	Thousand head	1 413.1	98.7	798.3	56.5	103.9
Poultry						
Total egg production	Million units	456.5	98.9	4.1	0.9	118.0
Eggs produced under modern industrial conditions	Million units	408.3	92.4	–	–	–
Population of laying hens	Thousand head	6 975.1	96.4	–	–	–
Egg/laying hen	One	59	96.7	–	–	–
Feed/10 eggs	Kg	1.7	106.3	–	–	–
Meat produced (peso pie)	Metric ton	2.4	120.0	–	–	–

Appendix 9. Livestock Production as of March 31, 2010 (continued)

	Measurement unit	Total	% 10/09	Non-state	Non-state % total	Non-state % fullfillment
Ovine–caprine						
Meat production	Metric ton	2.3	98.9	1.3	56.5	95.0
Slaughtered	Thousand head	83.5	44.3	95.1	53.1	90.0
Average weight	Kg	27.6	95.2	29.2	–	–
Slaughtered	Thousand head	1742.0	61.0	1309.0	75.1	54.0

Source: Elaborated by the author based on data found in *Principales Indicadores del Sector Agropecuario,* ONE, 2010.

Endnotes

1. Armando Nova González, "La agricultura cubana: medidas implementadas para lograr incrementos en la producción de alimentos. Análisis y valoración," in Proceedings of the Seminario Científico del Centro de Estudio de la Economía Cubana (CEEC), University of Havana, June 2010, CD.

2. ONE, "Sector Agropecuario, Indicadores Seleccionados," September 2010.

3. ONE, "Panorama Económico Social," January 2010.

4. *Proyecto de Lineamientos de la Política Económica y Social* prepared for discussion in advance of the Sixth Congress of the Cuban Communist Party. Havana, November 1, 2010.

5. In 2008, sweet potatoes were planted on 56,600 hectares, increasing in 2009 by 20.2% to 67,500 hectares. This was the highest cultivated acreage increase among the 15 categories specified in Principal Indicators of the Agricultural Sector, December 2009, by Cuba's national statistical office (ONE).

6. Assuming that planting takes place between July and January, the harvest season for sweet potatoes is from December to July. Sweet potatoes should be harvested four to five months after planting.

7. This is a pest that attacks sweet potatoes in the ground, affecting their quality and suitability for human consumption.

8. The productive forces include the means of production (machinery, equipment, tools, and inputs), technology, and the labor force, the latter being the most important component.

9. J. Varela, "Ceba de toros en su primer round," *Granma*, October 26, 2009. Eleven thousand producers participate, with more than 90,000 animals. An incentives regime has been established whereby 80% of net profits are distributed among the members of the cooperative. Since January 2010, producers who have over 200 animals get an additional incentive to sell directly to the meat industry.

10. Until recently, the fattening process was centralized in state enterprises dedicated exclusively to fattening bovine livestock.

11. Average weight on the hoof at the end of 2009 was 328.1 kilograms, when it should have been above 430 kilograms.

12. M. Martín and León H., "Experimentarán nueva fórmula para el Acopio and comercialización de productos agrícolas." *Juventud Rebelde*, June 7, 2009: digital@jrebelde.cip.cu.

13. According to ONE's 2008 Statistical Yearbook, there were 3,631,000 hectares of uncultivated land at the end of 2007, of which 2,398,000 hectares were in grass with a low ratio of animals per hectare, and 1,232,800 hectares were idle. Uncultivated agricultural land constituted 54.8% of the agricultural land and idle lands represented 18.6% of the agricultural area. The Ministry of Agriculture reported 1,758,962 hectares of idle land in its October 2009 report, *Resultados y Perspectivas*.

14. The land continues to be state property.

15. See Armando Nova González, *La agricultura en Cuba: evolución y trayectoria, 1959–2005*.

16. President Raúl Castro reported on July 26, 2009 that more than 110,000 applications had been filed of which approximately 82,000 were approved, comprising some 690,000 hectares or 39% of idle land. (It can be inferred, therefore, that there had been a total of 1,769,230 hectares of idle land.) Up to that date 225,000 hectares (32.6%) of the land assigned and transferred in usufruct had been planted. In his report to the National Assembly on December 20, 2009, the president reported the assignment and transfer of 920,000 hectares in usufruct, benefiting more than 100,000 applicants.

17. The quantity of land requested up to January 18, 2010, was 1,311,995 hectares, and 946,344 hectares had been assigned and transferred up to that date. Individuals ("natural persons") accounted for 1,145,297 of the hectares applied for, and 866,406 hectares had been assigned and delivered to them. Economic Directorate of ANAP, February 8, 2009.

18. The right of the producer to decide what to produce, to whom to sell, and at what price, and to have access to a market for inputs to buy at the appropriate time what is needed to complete the productive cycle successfully.

19. Armando Nova González, "La cadena agro-comercializadora en el sector agropecuario," *IPS* 22/13, July 15, 2009.

Commentary

A Comparative View of Cuban Agricultural Institutions and Reforms

Dwight H. Perkins

The reform of agricultural institutions has been a central feature of economic reform in socialist economic systems during the past three decades. Agricultural reforms in China and Vietnam were central to a reform process that has lifted the per capita incomes of these two countries by more than 12-fold and 3-fold respectively. Initially at least, these reforms also lowered inequality in the two countries as rural incomes grew faster than urban incomes for the first five or six years of the reform period. In contrast, the failure of the Soviet Union to reform agricultural institutions contributed to the economic recession that plagued the reform process there, although it was not the main reason for the steep recession of the 1990s. Cuba, as Armando Nova González describes in his two chapters, has begun an effort to reform institutions related to agriculture. Any agricultural economy that has large amounts of unused arable land and at the same time imports a substantial portion of its food needs still has a long ways to go, however, before reforms can be considered a success.

A variety of institutions are central to achieving an efficient and equitable agricultural sector. Broadly speaking, they divide into three parts: the health and education levels of the farm population, the way agricultural production is organized, and the way that production is purchased and distributed. Cuba scores well on the first part, with its well-developed public health and education systems, but clearly still has major problems in the latter two areas.

I see no country that has made a success of collective agriculture from a production perspective. The spurt in agricultural output in both China and Vietnam occurred when the two countries abandoned the collectives and returned to household-based agricultural production. In China's case, the rise in output was roughly 50 percent over the first six years of reform. In Vietnam, a shortage of food in the late 1980s led to widespread malnutrition, particularly in the north, and was followed after 1988 with reforms that led to a 41 percent rise in farm output by 1995.[1] Cuban agricultural output, in contrast, has fluctuated from year to year over the past decade, but the overall trend appears to have been flat. The most significant Cuban reform has clearly been the decision to open up the large amount of unused arable land to cultivation by different kinds of groups, but 1.1 million hectares of land with agricultural use potential was still idle in 2005 and 2.27 million hectares was in pasture. Of the total land with agricultural use potential of 6.6 million hectares in 2005, only 3.2 million hectares was under cultivation and only 7.8 percent of that land was cultivated by private units. In more recent years, reforms have led to roughly half of the idle land being put into cultivation, which is clearly a step in the right direction, although the process has been slow.[2] Less impressive is that most of this land is apparently still cultivated by state or collective entities that have very limited decision-making authority at the production unit level. By way of comparison, Vietnam, with a population of over 80 million, provides most of the food requirements of that population from 9.4 million hectares of cultivated land. Vietnam's exports of food are three times its food imports. Most Vietnamese food production comes from individual household producers who have wide discretion in deciding what to produce.

There are typically three justifications put forward for why the state should play a major role in managing the distribution of agricultural products. The most common one is the popular notion that private merchants use monopoly powers and superior information to gouge unsophisticated peasant farmers, paying them below market prices. A second reason is that the state can ensure a more equitable distribution of food. The third reason is that the state can even out the fluctuation in prices paid to farmers so that they don't go from boom to bust from year to year. There are several other reasons that are often not spoken about openly but may be more important. Marketing boards for agricultural products were a common feature in many European colonies and are still in widespread use in many African countries. The main purpose of these marketing boards today is to generate revenue for the state by paying low prices to domestic producers, particularly during boom times when high prices produce a windfall for the state. Of course, state control of the distribution of key products can also be used for political ends, and the employees of these state distribution systems also benefit from having well-paying jobs that they are understandably reluctant to give up.

Cuba's food distribution system appears to be testimony to the falsity of most of these arguments for state distribution. Plausibly there were times when Cuba needed the state to ensure that everyone got sufficient food—in the immediate aftermath of the end of Soviet sugar subsidies and the collapse of the sugar industry, for example, and for brief periods after natural disasters such as hurricanes. Yet there are far more efficient ways to ensure that those in poverty receive sufficient food during more normal times. Food stamps are the principal method used in the United States, but in developing countries it is not easy to identify who falls below a given poverty line and requires such a subsidy. Direct allocation of a limited supply of basic foods is sometimes used in developing countries, but is typically highly inefficient. Nutrition programs targeted to designated poverty areas are likely to be a better use of the resources available for this purpose and are the main methods in use in China.

The argument that a state monopoly of the purchase and distribution of agricultural products is superior to competitive market distribution finds no empirical support anywhere in the world. Cuba clearly pays very low prices to producers and sells at high prices. It is not clear to me from the data available to me that the Cuban distribution system even produces much revenue for the state. If the poorest people in the country, a majority of whom are farmers, receive prices far below the market rate, and if the profits of the state monopoly are not large, then the only real beneficiaries of this system are the employees of the state monopoly. In the Soviet Union, state marketing did for a time produce large revenues for the government. In China in the pre-reform period (before 1978), the state paid below-market prices to farmers, and the benefits of these below-market prices to the producers were then mostly distributed to the urban population through low prices that required use of ration coupons. These low prices to the collective farms hurt incentives to produce, and the urban rationing system was cumbersome and inefficient. The urban low-price rationing system also subsidized the highest income portion of the population. This Chinese rationing system did make it easier for the state to limit rural to urban migration, but it produced other kinds of serious inequities for the rural poor. China today still has pockets where nutrition is below acceptable norms, but these are dealt with using targeted nutrition programs, not by gearing the entire food distribution system to this end. For the past two decades plus, food in China and in Vietnam is mainly distributed through the market and there is no sentiment for a return to state distribution.

There are plausible reasons why Cuba chose to go down a path that relied on state and collective institutions to manage both the production and distribution of agriculture. The dominance of large sugar plantations—whether private or state controlled—had more in common with industry than with small-holder agriculture. Close ties with the Soviet Union and admiration of many aspects of the Soviet economic system would reinforce this view. But Cuba today has a farm population of over one million farming 3 plus million hectares of crop land and 2 plus million hectares of pasture; this would come to not much more than 20 hectares per farm family if this arable land were distributed to households. That is far more land per farm household than in China or Vietnam (less than one hectare per farm family), but far less than the 500 to 1000 hectares for the highly mechanized farms of the United States.[3] Household agriculture on limited land requires the right incentives if farmers are to exploit the full potential of their arable land, and factory or collective incentives simply cannot match the incentives of a farmer knowing that every improvement he or she makes will go directly into his own pocket. A distribution system that reaches these same small-holder farmers must also have the right incentives, and unfettered market forces and competitive small merchants are likely to be more efficient than any large organization, particularly any large organization run in accordance with bureaucratic rules with more than a little political interference.

Endnotes

1. The Chinese data are from National Statistical Bureau, *China Statistical Yearbook 2010* (Beijing: Statistical Publishers, 2010) and the Vietnamese data are from Nguyen Sinh Cuc, *Agriculture of Vietnam, 1945–1995* (Hanoi: Statistical Publishing House, 1995), p. 175. The Vietnamese data are for gross output of agriculture whereas the Chinese data are for value added so are not strictly comparable.
2. These data are from the two chapters by Armando Nova González in this volume.
3. The average farm size in the United States was only 176 hectares in 2008, but many of these are small and are only farmed part time. Much of the U.S. food production is from much larger farms.

PART

II

Opportunities for Outward-Oriented Growth

5

Cuban Monetary Policy and the Global Crisis[1]

Pavel Vidal Alejandro

The global financial and economic crisis of 2008–2009 intensified the weaknesses in the Cuban economy, which since 2008 has been experiencing slower growth and important external and internal disequilibria. In 2008, the economy sustained an abrupt drop in terms of trade and suffered the costly effects of several seasonal hurricanes, especially in housing and food production. As a result, gross domestic product (GDP) growth dropped to 4.1% in 2008 compared to 7.3% in 2007 and 12.1% in 2006. Imports grew by 43.3%; the economy incurred a large international trade deficit amounting to $2.3 billion worth of goods and services; and the foreign debt rose to $20.532 billion (152% in relation to exports); furthermore, the budget deficit was the highest of the decade.

The main effects of the global financial and economic crisis on the Cuban economy were felt in 2009. In that year, exports of goods and services dropped significantly, the terms of trade declined again, and the difficulty of obtaining external financing grew. With the increase in external constraints, deceleration of GDP growth intensified; in 2009 GDP grew by only 1.4%. The production of goods declined by 3.6% in that year, but a negative overall growth rate was prevented due to the large share of services (80%) as a share of total GDP.

When the global crisis took place, Cuba lacked the foreign reserves required to implement a counter-cyclical expansionary policy, which might have used such reserves to provide resources to cushion the economic slowdown and reactive growth. Instead, its government had to reduce spending to recover from the deterioration in macroeconomic equilibria that had started in 2008. In 2009, the fiscal deficit was reduced and a surplus in trade in goods and services was obtained as a result of austerity policies, principally a sharp cut in imports (–37.3%), a contraction in investment (–16%), and tight control on expenditures (0.8%).

In this chapter I seek to identify the monetary mechanisms that transmitted the global financial and economic crisis to Cuba, and Cuba's monetary policy response. We begin with the results of a structural vector autoregression (SVAR) econometric model, previously estimated by the author.[2] The chapter is organized in the following manner: Section 2 examines inflation. Section 3 presents some characteristics of monetary policy in Cuba. Section 4 summarizes the specifications and data from the SVAR model and discusses what these reveal about monetary transmission mechanisms in Cuba. On this basis, Section 5 examines the 2008–2009 monetary impacts as seen through a set of key indicators. Section 6 extends the analysis to the effect of the global crisis on currency exchange policy and the Cuban banking system. Finally, Section 7 presents the conclusions related to the chapter's main objective.

Inflation

Until the early 1990s, the Cuban family's basic market basket was obtained almost entirely from state retail markets. In this environment, monetary disequilibrium was reflected not in prices, but in the accumulation of excess liquidity. Thus, the processes of monetary instability did not result in price increases, but rather in repressed inflation or forced savings. The economic authorities, as their fundamental monetary strategy, monitored this variable—the amount of liquidity held by the population—and undertook actions to control it. The policy target was to maintain monetary liquidity within certain limits or ratios relative to the value of production. Various analysts have written works on excess monetary liquidity in the early 1990s in Cuba.[3]

As part of the economic policy changes undertaken in the 1990s, greater space was given to non-state enterprises operating under unregulated pricing schemes in private agricultural markets (*mercados agropecuarios*),[4] and informal markets.[5] Also, a new non-bank financial institution was created: the Casas de Cambio S.A. (CADECA), which organized a national network of exchange offices where individuals could buy and sell currencies. In the new conditions under which the Cuban economy operates—now with greater similarities to what occurs in a market economy—increases in the money supply no longer result in the accumulation of excess liquidity but rather in more inflation and greater purchases of hard currencies in the exchange market. In consideration of this development, the Central Bank of Cuba has been modifying the way it designs and modifies monetary policy. The monetary authorities have been transitioning from a strategy that emphasized the control of the liquid assets in the population's possession toward a strategy whose main goals are the control of inflation and market equilibrium in the currency exchanges that take place in CADECAs.

Since 1989, inflation in Cuba has passed through several periods. The informal market experienced hyperinflation in the early 1990s. The years of greatest price increases in that market were 1991 (more than 150%) and 1993 (more than 200%). This inflation resulted from the economic crisis associated with the collapse of the Soviet Union and of its special relationship with Cuba, as well as from the associated fiscal and monetary disequilibria. In the four years following 1990, GDP contracted by 34.8%. The average budget deficit from 1990 to 1993 equaled 24.9% of GDP. This budget deficit was financed through a loan from the Central Bank (at that moment, it was called the Banco Nacional) to the state budget. Monetization of the budget deficit provoked a growth in the money supply in the hands of the population to an annual rate of 27.6%. In the informal currency exchange market, the exchange rate for the Cuban peso rose to 150 Cuban pesos per dollar, while before the crisis this rate had been five pesos per dollar.

Since 1995, the National Statistics Office (Oficina Nacional de Estadísticas, ONE) has computed a Consumer Price Index (CPI) made up of the average prices in Cuban pesos that the population encounters in three different markets. The index of consumer prices reflects a combination of prices. The prices for goods and services sold by the state to the population through both rationed and non-rationed means account for 40% of the CPI. The other two markets included in the CPI are the *agromercado* or agricultural market sector, which operates under few regulations and in market prices in response to supply and demand, with a share of about 30%, and the informal market, which amounts to another 30%. Prices in the *peso convertible*[6] markets are not included in the CPI.

Since the triple-digit inflation of the early 1990s, monetary policy has managed to keep the inflation rate within the single-digit range. In the current decade, inflation in Cuban pesos has continued to be low (Figure 5.1). In 2008, the CPI in Cuban pesos dropped by 0.1%. In 2009 it dropped again by 0.1%, while the CPI in convertible pesos rose by 1.4%. (In 2009, CPI figures associated with convertible peso markets were publicly announced for the first time.) Inflation has stayed under control despite the impact of the global crisis and the deterioration in macroeconomic conditions.

In the inflation data presented in Figure 5.1, two issues stand out: the volatility of inflation, and deflation.[7] The variability in inflation reveals that monetary policy has not defined a clear target with respect to inflation, but rather follows a discretionary strategy whose purpose is to correct past dis-

Figure 5.1. Inflation in Cuban Pesos, 2000–2009

(Percentage of change in Consumer Price Index, CPI)

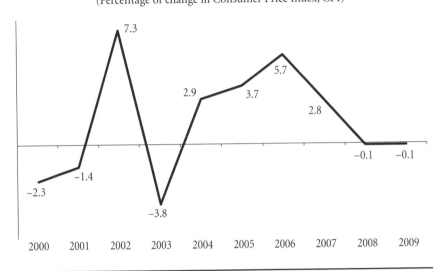

Source: Central Bank of Cuba (2008) and ONE (2008, 2009a and 2009b).

equilibria. While the Central Bank has become steadily more concerned about inflation, the setting of an inflation target remains a pending issue for Cuban monetary policy. The policy makers seek a low inflation rate, but are not much concerned by deflation; in fact, price declines are sometimes favorably viewed by some sectors, given that they increase the real value of salaries and pensions. In Cuba, deflation does not carry such heavy costs as in market economies; nonetheless, a set of negative effects can be identified, particularly in providing a negative incentive for the agricultural sector.[8]

Other Characteristics of Monetary Policy in Cuba

Stability in GDP does not figure among the ultimate objectives of Cuban monetary policy. Several particularities of the Cuban economy limit the effects that money supply and monetary policy tools have on GDP. First, there is the effect of how the state-enterprise[9] sector is managed. Production of most Cuban enterprises is carried out according to a central plan. Planning and centralization orient enterprises' spending and intervene in the allocation of resources. Enterprises do not have complete autonomy in making decisions on their activity solely based on prices.

Second, the state enterprise sector does not have access to any exchange market for Cuban pesos. Unlike individuals, "legal persons" cannot use

Cuban pesos to buy hard currency to purchase imports; they are prohibited from using the CADECA exchange markets. Rather, one of the main functions of the economic plan is to assign and distribute hard currency reserves centrally. Therefore, an enterprise's production level does not depend solely on demand for its goods and services and on prices, but also on the availability of hard currency assigned to it by the plan.

Third, there is the issue of market segmentation between the enterprise sector and the population. Individuals and enterprises do not have recourse to the same markets for goods, currencies, or financing. Though connections between the segments exist, there are also regulations that impede the free flow of money between them. Therefore, monetary analyses concerning Cuba generally speak of the "population sector" and the "enterprise sector." This distinction is usually not made in market economies, but in the case of Cuba a separate assessment of the two spheres is necessary, and thus we may also speak of segmented monetary policy.

In sum, planning and centralization have been the principal instruments employed to regulate demand and production in the enterprise sector. In practice, monetary policy instruments have been more oriented toward affecting monetary equilibria in the population sector.

Cuba does not carry out open-market operations. There is no market for public debt, nor has the Central Bank issued its own bonds or notes that could be used as an instrument to regulate the money supply. The budget deficit continues to be monetized by way of the Central Bank and, consequently, a fiscal disequilibrium has a direct and immediate impact on monetary stability. Discount rates or reserve requirements are not employed as monetary policy tools.[10] To maintain price stability and equilibrium in the exchange market, the Central Bank's main tools have been direct control of exchange and interest rates. It has also carried out operations such as selling dollars to the Ministry of Internal Commerce (MINCIN) to stimulate the supply of consumer goods for sale in Cuban pesos and to contribute to equilibrium between the supply and demand of goods and services. Also, the Central Bank participates in the coordination of various economic policies and decisions that affect monetary equilibria.

Design and implementation of monetary policy is in the hands of a Monetary Policy Committee composed exclusively of Central Bank administrators. A body called GASFI (Spanish acronym for Group for Analysis of the Prophylaxis of Internal Finances) coordinates among the various institutions and policies involved in monetary stability. GASFI meetings are attended by administrators of the Ministry of Economics and Planning, the Ministry of Finance and Pricing, MINCIN, and the Central Bank.

A fundamental characteristic of Cuban monetary policy is the existence of a dual currency regime. In 2003 and 2004, the convertible peso (CUC) replaced the U.S. dollar as a medium of exchange. Since then, two locally issued currencies have circulated in the economy: the Cuban peso (CUP) and the convertible peso. In the eight state-owned Cuban commercial banks, members of the public and enterprises alike maintain deposits in these two local currencies, but bank accounts in dollars and other hard currencies have continued to exist as well. Monetary statistics related to the convertible peso are scarce, and the monetary policy actions with respect to this currency are carried out with little transparency. Starting in 1994, when the convertible peso was first issued, the goal of monetary policy has been to maintain a currency-board exchange-rate regime with international reserves to support the CUC's monetary base and its parity with the U.S. dollar. Since 2003–2004, however, that mechanism ceased to operate. The sources and uses of the monetary base of this currency are unknown, as are the degree and manner in which they are backed by international exchange reserves.

SVAR Model and Monetary Transmission Mechanisms

This section presents the key results of the structural vector autoregression model (SVAR) of 2008 mentioned above, on which the subsequent analysis of the monetary transmission mechanisms of the global crisis will be based. The SVAR model supports an understanding of the sources of pressures that impact the goals of monetary policy to keep inflation low and bring the CADECA currency exchange market into equilibrium. Given the lack of available data, monetary statistics in convertible pesos have not been included.

In general, vector autoregression models (VAR) allow for an estimation of dynamic relations among the variables related to monetary policy, without requiring *a priori* theoretical restrictions, which is quite convenient in the Cuban case given the previously discussed peculiarities of Cuban markets.[11] Because of the previously noted segmentation, the estimates refer to the population sector, that is, to the relations closest to the phenomenon of inflation and to the CADECA exchange market.

Table 5.1 summarizes the definitions and sources of the data employed in the model. The variables that are employed are used by the Central Bank to monitor and design monetary policy. The series are monthly in frequency and cover the period from January 1996 to December 2004. Logarithms were used for all variables except the interest rate. These data, excluding the exchange and interest rates, were seasonally adjusted using the TRAMO-SEATS program. Though the variables follow a non-stationary trajectory,

Table 5.1. Data Used in SVAR Model

Variable	Definition	Source[*]
Unregulated Prices (P)	Simple average of the CPIs of *agromercados* and informal markets, which together total approximately 60% of the full CPI in Cuban pesos.	ONE
Regulated Prices (PR)	CPI of the formal market, which represents approximately 40% of the full CPI in Cuban pesos.	ONE
Salary Payments (SAL)	Nominal salary paid by enterprises in Cuban pesos. This is not the average salary, but the monthly sum disbursed by enterprises for this category in a month.	BCC
Retail Mercantile Circulation (CMM)	Nominal value of sales of services and consumer goods to the population, by state enterprises, in Cuban pesos; most of these enterprises belong to MINCIN.	BCC
Money Supply (M)	The aggregate M_0, which calculates cash in the hands of the population, in Cuban pesos.	BCC
Exchange Market Balance (CAM)	Difference between the purchase and sale of other currencies, in return for Cuban pesos, carried out in the CADECA network. The currencies most often exchanged by the population for Cuban pesos are: U.S. dollars, convertible pesos, and euros. A positive balance for this variable indicates that, during the month, the population sold more of these currencies in the CADECAs than it bought there with Cuban pesos.	BCC
Exchange Rate of Cuban Peso in CADECA (TC)	Exchange rate of Cuban peso with respect to the dollar and the convertible peso. These are the same exchange rate because, until March 2005, one convertible peso equaled one U.S. dollar.	BCC
Interest Rate (TI)	Interest rate for one-year fixed-term deposits of Cuban pesos.	BCC

* ONE: Oficina Nacional de Estadísticas. BCC: Central Bank of Cuba

the VAR estimation was made with variables in levels so as not to lose information about long-term relations.

The VAR model can be summarized in matrix form:

$$AX_t = C(L)X_{t-1} + u_t$$

where X is a vector with all the described variables. The matrix A is made up of the coefficients a_{ij} which capture the contemporaneous relationships among the variables. $C(L)$ is a polynomial in the lag operator, which contains the coefficients that relate each variable to the lags of the rest of the variables and to its own lags. Four lags are included, following the Likelihood Ratio (LR) test. The u_t represent the shocks associated with each of the variables (structural shocks), which are assumed to be uncorrelated white noise residuals (it is assumed that $E(u_t u_t')$ is a diagonal matrix).

As a first step, Granger causality tests were performed to test each variable's capacity to explain the rest of the variables in the model.[12] The results indicated that interest rates do not Granger-cause the rest of the variables. Based on this result, and understanding the particular characteristics of interest rates in the Cuban case, it was decided not to include these in the final estimation of the model, with a consequent gain in the degrees of freedom used to derive statistical results. It may be surprising to interpret the results of a monetary VAR model that excludes interest rates, but it must be recalled that these are fixed-term interest rates, which are, in addition, a relatively new feature of the Cuban financial system. There were only four changes in the interest rate during the sample period used for the estimation. Evidently this result must be viewed with caution; it is likely that interest rates will become increasingly important to the extent that the population continues to become acquainted with, and makes use of, fixed-term deposits.[13]

Finally, the SVAR was estimated based on the remaining seven variables. The reduced-form VAR (without contemporaneous relationships) was estimated, and the restrictions required to identify the system and recover the structural parameters were defined. A structural identification was used, which is to say an SVAR variant with the following restrictions in matrix A[14]

$$
A = \begin{bmatrix}
1 & -a_{12} & -a_{13} & -a_{14} & -a_{15} & -a_{16} & 0 \\
0 & 1 & 0 & 0 & 0 & 0 & 0 \\
0 & 0 & 1 & 0 & 0 & 0 & 0 \\
-a_{41} & -a_{42} & -a_{43} & 1 & 0 & -a_{46} & -a_{47} \\
-a_{51} & -a_{52} & -a_{53} & -a_{54} & 1 & -a_{56} & -a_{57} \\
-a_{61} & -a_{62} & -a_{63} & -a_{64} & 0 & 1 & -a_{67} \\
0 & 0 & 0 & 0 & 0 & 0 & 1
\end{bmatrix}
$$

in which every row defines a contemporaneous effect on P, PR, SAL, CMM, M, CAM, and TC, in that order.

The majority of the restrictions are concentrated in rows two, three, and seven, which represent the contemporaneous impact of the variables on regulated prices, salaries, and exchange rates. These are the three variables primarily determined by the economic authorities. In setting the coefficients to zero, it is assumed that regulated prices, salaries, and exchange rates lag at least one period in reacting to shocks in the rest of the variables.[15] Furthermore, the contemporaneous impacts of the monetary aggregate on retail mercantile circulation and on the exchange market coefficients (a_{45} and a_{65}) are also set at zero, because by accounting identity they are sources of liquidity growth during the month. Since convertible peso prices are not included in the CPI, the contemporaneous effect of exchange rates on unregulated prices (coefficient a_{17}) is also assumed to be zero. As a result, the matrix contains twenty-one restrictions, which render the system exactly identified.[16]

Figure 5.2 summarizes the evidence found in the SVAR model about monetary transmission mechanisms affecting inflation and the CADECA exchange market. The mechanisms that may be empirically supported by impulse-response functions of inflation are considered significant, as are—in accordance with the variance decomposition results—those affected by

Figure 5.2. Monetary Transmission Mechanisms in the Population Sector (see Table 5.1 for definitions of the variables)

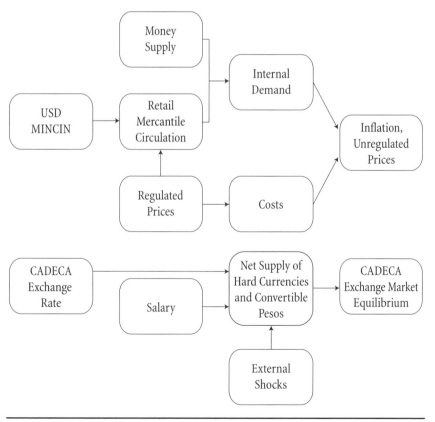

the shocks that explain more than 10% of the variation in unregulated prices and in the exchange market.[17] Interest rates do not appear in Figure 5.2 because of the above-mentioned Granger-causality result. Each net effect is associated with a possible channel through which it might operate, whether that be internal demand, costs, or the supply and demand of convertible peso and hard currency in exchange for Cuban pesos in CADECA.

It is clear that monetary aggregates, retail mercantile circulation, and regulated prices are the variables that show a significant impact on unregulated prices. By way of the internal demand mechanism and the cost channel, these variables exert pressure on inflation. Through the sale of dollars to MINCIN, the Central Bank can influence this mechanism and contribute to price stability.

Exchange rates, salaries, and external shocks have a significant impact on exchange market equilibrium in the population sector, which is to say in CADECA. A rise in salaries translates into increased demand for convertible pesos and hard currencies, exerting pressure on the equilibrium of this market. The diagram also includes external shocks, reflecting the fact that the Central Bank must monitor tourism, remittances, and other sources of hard currencies and convertible pesos in CADECA.

No evidence was found that the Central Bank can influence the population sector exchange market by way of sales of dollars to MINCIN. Nor did the SVAR estimates suggest a significant pass-through effect from exchange rates to unregulated prices. Nonetheless, it is important to bear in mind that the sample does not include the 1990–1994 period, during which more evidence of this type of transmission mechanism was present.[18]

Monetary Impacts in 2008–2009

Monthly data are not available to simulate the monetary effects of the various shocks that affected the Cuban economy in 2008–2009 using the SVAR model. With the information available, it is only possible to analyze the annual evolution of some of the key monetary policy variables that were identified as significant in the transmission mechanisms of the SVAR model estimated for the 1996–2004 period. To assess the pressures affecting the goal of low inflation, Figure 5.3 shows the annual evolution of retail mercantile circulation and of the money supply in the hands of the population. To assess the pressures affecting the equilibrium of the CADECA exchange market, Figure 5.3 shows the annual evolution of salaries and of the Cuban peso exchange rate.[19]

Figure 5.3 shows that retail mercantile circulation fell in 2008 (−2.8%) and rose somewhat in 2009 (5.6%). The sharp deceleration of GDP growth

Figure 5.3. Important Indicators for Monetary Policy, 2000–2009
(Index 2000 = 100)

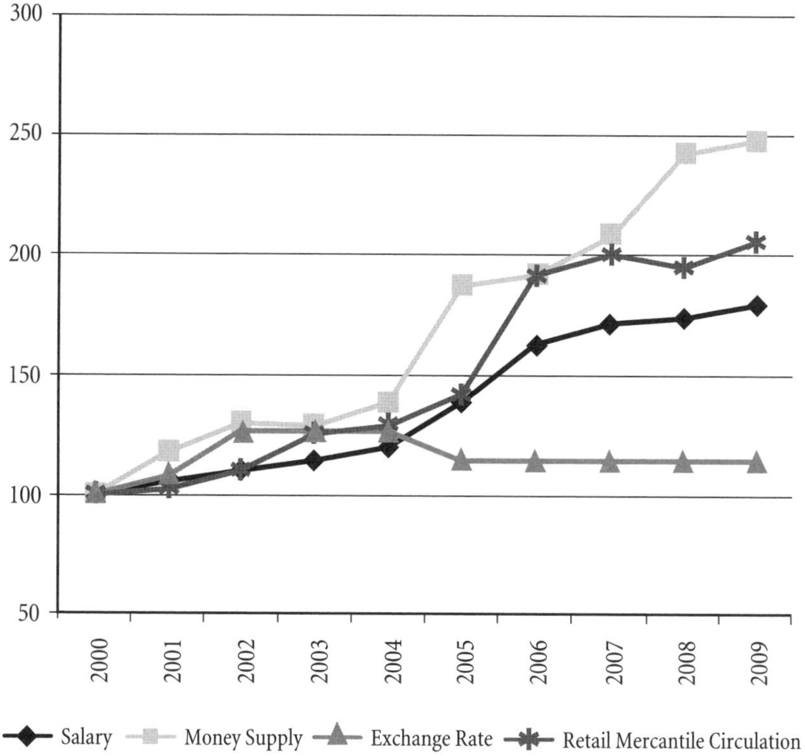

◆ Salary   ■ Money Supply   ▲ Exchange Rate   ✳ Retail Mercantile Circulation

Source: Calculated by the author on the basis of ONE (2009a and 2009b)

in those years, along with worsening macroeconomic conditions, limited the ability of the government and the Central Bank to continue to stimulate the supply of goods and services to the population, as they did in 2005 and 2006. A drop or slowdown in state sales (retail mercantile circulation) tends to raise demand in non-state markets and pushes unregulated prices upward. At the same time, the money supply grew significantly in 2008 (16.8%), corresponding to the monetization of the largest budget deficit of the decade (equal to 6.7% of GDP and driven primarily by food-price subsidies that absorbed the increase in international food prices, and expenditures undertaken in response to hurricane damage). Nonetheless, the monetary aggregate only increased 2.1% in 2009, a year in which the budget deficit was reduced, though it still remained the second-highest of the decade (4.8% as a percentage of GDP). That is, in 2008 inflationary pressures were generated through the channel of internal demand, due to the drop in retail mercantile circulation and to the growth in the money supply. In 2009 inflationary pressures were reduced by controlling the growth of monetary aggregates.

It is worth devoting some attention to the transmission mechanism of costs into inflation, even though the data are unavailable. In 2008, the price of fuel in state-owned gasoline stations rose by more than 50% in response to the international rise in oil prices. This increase in fuel prices, in turn, exerted pressure on the prices of *agromercado* products because this input represents a significant share of transportation and agricultural production costs for farmers. Nonetheless, neither this pressure nor the others mentioned as part of the internal demand mechanism resulted in price increases in the *agromercados* because the government declared a price freeze on major goods sold in these markets in 2008.

As for the CADECA exchange market, Figure 5.3 indicates that there was not much pressure exerted through the salary channel because salary growth slowed to 1.7% in 2008 and 3.4% in 2009, as compared to increases of 16.2% in 2005 and 17.3% in 2006. Given the improvement in economic performance since 2004 and the increase in GDP growth, the government began to raise minimum wages and salary scales in the majority of enterprises and institutions. As economic growth has slowed since then, salary increases have been limited to select economic sectors. In 2009, the government of Raúl Castro implemented a reform intended to bring more flexibility in salary policies, allowing enterprises to make autonomous decisions about their workers' pay in relation to individual performance. So far, this reform has not provoked an important increase in average salaries.

Exchange rates in CADECA are a null factor in 2008–2009 because they remained fixed. Since the currency exchange regime was established in 1995, and up until 2002, the exchange rate for the Cuban peso in CADECA followed a managed-floating regimen. That is, the Central Bank intervened to avoid short-term volatility, but it adjusted the rates in the presence of sustained disequilibrium. Nonetheless, as can be seen in Figure 5.3, exchange rates have been held fixed since 2005.

To conclude the analysis of the exchange market, Figure 5.4 summarizes some of the most important external indicators affecting this market: tourism, total exports of goods and services, and terms of trade. These variables contribute more or less directly to the supply of hard currencies reaching the exchange market. Earlier, Figure 5.2 described how external shocks also influence the share of the exchange market controlled by CADECA.

As seen in Figure 5.4, exports of goods and services plummeted 16.6% after having grown for six consecutive years, supported as they had been by the export of professional services, principally the commercialization of medical services to Venezuela. The global crisis, and especially its effects on Venezuelan GDP, negatively affected demand for Cuban exports. The repercussions of the crisis in major tourist-providing areas, such as Canada and Europe, negatively impacted the revenue from tourist services, which dropped by 10.7% in 2009. Changes in terms of trade (dropping by 31.6% in 2008 and 5.8% in 2009) also brought about a decline in the net hard currency supply in the exchange market. This trend is explained by a collapse in the price of nickel, which is Cuba's leading goods export, alongside with the growth in the international prices of petroleum and food, which are Cuba's key imports.

Due to the lack of data, remittances from abroad have not been included in this analysis, although they are also an important source of the level of

Figure 5.4. Important External Indicators for the Exchange Market, 2000–2009 (Index 2000 = 100)

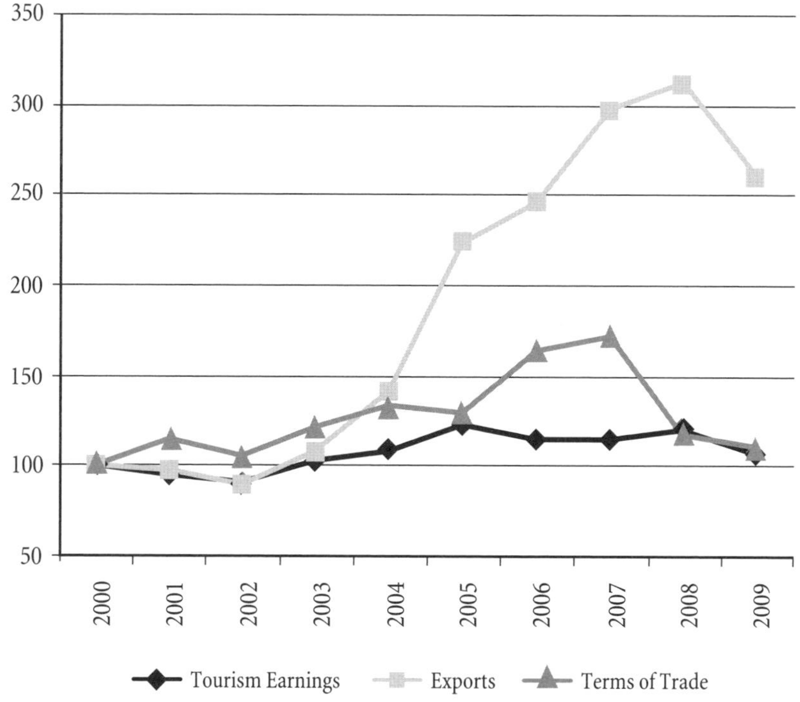

Source: Calculated by the author on the basis of ONE (2008, 2009a, and 2009b).

hard currencies held by the population and influence the CADECA exchange market (a variety of sources estimate that remittances total on the order of $1 billion a year). Two opposite forces have had an impact on the flow of remittances to Cuba during the crisis. On the one hand, flows have eased by the Barack Obama administration's reduction of restrictions on the sending of remittances to Cuba from the United States. On the other hand, the recession and rising unemployment in the United States restricted the level of resources directed to families living in Cuba. Based on the assumption that these two events cancel each other out, remittances probably did not vary significantly in 2008–2009.

In sum, the population sector exchange market has been subject to deficit pressures exerted by external shocks, most of them linked to the global crisis. The Central Bank has not resorted to devaluation to correct the deficit in the supply of hard currency. Therefore, most likely the CADECA market has been in a state of disequilibrium since at least 2008, when the effects of the external shocks began to be felt. To maintain the exchange value of Cuban currencies and cover the hard currency deficit, the Central Bank has been forced to intervene in the exchange market, using its foreign currency reserves. Sales of hard currency in the exchange market imply sterilization of the money supply in local currency, which is consistent with the drop of the monetary aggregate growth for 2009 (2.1%).

Considering these events, it is now possible to understand better why inflation did not accelerate in 2008–2009 despite the impact of the global crisis and the deterioration of macroeconomic equilibria. In 2008, real inflationary pressures were exerted on the Cuban economy through the channels of internal demand and costs, but these pressures were blocked primarily by the decision to freeze prices in the *agromercados*. The fixed exchange rate policy dampened inflationary pressures, avoiding a possible transmission of these pressures to final prices and leading to a sterilization of the money supply in 2009. The Central Bank's fixed exchange rates policy, therefore, contributed to its goal of low inflation. The resulting monetary policy, however, was not able to achieve the goal of maintaining the CADECA exchange market in equilibrium.

The Convertible Peso and the Banking Crisis

The policy of fixed exchange rates may be questioned not only because it fails to counter the disequilibrium in CADECA but also because it does not contribute to an external equilibrium or to preventing a Cuban banking crisis. The major error may have been the extension of the policy of fixed exchange rates to the convertible peso. Besides maintaining a fixed exchange rate for the Cuban peso, the Central Bank has also defended the exchange value of the convertible peso at a rate of US$1.08 per 1 CUC in spite of the disequilibrium in the balance of payments.

The decision to continue with a fixed exchange rate for the Cuban peso in CADECA is somewhat understandable, given its great importance to the population sector and its direct effect on the purchasing power of low salaries. Nonetheless, a greater share of the exchange rate of the convertible peso is linked to foreign commerce, and it has become a potential instrument for adjusting external economic balances since the U.S. dollar was replaced by the convertible peso in 2003–2004. The convertible peso was created in 1994 with a fixed parity to the U.S. dollar and a currency board to back it up. In response to a balance of payments surplus in 2005, the convertible peso was revalued upward by 8%. However, no such inverse adjustment has been made in response to the subsequent balance of payments deficit. A convertible peso devaluation (for instance, to 1.10 CUC per 1 USD) would favor import substitution, promote exports, and increase the competitiveness of the tourist industry.

The network of state-owned convertible peso retail stores, which operate with a high profit margin, could reduce their margins to lessen the inflationary effects of a convertible peso devaluation. Interest rates for fixed-term deposits could be increased and could broaden their differential in favor of local currencies in order to promote savings in local currencies and also contribute to decreasing demand for hard currencies, thereby lowering inflationary pressures (even though there is no evidence as to the significance of this mechanism).

The fixed-exchange rate policy did not contribute to equilibrium in the balance of payments and in the exchange market. Rather, it merged with other, previously enacted economic policy decisions, to provoke a crisis in the Cuban banking system. The recent deterioration in macroeconomic conditions and the global crisis have had a severe effect on Cuban banks because, since 2005, these banks have been affected by the centralization of national hard currency revenues in the so-called *Cuenta Única* (sole account) of the state.[20] This has implied the concentration of financial risk within a single economic agent—in this case, the central government. Another determinant of the banking crisis has been the de-dollarization of the economy and the failure to maintain the currency board that backed up the convertible peso, without creating any substitute rule to govern the issuance of this currency. Monetization of the budget deficit in Cuban pesos is accounted for in each year's budget, and the deficit is approved by the National Assembly. In the case of the convertible peso, however, not even this limit exists, and there is less transparency in the statistics and in the decisions that have been made in this area since de-dollarization.[21]

Thus, with the deterioration in the macroeconomic context and the shocks produced by the global crisis, the indebted government observed a deterioration of its finances, which, it seems, brought about unlimited printing of convertible pesos, in turn provoking an excess supply of this currency. This process had direct repercussions on the balance sheets of Cuban banks, which found themselves unable to carry out international payments from the accounts of their clients.

Since early 2009, payments to foreign entities almost ceased, as have any capital flows out of the Cuban banking system. Bank transfers that would normally require a few days' delay took several months to carry out. This phenomenon was the result of convertible-peso deposits' loss of their backing and convertibility into hard currencies at the Central Bank. Meanwhile, the remaining foreign-currency bank deposits suffered from similar lack of liquidity in the commercial banks themselves. Thus, the effects of the exchange crisis and the banking crisis were combined. CEPAL estimates the defaulted or delayed payments by Cuban banks currently range between US$600 million to US$1 billion.[22]

The fixed-exchange policy became a co-factor in the banking crisis to the extent that it weakened the Central Bank and did not contribute to reestablish an equilibrium in the balance of payments or the exchange market. Monetary policy interventions to support existing exchange rates implied a reduction in international reserves and left the Central Bank with less liquidity to support the convertibility of the convertible peso or to allow the institution to act as a lender of last resort for the banking system.

Some of the consequences for the banking system are now irreversible: international confidence in Cuban banks will not be easily restored in the short or mid term. This crisis of confidence itself complicates the banking system's recovery because it gives rise to a vicious cycle in which there is a disincentive for new capital flows to enter the country, while the scarcity of hard currency liquidity therefore deepens. The global crisis makes sources of financing in international markets still more difficult to secure. Stabilization of the banking system requires an international lender of last resort, particularly difficult in the case of Cuba because it is not a member of the major international finance institutions. The effects of the global crisis on Venezuela seem to have made that type of relationship with Cuba's major economic ally impossible, and the same is true of the recently created Bank of the Bolivarian Alliance for the Americas (Banco del ALBA).

Conclusions

On the basis of the available evidence, the monetary transmission mechanisms of the global crisis to Cuba may be summarized as follows:

- The slowdown in GDP growth has become more dramatic, and the government and Central Bank have less ability to continue stimulating the supply of state goods and services to the population (retail mercantile circulation). This in turn leads to higher demand in non-state markets, creating inflationary pressures.

- Worsening macroeconomic conditions kept pressures on the fiscal balance. In 2009, the budget deficit shrank but still remained high, with the result that its monetization continued to expand the money supply, also generating inflationary pressures through the internal demand channel.

- Because of the effects of the global crisis on Venezuela and other foreign partners, exports dropped, including revenues from tourism. Furthermore, the terms of trade declined again. The net supply of hard currencies through this channel of transmission shrank in the Cuban exchange market.

- The global crisis combined with other negative external shocks and with previous errors in economic policy to set off an exchange and banking crisis. The banks and the convertible peso exchange system were previously subjected to financial centralization and the lack of transparent rules to govern the issuance of this currency. The resulting situation amplified the impact of the shocks of 2008 and the global crisis of 2009.

- Cuba has limited access to financing in the international market and few possibilities of finding a lender of last resort to solve the current financial crisis.

By way of controls on exchange rates for the Cuban peso and the convertible peso and the monetary sterilization of 2009, the Cuban monetary policy response maintained inflation low (also, some prices in the *agromercados* were frozen in 2008). However, this policy could not avoid exchange disequilibrium, damage to the convertibility of the convertible peso, and a banking crisis. The Central Bank supported the value of Cuban currencies but, as a result, it weakened its international-reserves support for the monetary base of convertible pesos and its role as lender of last resort for the domestic banking system. The devaluation of the convertible peso could have been a possible alternative, which would have contributed to restoring equilibrium in the balance of payments and the exchange balance. The eventual inflationary effects of this measure could have been compensated with other monetary policy actions.

The impossibility of counting on any international lender of last resort suggests that a solution to the current financial crisis will be very slow, with negative effects on the real economy. Without economic reserves to support a counter-cyclical expansion, the belt-tightening policy begun in 2009 seems to be the best option, given that reestablishing macroeconomic equilibrium contributes to monetary and financial stability and thus to growth in the long run. In the short term, however, the financial crisis and the spending cuts will have a negative impact on economic growth. The lack of supply of goods to local markets is already noticeable, stemming in part from the withdrawal of international investors and suppliers from the Cuban market. Therefore, the new challenge facing monetary policy is how to overcome the renewed inflationary pressures that will emerge within this scenario. The financial and monetary framework of the Cuban economy has become more complicated since the onset of the global crisis. The banking crisis, the convertible peso crisis, and the eventual inflationary pressures make the elimination of monetary duality even more difficult.

Endnotes

1. This essay was prepared for a workshop sponsored by the David Rockefeller Center for Latin American Studies at Harvard University on "Cuba's Development Agenda for 2030" in Cambridge, MA, April 30, 2010. It is part of a research program supported by the Center's Cuban Studies Program with funding from the Ford Foundation.

2. Pavel Vidal, "Monetary Policy in Cuba. A Structural VAR Model Estimation," *Revista Principios* 12 (2008): 85–102.

3. For a discussion, see Julio Carranza, Luis Gutiérrez, and Pedro Monreal, "La desmonetización de la economía cubana: una revisión de las alternativas," *Economía y Desarrollo* 118/ 2 (1995): 44–67; Alfredo González, ed., *La economía cubana en 1994 y los escenarios para 1995; Economía y Reforma Económica en Cuba* (Caracas: Editorial Nueva Sociedad, 1995); Comisión Económica para América Latina y el Caribe (CEPAL), *La economía cubana. Reformas estructurales y desempeño en los noventa* (Santiago: CEPAL, 1997); and Vilma Hidalgo, Pavel Vidal, and Lourdes Tabares, "Equilibrios monetarios y política económica," *Economía y Desarrollo* 127/2 (2000): 75–107.

4. *Mercados agropecuarios*—hereafter *agromercados* following popular usage—offer vegetables, fruits, tubers, rice, beans, some meats, and a few processed foods or cooking ingredients.

5. The informal markets include the self-employed sector and part of the black market.

6. *Pesos convertibles*—hereafter "convertible pesos" or CUCs—are a currency issued by the Cuban state, which can be purchased in the CADECA for Cuban pesos (often referred to as MN or *moneda nacional,* and more formally as CUP) or for various external hard currencies including U.S. dollars, Canadian dollars, and euros. They are redeemable for goods and services in a distinct network of stores and other venues. The exchange rate for *moneda nacional* is approximately 25 Cuban pesos per convertible peso. The rates for foreign currencies were originally pegged to the U.S. dollar at 1:1, followed by changes described by the author.

7. The data are based on Banco Central de Cuba, "Informe Económico 2007" (Havana: Banco Central de Cuba, 2008); Oficina Nacional de Estadísticas (ONE), "Serie de Cuentas Nacionales 1996–2007" (Havana: ONE, 2008); ONE, *Panorama Económico y Social: Cuba 2009* (Havana, ONE, 2009); and ONE, *Anuario Estadístico de Cuba 2008* (Havana, ONE, 2009).

8. Determinants and costs of deflation in Cuba are analyzed in Pavel Vidal and Yaima Doimeadios, "Deflación vs. inflación en la economía cubana," *Economía y Desarrollo* 134 (2003): 59–72.

9. The universal term in Cuba for what in the U.S. might be called either a "company" (if private) or an "agency" or "institution" (if public or non-profit) is *empresa* (enterprise), whether the body in question is state-owned (most often the case), foreign-owned, joint-venture, etc. To maintain this usage, *empresa* is rendered "enterprise" throughout. Generally, as here, the author is referring to state-owned enterprises.

10. The reserve ratio is 10% for on-demand deposits in Cuban pesos and 5.5% for deposits in hard currencies or convertible pesos.

11. Probably one of the largest uses of VARs has been in area of monetary policy. VAR systems have allowed empirical study of the mechanisms of transmission of monetary policies as well as predictions of inflation rates. Relevant works are David Gordon and Eric Leeper, "The Dynamic Impacts of Monetary Policy: An Exercise in Tentative Identification," *Journal of Political Economy* 102/6 (1994): 1228–47; Lawrence Christiano, Martin Eichenbaum, and Charles Evans, "The Effects of Monetary Policy Shocks: Evidence from the Flow of Funds," *The Review of Economics and Statistics* 78/1 (1996): 16–34; and Ben Bernanke and Ilian Mihov, "Measuring Monetary Policy," *Quarterly Journal of Economics* 113/3 (1998): 869–902, among many others. In Latin America, for the case of Chile, see, for instance, Rodrigo Valdés," Transmisión de política monetaria en Chile," *Documentos de Trabajo,* 16 (Santiago: Central Bank of Chile, 1997); and Verónica Mies, Felipe Morandé, and Matías Tapia, "Política monetaria y mecanismos de transmisión: nuevos elementos para una vieja discusión," *Working Paper* 181 (Santiago: Central Bank of Chile, 2002). For an estimate of a structural VAR

for mechanisms of transmission in Venezuela, see Adriana Arreaza, Norka Ayala, and María Fernández, "Mecanismos de transmisión de la política monetaria en Venezuela," VII encuentro de la Red de Investigadores de Bancos Centrales de las Américas. André Minella, "Monetary Policy and Inflation in Brazil (1975–2000): A VAR Estimation," *Revista Brasileira de Economia* 57/3 (2003): 605–35, has studied monetary policy in Brazil using an estimated VAR for three periods since 1975. Alejandro Gaitán and Jesús Gonzáles, "Structural Changes in the Transmission Mechanism of Monetary Policy in Mexico: A Non-linear VAR Approach," *Documentos de Investigación* 6 (Mexico D. F.: Banco de México, 2006), have analyzed changes in Mexico. Since 2005, the Office of Monetary Policy of the Central Bank of Cuba has used a VAR, very similar to the one presented in this paper, to make predictions a year in advance about unregulated prices and about the exchange market for the population sector.

12. The tests to determine whether a variable "Granger-causes" the other variables in the system (block causality test) are useful in detecting whether or not the given variable should be included in the VAR. For a discussion, see Walter Enders, *Applied Econometric Time Series* (New York: Wiley, 1995), and Thomas Doan, *Rats Version 5 User's Guide* (Evanston: Estima, 2000).

13. At the end of 2004, 36% of savings in Cuban pesos on the part of the population were held in fixed-term deposits.

14. Ben Bernanke, "Alternative Explanations of Money-Income Correlation," *Carnegie-Rochester Conference Series on Public Policy* 25 (Pittsburgh: 1986): 49–100; Christopher Sims, "Are Forecasting Models Usable for Policy Analysis?" *Quarterly Review of the Federal Reserve Bank of Minneapolis* (1986): 2–16.

15. Such assumptions about variables controlled by economic authorities have been broadly used and are supported by various lines of argument. On the one hand, delays in data collection by departments of statistics make it difficult for the authorities to become immediately aware of the occurrence of shocks in the economy. On the other hand, these institutions are thought to make decisions with a certain prudence and to prefer confirming the occurrence of shocks before modifying the conditions of economic policy. With monthly data, this form of identification is quite defensible.

16. On the identification of VAR systems, see Enders, *Applied Econometric Time Series*, and Doan, *Rats Version 5 User's Guide*.

17. Vidal, "Monetary Policy in Cuba."

18. Eduardo Hernández, Anaís Chuairey, and Susset Rosales, "El traspaso del tipo de cambio a los precios: Una aproximación al caso de Cuba," Paper presented at the 42 Aniversario de los Estudios Económicos en la Facultad de Economía de la Universidad de la Habana (Havana, 2004). In considering those years, these authors did find a significant pass-through effect.

19. The breakdown of the CPI into regulated and non-regulated prices is also unavailable. Salaries are measured as the average salary per worker, and the monetary aggregate is made up of Cuban-peso savings and cash in the hands of the population.

20. See Central Bank of Cuba, "Resolución 92/2004" (Havana: Central Bank of Cuba, 2004).

21. For a more detailed explanation of the banking crisis, see Pavel Vidal, "Cuban Economic Policy under the Raúl Castro Government," in *Cuba under the Raúl Castro Government*, ed. Kanako Yamaoka (Tokyo: Institute of Developing Economies, 2010).

22. Comisión Económica para América Latina y el Caribe (CEPAL), "Preliminary Overview of the Economies of Latin America and the Caribbean 2009" (Santiago: CEPAL, 2009).

6

Cuba's Agricultural Sector and Its External Links

Anicia García Álvarez

Many economic development theorists have attributed a secondary role to agriculture, yet there is more than a little evidence to support the thesis that agriculture can give rise to important processes of modernization and structural change. Two particular topics have generated considerable controversy as well as quite varied interpretations in economic practice and in academic debate: the agricultural sector's links with the external economy, and its possible contribution to mitigating balance of payments problems in underdeveloped countries. As part of the development process, the GNP share of agriculture decreases along with the volume of farm production in international trade. But the importance of agriculture is not limited to its relative contribution to total production or foreign trade.

According to Johnston and Mellor, the five basic functions of agriculture in the development process are: 1) to increase the supply of food for domestic consumption; 2) to release a share of its labor force to manufacturing and the service sector; 3) to increase demand for industrial products and services; 4) to increase domestic savings that can finance investments; and 5) to earn foreign exchange by selling to foreign markets.[1] The first and third functions are related to the role of agriculture as a supplier of consumer goods and as a source of demand for industrial inputs or particular services; that is, they depict the sector as a source of input and outputs linked to the rest of the country's economy. The other functions stem from an "extractive" approach that regards the agriculture sector as a supplier of surplus labor, savings, and foreign exchange, which might be directed toward the promotion of other economic sectors such as industry and services.

Among agriculture's essential contributions to a country's development is that it is a source for earning foreign income, which is needed both to underwrite the functioning of the sector itself and to help expand other sectors of goods and service production. The linkages of agriculture with global markets should not be understood, however, as merely driven by the need to earn income from agricultural exports. The agricultural sector also consumes inputs, such as seeds, fertilizers and machinery, which are often purchased from other countries. In addition, opportunities offered by foreign trade can lead to product specialization, and as a result countries can supplement their own production with imports; a country that exports agricultural products may also need to import goods that it cannot efficiently produce. Therefore, the extent to which agriculture generates foreign earnings depends upon government officials making correct decisions about what product lines to export and to import. With effective management, a surplus can be generated and channeled to enable the structural changes necessary for economic development.

This chapter seeks to analyze the contribution of Cuban agriculture to the country's economic development. After providing a general overview of the contribution of agriculture to this development in comparative terms, it seeks to deepen understanding of how and how well Cuban agriculture carries out the functions that are specifically related to the external sector. Given that Cuba's international balance-of-payments limitations constitute one of the greatest obstacles to the country's ability to achieving a more dynamic economic development trajectory, this focus is especially relevant and timely.

In examining the relationship between the agricultural and external markets, we will concentrate on the potential that agriculture may have for overcoming the obstacles facing the Cuban economy. We identify agricultural exports that could improve Cuba's balance of payments and discuss the potential for efficient import substitution which could help to ease the pressures on Cuba's balance of payments that are due to the high costs of imported food products. In addition, we propose the types of imports of inputs and machinery that could promote greater productivity and competitiveness in Cuban agricultural product lines. Finally, with respect to food imports, we direct some attention to the imports of food from the United States, which began in 2001. The opening of this trade offers an opportunity, but at the same time it represents a challenge. The opportunity lies in obtaining lower-priced imported goods in some cases. The challenge is that, for the same reason, domestic products face even greater competition.

Agriculture and Economic Development in Cuba

Our analysis of the current contribution of agriculture to development will focus on the functions that this sector ought to carry out in such a process, and on how well the Cuban agricultural sector is fulfilling them. In addition to the outline by Johnston and Mellor,[2] we offer some further observations on the subject.

Johnston and Mellor insist that all the functions of their framework are equally important: that agriculture, as part of the development process, must generate increasing amounts of food and also raise rural incomes to expand demand for industrial products and services. At the same time, the sector must provide resources to increase the production of the secondary and tertiary sectors. About the interrelation among these functions of the agriculture sector in development, they write:

> It is our contention that "balanced growth" is needed in the sense of simultaneous efforts to promote agricultural and industrial develop-ment. We recognize that there are severe limitations on the capacity of an underdeveloped country to do everything at once. But it is pre-cisely this consideration which underscores the importance of devel-oping agriculture in such a way as to both minimize its demand on resources most needed for industrial development and maximize its net contribution required for general growth.[3]

Similarly, Rao asserts a need to develop the agricultural sector at a proper pace, because lags could become an impediment to the development of industry and other sectors.[4]

Many other authors have emphasized the interdependence of the agri-cultural and industrial sectors, emphasizing the fundamental role of agri-culture for economic development. However, this emphasis is in a certain sense inconsistent with the function of obtaining foreign exchange put for-ward by Johnston and Mellor, which implies that the economy should be open to international trade. This last consideration is of great importance in the cases of many underdeveloped countries whose economies depend on such trade.

Despite many agricultural economists' insistence on the interdepend-ence of agriculture and other economic sectors, the prevailing notion in the development models elaborated since the Second World War has been one in which agriculture is viewed as a resource supplier for the economy.[5] The limited understanding of agriculture's role in development obscures an important aspect of the process of transferring resources from one sector to another: its dynamic character. As Reynolds argues:

> (1) It is one thing to assert that, in an economy where agricultural out-put is not rising, the agricultural sector contains potential surpluses of labor time, food output, and saving capacity requiring only appro-priate public policies for their release. This we may term the static view

of resource transfer. (2) It is quite a different thing to assert that, in an economy where agricultural output is being raised by a combination of investment and technical progress, part of the increment in farm output and income is available for transfer to non-agriculture. This we may term the dynamic view of resource transfer. The model-building implications of this approach are different, and its policy implications are decidedly different.[6]

An interesting point of view regarding the agricultural sector's possible contribution to economic growth can be found in the work of Sheila Amin, who examines the positive spillovers that can be generated by its exports.[7] The author underscores the significance of non-traditional agriculture exports,[8] an activity whose success requires complex infrastructure and a considerable investment in human capital. Economies that specialize in this type of export activity and also engage in research on exportable native products can generate increases in a country's knowledge base and achieve economic growth.

Agriculture has already contributed—in the case of today's developed countries—and should contribute—in the case of countries trying to climb the development ladder—to the promotion of an economic structure that privileges the secondary and tertiary sectors. But if the agriculture sector itself does not grow vigorously, how can it fulfill that mission?

Statistics show that despite agriculture's decreasing share in total production—in both developed and underdeveloped countries—the trade of goods of agricultural origin still represents a significant share of total trade (see Table 6.1). The selection of countries included in Table 6.1 is not arbitrary. These were the world's twenty largest exporters of farm products in 2008, according to the United Nations Food and Agriculture Organization (FAO), contributing almost 76% of world agro-exports in that year.

Even in several of the most developed countries, with their agricultural sectors' declining share of GDP, trade originating in this sector represents a significant fraction of total merchandise trade, much higher than the sector's contribution to GDP. For some underdeveloped countries, such as Brazil and Argentina, the share of agriculture relative to merchandise exports is more than four times greater than the sector's share of 2008 GDP.

Finally, authors such as Hardt and Negri recognize that a purely quantitative view of shifts among the three economic spheres of the economy— that is, successive dominance of the primary, secondary, and service sectors—can lead to serious misunderstanding.[9] A sector which loses its dominant role does not cease to be an essential component of an economy;

Table 6.1. The Role of Agriculture in the Economy and in Trade in 1990, 2000 and 2008

	Agriculture (as a % of GDP)			Agriculture exports (as a % of total exports)			Agriculture imports (as a % of total imports)		
	1990	2000	2008	1990	2000	2008	1990	2000	2008
Argentina	8.1	5	9.8	56.5	40.9	51	5.6	5.3	4.9
Australia	4.9	3.5	2.5	31.1	27.3	12.9	4.3	4.7	4.2
Belgium*	2.1	1.4	0.8	10	9.1	8.7	10	8.2	8
Brazil	8.1	5.6	6.4	27.9	23.2	28	10.1	7.3	4.4
Canada	2.9	2.3	2.2	7.2	5.6	8.1	6.1	4.8	6.1
China	27.1	15.1	10.7	7.9	3.3	1.8	9.1	4.2	4.9
Denmark	4	2.6	1.3	23.4	17.1	16	9.5	9.4	11
France	4.2	2.8	2	15.1	10	11.3	9.3	6.5	7.6
Germany	1.5	1.3	0.9	4.8	4.4	4.9	10.8	6.9	7
India	29.3	23.4	17.2	16.9	10.9	8.9	4.5	5.6	2.8
Indonesia	19.4	15.6	14.4	10.9	8	21.3	7.3	12.1	8.9
Italy	3.5	2.8	2	6.5	6.5	6.9	13	9	8.1
Malaysia	15.2	8.6	10.3	14.8	5.9	12.5	7.3	4.6	7.5
Mexico	7.8	4.2	3.8	10.9	8.5	5.3	15.3	8.2	7.2
Netherlands	4.4	2.6	1.7	22.7	12	12.4	13.2	7.3	8.5
Poland	8.3	5	4.5	11.4	7.6	9.1	10.4	6.2	6.5

* Data for Belgium-Luxembourg, 1990.

Table 6.1. The Role of Agriculture in the Economy and in Trade in 1990, 2000 and 2008 (continued)

	Agriculture (as a % of GDP)			Agriculture exports (as a % of total exports)			Agriculture imports (as a % of total imports)		
	1990	2000	2008	1990	2000	2008	1990	2000	2008
Spain	5.6	4.4	2.8	14.1	12.1	13	9.2	6.7	7.5
Thailand	12.5	9	11.6	23.4	10.7	13.4	4.9	4.3	4
United Kingdom	1.8	1	0.7	7	5.8	5.4	10.3	7.5	9.2
United States	2.1	1.2	1.3	11.5	7.2	9.2	5.2	3.6	3.8
Cuba**	9.2	6.2	3.8	87.6	44.7	16.2	14.6	15.3	14.0

** For Cuba, the trade data is reported by the World Bank, and the GDP data is reported by the Oficina Nacional de Estadísticas (ONE).

Sources: Constructed by the author on the basis of FAOSTAT (2010), World Bank (2010), and ONE (1998, 2006a, 2010).

rather, the emerging sector imbues the rest of the economy with its distinctive characteristics. For example, when agriculture was displaced from its leading role by industry, agricultural production itself became industrialized. Currently, with the service sector driving economic growth and structures, it too leaves its imprint on agriculture and industry.

Having put forward the criteria we will use to evaluate the agriculture sector's contribution to national economic development, we will proceed to examine the current situation of Cuban agriculture. We begin with the function of increasing food supplies. In the 1990s, Cuba certainly went through a very difficult situation in terms of its food provision capabilities. This stemmed from the loss of commercial ties with the former USSR—from which Cuba imported a considerable quantity not only of food, but also of machinery, equipment, and inputs for domestic farm production—and from the development model that preceded that loss, in which the economy was excessively dependent on food imports. This dependency made Cuba extremely vulnerable to external shocks.

For a time after 1989, domestic production plus imports of food remained below the population's nutritional requirements. The result was an increase of associated health problems during this period, such as a neuritis epidemic and the rise in low birth-weight newborns. Starting in 1994, this picture gradually began to improve (see Figure 6.1). From 2000 to 2003, food supply as measured by per capita daily calories recovered and again surpassed the levels recommended by the FAO for a comparable population. Since 2004, food supply has surpassed FAO recommendations in both calories and protein.

However, the rise of nutritional levels was achieved largely through food imports (see Figure 6.2). Cuba has historically been a food-importing country, due to its specialization in sugar and other export crops that have occupied an important share of the country's farmland. According to our estimates, the contribution of food imports to the provision of calories was at a level similar to that of the 1950s in 2006; the contribution of imports to protein levels was greater than that of the 1950s or the 1980s.

Food production has expanded since 1994, but some products have still not recovered their pre-crisis level (see Figure 6.3). The most important deficits are in the production of rice, the principal grain in the Cuban diet, which remains at 1980s level. There is also considerable deficiency in the production of both meat and milk. Chicken production remains depressed as this industry is not competitive by world market standards, a situation which has not improved since Cuba began to import food from the United States in 2001.

Figure 6.1. Daily Per Capita Food Supply, 1965–2008

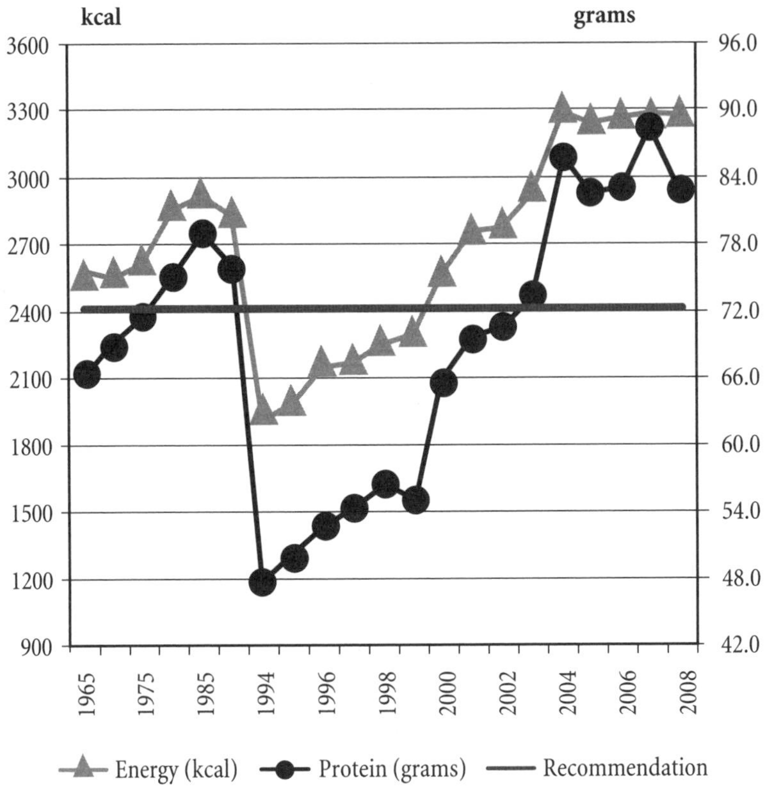

Source: Constructed by the author based on MEP (n/d) and ONE (2005, 2006b, 2007, 2009).

Figure 6.2. Imports as Share of Food Supply, 1950–2006
(in terms of food energy and protein)

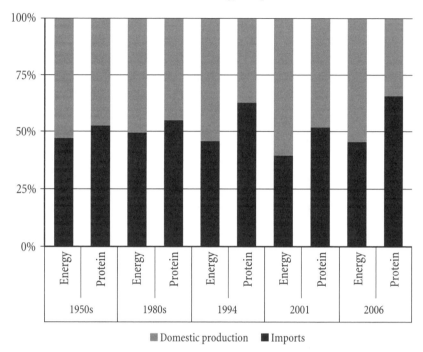

Source: Constructed by the author based on Marcos (1987), MEP (n/d), and ONE (2005, 2006b, 2007, 2009).

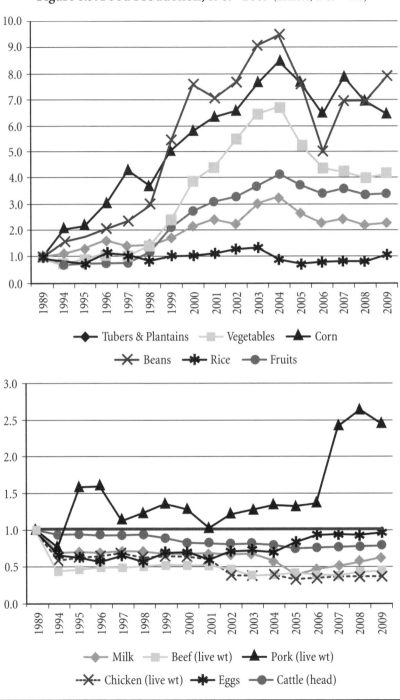

Figure 6.3. Food Production, 1989–2009 (indices, 1989 = 1.0)

Source: Constructed by the author based on ONE (1998, 2006a, 2010).

In general, the foods that have shown the best production results are those whose sale is permitted in farmers' markets (including root crops, plantains, vegetables, beans, corn, and fruits), as well as those benefiting from government programs. Outstanding in the latter category are pork and eggs, which benefited from special government price supports because they offered quick response times and because efficient technologies were available.

In addition to the large import share of the food supply, another problem lies in the distribution mechanisms and the high prices of non-subsidized food (see Figure 6.4). The food basket to which all Cubans have access through the ration system does not completely satisfy nutritional needs. Other subsidized food sources—social consumption (institutional), public food supply (state sales), and *autoconsumo*[10] (self-produced food for personal consumption)—are not available to everyone. Depending on how much households benefit from state-distributed or subsidized food sources, individuals must supplement their consumption in commercial outlets to a greater or lesser degree with corresponding impacts on the household budget.

We have estimated per capita food spending based on official data for food distribution in 2006 and its breakdown according to subsidized or unsubsidized source (see Figure 6.5).[11] To estimate spending in commercial outlets, we have employed the prices prevailing in the farmers' markets for that year.

Figure 6.4. Food Consumption in Cuba by Distribution Source, 2004–2007

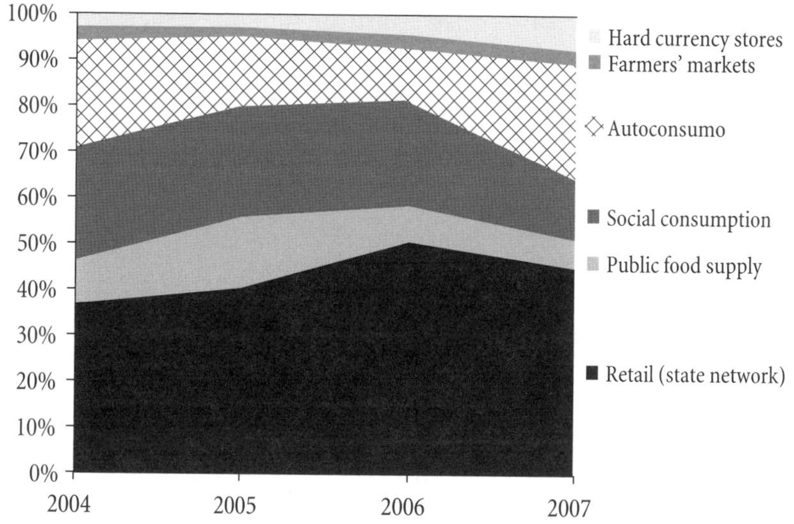

Legend:
- Hard currency stores
- Farmers' markets
- ◇ Autoconsumo
- Social consumption
- Public food supply
- Retail (state network)

Source: Constructed by the author based on ONE (2005, 2006b, 2007, 2009).

Figure 6.5. Food Expenditures and Composition by Access to Subsidized Sources, 2006

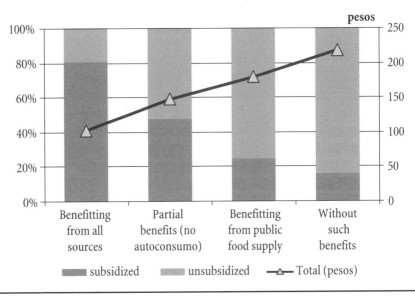

Source: García and Anaya (2009).

Access to other subsidized food sources above rations determines food consumption and expenditures. For urban households, which generally have no access to *autoconsumo* (only to social and public consumption), subsidized sources represent from 16% to 47%, and market purchases from 84% to 53%. Food prices for items available through subsidized channels (rations, social consumption, public food supply) or equivalently priced channels (*autoconsumo*) are lower than those available through commercial outlets (farmers' markets, foreign currency stores, and informal markets).

Food purchases have been estimated to represent from 62% to 75% of total personal consumption spending for Cubans living in urban areas.[12] Ferriol et al. reported that the figure was 66.3% for Havana City in 2001.[13] Devoting such a high share of income to food purchases is characteristic of economies with low levels of development and represents a situation of high stress for Cuban families.

Moreover, the persistence of high prices in existing commercial outlets is closely related to how these markets are structured. Certain limitations still restrict competition and potential efficiency in farmers' markets. Food supply also remains low given the rules limiting entry, the lack of markets where farmers can buy farm inputs, and credit. In addition, there is tacit collusion on prices charged by sellers that results from restrictions placed on market entry and the lack of food transport services.

Moreover, the agriculture sector's ability to free up workers for the development of the manufacturing and service sectors has been limited. Significant competition for laborers arose among agricultural, industrial and service sectors in Cuba during the post-1959 years. As a result, the agricultural workforce has been aging, though, as Fernández points out, over this entire period the labor force per hectare has remained nearly constant.[14] The introduction of machinery and other equipment, in an attempt to humanize the rough working conditions in this sector and also to achieve economies of scale, did not yield the expected results in terms of increasing productivity per worker. Thus, about 20% of workers are employed in agriculture (see Figure 6.6), and productivity remains low.

Figure 6.6. Structure of Employment by Type of Economic Activity in 1954, 1989 and 2009

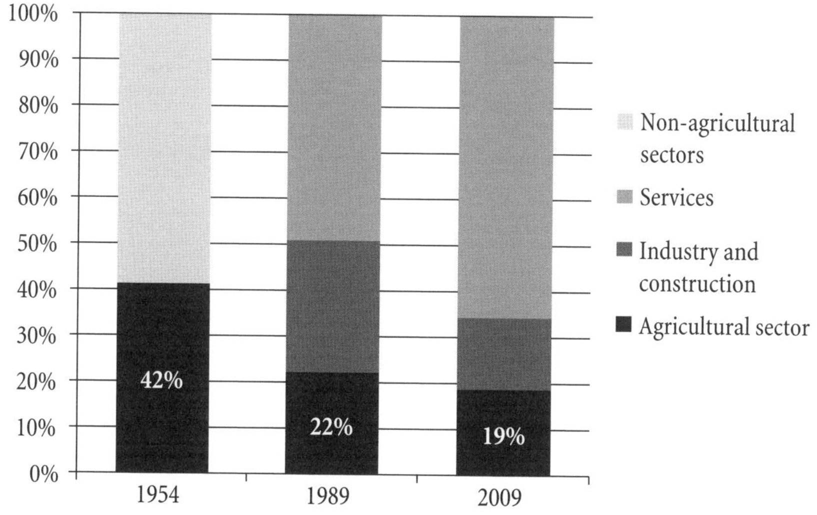

Source: Constructed by the author based on Fernández (2002), Figueras (1999) and ONE (2010).

The productivity difference between agriculture and the rest of the economy is large enough to conclude that far from contributing to economic development in Cuba, agriculture has become a major stumbling block (see Figure 6.7).

This lag in agricultural productivity may be due, in part, to important price distortions present in the Cuban economy, especially for food crops

Figure 6.7. Labor Productivity by Sectors of Economic Activity, 2001–2009 (pesos per worker)

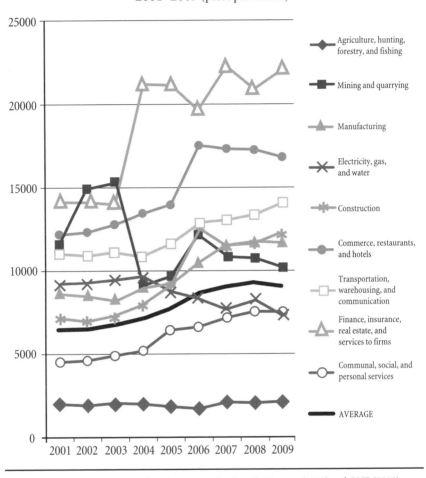

Source: Constructed by the author based on Fernández (2002), Figueras (1999) and ONE (2010).

and some livestock products, which vary greatly according to whether they are sold in state or informal markets.[15] Most farm production is sold in state markets at official prices, which are substantially lower than those predominating in farmers' markets.

Cuban agricultural productivity is low not only in comparison to that of other sectors of domestic goods and services production. If we compare the island with other countries with the same density of agricultural workforce per hectare of agricultural land,[16] or of land available for agricultural work,[17] Cuba also ranks poorly (see Figure 6.8).[18]

Figure 6.8. Agricultural Productivity and Resources for Production, Per Unit of Land Available for Agricultural Work (Cuba = 1)

a) Countries with Comparable Economically Active Population (EAP) Per Unit of Agricultural Land

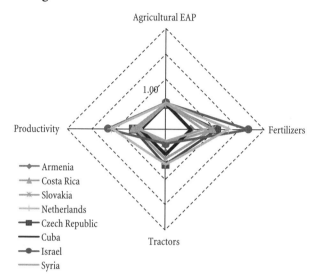

b) Countries with Comparable Economically Active Population (EAP) Per Unit of Available Land

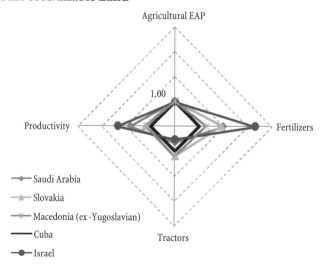

Notes: We are applying logarithms to the indices to smooth out differences. EAP = economically active population.

In order to realize its potential for generating wealth, the labor force must be adequately complemented. If, in addition to indices of productivity and of labor force in relation to land area (whether by unit of agricultural land or by unit of available land), we compare indices of other resources devoted to farming activities, such as equipment per worker, the resulting contrast helps to explain the productivity gap.

The lackluster output of the Cuban agriculture sector is also manifest in the systematic increase in idle land since 1989 (see Figure 6.9). In the early 1990s, this trend could be explained by the shock resulting from the fall of the socialist bloc and the reduced access famers had to inputs and equipment. The 2002 decision to restructure the sugar industry by sharply reducing the number of operating mills and by shifting some of the cane-growing land to food crops, a transfer which has not occurred with the necessary speed due to the investment and resources that were required, has also contributed to the continued rise in idle land.

The scarcity of inputs and equipment needed to boost the productivity of farmland and the labor force is a major problem confronting Cuban agriculture. This shortage, moreover, has also, since 1989, negatively affected agriculture's ability to stimulate other economic activities. In recent years, the state attempted to mitigate this problem (see Figure 6.10), but without formulating an adequate model of agricultural organization that would guarantee effective use of resources—and in the midst of a global crisis that has severely impacted Cuba's import capacity—such efforts are difficult to sustain. The point is not to re-introduce the "classic"[19] model of agricultural development promoted in Cuba in the 1970s and 1980s, which would allow

Figure 6.9. Idle Land in Cuba and Its Composition by Type of Farm,[20] 2007

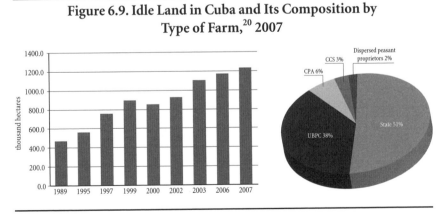

Source: Constructed by the author based on ONE (2008).

Figure 6.10. Imports of Selected Agricultural Inputs, 1989–2008
(1989 = 1.0)

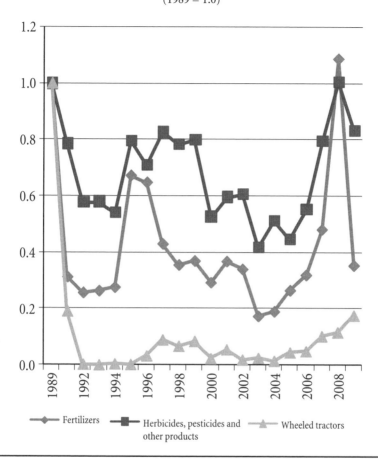

Source: Constructed by the author based on ONE (2006a, 2010).

important growth in this sector, but at the cost of excessive spending and prejudicial effects on the environment. Nonetheless, there is no denying that a certain number of complementary productive factors is required to obtain competitive results. The image conveyed by Figure 6.8 is quite eloquent.

An adequate balance must be found in the agricultural sector between resource allocation and results. In the last decade, the country has devoted considerable resources to agriculture, but such allocation has not produced greater output. This disparity should provoke a radical change in the model of agricultural organization and management, which, "in tune with the greater presence of non-state forms of production [in the sector] . . . should be based on a more effective use of monetary-mercantile relationships,

Figure 6.11. Agriculture Sector Losses, 1991–1996 (millions of pesos)

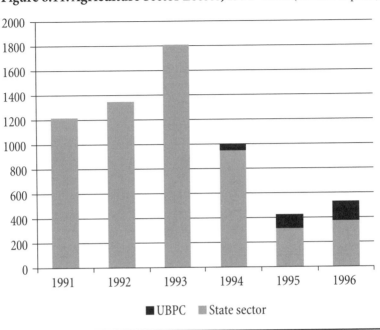

Source: Constructed by the author based on Ministry of Agriculture, MINAG (1997).

limiting the function of the state and of enterprise managers, with the goal of promoting greater autonomy among producers, increasing efficiency, and allowing for gradual decentralization toward local government bodies."[21] Without such a policy, Cuba is at risk of falling into the same pattern that plagued the Cuban agriculture sector in the 1980s.[22]

Finally, at least in the early 1990s, the Cuban agricultural sector has been unable to generate surpluses which could serve as a source of accumulation for the promotion of other economic activities (see Figure 6.11). Rather than earning foreign exchange, agriculture has caused a constant erosion of the country's internal finances.[23] Any path toward national economic recovery must include a reversal of this pattern.

While the Cuban economy as a whole has surpassed the production level of 1989, the agriculture sector has failed to produce at more than 60% of 1989 levels.

As Armando Nova González discusses in greater depth (see Chapter 3), the losses accrued by the agricultural sector (which excludes sugarcane farming) increased rapidly until 1993. That unsustainable level of losses resulted in a change in the administrative structure of state lands through

**Figure 6.12. GDP and Agriculture Sector Production in Cuba,
1989–2009** (1989 = 1.0)

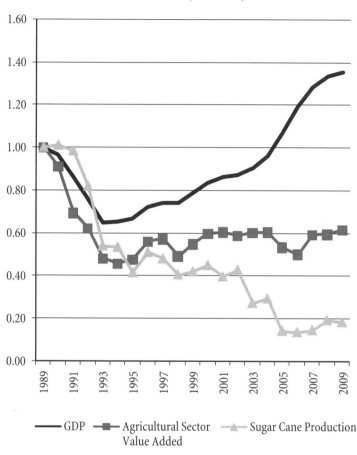

—— GDP   —■— Agricultural Sector   —▲— Sugar Cane Production
                 Value Added

Source: Constructed by author based on ONE (1998, 2006a, 2010)

the creation of the Basic Units of Cooperative Production (Spanish initials
UBPC) in that same year. The general trend in the agriculture sector
between the first set of reforms in 1993–94 and the year 2000 was one of
growth. Nonetheless, the failure to complement the initial measures with
others that would have taken better advantage of the opportunities in foreign and domestic markets led to stagnation and even backsliding (see Figure 6.12). In 2007, the administration made a new effort to jolt the
agricultural sector out of inertia.[24]

In sum, given its current state, Cuban agriculture cannot contribute to
growth as it needs to do—let alone contribute to economic development.

Food production is insufficient, with imports growing as a result. The sector's main export product—sugarcane—dwindled, first for lack of resources to maintain and exploit the crop, and then because of a voluntary reduction in production. It is no accident, therefore, that agriculture has been chosen as the battlefield on which a reform of the Cuban economic model will begin. New measures announced in early 2011 include a distribution of idle land, an increase in the wholesale prices the state pays for farm products, and a decentralization of decision-making to the municipal assembly level. The year 2007 had already marked a watershed in that sense, and some encouraging results can already be seen. These are sure to be further strengthened as part of the process of generalized economic reform now under way.

Cuban Agriculture and the External Sector

Cuban agriculture is running deficits in its external balances. Agricultural exports have continued to shrink, due not only to reductions in world demand but also to production shortages, an area that has been substantially depressed since 1990. At the same time, food import bills have shot up in recent years, because of rising prices for imported products and the need to buy in greater quantities given insufficient domestic production.

The balance of trade in the agriculture sector suffered considerable deterioration after 1991 as a result of Cuba's loss of its major export markets and of the preferential prices it had received for products imported from the CMEA (Council for Mutual Economic Assistance)—both destroyed by the collapse of socialism in Europe. Thus, since 1993, Cuba's farm-based exports have lost their capacity to earn the foreign exchange needed to guarantee the sector's strategic goal of feeding the populace. Export earnings are insufficient to cover current inputs for the agriculture sector and for food that must be imported (see Figure 6.13), let alone to stimulate new productive activities. In fact, just the opposite occurs. Ever more foreign exchange must be used to fulfill the functions that Cuban agriculture is incapable of carrying out, or that it cannot carry out under the current institutional arrangements. Yet there are opportunities for some Cuban agricultural products to change this situation; we will examine both their export trajectories and their potential to serve as substitutes for food imports.

Cuban Agricultural Exports: Evolution and Prospects

With the collapse of socialism in Eastern Europe and Cuba's consequent loss of its major trade partners,[25] trade deficits for products of agricultural origin suddenly surged. As a result of the largely agricultural character of the country's exports in the late 1980s, Cuba faced an extremely tense moment

Figure 6.13. Cuban Agriculture International Trade Balance, 1989–2009

(millions of pesos)

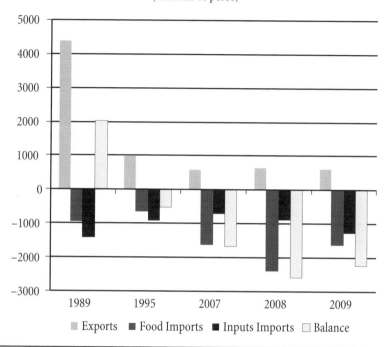

■ Exports ■ Food Imports ■ Inputs Imports □ Balance

Source: Constructed by the author based on Fernández (2002, p. 131) and estimates.

in the early 1990s (see Figure 6.14). Agro-exports plummeted, and their share of Cuban exports dropped from over 80% to barely 20% (see Figure 6.15).

Given the radical change in the international context and its catastrophic impact on Cuba, it was impossible to postpone implementation of a set of measures which, to begin with, were focused on redirecting exports and utilizing imported resources more efficiently. The priority accorded to trade policy changes was a logical consequence of that sector's importance, considering the open nature of the Cuban economy as well as the size and depth of the external shock that had hit the country.

A wide array of policy measures was implemented.[26] Among them was the so-called system of foreign currency self-financing, which later developed into foreign currency income and spending budgets (Spanish initials PIGD) that granted greater enterprise autonomy in the management of foreign currency resources. The administration also introduced sectoral policies intended to stimulate activities that would generate foreign currency income in traditional agro-export lines such as sugar, coffee, citrus, and tobacco. The institutional framework underwent important improvements

Figure 6.14. Structure of Cuban Merchandise Exports, 1958–2009

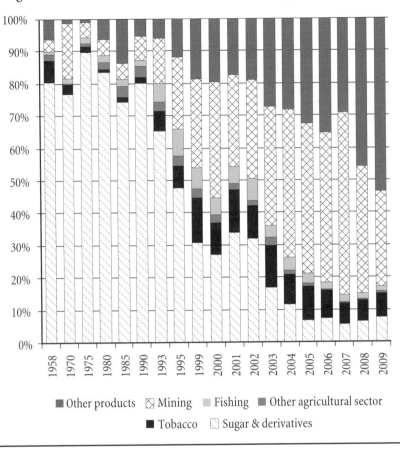

Source: Constructed by the author based on ONE (1998, 2006a, 2010).

and modifications, such as the decentralization of foreign trade activities, the creation of the Center for Promotion of Cuban Exports, and the strengthening of the Chamber of Commerce. Along with these initiatives, the government instituted some qualitative improvements in management: for example, special customs procedures for exporters and differentiated mechanisms for financing exports. Producers of exportable goods were encouraged to attend national and international trade fairs with the support of a new National Incentives Program for Promotion of Exports (Spanish initials PNIFE), intended to promote non-traditional exports (excluding traditional exports such as tobacco, raw sugar, molasses, and rum). The reformers spurred joint-venture investments in enterprises and in distribution chains.[27]

Figure 6.15. Cuban Agricultural Exports and Their Share of Total Exports, 1989–2009

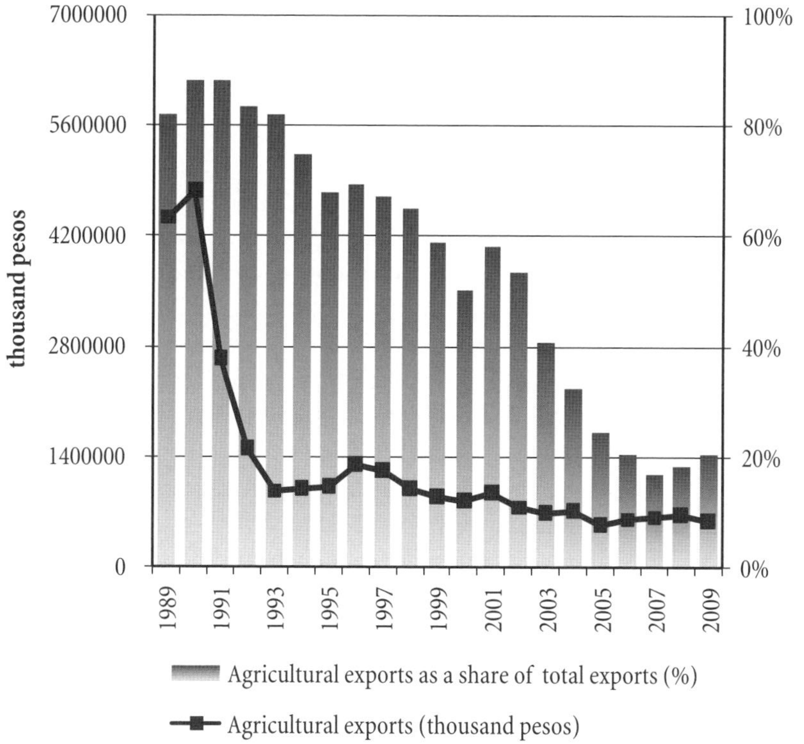

Agricultural exports as a share of total exports (%)

Agricultural exports (thousand pesos)

Source: Constructed by the author based on ONE (1998, 2006a, 2010).

Specifically related to the agro-export sector were measures such as the partial cooperativization of state farms, which gave rise to the UBPCs, and grants of usufruct rights of state lands to new producers growing exportable crops including tobacco and coffee.[28]

The sugarcane sector, however, was denied the opportunities provided by self-financing schemes that helped other enterprises stabilize the supply of imported supplies, nor was the sector permitted to take advantage of the growing domestic foreign currency market. The result is evident in this sector's persistent diminished performance. Finally, as mentioned above, in 2002 a decision was made to restructure this sector, concentrating production in approximately half of the sugar mills and using half the land previously planted with cane.

These decisions help to explain why the performance of the sugar agro-export sector contrasts so sharply with those of other agro-exports (see Figure 6.16). Non-sugar agro-exports have responded favorably to the incentives implemented to stimulate production. Since 1994, both the volume and value of production have shown positive trends, though performance improvements have been especially marked in traditional product lines of tobacco and beverages, which have benefited from special support programs.

Because the sugar industry had been the main source of external financing of the Cuban economy, it was initially excluded from the initiatives introduced to stimulate exports and production, such as the self-financing systems authorized for non-sugar export production lines. This is because Cuba sought to reinsert its economy in the international arena by seeking new markets for traditional products as well as promoting exports of more dynamic activities (which had to develop in an accelerated fashion and almost entirely with their own resources),[29] while also hoping to depend on sugar export earnings as the main source of foreign income. In the long run, the tension between the need for this source of earning foreign currency and the need to finance investments in the rest of the economy impeded the development of this industry, which is predominantly oriented toward exporting its production abroad. The denial of foreign currency self-financing to the sugar industry could be interpreted as an enormous tax on this activity. In the long run, the main consequence of this policy was the progressive de-capitalization and the loss of international competitiveness of this sector.

In earlier studies, we have shown why international demand and domestic supply both determine the competiveness of Cuban exports.[30] Our findings indicate that supply side factors, expressed through indices of diversification and competitiveness, are relatively more important. This chapter updates these earlier studies of trends in international trade in agriculture and in a potential demand for Cuban agricultural exports to show which international market niches are growing.

During the 1980s and 1990s, international agricultural trade grew more slowly than overall global trade in manufactured products. The share of merchandise trade of agricultural products dropped from over 17% in the early 1970s to about 7% in 2008 (see Figure 6.17). However, even if this trend suggests that international agricultural trade as a whole was regressing, its share of global merchandise trade has stopped falling in recent years. Moreover, not all sub-sectors have followed the same pattern.

For example, in the 1990–2008, sales of miscellaneous food products,[31] oil-containing seeds, processed oils,[32] and vegetable oils grew faster than

Figure 6.16. Cuban Sugar and Non-Sugar Agro-Exports, 1970–2008
(millions of pesos)

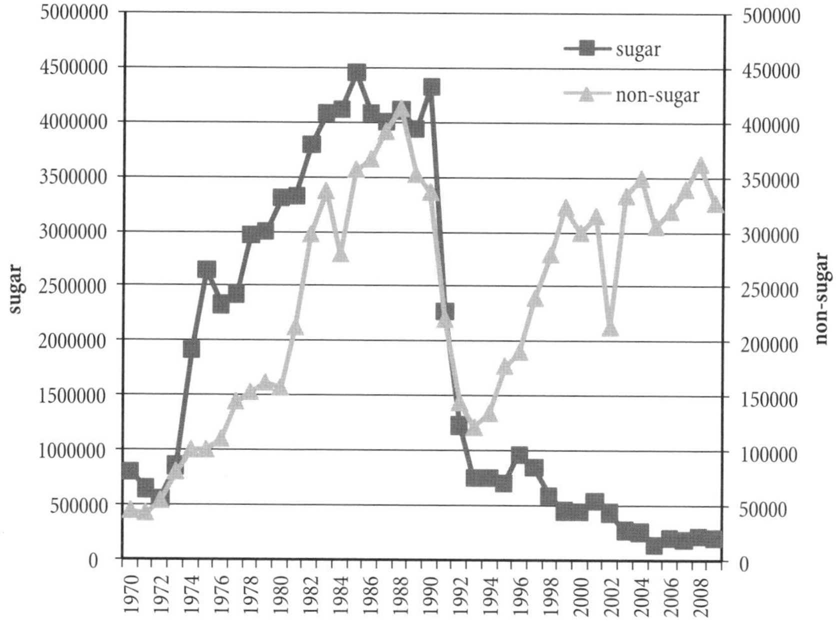

Source: Constructed by author based on ONE (1998, 2006a, 2010).

merchandise trade; similarly honey, beverages, fruits, and vegetables, though growing more slowly than merchandise trade, have grown faster than agricultural goods as a whole. And within that group, certain tropical fruits and vegetables have shown faster growth than merchandise trade; these include mangos, guavas, pineapples, papayas, avocados, chilies and sweet peppers, frozen potatoes, and plantains (see Figure 6.18). Many of these products are grown in Cuba and are potential export lines.

A more detailed study of international agricultural trade might reveal some unexploited advantages for Cuba. With this goal in mind we examined three groups of products: traditional ones,[33] fresh and processed citrus fruits, and other lines that would constitute non-traditional agricultural exports.[34] Some of the latter began to figure in the Cuban agricultural export lexicon already in the 1980s, such as peppers and potatoes. Our goal is to find possible market niches for products that Cuba already exports or potentially could export. The period of analysis encompasses the years between 1998 and 2008.

Figure 6.17. Agricultural and Merchandise Trade: Trends* and Shares, 1970–2008

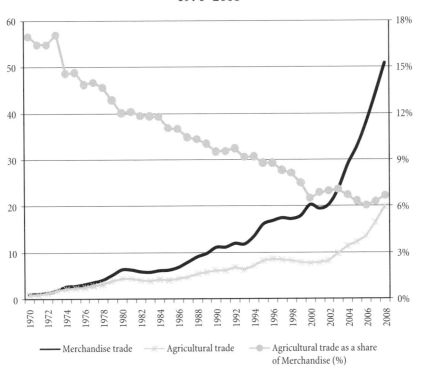

——— Merchandise trade   ⸻ Agricultural trade   ⸺●⸺ Agricultural trade as a share of Merchandise (%)

* trends are expressed as indices with 1970 as base year.

Source: Constructed by the author based on FAOSTAT (2010).

The method applied in this analysis is one devised by Rodrígues and Torres, with modified criteria for classifying the growth rates of the markets and products.[35] As reference points, we use the average annual growth rates of world merchandise imports and those of agricultural imports for the period covered. The rate of growth of imports for a given product in a given market is compared with the overall referents, categorizing them as follows: *very dynamic* when the rate for the product exceeds the rate for worldwide merchandise imports; *dynamic* when it exceeds the world agricultural import growth rate, but is equal to or less than the world merchandise rate; *stagnant* when the rate is positive but equal to or less than world agricultural imports; and *regressing*, when the rate is negative.

The countries selected include some markets with which Cuba already has ties, such as Canada, China, the Russian Federation, Japan, the European Union (EU), and the islands of the Caribbean other than Cuba.[36] They

Figure 6.18. Average Annual Growth for Selected Agriculture Exports in World Trade, 1990–2008

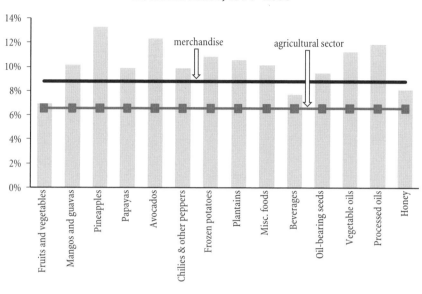

Source: Constructed by the author based on FAOSTAT (2010).

also include the United States, because despite the current economic embargo, this would be the largest nearby market and it is important to be aware of the agricultural goods imported by its economy.

Comparing the results of this analysis with the portfolio of agricultural goods currently exported by Cuba, we draw the following observations:[37]

- Among traditional products, honey is dynamic or very dynamic in all the markets studied with the sole exception of the Russian Federation. However, after a rise in the volume of exports between 1997 and 2003, it has turned unstable with a tendency toward contraction.

- The outstanding product within traditional agricultural exports is alcoholic beverages, which have been very dynamic in Canada, China, Russia, and the Caribbean. Cuba has been able to take advantage of this opportunity, and its volume of exports has tended to grow since 1998, though certain instability is visible since 2005.

- Hand-rolled cigars are very dynamic in Canada, Russia, and the Caribbean. In the rest of the markets studied this product is stagnant. Cigar production has benefited from special support in Cuba, and its exports have grown steadily. However, since the incorporation of Habanos into the transnational Altadis S.A. in 1999 and the restrictions on importation of Cuban cigars into the United States, the probable major destination is the EU, a market which, overall, does not present a favorable dynamic.

- Cocoa butter is very dynamic in China and Russia, and dynamic in the EU. However, Cuban exports have been unstable, with a tendency to drop in volume.

- The rest of the traditional products show less favorable patterns in the markets studied, but even so, some very dynamic opportunities exist. Examples are demand for cigarettes and leaf tobacco in Canada and the Caribbean, machine-made cigars in Japan and the Caribbean, and coffee (both roasted and unroasted) in China and Russia.

- Among fresh citrus fruits, the standouts are limes and lemons, which are very dynamic in all the markets studied except for Japan.

- Other fresh citrus fruits offer growing opportunities in particular markets: oranges, mandarin oranges, and tangerines are very dynamic in China and Russia; grapefruits are very dynamic in Russia and the Caribbean, and tangerines and mandarines are dynamic in the United States.

- Among processed citrus, very dynamic patterns apply to concentrated grapefruit juice in China, Russia, and European Union; non-concentrated lemon juice in the United States, Russia, and the Caribbean; and non-concentrated orange juice in China, the United States, and Russia.

- Other processed citrus products show much less favorable dynamics, but there are some exceptions in some markets: non-concentrated grapefruit juice is very dynamic in the United States, as is concentrated orange juice in the EU.

- Among non-traditional products, the highest proportions of very dynamic and dynamic opportunities among the markets studied are: avocados, very dynamic in all markets except China; pineapples, very dynamic in Canada, the United States, Russia, the EU, and the Caribbean, and dynamic in Japan; frozen potatoes, very dynamic in Canada, China, Russia, and the Caribbean, and dynamic in the United States and the EU.

- Second-best, according to their growth rates, are: pineapple juice, very dynamic in Canada, the United States, Russia, and the Caribbean; papayas, very dynamic in Canada, Russia, and EU, and dynamic in the United States; and chilies and sweet peppers, very dynamic in Russia and the Caribbean, and dynamic in Canada and the EU.

- Most very dynamic and dynamic products are within the non-traditional group. However, these are not among Cuba's principal exports: altogether they made up a little more than 7% of total agriculture exports between 1998 and 2008.[38]

- In general, the markets demanding a greater proportion of dynamic and very dynamic products are Russia, the Caribbean, and China. What stands out in Russia is the growth in importation of non-traditional products and citrus. For the Caribbean, the traditional and non-traditional groups are most important; for China, traditional and citrus.

- Even the market for refined sugar is very dynamic in China and the United States.

It should be noted that Canada, China, and Russia are among Cuba's major trading partners and also among the major sources of tourism to Cuba. Cuba has significant trade deficits with all of these countries. The Caribbean islands are not such an important market as the others, but they offer a nearby opportunity. Market trends in these markets should be followed to help identify possible niches in which to expand Cuba's exports. This type of market analysis has been successfully applied in Cuba for some traditional products such as cigars and beverages, and should be extended to other promising product lines.

There is a more favorable demand potential for non-traditional and not yet exported agricultural goods, and therefore these products should be prioritized. Specific studies with respect to the production chains behind each promising group of products should be undertaken to detect bottlenecks which may interfere with the improvement in the positioning of these goods as part of Cuba's export portfolio. However, what is most needed to ignite the country's export potential in agriculture is a change in the farm management model and in macroeconomic policies which directly affect export incentives and import substitutions. In order to increase exports so as to broaden opportunities and offer producers greater benefit from these very-much-needed foreign sales, greater alignment of policies in foreign trade, investment, science, technology, and innovation are needed.[39]

Cuban Food Imports and Potential Import Substitution

In recent years, the share of food imports as a part of Cuba's total merchandise imports has dropped, returning to levels similar to those of 1980. Still, the chances of maintaining these levels are uncertain in the currently unsettled world context. Around 2008, Cuban food imports experienced a surge (see Figure 6.19) caused by increased purchases in terms of both physical volume and by the upward trend in food prices (see Table 6.2), a trend

Figure 6.19. Cuban Food Imports and Their Share of Total Imports, 1989–2009

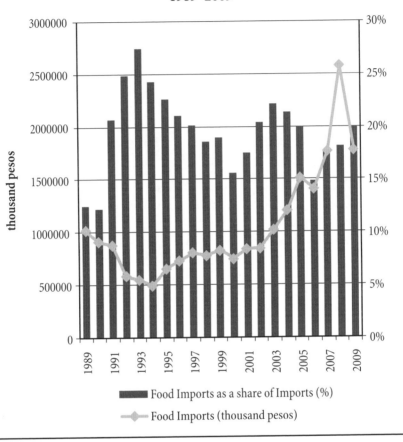

Source: Constructed by the author based on ONE (1998, 2006a, 2010).

sparked by the partial elimination of subsidies on the part of the developed countries (applying the agreements of the Uruguay Round) and more recently reinforced by a variety of other factors.[40]

In the historical composition of Cuban food imports (see Table 6.3), the category "other grains"[41] stands out. These have been predominantly wheat, corn, barley, and oats used in making balanced animal feed and also for human consumption. Other important components have been fats and oils as well as proteins for cattle feed, which are not produced on the island.

This import picture shows that in recent years more than 50% of food purchases from abroad has been items such as rice, milk products, eggs, fish and fish-based products, meat and meat-based products, and even coffee—

Table 6.2. World Prices for Selected Foods (indices, Jan. 2004 = 1.0)

	Wheat (unmilled)	Rice (for human consumption)	Corn (unmilled)	Soybean cake	Soybeans	Soybean oil	Meat, chicken
Jan-04	1.0	1.0	1.0	1.0	1.0	1.0	1.0
Feb-04	1.0	1.0	1.1	1.0	1.1	1.0	0.9
Mar-04	1.0	1.1	1.1	1.1	1.2	1.1	0.9
Apr-04	1.0	1.2	1.2	1.1	1.0	1.0	0.9
May-04	1.0	1.1	1.1	1.0	0.9	1.0	1.1
Jun-04	0.9	1.1	1.1	0.9	0.8	0.9	1.1
Jul-04	0.9	1.1	0.9	0.8	0.8	0.9	1.1
Aug-04	0.8	1.2	0.9	0.7	0.8	0.9	1.2
Sep-04	0.9	1.1	0.8	0.7	0.7	0.9	1.2
Oct-04	0.9	1.2	0.8	0.7	0.7	0.8	1.1
Nov-04	0.9	1.2	0.8	0.7	0.7	0.9	1.1
Dec-04	0.9	1.3	0.8	0.7	0.8	0.8	1.1
Jan-05	0.9	1.4	0.8	0.7	0.7	0.8	1.1
Feb-05	0.9	1.4	0.8	0.7	0.7	0.8	1.1
Mar-05	0.9	1.4	0.9	0.8	0.8	0.8	1.1
Apr-05	0.8	1.4	0.8	0.8	0.8	0.8	1.1
May-05	0.9	1.4	0.8	0.8	0.8	0.8	1.1
Jun-05	0.9	1.3	0.8	0.8	0.9	0.8	1.1
Jul-05	0.9	1.3	0.9	0.8	0.9	0.9	1.1
Aug-05	0.9	1.3	0.9	0.8	0.8	0.8	1.1
Sep-05	1.0	1.3	0.8	0.8	0.8	0.8	1.1
Oct-05	1.0	1.3	0.9	0.7	0.7	0.9	1.1
Nov-05	1.0	1.3	0.8	0.7	0.7	0.8	1.1
Dec-05	1.0	1.3	0.9	0.8	0.8	0.8	1.1
Jan-06	1.0	1.3	0.9	0.7	0.7	0.8	1.1
Feb-06	1.1	1.4	0.9	0.7	0.7	0.8	1.1
Mar-06	1.0	1.4	0.9	0.7	0.7	0.8	1.0
Apr-06	1.1	1.4	0.9	0.7	0.7	0.8	1.0
May-06	1.2	1.4	1.0	0.7	0.8	0.9	1.0
Jun-06	1.2	1.4	0.9	0.7	0.8	0.9	1.0
Jul-06	1.2	1.4	1.0	0.7	0.8	1.0	1.1
Aug-06	1.1	1.4	1.0	0.7	0.7	1.0	1.1
Sep-06	1.2	1.4	1.1	0.8	0.7	0.9	1.1
Oct-06	1.3	1.4	1.2	0.8	0.8	0.9	1.1
Nov-06	1.3	1.4	1.4	0.8	0.9	1.0	1.1
Dec-06	1.2	1.4	1.4	0.8	0.8	1.1	1.1

Table 6.2. World Prices for Selected Foods (indices, Jan. 2004 = 1.0) (continued)

	Wheat (unmilled)	Rice (for human consumption)	Corn (unmilled)	Soybean cake	Soybeans	Soybean oil	Meat, chicken
Jan-07	1.2	1.4	1.4	0.9	0.9	1.1	1.1
Feb-07	1.2	1.5	1.5	0.9	0.9	1.1	1.1
Mar-07	1.2	1.5	1.5	0.9	0.9	1.1	1.1
Apr-07	1.2	1.5	1.3	0.9	0.9	1.2	1.1
May-07	1.2	1.5	1.4	0.9	1.0	1.2	1.1
Jun-07	1.3	1.5	1.4	1.0	1.0	1.3	1.1
Jul-07	1.4	1.5	1.3	1.0	1.1	1.3	1.1
Aug-07	1.6	1.5	1.3	1.1	1.1	1.4	1.1
Sep-07	2.0	1.5	1.4	1.2	1.2	1.5	1.1
Oct-07	2.0	1.6	1.4	1.4	1.3	1.5	1.1
Nov-07	1.9	1.7	1.5	1.4	1.4	1.7	1.1
Dec-07	2.2	1.8	1.6	1.5	1.5	1.8	1.1
Jan-08	2.2	1.9	1.8	1.6	1.5	1.9	1.3
Feb-08	2.6	2.2	1.9	1.6	1.6	2.1	1.3
Mar-08	2.6	2.8	2.0	1.6	1.6	2.2	1.3
Apr-08	2.2	3.9	2.1	1.7	1.6	2.2	1.3
May-08	2.0	3.7	2.1	1.7	1.6	2.2	1.4
Jun-08	2.1	3.0	2.5	1.8	1.8	2.3	1.4
Jul-08	2.0	2.8	2.3	1.8	1.8	2.3	1.4
Aug-08	2.0	2.4	2.0	1.6	1.6	2.0	1.4
Sep-08	1.8	2.2	2.0	1.5	1.5	1.9	1.4
Oct-08	1.4	1.8	1.6	1.2	1.1	1.4	1.4
Nov-08	1.4	1.6	1.4	1.2	1.1	1.3	1.4
Dec-08	1.3	1.5	1.4	1.1	1.0	1.1	1.4
Jan-09	1.4	1.6	1.5	1.3	1.2	1.2	1.4
Feb-09	1.4	1.6	1.4	1.4	1.1	1.1	1.4
Mar-09	1.4	1.7	1.4	1.2	1.1	1.1	1.4
Apr-09	1.4	1.7	1.5	1.4	1.2	1.2	1.4
May-09	1.6	1.7	1.6	1.6	1.3	1.4	1.4
Jun-09	1.5	1.6	1.6	1.6	1.4	1.4	1.4
Jul-09	1.4	1.6	1.3	1.5	1.3	1.3	1.4
Aug-09	1.3	1.6	1.3	1.6	1.4	1.3	1.4
Sep-09	1.1	1.6	1.3	1.5	1.2	1.3	1.4
Oct-09	1.2	1.5	1.4	1.5	1.4	1.4	1.3

Table 6.2. World Prices for Selected Foods (indices, Jan. 2004 = 1.0) (continued)

	Wheat (unmilled)	Rice (for human consumption)	Corn (unmilled)	Soybean cake	Soybeans	Soybean oil	Meat, chicken
Nov-09	1.3	1.7	1.5	1.5	1.3	1.4	1.3
Dec-09	1.2	2.1	1.4	1.4	1.3	1.4	1.3
Jan-10	1.2	2.2	1.4	1.5	1.2	1.4	1.3
Feb-10	1.2	2.1	1.4	1.3	1.2	1.4	1.3
Mar-10	1.1	1.9	1.4	1.2	1.2	1.4	1.4
Apr-10	1.2	1.8	1.4	1.2	1.2	1.4	1.4
May-10	1.1	1.7	1.4	1.3	1.2	1.3	1.4
Jun-10	0.9	1.7	1.3	1.2	1.2	1.3	1.4
Jul-10	1.2	1.8	1.4	1.3	1.2	1.4	1.4
Aug-10	1.5	1.9	1.5	1.4	1.3	1.5	1.4
Sep-10	1.6	2.1	1.8	1.4	1.3	1.6	1.4
Oct-10	1.6	2.2	2.0	1.5	1.4	1.8	1.4

Source: Constructed by the author based on World Bank figures (2002–2010).

all areas in which Cuba does have productive potential. This potential has been reduced by a lack of incentives, inputs, and investments, while the foreign exchange devoted to imports of these items ends up in the pockets of international food traders instead of being used to expand production and offer incentives to producers.

Until the Cuban agriculture sector fully recovers, the country will have to spend some of its foreign currency income on food, because it is a basic necessity that cannot be put aside. This same level of resources would be required to expand other kinds of production or to undertake new initiatives. The OECD-FAO projections for major food product prices predicted that levels would remain above those of 2005.[42] That is, in spite of deflation after the commodity price boom of 2008, prices would climb again (as they have in fact done, see Table 6.2), and should not be expected to return to pre-crisis levels (see Figure 6.20). These trends should be taken into account.

In previous studies we have discussed the issue of food import substitution in Cuba.[43] In particular, we have closely examined the cases of rice, dried legumes (black and red beans, split peas, and others), and milk products, as well as the potential for vegetable oils. In all these cases, imports have not only grown in value terms, but have also shown a tendency to grow in terms of physical volume (see Figure 6.21).

Table 6.3. Product Structure of Cuban Food Imports

	Rice (for human consumption)	Milk products and eggs	Beans	Fish and fish products	Meat and meat products	Coffee, tea, cocoa, spices, and derivatives	Other grains	Fruits and legumes (except beans)	Proteins for animal feed	Fats and oils	Other foods
1958	39252	2736	14690	7334	709	23	25716	13256	3159	28543	29252
1965	40231	24789	10671	5608	5392	718	61727	13789	5527	35293	0
1970	31746	37505	19142	13321	18758	12379	71498	16092	13727	42092	6623
1975	76885	63709	36165	31183	50120	27467	217457	12506	32730	77997	9685
1980	71576	67822	45561	27075	60742	20467	307106	26736	67202	98750	10490
1981	75581	63557.8	59772	38569	76933	20270	311437	25447	60970	96653.1	0
1982	87394	61720.6	46703	35090	107665	10010	314515	26365	49497	90473.4	28716.7
1983	61057	79866.7	28772	41093	97968	2734	295624.9	34824	61209	114397.4	33783.1
1984	63065	80975	41826	28991	105978	4885	330145	30446	75962	118594	29188
1985	92658	84715	53592	53841	106060	5346	352941	27515	48883	130269	21775
1986	44937	85711	38939	40974	76341	8593	249183	25604	68443	113404	37693
1987	49425	83933	43007	43468	69567	11368	232436	31709	78592	106336	35064
1988	48080	80808	35467	45711	82929	11254	225397	21766	96745	119044	44171
1989	65386	83978	54785	42874	116340	10150	318766	18917	122040	121192	53077
1990	82486	98517	50638	40114	104602	9717	247627	21370	98122	112350	34627
1991	69584	162313	51838	16146	200712	3268	215629	13457	49567	79668	12521
1992	83316	80153	64255	5449	52124	2210	175129	7304	3063	45708	56625
1993	109784	78637	54079	17106	24873	746	176148	8063	2433	19281	59172
1994	72459	72079	55963	17123	13075	9620	164568	4604	56522	16564	3515
1995	107247	90370	49798	28915	23657	10204	224267	7319	62232	24863	10355

Table 6.3. Product Structure of Cuban Food Imports (continued)

	Rice (for human consumption)	Milk products and eggs	Beans	Fish and fish products	Meat and meat products	Coffee, tea, cocoa, spices, and derivatives	Other grains	Fruits and legumes (except beans)	Proteins for animal feed	Fats and oils	Other foods
1996	126494	84941	49580	25854	33994	7788	273111	30084	79737	32122	11939
1997	94104	79601	66292	19679	58301	9001	247888	19926	88038	39957	51817
1998	99382	83946	42517	28924	65446	16294	248878	29604	63511	45430	30683
1999	141163	76534	64809	28306	94304	18016	172592	31090	63724	73334	40393
2000	100772	87677	45186	39869	91170	14700	184769	29112	56830	47151	32453
2001	98921	105743	52757	34009	129115	10873	211177	32969	57335	47390	45321
2002	120160	99017	42430	28770	127595	11370	202462	39075	64851	39953	51553
2003	85062	113436	83309	35666	130216	15184	262900	36779	85824	66816	82928
2004	170432	127413	83335	51222	186817	14176	278624	43841	109920	60217	56206
2005	246118	181297	84392	50884	201958	58531	299630	49714	136891	93456	87992
2006	172437	168842	81001	35832	228469	27310	315433	49186	92046	44819	176553
2007	229239	189795	109376	48420	244132	48854	442556	50678	124402	71096	186407
2008	478830	265189	148191	70039	280166	62586	649908	71211	195518	154044	168468
2009	238411	224304	86023	50285	285128	47530	409271	48789	171643	85999	108221

Source: Constructed by the author based on ONE (1998, 2006a, 2010).

Figure 6.20. Projected World Prices for Selected Foods, 1996–2017

(index of nominal prices, 1996 = 1.0)

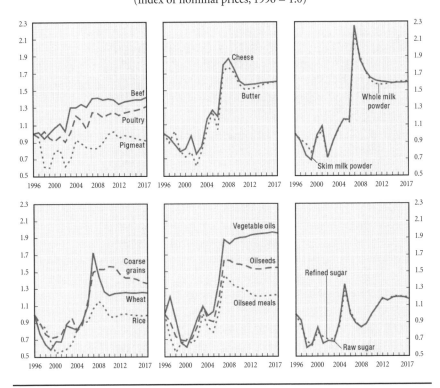

Source: OCDE-FAO (2008)

Since 2007, milk import growth has been restrained, and rice imports have even dropped, as did those of beans in 2009. These new patterns reflect foreign currency income shortages, which has become more severe as a result of the impact of the global crisis on the Cuban economy. This scarcity has led to the implementation of many adjustment measures including budget cuts for social food consumption. At the same time, the reduction in food imports is also the result of the increases in production in the Cuban agriculture sector responding to stimulus programs, which were mentioned earlier in this chapter.

Since the external shock of 1989–93, and specifically beginning in 1994, modest advances were made in the contribution of domestic output to the availability of these foods for domestic consumption. This trend ended in 2000. Fortunately, since 2006 domestic agricultural production has managed to improve once again, and in that sense the country now finds itself

Figure 6.21. Evolution of Selected Cuban Imports by Volume, 1989–2009

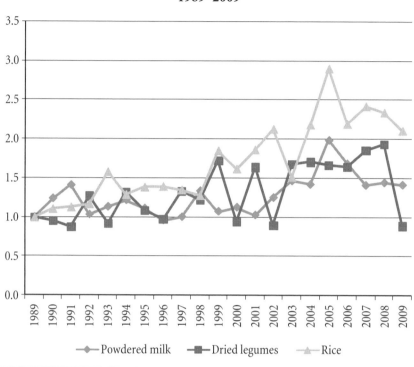

—◆— Powdered milk   —■— Dried legumes   —▲— Rice

Source: Constructed by the author based on CEE (1986 and 1991) and ONE (1998, 2006a, 2010).

with a greater capacity to supply food to its population (see Figures 6.22, 6.23, and 6.24).

Studies on the viability of import substitution for these foods show that the domestic production costs of milk and rice (either *Acopio* or farmers' market prices) exceed the total production cost from imported sources if the Cuban peso is seen as having equal value to the US dollar (see Figure 6.25, panel b).[44] This resulted from low domestic milk yields per cow, and low rice yields per unit of agricultural land.

If we limit the comparison to the foreign currency component of domestic costs, however, there appears to be maneuvering room for domestic production to supply consumer demand (see Figure 6.26, panel b). For milk and beans, the foreign currency component of domestic production (measured in US$) is less than the import price. For rice, improvement of yields to potentially achievable levels would reduce costs to the point where domestic rice could compete with imports, even considering the overvalued official exchange rate.

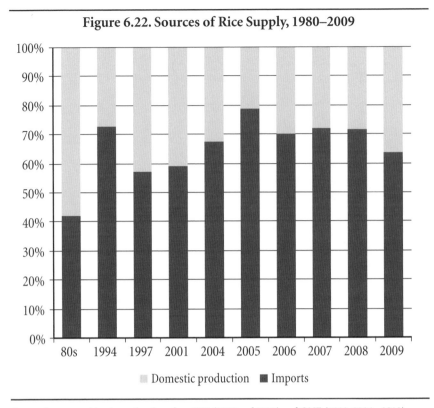

Figure 6.22. Sources of Rice Supply, 1980–2009

■ Domestic production   ■ Imports

Source: Constructed by the author based on CEE (1986 and 1991) and ONE (1998, 2006a, 2010).

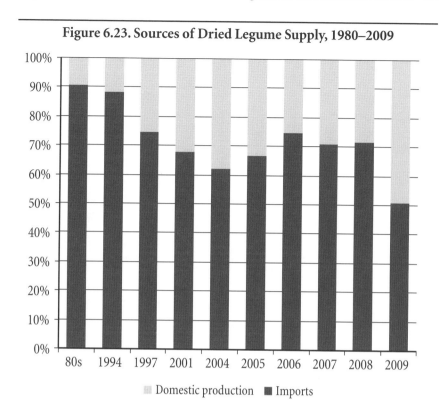

Figure 6.23. Sources of Dried Legume Supply, 1980–2009

Domestic production   Imports

Source: Constructed by the author based on CEE (1986 and 1991) and ONE (1998, 2006a, 2010).

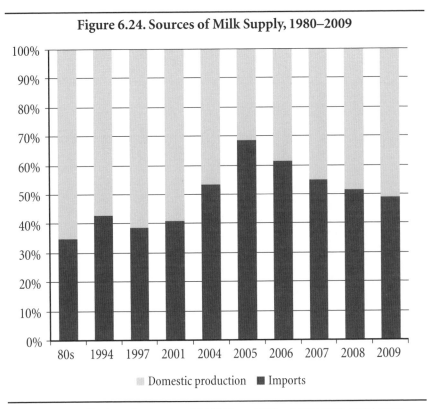

Figure 6.24. Sources of Milk Supply, 1980–2009

☐ Domestic production   ■ Imports

Source: Constructed by the author based on CEE (1986 and 1991) and ONE (1998, 2006a, 2010).

Over the more than ten years that we have been following this issue, the cost-price comparisons have evolved in a way (as shown in Figures 6.25 and 6.26) that is notably more favorable for import substitution. Several factors should be noted, including:

- The introduction of a new pricing policy for agricultural goods has narrowed the gaps that existed between official wholesale prices (*Acopio*) at which the state purchased goods, and consumer prices in farmers' and informal markets. Therefore, it has become more attractive now to sell agricultural good to the state, and there is a direct connection between such sales and import substitution.

- In all the cases studied, official wholesale prices now cover estimated production costs, so that producers may obtain a favorable profit margin through such sales. This change results from the increase in wholesale prices and also from a reduction in estimated costs.

Figure 6.25. Estimated Production Costs, Wholesale Prices (*Acopio*), and Prices in Farmers' and Informal Markets in 1997 and 2007

(indices, *Acopio* price = 1.0)

a) 1997

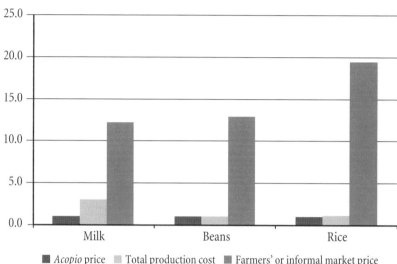

b) 2007

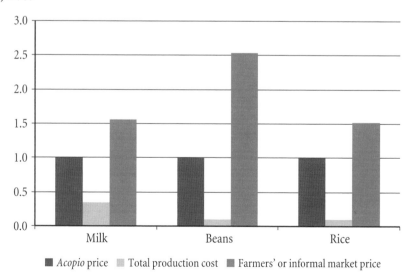

Source: Constructed by the author based on CEE (1986 and 1991) and ONE (1998, 2006a, 2010).

Figure 6.26. Estimated Production Costs, Foreign Currency Component of Those Costs, and Import Prices in 1997 and 2007

(Indices, import prices = 1.0)

a) 1997

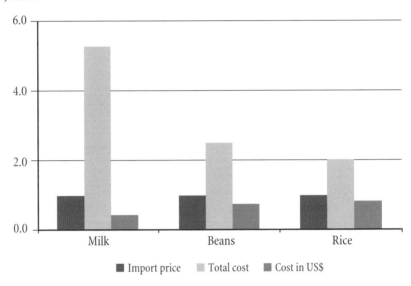

b) 2007

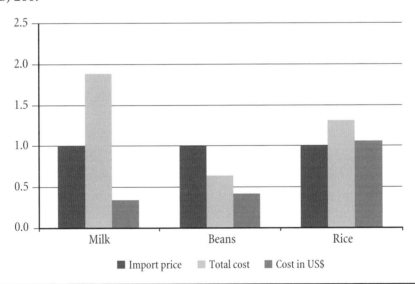

Source: García (2008).

- The gap between estimated production costs and import prices has also narrowed, thanks to movements in both directions: rising prices and lower costs.

To bring these reflections on Cuban food imports to a close, we must comment on one particular source of those imports: the United States. Purchases of food products from U.S. companies constitute an opportunity for Cuba, but at the same time they represent a challenge. The opportunity lies in reducing the prices paid for some imports such as poultry and rice. The lower prices, however, have practically caused a hiatus in chicken-raising in Cuba, making it much harder for domestic producers to compete.

Food purchases from the United States grew at such a rate from 2001 on that Cuba rose from the 114th rank (out of 226 importing countries) in that year to the 29th rank (out of 228 countries) in 2008 (see Table 6.4).

Table 6.4. U.S. Food Exports to Cuba, 2001–2009

Year	Ranking (among export markets)	U.S. exports to Cuba (US$ million)
2009	*36 (out of 232)*	528
2008	*29 (out of 228)*	710
2007	*37 (out of 230)*	438
2006	*34 (out of 227)*	340
2005	*30 (out of 228)*	350
2004	*25 (out of 228)*	392
2003	*35 (out of 219)*	257
2001	*144 (out of 226)*	4

Source: U.S.-Cuba Trade and Economic Council, USTEC (2010).

In 2009, these imports dropped as a result of the adjustment measures already discussed, the revival of domestic production in some areas, and a return to purchasing from some previous suppliers who offer better financing conditions. It should not be forgotten that purchases from the United States must be paid for in advance, without credit arrangements. In 2010, under the same conditions, purchases from this market have continued to drop (see Figure 6.27).

Four groups of products stand out of the total portfolio of Cuban imports from the United States: chicken (representing 82% of total value of Cuba's 2009 chicken imports), corn (75%), soybeans (96%) and soy oil (47%), and pork (47%). Figure 6.28 shows the ten most important products according to the level of U.S. sales to Cuba as a percentage of Cuban purchases abroad.

Figure 6.27. Food Exports from the United States to Cuba, 2006–2010

(data through September of each year, in millions of US dollars)

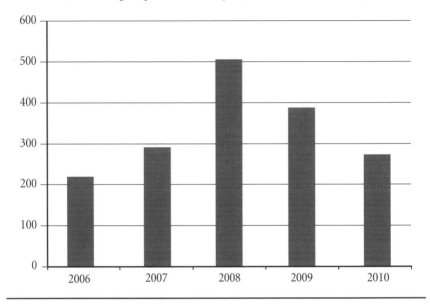

Source: Constructed by the author based on International Trade Administration (2010).

Six foods appear continuously in these rankings: corn, chicken, wheat, soybeans, soybean oil cake, soy oil, and pork (see Table 6.5). All of these, except for wheat, could be domestically produced.

In sum, for many years policy-makers have stated that import substitution is a national economic priority, but in order to convert this declaration into reality, specific actions to promote ever more efficient activity by producers in the agrarian sector must be implemented. Policies must favor producers and foster a perception for farmers that it is possible for them to achieve favorable economic results from the vital activities related to food production for domestic consumption.

Figure 6.28. Main Food Imports from the United States to Cuba in 2009

(% of Cuban imports)*

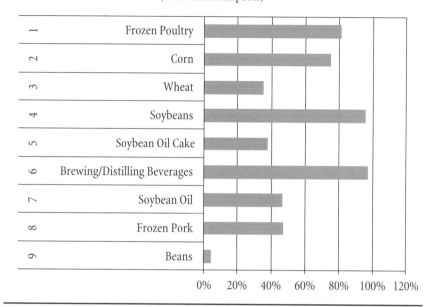

* The products are ranked by order of importance in the share of U.S. exports purchased by Cuba in 2009. These rankings are denoted by the first number in the first column.

Source: Constructed by the author based on USTEC (2010). Includes animal feed.

Table 6.5. U.S. Food Exports to Cuba: The Ten Major Products in 2007, 2008 and 2009

(includes food for direct human consumption and animal feeds)

Ranking	2009	2008	2007
1	Frozen Poultry	Corn	Corn
2	Corn	Wheat	Chicken
3	Wheat	Chicken Leg Quarters and Other Parts	Wheat
4	Soybeans	Soybeans	Soybean Oil Cake
5	Soybean Oil Cake	Soybean Oil Cake	Soybeans
6	Brewing/Distilling Dregs	Soybean Oil	Rice
7	Soybean Oil	Brewing/Distilling Dregs	Soybean Oil
8	Frozen Pork	Powdered Milk	Wood Products
9	Beans	Animal Feed	Brewing/Distilling Dregs and Waste
10	Turkey	Pork Products	Pork Products

Source: Constructed by the author based on USTEC (2010).

Conclusion

It is clearly necessary to reevaluate the role assigned to the agriculture sector in Cuban economic development. The difficult circumstances of the 1990s associated with the fall of socialism in Europe, the sector's meager results in the 1980s in terms of efficiency, along with changes in the country's export structure, all led to a lower priority for this sector and to drawing too many resources away from sugar exports for other financing needs. The consequences of this approach resulted in agricultural foreign trade deficits that have strained Cuba's finances and interfered with strategic visions to reorient the country's economic development paradigm.

The agro-industrial sector is cast in a leading role in the Guidelines on Cuba's Economic and Social Policy recently put forward for approval by the Sixth Congress of the Cuban Communist Party. Indeed, the first guideline in the chapter devoted to this sector refers to the need to reverse the deficit situation described above.

This chapter has attempted to shed light on the pathways that could contribute to reverse Cuba's meager exports of agricultural products and high dependency on imports for internal consumption. On the export side, there are potentials that other countries have already exploited to their advantage. If, for example, Cuba had managed to capture only one percent of the market growth experienced between 1990 and 2008 (excluding the United States, where Cuba is not allowed to sell) in traditional exports, in citrus fruits and derivatives, and in non-traditional products, its exports would have been almost twice the 2009 levels. On the food import side, if Cuba had been able to replace half of its foreign purchases with domestically produced goods, total imports would have been reduced by one-fourth. As a result of both of these measures, the deficit in Cuban agriculture sector would have been only 17% of 2009 levels.

The proposals that have been raised as key discussion points for the Sixth Party Congress all point in this direction.[45] Still pending is their wide discussion by the public and especially by researchers and technicians from this important sector. Their input will surely enrich the proposals that have been put forward, especially when it comes to putting policies into practice. Cuba now more than ever needs an agriculture sector that is able to fulfill its functions for national economic development. The global food crisis should be viewed as an opportunity for the revival of farm production to replace food imports. The goals of achieving higher growth rates, import substitution, and food security can only be achieved by significant policy changes.

Appendix 1.

Classification of Products-Markets by Dynamism of Import Markets, 1998–2008

Products	World + (Total)	Canada	China	United States of America	Russian Federation	Japan	European Union + (Total)	Caribbean (without Cuba)
Sugar (centrifuged)	STAGNANT	STAGNANT	STAGNANT	REGRESSIVE	REGRESSIVE	STAGNANT	STAGNANT	STAGNANT
Sugar (refined)	STAGNANT	STAGNANT	VERY DYNAMIC	VERY DYNAMIC	REGRESSIVE	STAGNANT	STAGNANT	STAGNANT
Alcoholic beverages	DYNAMIC	VERY DYNAMIC	VERY DYNAMIC	STAGNANT	VERY DYNAMIC	REGRESSIVE	STAGNANT	VERY DYNAMIC
Cocoa beans	STAGNANT	STAGNANT	VERY DYNAMIC	STAGNANT	STAGNANT	REGRESSIVE	STAGNANT	VERY DYNAMIC
Cocoa butter	DYNAMIC	STAGNANT	VERY DYNAMIC	STAGNANT	VERY DYNAMIC	STAGNANT	DYNAMIC	STAGNANT
Cigarettes	STAGNANT	VERY DYNAMIC	REGRESSIVE	STAGNANT	REGRESSIVE	STAGNANT	STAGNANT	VERY DYNAMIC
Molasses	STAGNANT	STAGNANT	REGRESSIVE	STAGNANT	REGRESSIVE	REGRESSIVE	STAGNANT	DYNAMIC
Honey	DYNAMIC	VERY DYNAMIC	VERY DYNAMIC	DYNAMIC	STAGNANT	DYNAMIC	DYNAMIC	VERY DYNAMIC
Hand-rolled cigars	STAGNANT	VERY DYNAMIC	STAGNANT	STAGNANT	VERY DYNAMIC	STAGNANT	STAGNANT	VERY DYNAMIC
Leaf tobacco	STAGNANT	STAGNANT	VERY DYNAMIC	REGRESSIVE	STAGNANT	REGRESSIVE	STAGNANT	VERY DYNAMIC
Machine-made cigars	STAGNANT	STAGNANT	STAGNANT	STAGNANT	STAGNANT	VERY DYNAMIC	STAGNANT	VERY DYNAMIC
Coffee (green and roasted)	STAGNANT	STAGNANT	VERY DYNAMIC	STAGNANT	VERY DYNAMIC	STAGNANT	STAGNANT	STAGNANT

TRADITIONAL

Classification of Products-Markets by Dynamism of Import Markets, 1998–2008 (continued)

Products	World + (Total)	Canada	China	United States of America	Russian Federation	Japan	European Union + (Total)	Caribbean (without Cuba)
Lemon juice (concentrated)	STAGNANT	REGRESSIVE		STAGNANT			REGRESSIVE	REGRESSIVE
Lemon juice (non-concentrated)	DYNAMIC	STAGNANT	REGRESSIVE	VERY DYNAMIC	VERY DYNAMIC		STAGNANT	VERY DYNAMIC
Grapefruit juice	REGRESSIVE	STAGNANT	REGRESSIVE	VERY DYNAMIC	REGRESSIVE	REGRESSIVE	REGRESSIVE	STAGNANT
Concentrated orange juice	STAGNANT	REGRESSIVE	REGRESSIVE	STAGNANT	STAGNANT	REGRESSIVE	VERY DYNAMIC	REGRESSIVE
Concentrated grapefruit juice	VERY DYNAMIC	REGRESSIVE	VERY DYNAMIC	REGRESSIVE	VERY DYNAMIC	REGRESSIVE	VERY DYNAMIC	STAGNANT
Lemons and limes	DYNAMIC	VERY DYNAMIC	VERY DYNAMIC	VERY DYNAMIC	VERY DYNAMIC	REGRESSIVE	VERY DYNAMIC	VERY DYNAMIC
Orange juice	STAGNANT	STAGNANT	VERY DYNAMIC	VERY DYNAMIC	VERY DYNAMIC	STAGNANT	STAGNANT	STAGNANT
Oranges	STAGNANT	STAGNANT	VERY DYNAMIC	STAGNANT	VERY DYNAMIC	REGRESSIVE	STAGNANT	STAGNANT
Tangerines, mandarin oranges, and clementines	STAGNANT	STAGNANT	VERY DYNAMIC	DYNAMIC	VERY DYNAMIC	STAGNANT	STAGNANT	STAGNANT
Grapefruits (including pomelos)	STAGNANT	STAGNANT	REGRESSIVE	STAGNANT	VERY DYNAMIC	REGRESSIVE	STAGNANT	VERY DYNAMIC

CITRUS

Classification of Products-Markets by Dynamism of Import Markets, 1998–2008 (continued)

Products	World + (Total)	Canada	China	United States of America	Russian Federation	Japan	European Union + (Total)	Caribbean (without Cuba)
OTHER NON-TRADITIONAL								
Avocados	VERY DYNAMIC	VERY DYNAMIC	STAGNANT	VERY DYNAMIC	VERY DYNAMIC	VERY DYNAMIC	VERY DYNAMIC	VERY DYNAMIC
Bananas	STAGNANT	STAGNANT	REGRESSIVE	REGRESSIVE	VERY DYNAMIC	STAGNANT	STAGNANT	VERY DYNAMIC
Eggplant	DYNAMIC	STAGNANT	STAGNANT	STAGNANT	VERY DYNAMIC	REGRESSIVE	DYNAMIC	VERY DYNAMIC
Squash, pumpkin, etc.	STAGNANT	REGRESSIVE	REGRESSIVE	STAGNANT	VERY DYNAMIC	REGRESSIVE	VERY DYNAMIC	VERY DYNAMIC
Peppers (chilies and sweet peppers)	DYNAMIC	DYNAMIC	STAGNANT	STAGNANT	VERY DYNAMIC	STAGNANT	DYNAMIC	VERY DYNAMIC
Pineapple juice	REGRESSIVE	VERY DYNAMIC	VERY DYNAMIC	STAGNANT	VERY DYNAMIC	REGRESSIVE	REGRESSIVE	VERY DYNAMIC
Tomato juice (concentrated)	REGRESSIVE		REGRESSIVE		REGRESSIVE		STAGNANT	STAGNANT
Tomato juice	STAGNANT	VERY DYNAMIC	STAGNANT	REGRESSIVE		REGRESSIVE	STAGNANT	STAGNANT
Mangos, mangosteens, and guavas	DYNAMIC	VERY DYNAMIC	VERY DYNAMIC	STAGNANT	VERY DYNAMIC	STAGNANT	VERY DYNAMIC	STAGNANT
Melons (besides watermelons, including cantaloupes)	STAGNANT	STAGNANT	VERY DYNAMIC	REGRESSIVE	VERY DYNAMIC	STAGNANT	STAGNANT	STAGNANT

Classification of Products-Markets by Dynamism of Import Markets, 1998–2008 (continued)

Products	World + (Total)	Canada	China	United States of America	Russian Federation	Japan	European Union + (Total)	Caribbean (without Cuba)
Potatoes (frozen)	DYNAMIC	VERY DYNAMIC	VERY DYNAMIC	DYNAMIC	VERY DYNAMIC	STAGNANT	DYNAMIC	VERY DYNAMIC
Potatoes	STAGNANT	STAGNANT	DYNAMIC	STAGNANT	VERY DYNAMIC	VERY DYNAMIC	STAGNANT	STAGNANT
Papayas	STAGNANT	VERY DYNAMIC	REGRESSIVE	DYNAMIC	VERY DYNAMIC	REGRESSIVE	VERY DYNAMIC	REGRESSIVE
Cucumbers	STAGNANT	STAGNANT	VERY DYNAMIC	STAGNANT	VERY DYNAMIC	REGRESSIVE	STAGNANT	VERY DYNAMIC
Pineapples (fresh)	VERY DYNAMIC	VERY DYNAMIC	STAGNANT	VERY DYNAMIC	VERY DYNAMIC	DYNAMIC	VERY DYNAMIC	VERY DYNAMIC
Pineapples (canned)	STAGNANT	STAGNANT	STAGNANT	STAGNANT	VERY DYNAMIC	REGRESSIVE	STAGNANT	VERY DYNAMIC
Plantains	STAGNANT			STAGNANT			VERY DYNAMIC	STAGNANT
Watermelons	STAGNANT	STAGNANT	VERY DYNAMIC	VERY DYNAMIC	STAGNANT	REGRESSIVE	DYNAMIC	STAGNANT
Tomatoes	STAGNANT	STAGNANT	VERY DYNAMIC	STAGNANT	VERY DYNAMIC	REGRESSIVE	STAGNANT	REGRESSIVE

OTHER NON-TRADITIONAL (continued)

Source: Constructed by the author based on FAOSTAT (2010). For boxes in black the data for some years was unavailable.

Endnotes

1. Bruce F. Johnston and John W. Mellor, "The Role of Agriculture in Economic Development," *The American Economic Review* 51/4 (1961): 566–93; Peter C. Timmer, "Agriculture and Economic Development," in *Handbook of Agricultural Economics, Vol 2*, edited by Bruce L. Gardner and Gordon C. Rausser, 1487–546 (Amsterdam: Elsevier, 2002). It should be recalled that at the time Johnson and Mellor were writing, services did not yet constitute the preponderant sector in many economies.

2. Johnston and Mellor, "The Role of Agriculture in Economic Development."

3. Timmer, "Agriculture and Economic Development."

4. S. K. Rao "Agriculture and Economic Development," in *The New Palgrave: a , Dictionary of Economics*, edited by John Eatwell, Murray Milgate and Peter Newman, 4 v. (London: Macmillan, 1987).

5. Timmer, "Agriculture and Economic Development."

6. Lloyd George Reynolds, *Agriculture in Development Theory*, A Publication of the Economic Growth Center at Yale University (New Haven: Yale University Press, 1975).

7. Sheila Amin Gutiérrez de Piñeres, "Externalities in the Agricultural Export Sector and Economic Growth: A Developing Country Perspective," *Agricultural Economics* (1999): 257–67.

8. This refers to farm products outside the traditional areas of specialization of developing countries such as bananas, cotton, coffee, and sugar. For example, non-traditional products include flowers, fruit, and fresh vegetables for export.

9. Michael Hardt and Antonio Negri, *Empire* (Cambridge, Mass.: Harvard University Press, 2000).

10. Social consumption includes consumption of food in public institutions including schools, hospitals, senior homes, etc. Public food supply includes sales of food through the state restaurant network, other sales of prepared food to the public as a secondary activity outside that network, and sales in workplace cafeterias and snack bars. *Autoconsumo* (personal consumption) refers to food that is produced for consumption within the producing entity (e.g., for cafeterias of the workers and/or members in enterprises and cooperatives that provide this service) and food for the consumption of the farm family in the private sector.

11. Oficina Nacional de Estadísticas (ONE), "Consumo de alimentos 2005," Oficina Nacional de Estadísticas (ONE) (Havana: 2006).

12. Anicia García and Betsy Anaya, "Política social en Cuba, nuevo enfoque y programas recientes," in *Centro de Estudios de la Economía Cubana, Publicaciones 2006–2007* (Havana: Centro de Estudios de la Economía Cubana, 2006).

13. Angela Ferriol, Maribel Ramos, and Lía Añé, *Reforma económica y población en riesgo en Ciudad de Havana, Research report for the Programa Efectos Sociales de las Medidas de Ajuste Económico sobre la Ciudad—Diagnósticos y Perspectivas* (Havana: INIE-CEPDE/ONE, 2004).

14. Pablo Fernández Domínguez, "El sector agropecuario en Cuba: evolución y perspectivas," in *Cuba: el sector agropecuario y las políticas agrícolas ante los nuevos retos* (Montevideo: INIE-MEP-ASDI-Universidad de la República Oriental del Uruguay, 2002).

15. To illustrate this statement, we compare the market prices of some products, as we do in the second part of this chapter. Although in 2007 the state began to introduce increases in the official state prices for some products, during most of the period under consideration these prices remained low and far below the corresponding prices in the farmers' markets (which we are classifying in the informal market category). If the supply of products were to remain the same, and if all were sold through a single market, the resulting average prices would probably fall somewhere between the two extremes of the official prices and those of the current farmers' markets (which do not exactly represent a perfect market). See Lisset Robaina González and Anicia García, *La distribución de alimentos en Cuba: posibles impactos de eliminar su segmentación*. Paper presented at conference of the VI Escuela de Verano Humboldt Universität—Universidad de la Habana: 2010.

16. The FAO definition of agricultural area includes:

    a) arable land: land under temporary agricultural crops (multiple-cropped areas are counted only once), temporary meadows for mowing or pasture, land under market and kitchen gardens, and land temporarily fallow (less than five years). The abandoned land resulting from shifting cultivation is not included in this category. Data for arable land are not meant to indicate the amount of land that is potentially cultivable, *but rather that which is really under cultivation (author's note)*;

    b) permanent crops: land cultivated with long-term crops which do not have to be replanted for several years (such as cocoa and coffee and rubber); this category also includes land under trees and shrubs producing flowers, fruit trees, and trees producing nuts and grape vines, but excludes land with trees grown for wood production; and

    c) permanent meadows and pastures: land used permanently (five years or more) to grow herbaceous forage crops, either cultivated or growing wild (wild prairie or grazing land).

17. According the FAO, this refers to arable land and land under permanent crops.

18. We are aware of the complexities involved in international comparisons, but Cuba is developing in a world context, and that is the environment in which it must compete and systematically measure its performance. Therefore, and based on the assumption that labor force is the fundamental productive force, we are comparing Cuba only to countries with similar indices of economically active population (EAP) in the farm sector per hectare of agricultural land or hectare of land available for agricultural work. For this purpose we have used data from the FAO database FAOSTAT, drawn from that source between May 31 and June 1, 2008.

19. Also known as the "conventional" or the "high-input, high-capital" model. See Sara Oppenheimer, "Alternative Agriculture in Cuba," *American Entomologist* (2001): 216–27.

20. The acronym UBPC (in English, Basic Unit of Cooperative Production) denotes the cooperatives formed in 1993, when state lands were granted in usufruct to collectives of workers for an indeterminate time period, and so transformed into cooperatives. Property rights in the buildings and other means of production were transferred to the members of the cooperatives, who thus acquired an initial debt. The initials CPA stand for (in English) Farm Production Cooperatives; these emerged in the mid-1970s from the voluntary unification of individual peasants' lands and tools. The CCSs are Credit and Service Cooperatives, which emerged in the 1960s to allow independent peasants to share access to such services, in return for lower charges.

21. See page 22 of Partido Comunista de Cuba, "Proyecto de lineamientos económicos del VI Congreso del Partido Comunista de Cuba" (Havana: PCC, 2010).

22. Fernández Domínguez, "El sector agropecuario en Cuba: evolución y perspectivas." and Anicia García. "El sector agropecuario cubano: cambios en su paradigma de desarrollo," in *15 Años del Centro de Estudios de la Economía Cubana* (Havana: Editorial Félix Varela, 2004).

23. And also its external finances, as we shall see later in this chapter.

24. For a discussion of the outcomes of these reforms, see Chapter 4 by Armando Nova González in this volume.

25. It should be noted that more than 80% of Cuba's merchandise trade was carried out with countries belonging to this bloc.

26. See Nancy Quiñones and Isis Mañalich, "Fomento exportador: resultados y retos para la economía cubana," in *Primer Fórum Científico de la Rama del Comercio Exterior,* Centro de Información del Instituto de Comercio Exterior (Havana: MINCEX, 2002).

27. Among the best-known examples is the agreement reached between the Corporación Habanos S.A. and the European company Altadis (fourth-largest international seller and world leader in the distribution of fine cigars), and the partnership with the Pernaud Ricard firm for foreign distribution of Havana Club rum.

28. This mechanism has continued to grow, and today there are more than 160,000 such units.

29. Cuba does not have access to the international bodies that offer international financing, as a result of the policies of exclusion and economic embargo of which it has been a victim for more than forty years.

30. Anicia García, "Las agroexportaciones cubanas: factores determinantes." Paper presented at the Latin American Studies Association Annual Congress, Washington D.C., 2001; *El sector agropecuario y la restricción externa: el caso de las agroexportaciones cubanas, doctoral thesis*, Centro de Estudios de la Economía

Cubana (Havana: Universidad de La Habana, 2004); and "Las agroexportaciones cubanas: demanda y competitividad," in *Cuba, crecer con el conocimiento* (Havana: Editorial de Ciencias Sociales, 2005).

31. This refers to a group of foods not included in other categories, such as soy products (sauce and paste), peanut butter, frozen prepared sweet corn, reconstituted milk, ice cream, edible ice, lard, rendered poultry fat, solid and liquid margarine, and other prepared shortenings.

32. These include, among other items, beeswax and vegetable waxes; cooked, acidified, and hydrogenated oils; and fatty acids.

33. That is, sugar, tobacco, coffee, and alcoholic beverages.

34. Among the other non-traditional products are avocados, bananas, eggplants, squash, chilies and sweet peppers, pineapples and pineapple juice, tomatoes and tomato juice, mangos, guavas, watermelon and other melons, potatoes and frozen potatoes, papayas, cucumbers, and plantains.

35. Mónica Rodrígues and Miguel Torres, "La competitividad agroalimentaria de los países de América Latina y el Caribe en una perspectiva de liberalización comercial," *Serie Desarrollo Productivo de CEPAL* 139 (2003).

36. Henceforth, any mention of "the Caribbean" should be understood as the Caribbean islands other than Cuba.

37. For more details, see the Appendix.

38. Author's calculation based on ONE Oficina Nacional de Estadísticas (ONE), "Consumo de alimentos 2004," Oficina Nacional de Estadísticas (ONE) 2005, and *Anuario Estadístico de Cuba* (Havana: ONE, various years).

39. Partido Comunista de Cuba, "Proyecto de lineamientos económicos del VI Congreso del Partido Comunista de Cuba." See esp. pp. 11–18.

40. Institute for Agriculture and Trade Policy (IATP), "Seven Reasons Why the Doha Round Will Not Solve the Food Crisis," *IATP in Fact* (2008). The Institute for Agricultural and Trade Policy lists among the most important causes: concentration of market power in a group of transnational corporations that can fix prices at their convenience by controlling supply; the significant rise in the price of oil, which is a basic input in industrial-type agriculture; diversion of an ever-growing portion of grain and seed production to the making of biofuels; financial speculation in commodity markets; and climate change, which generates extreme weather patterns highly prejudicial to food production.

41. All cereals other than rice.

42. OECD-FAO, "Agricultural Outlook 2008–2017." OECD and FAO, 2008.

43. Anicia García, Isis Mañalich, Nieves Pico, and Nancy Quiñones, "La sustitución de importaciones de alimentos: una necesidad impostergable (primera parte)," *CUBA: Investigación Económica INIE* 3/1 (1997); "La sustitución de importaciones de alimentos: una necesidad impostergable (segunda parte)," *CUBA: Investigación Económica INIE* 3/1 (1998); Anicia García, Pablo Fernández, and Adria Loaces, "La sustitución de importaciones de alimentos en Cuba: estudio

de casos" (Havana: INIE, 1998); Anicia García, "La sustitución de importaciones de alimentos: necesidad vs. posibilidad," in *Reflexiones sobre Economía Cubana*, edited by Omar Everleny Pérez Villanueva (Havana: Editorial de Ciencias Sociales, 2006); García, "Sustitución de importaciones de alimentos en Cuba, una década después," in *XX Aniversario del CEEC* (Havana: Centro de Estudios de la Economía Cubana, 2008); and Anicia García, Rafael Barrios, and Lisset Robaina, "La sustitución de importaciones de alimentos en Cuba: una aproximación al caso de las grasas comestibles," in *Seminario Anual sobre Economía Cubana y Gerencia Empresarial*. Centro de Estudios la Economía Cubana (Havana: 2010).

44. García, "Sustitución de importaciones de alimentos en Cuba, una década después."

45. Partido Comunista de Cuba, "Proyecto de lineamientos económicos del VI Congreso del Partido Comunista de Cuba."

7

Foreign Direct Investment in China, Vietnam, and Cuba: Pertinent Experiences for Cuba

Omar Everleny Pérez Villanueva

The subject of this chapter has been hotly contested in the economic literature. On a spectrum ranging from liberal economic theory to Marxist approaches, many analysts have been critical of the role of foreign capital as a factor that may contribute to development. In recent times, however, new views about foreign direct investment (FDI) flows and their role as catalysts to underdeveloped economies have evolved in response to the study of positive experiences in several countries, especially in Southeast Asia.

The costs and benefits of FDI flows have been a traditional subject of controversy. Supporters point to the positive role FDI plays for the investment-receiving countries in technology transfer, economic and job growth, and acceleration of both economic development and integration into world markets. Its critics accuse it of causing balance of payment problems, allowing foreign investors to exploit the markets of the receiving countries, and reducing those countries' capacity to manage their own economies and other spheres of life. In recent years the debate has tilted in favor of FDI's merits, given the increasing number of countries whose development strategies are based on greater integration into the world market, though criticisms remain, stating that, "as a historical fact, in the socialist economies that have existed up until now, foreign investments were long identified as bearers of bourgeois penetration during the imperialist phase of the capitalist system. For many years this was the reigning view of the presence of foreign capital within such economies."[1]

The changing attitude toward FDI in developing countries stems from the belief and evidence that such investment can be important for technology transfer understood in its broadest sense: not only as scientific processes, but also as techniques of organization, administration, and commercialization. Developing countries need foreign financing in all its senses;

Cuba is not exempt from this need, though it differs from other countries because it does not have access to multinational financing sources, and its access to bilateral credit is limited by its foreign debt.

Starting in the late 1980s, Cuba reexamined its policies toward foreign capital investment and sought to expand the role of FDI in the economy, because its former sources of financing had disappeared and it was impossible to obtain access to new foreign bilateral or multilateral credit. For numerous reasons, the policy seeking to attract foreign capital has not succeeded. In view of the unfavorable situation of Cuban macroeconomic indicators and the deterioration and obsolescence of its productive base, it might be helpful to analyze the positive experiences of China and Vietnam.

The main objective of this chapter, therefore, is to characterize the role FDI has played in the economic evolution of developing economies in Asia, with a particular emphasis on China and Vietnam. This analysis is used as a reference framework to suggest alternative possibilities for the necessary use of such capital in Cuba, bearing in mind the specifics of the Cuban economy and the impact of these resources on the structural changes that must occur in Cuba in the future. Within the spectrum of social sciences, there are no definitive established values. Conclusions are always partial and permanently subject to change over time, especially in the case of a complex subject that is, to some degree, in contradiction with classic Marxist approaches. Therefore, this essay seeks to validate its conclusions scientifically through experiential data and logical arguments, but it does not contain definitive proposals for the long term. Like any scientific investigation, it may stimulate wide discussion. If that discussion takes place within Cuban academic circles, one of the study's objectives will have been fulfilled.

International Context

FDI remains a centerpiece of world economic attention for many and varied reasons. One is its spectacular rise. Annual flows have grown from some $60 billion in 1985 to $1.86 trillion in 2008. The accumulated world total of FDI multiplied more than nine-fold between 1990 and 2008, rising to a total of $14.9 trillion. The current financial crisis has modified the FDIdirection; investments in developing and transition economies grew rapidly, increasing their share of world FDI inflows to 43% in 2008, while FDI flows to developed countries diminished considerably (29%). Between 2008 and 2009, developing countries confronted the financial crisis in better circumstances than developed countries because their financial systems were less interrelated with the U.S. and European banking systems, which were passing through difficult times.

Figure 7.1. FDI Inflows by Groups of Economies, 1970–2008

(billions of US dollars)

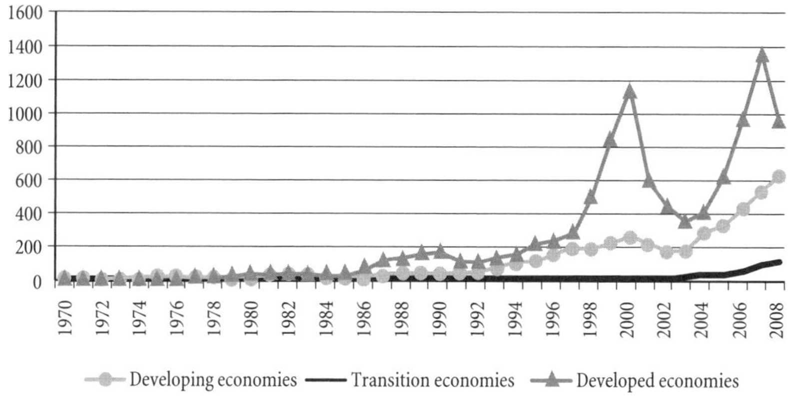

Source: UNCTAD (2009).

In 2008, developing countries received \$620.7 billion worth of FDI in current dollars, one of the highest such figures ever seen. The direction of international flows toward developing countries has meant that their participation in the worldwide FDI flows rose to 36.5%, up from 30% in 1995. The main recipients over the decade have been Asian developing nations (63% of FDI inflows in 2008) and those in Latin America and the Caribbean (23%). Among the main recipients of FDI in developing countries in 2008, the People's Republic of China received \$108 billion in FDI, the top FDI receiver among developing countries (see Figure 7.2).

The trend toward increased liberalization in foreign investment laws has been another characteristic of the past twenty years. Between 1991 and 1996, out of a total of 599 changes of worldwide government regulations affecting FDI, 562 were in the direction of liberalization and promotion of investments—that is, 95% of the regulatory changes affecting FDI. In 2008 and 2009, despite signs of possible rising protectionism with respect to investment, the general trend of FDI policies continued to point toward more opening, including limits on barriers to FDI and lower taxes on business profits. UNCTAD's (United Nations Conference on Trade and Development) annual survey of legal and regulatory changes affecting FDI shows that 110 new measures were adopted in 2008, of which 85 fostered it (see Table 7.1).[2] This trend resulted from governments' desire to facilitate the search for such foreign capital, as it is reflected in the growth in bilateral treaties to protect and promote investment in the 1990s. On January 1, 1997,

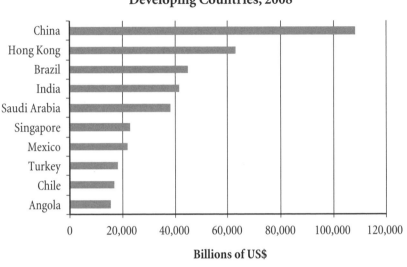

Figure 7.2. The 10 Largest Recipients of FDI among Developing Countries, 2008

Billions of US$

Source: UNCTAD (2009).

Table 7.1. National Regulatory Changes to FDI, 2000–2008

	2000	2001	2002	2003	2004	2005	2006	2007	2008
Number of countries that introduced changes	70	71	72	82	103	92	91	58	55
Number of regulatory changes	150	297	246	242	270	203	177	98	110
More favorable	147	193	234	218	234	162	142	74	85
Less favorable	3	14	12	24	36	41	35	24	25

Source: UNCTAD (2009).

there were 1,330 such treaties in effect in the world, involving 162 countries, which represented a tripling in their number in five years.

The current financial and economic crisis has not had serious repercussions on the policies affecting FDI because these capital flows are not seen as the cause of the crisis. Nonetheless, the farthest-reaching national policies adopted in response to the crisis (national economic recovery programs, economic stimulus plans) have indirectly affected FDI flows and the operations of transnational companies. National policy measures have provoked a degree of protectionism regarding investment, favoring domestic over foreign investors, or erecting obstacles to nationals investing abroad, in order to keep capital at home.[3]

Foreign Direct Investment in Asia: China and Vietnam

Of the FDI directed toward Asian developing countries in 2008, 86% was concentrated in East and Southeast Asia—especially China, Hong Kong, Indonesia, South Korea, Malaysia, Singapore, Thailand, and recently Vietnam. These countries are important markets and also offer advantages in terms of infrastructure, low labor costs, and relative abundance of natural resources. The investment funds generally come from Japan and the United States and to a lesser extent from Western Europe. The so-called newly industrialized countries of Asia (Newly Industrializing Countries, hereafter NICs: South Korea, Hong Kong, Singapore, and Taiwan) are now themselves investing in what might be called a new generation of NICs (Southeastern Asian countries like the Philippines, Indonesia, Malaysia, Thailand, Vietnam, and the great dragon of China), using the previous Japanese strategy of seeking low labor costs.

Great differences in accumulated foreign direct investment distinguish the economies of China, Hong Kong, and Singapore from the rest (see Table 7.2). Vietnam, however, stands out because of its accelerating rate of FDI, which caused accumulated investment to grow by a factor of twenty-nine in the 1990–2008 period, more than matching China, whose accumulated FDI grew by a factor of eighteen. The Asian region illustrates how companies in developing countries have accelerated their pursuit of comparative advantage, contributing to a redistribution of resources toward

Table 7.2. Stocks of FDI Inflows in East and Southeast Asian Economies, 1990, 2000 and 2009 (millions of US dollars)

	1990	2000	2008
Hong Kong	201,653	455,469	835,764
China	20,691	193,348	378,083
Singapore	30,468	110,570	326,142
Thailand	8,242	29,915	104,850
South Korea	5,186	38,110	90,693
Malaysia	10,318	52,747	73,262
Indonesia	8,732	25,060	67,044
Vietnam	1,650	20,596	48,325
Taiwan	9,735	19,521	45,458

Source: UNCTAD (2009).

more productive economies, moving to the recipient countries activities that may have ceased to be productive in their home countries but that significantly increase the marginal productivity of the recipient countries. What follows is an analysis of the People's Republic of China and Vietnam as recipients of foreign direct investment. Both countries maintain a "socialist" regime, a single party, and a mixed economy, which began from a relatively low level of development. Each has achieved favorable results after transforming its economic system.

Characteristics of FDI in China

During the first thirty years of Chinese socialism, Soviet-style central planning predominated. In July 1979, the Central Committee of the Chinese Communist Party decided to implement economic reforms that would gradually provide benefits to commerce, agriculture, financial and monetary exchange systems, prices, salaries, the income side of the state budget, and FDI, among other aspects. They decided on a series of changes to reintegrate China in the world economy by allowing an open door policy.[4] The Chinese economic reforms permit nearly free activities to internal and external economic actors, including the central, provincial, and local governments, in order to accelerate the fulfillment of the economic development goals within a regime deemed essentially socialist but with "Chinese peculiarities."

Under Deng Xiaoping—regarded as a radical reformer—Chinese officials took measures to open the economy gradually to the outside world. The entrance of transnational corporations and FDI was encouraged in hopes of their potential contribution to resolving existing problems in the quest for development. Deng's policy of external opening accompanied a thoroughgoing economic reform that sought to reconcile national interests with those of foreign capital. Before the 1979 opening, there was practically no foreign investment in China. According to the World Bank, total accumulated FDI was minuscule in comparison to the size of the economy.[5] On July 8, 1979, the Joint Venture Law, governing companies with a mixture of domestic and international capital, went into effect. It was followed by several specific laws and regulations covering the processes of negotiation, approval, and registration of such companies, procedures governing employment, taxes, and sales, and so forth. This open door policy led to a gradual opening of various geographic areas in China to FDI and international trade that may be divided into four stages:[6] a) introductory (1978–1983); b) expansionary, from coastal areas to interior regions (1984–1991); c) a rapid and deep opening across all regions (1992–2000); and, d) the entrance of China into the World Trade Organization (WTO) (2001–present).

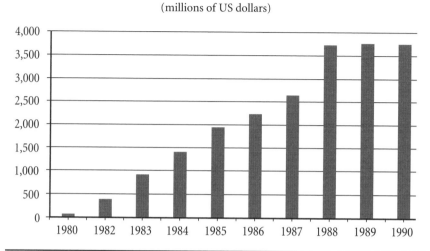

Figure 7.3. Foreign Direct Investment in China, 1980–1990
(millions of US dollars)

Source: Castro (2009) and *Beijing Informa* (1997).

The role played by FDI is striking. In 1979, FDI flows to China were only $57 million; between then and 1984, foreign capital still played a minor role (some $500 million annually, on average, directed toward small-scale projects, of which more than half were less than $500,000 each).[7] But, as Figure 7.4 confirms, a foreign capital boom in China began in 1991.[8]

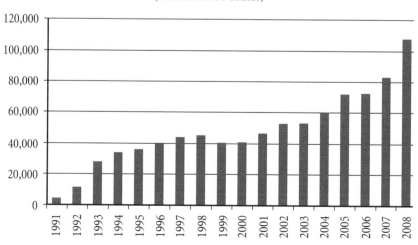

Figure 7.4. Foreign Direct Investment in China, 1991–2008
(millions of US dollars)

Source: UNCTAD (various years).

By 2008, China had absorbed $378 billion in FDI. For sixteen consecutive years, it occupied first place among FDI recipients on the list of developing countries and Eastern European countries in transition. Most of the world's five hundred largest companies have invested in China, and 20% to 25% of the FDI has been investments made in the home country by Chinese entities abroad, principally those in Hong Kong before its reintegration into China.

According to region of origin of FDI in China in 2008, Hong Kong was the leading supplier of foreign capital, amounting to more than $41 billion of the total FDI received. This was followed by investments from the "fiscal paradises" such as the Virgin Islands and the Cayman Islands. The combined flow of investment from the Asian region (Hong Kong, Macao, Taiwan, Japan, the Philippines, Thailand, Malaysia, Singapore, Indonesia, and South Korea) amounted to 60% of the total FDI that China received.

In 1987, Hong Kong invested 68.64% of the total FDI entering China, with a value of approximately $1.6 billion. But its share of the total dropped to 44% by 2008, when the total value of FDI entering China was approximately $41.4 billion.

FDI in China may take various forms. The most common are equity joint ventures, cooperative businesses (also called contractual participation or contractual cooperation businesses), wholly foreign-owned companies, and joint exploration contracts. Other variations for foreign investors are the

**Figure 7.5. Foreign Direct Investment in China in 2008
from Asian Countries**

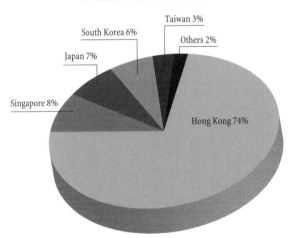

Source: People's Republic of China, Ministry of Commerce (2009).

creation of foreign-funded shareholding companies (also known as lim-ited-liability companies) with foreign and Chinese share owners, or the pur-chase abroad of stock in Chinese companies, or the purchase of corporate bonds. Analysis of the pattern of FDI in China through 2007 reveals a pref-erence for investment projects developed through wholly foreign-owned companies. In 2007, 70% of the FDI received by China was directed to cre-ate these sorts of enterprises, with a total of 29,543 new projects, as com-pared to 8,290 new joint ventures. In cumulative statistics on forms of FDI through the end of 2007, wholly foreign-owned companies predominated with a 49.03% share, followed by equity joint ventures with a 33.79% share.

Looking at investment sectors, manufacturing (still attractive because of low labor costs) received 49% of effective investment in 2007. Within man-ufacturing, the leading areas were electronic and telecommunications prod-ucts; metal products; clothing and other textile products; plastics; leather, hide, and feather goods; and food products. According to statistics from the Chinese Ministry of Commerce, real estate ranks second in terms of vol-ume of effective investment, accounting for 20.46% of the total, followed by finance with about 12%. Nonetheless, foreign investment in real estate remains restricted according to the regulations in the 2007 New Industrial Catalogue for the Guide to Foreign Investment.[9]

Figure 7.6. Forms of Accumulated Foreign Investment in China through December 2007

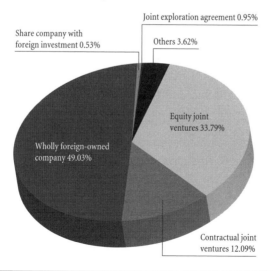

Source: People's Republic of China, Ministry of Foreign Commerce (2009).

Figure 7.7. Foreign Investment in China by Sectors, 2007

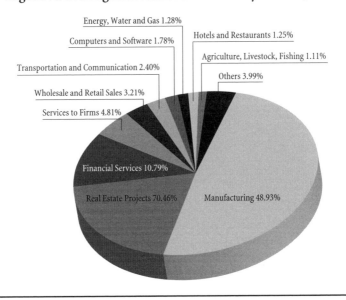

Source: People's Republic of China, Ministry of Foreign Commerce (2009).

The results of foreign investment are evident in China's foreign trade figures. The share of foreign trade by foreign firms investing in China rose from 4% in 1986 to 55% in 2008. In terms of exports, in 1986 foreign firms contributed 1.8% of the country's total exports while by 2008 their contribution had risen to 55.34%. Yet this share has declined in recent years, as may be seen in Figure 7.8. Of the total exports by foreign firms, machinery and electronic appliances make up a 70% share, followed by high technology products.

China's FDI policy is based on:[10]

- A favorable national economic environment since the reform of 1979.
- Creation of Special Economic Zones (SEZs) and open cities to focus the attraction of foreign capital geographically.
- Construction of infrastructure (starting from small villages almost completely lacking in urban development).
- Relatively low-cost labor force, with direct contracting.
- Diversified and attractive tax policy; similarly for the SEZs in relation to the rest of the country.
- Growing opportunities to participate in the domestic market.

Figure 7.8. Exports of Foreign Companies as a Percentage of China's Total Exports, 1986–2008

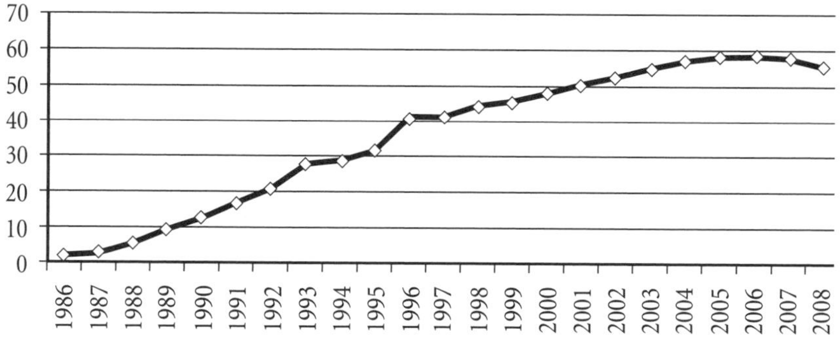

Source: People's Republic of China, Ministry of Foreign Commerce (2009).

- Political stability.
- Flexible policies regarding import and export facilities.
- Abundant natural resources.
- Policies that favor closer relations between the country and the overseas Chinese.
- Policy of "One country, two systems" to accommodate Hong Kong's capitalism.

China's broad body of law has, over time, adapted to the new laws and regulations. The laws establishing joint ventures between domestic and foreign investment were implemented in 1979, and the regulations to implement them were passed in 1983. A subsequent law allowed foreign investment companies, and the joint-venture law was amended in 1990. At first, the duration of such associations was limited to ten to thirty years, later extended to fifty to seventy years. Now foreign investment companies have direct access to both domestic and foreign markets but, in the initial phase, there were "bridge companies" to facilitate links with other domestic entities.

Foreign owners who reinvest their profits for a minimum of five years receive rebates of 40% of the taxes paid on profits; moreover, if that reinvestment is to increase exports or introduce advanced technology, they may obtain a complete rebate (corresponding to the portion of profit reinvested).The fiscal advantages granted to FDI are reflected in two documents: "Stipulations to Orient FDI" and the "Catalogue-Guide to Industrial

Activities for FDI" of 1995. In December 1997, the precepts of the Catalogue-Guide were further defined to refer to 330 production lines in which the state expressed a national interest to attract foreign direct investment.

Since the initial years, China has continued gradually to modify its FDI policies, introducing such changes as:

- Reorientation of foreign investment.
- Adjustment of customs duties to better adapt them to a world market.
- Financial administration and foreign commerce reforms to favor companies that have made foreign investments.
- Stimuli to foreign businesses to invest in central and western China.
- Protection of the interests of foreign businesses through legislation and enforcement.

Following the results of the initial foreign capital investment and the passage of considerable time, the Chinese government today is promoting foreign investment in:

- Renewal, modernization, and industrialization of agriculture.
- New and high technology industries: information and electronics, biotechnology, new materials, aerospace, and research and development centers.
- Infrastructure and basic industry such as transportation, energy, and raw materials.
- Protection of the environment and public works.
- Industries of the central, western, northeast regions of China that possess comparative advantages.

In general, Chinese policies to guide foreign investments are to:[11]

- Accord priority to foreign direct investment.
- Inject technological improvements and new administrative and professional experience.
- Broaden the use of foreign capital and improve its structure.
- Guide foreign investment to modernize the national industrial structure.
- Comply with the deadlines agreed upon with the WTO for opening the market for services: banking, insurance, telecommunication, domestic and foreign commerce, tourism, transportation, accounting, and law.

- Investigate new forms of utilizing foreign capital, including transnational acquisitions, transfer of rights and benefits over property, new kinds of international transactions, and investment reserves for the various sectors and attracting new projects.

- Attract transnational corporation investments and encourage their setting up regional headquarters in the country.

- Encourage these firms to move toward larger-scale production and exportation to the world market.

- Stimulate transnational companies to involve themselves—through mergers or acquisition of stocks—in the transformation and restructuring of Chinese state companies.

To accomplish these proposed policies, preferential tax policies for foreign investment have been established, including:[12]

Low tax rates on profits

- In general: **30% national** and 3% local;

- In the Special Economic Zones and for production companies in the Economic and Technological Development Zones: **15%;**

- In Coastal Open Economic Zones and/or old urban areas in cities that are parts of Special Economic Zones or Economic and Technological Development Zones: **24%;**

- Between 2001 and 2010, companies located in the western part of the country with economic sectors listed in the "Sectoral Catalogue for Foreign Investments" and the "Catalogue of Sectors with Comparative Advantage for Foreign Investment in the Central and Western Regions of China": **15%.**

Reduced rates or exemptions from profit taxes on long-term investments, including:

- Production projects lasting over ten years: **two years' exemption and 50% reduction for the next three years;**

- Sino-foreign joint ventures in port facility construction over more than fifteen years: **five years' exemption and five more years at 50% reduction** (this preferential policy includes airport, railroad, highway, and electric plant construction, and the Special Economic Zone of Hainan and the new zone in Pudong, Shanghai);

- Companies exporting more than 70% of their total production: **50% after period of exemption;**

- Companies making use of advanced technology: + **three years at 50% reduction.**

China's economic reforms have shown positive quantitative results. The 1979 goal of quadrupling GDP was met in 1995, ahead of the projected date of 2000. By 1996, GDP had risen to 4.4 times the 1978 level. Since 1978, China has generated one of the most intense processes of transformation in the world's economic history of the last three decades. It adopted a strategy of gradual liberalization and opening to foreign direct investment through implementation of policies that yielded results, whether or not these policies were consistent with Communist ideology.[13] In general, FDI in China is part of an integrally conceived system and is subject to continual adjustments. It plays an important role in the country's economic achievements. FDI is not the panacea of Chinese development, but it has brought more achievements than difficulties. It has been an essential component in China's takeoff as a world power, which should serve as an example to other economies.

FDI in Vietnam

The Republic of Vietnam is approximately three times the size of Cuba, with a current population of more than 86.2 million inhabitants. Its fundamental economic activity is agriculture, with 80% of the population living in rural areas. Twenty percent of the land area is arable, and more than half of it is devoted to growing rice. Other important activities include mining, lumber production, fishing, and tourism. Vietnam has abundant natural resources, oil deposits, natural gas, coal, iron, and tin; the coastline measures more than three thousand kilometers.[14] Vietnam's developing economy has performed well in recent years. Currently, it is going through a large-scale transformation in which, without ceasing to be a planned, socialist, and self-directed economy, it has been directed toward becoming a market-based economy as well. It has demonstrated potential to succeed in terms of development and the efficacy of foreign capital.

In the 1976–1987 decade, Vietnamese economic growth was limited by a number of factors. Among these were excessive centralization and planning, problems in management mechanisms, effects of the U.S. economic embargo, high defense costs, and others. In the mid-1980s, the economy grew slowly and suffered from hyperinflation, in spite of massive assistance from socialist countries.[15] After the country's reunification in 1975, Vietnam was considered one of the world's poorest nations, with per capita income under $200. In this context, many reforms were carried out with the goal of eradicating poverty and confronting old obstacles such as underdevelopment, the effects of the long war, the U.S. embargo, and border disputes with neighboring countries.

Not until 1986, as a result of the decisions taken during the Sixth Congress of the Communist Party of Vietnam, did the economy begin to undergo important transformations with the introduction of reforms, the application of market mechanisms, and overall restructuring. In that context, the lifting of the United States embargo also created a favorable climate to implement the reforms. Specifically, in 1986 the Vietnamese authorities undertook a program of reform (Doi Moi) that began with small changes in the rural sector. The goal of the development strategy was to establish a "socialist-oriented market economy" capable of inserting itself in the existing dynamic of the world economy, and to find solutions to economic and social problems along with sources of financing to carry out the new strategy. Vietnam thus adapted to the collapse of the Soviet-led Council for Mutual Economic Assistance (COMECON) and the loss of Soviet aid without a drop in production. Within a very short time, the reforms eliminated collective farms and restored the system of family farms; liberalized most price controls; authorized and created new private enterprises in various fields; liberalized regulation of commerce and investment; set up a single exchange rate; reduced budget deficits; and subjected state enterprises to financial discipline.

Vietnam began to integrate rapidly into the world economy, thanks to considerable growth in productive capacity generated by the changes in economic structure, institutions, development policy, and administration. In 1988, the National Assembly approved a policy of external economic opening and adopted the first foreign investment law. The next year, the reform plan described above began implementation. Although Vietnam was not a member of the International Monetary Fund (IMF) at that time, the plan was discussed with IMF experts because creditor nations continued demanding payment of the country's debt.

In 1990 a law for protection of private property was approved, as was a new constitution. In 1993, an agrarian reform law granted peasant families usufruct rights to land for twenty years, and for up to fifty years in some cases. In the foreign sector, in 1991 the state eliminated its former monopoly on foreign trade, which made it easier for enterprises to trade abroad. As part of the pursuit of new financing sources, new policies favored savings and investment. These included the creation of a capital market, higher interest rates, and permission to open individual hard-currency savings accounts in commercial banks. The foreign debt was renegotiated and ties were made with international financial institutions including the IMF and

Figure 7.9. Foreign Direct Investment in Vietnam, 1990–2008
(millions of U.S. dollars)

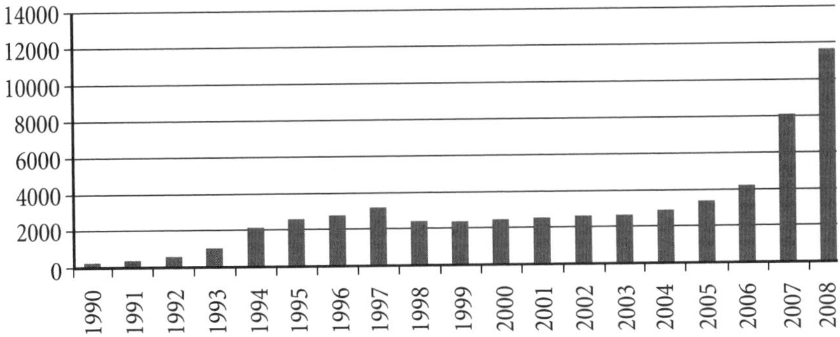

Source: Vietnam, General Statistics Office (2009).

the World Bank; Vietnam joined the Association of South East Asian Nations (ASEAN) as well.

Since 1986, growth in Vietnam's exports has been impressive, with an annual rate exceeding 25%. Though domestic companies have driven this growth in many fields, FDI provided capital, technology, knowledge of business administration, and access to markets, as well as other less tangible contributions, such as the importation of new ideas. Policies implemented to attract investment have made growing capital flows possible. Thus, from unimpressive levels in 1990, the flow of capital into Vietnam grew in six years to $2 billion a year and it is now over $11 billion a year (see Figure 7.9).

The first FDI law was approved in 1987, followed in 1990 and 1992 by two more laws containing amendments and additions. The second of those recognized new forms of investment, lengthened the time horizon of the associations, and introduced changes that implied a wider opening and a more flexible foreign investment process. Other rulings and regulations have complemented these laws, giving rise to the following basic forms of investment: contractual associations, joint ventures, wholly foreign companies, companies that operate with the EPZs (Export Processing Zones), and construction-operation-transfer contracts.

The sector with the fastest FDI growth has been manufacturing, which represents 50% of total effective investment. Other projects that stand out are in real estate, mining, and services (including investment growth in transportation, postal services, communications in general, and tourism). The main investing countries are Taiwan, South Korea, Malaysia, Japan, Singapore, British Virgin Islands, United States, Hong Kong, and Thailand.

Table 7.3. Foreign Direct Investment Projects in Vietnam by Type of Economic Activity, 1988–2008

	Number of Projects	Registered Capital (millions of USD)
Total	10,981	163,607.2
Manufacturing	6,778	81,247.8
Real estate, rentals to firms	1,788	37,894.6
Mines and quarries	126	10,583.6
Hotels and restaurants	308	8,970.8
Construction	396	7,300.1
Transportation; warehouses and communication	295	6,954.4
Agriculture and forestry	535	3,600.7
Electricity, gas and water	31	1,941.4
Recreation, culture, and sports	116	1,689.3
Health and social work	61	994.3
Financial intermediaries	66	925.3
Wholesale and retail sales	137	696.7
Fishing	162	535.4
Education and training	113	233.5
Community, social, and personal activities	69	39.3

As in China, the regional distribution of these projects is not very equitable. The southeast, north-central, north-central coast regions and the Red River and Mekong River deltas absorb 90% of the invested capital. Nonetheless, in June 2009, not including petroleum and natural gas investment, fifty-eight localities had direct investment of foreign capital. The most attractive area was Ho Chi Minh City, followed by Ba Ria-Vung Tau, and the capital city of Hanoi in third place. There are evident asymmetries between the north and south of the country in terms of total investment received. This is a result of the different levels of existing development, including in the period before the United States was at war against Vietnam, and also because of the financial resources given to the south, where the Saigon regime had been supported by the United States.

Legal environment for foreign investment

Companies with 100% foreign capital operate as "limited responsibility societies," and the non-resident owner may appoint a duly authorized representative in Vietnam. Companies operating in the EPZs develop support services for production of exportable goods and for the export business itself. They are structured as limited responsibility societies as well. Construction-operation-transfer contracts are variants used to attract large sums of capital, principally for infrastructure construction. The foreign partner builds the infrastructural component and puts it into operation. Once the investors have recovered their investment and obtained a margin of profit, the component becomes state property without the state having to expend any money. It is worth pointing out that FDI by persons born in Vietnam is restricted. However, there are no restrictions as to who can be a foreign investor, with the exception of emigrants who have criminal cases pending in Vietnamese courts. In general, participation of Vietnamese residing abroad is encouraged "as their contribution to national reconstruction."

Sectors toward which investment is guided
Foreign capital is channeled toward large economic programs (food production, consumer goods, and export lines), production that makes intensive use of Vietnam's available resources (especially the labor force), and infrastructure construction. Investment in tourism is also stimulated, as well as in ship repair, port and airport services, and other areas. The law allows investment in any sector of the Vietnamese economy, however, although that investment is regulated through the various levels of the project approval process.

Approval processes vary depending on the size of the investment and the area toward which it is directed, with three categories of investment labeled A, B, and C. Contract lengths may extend to a maximum of fifty years, although in necessary cases this may be further extended to seventy years by government authorization with approval from the Council of State. In the hiring practices of firms associated with foreign capital, Vietnamese citizens must have priority. Foreigners may be hired only for positions requiring technical qualifications that the domestic labor force cannot meet. An employment agency sorts out these issues.

Fiscal environment
Companies with foreign investment and individuals and organizations participating in these companies are taxed at a rate of 15%-25% on profits. If part of the earnings is reinvested for three or more years, the company receives a rebate equivalent to the share of taxes already paid on the reinvested profits. Tax exemptions may be granted for a maximum term of two years dating from the time when profits begin. Such benefits are distributed in accordance with the area of the investment, the amount of capital supplied, the exports resulting from the business, its nature, and its duration. There is also a required contribution to Social Security in accord with Vietnamese law, which amounts to a 10% payroll tax paid by the company. In addition, foreign individuals or organizations must pay a tax on earnings remitted abroad, which varies according to the individuals' or organizations'

Figure 7.10. GDP Growth Rates in Vietnam, 1978–2009 (percent)

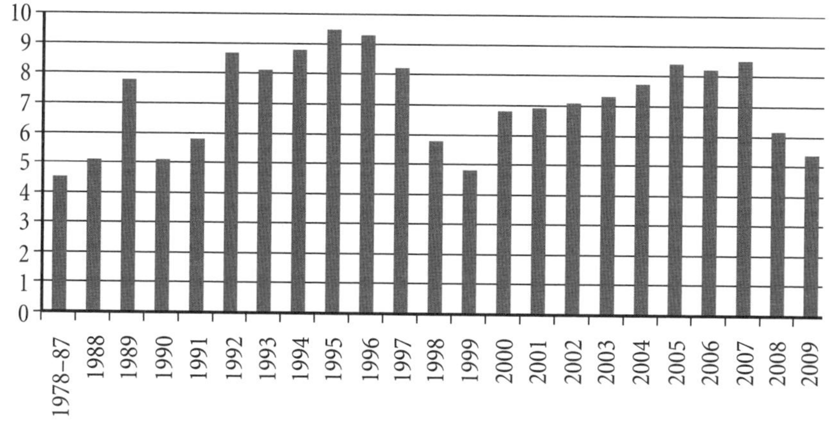

Source: Vietnam, General Statistics Office (2009).

contribution to the company. Domestic or foreign employees of any company with foreign investment (including contractual organizations) pay taxes on their personal incomes in accordance with Vietnamese tax law. Apart from the company's payroll tax, they also pay 10% of their salaries as their contribution to a local Social Security fund. Foreign investors receive guarantees that they may repatriate their share of business earnings as well as payments for technology transfer and other services. Investors and foreign workers are allowed to buy houses while they are living in Vietnam.

As a result of the Vietnamese reforms, its economic indicators show positive results in which FDI continually increases. The year 1991 marked the beginning of an era of recovery in which the average rate of growth reached 7.5%. This growth rate rose at a time when commercial relations with formerly socialist countries deteriorated most sharply, even though these had previously represented 46.3% of Vietnam's exports and 73.5% of its imports.[16] Real income has grown at an annual rate of 7.3% over the last ten years. When the World Bank resumed relations with Vietnam in 1993, per capita income was $170. It rose to $620 in 2007 and could reach $1,000 in 2010.[17] Industry plays an increasing role in the structure of Vietnam's GDP. From a 22.7% share in 1990, it doubled by 2008. Services also occupy a significant place in the Vietnamese economy, although their share is nearly constant; the service sector has seen a notable increase in transportation, postal, and telecommunications activity. Agriculture's share of GDP has been declining, in spite of the country's undeniable successes as a producer and world exporter of farm products including coffee and rice.

According to Vietnam's General Statistics Office, in 2008 industrial production in the state sector grew by 8.7%, in the non-state sector by 24.1%, and in the foreign investment sector by 20.9%. The foreign investment sector accounts for 37.2% of Vietnamese industrial production and 57.4% of total exports. As in the case of China, Vietnam's transition toward a competitive market economy is quite advanced and promotes the country's economic growth. Private firms, which had no significant activity in 1993, are currently responsible for more than 47% of the yearly investments. In recent years, state enterprises have also grown in spite of internal and external competition. More than 75% of state enterprises are profitable, with net earnings, and with margins of profit on capital between 7% and 8% a year.

Privatization has been limited to certain sectors, but many enterprises have been privatized over the past five years. The number of state enterprises was cut in half, to fewer than 3,000, thus making room for expansion of private companies. Today, private firms supply 65% of manufactured goods and more than 70% of non-petroleum exports, as Vietnam is becoming an integral part of international production and distribution chains. Vietnamese authorities attach special importance to private domestic investment, especially to develop small and medium-sized firms. In real terms, investment by state enterprises probably does not exceed 15% of annual GDP.

Vietnam's accomplishments in the economic sphere are beyond question. Nonetheless, other difficulties remain: insufficient development of

Figure 7.11. Vietnam's International Reserves, 1990–2008

(millions of dollars)

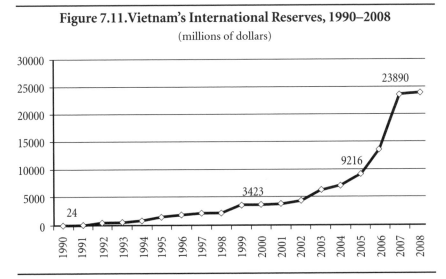

Source: Asian Development Bank (2008).

financial markets, weak competition in the domestic market, and growing imbalance in income distribution with a resulting widening gap between higher- and lower-income sectors. One striking statistic is international currency reserves. Vietnam had practically no foreign reserves in the early 1990s, but it has now accumulated approximately $23 billion.

To summarize, the Asian region illustrates how foreign companies have accelerated these countries' progress in the realm of dynamic comparative advantage. In recent years, we see a predominance of Asian FDI entering China and Vietnam, which demonstrates a world tendency toward the formation of large economic blocs. In the Chinese economy, the opening to foreign participation has spread to the entire country and all economic areas; from the coast to the interior, from agriculture and processing industries to basic industry, infrastructure, finance, insurance, and commerce. The Special Economic Zones in the countries under study showed satisfactory results from the beginning.

FDI flows evolved upwards in all the countries under study, especially in China, which in 2008 received more than $108 billion. In the past four years, China has ranked third in the world in volume of FDI received, and first among underdeveloped countries. Investments made in their countries of origin by overseas Chinese societies or Vietnamese individuals resident abroad have been significant over these years as a result of national policies designed to stimulate such investment. In the structure of FDI by sectors in China, we note a preponderance of investment in the secondary sector, largely in textiles, clothing, communication devices and electronic appliances, toys, processed food, chemicals, rubber, hydrocarbons, minerals, iron and steel, machinery, and transportation equipment. In recent years, there has also been investment growth in insurance and real estate.

Both China and Vietnam established strategies to acquire foreign technology as an input to achieve delayed industrial transformation. They imported primarily materials such as food and energy, and undertook large-scale export of manufactured goods—and Vietnam has seen a notable development of agricultural exports. FDI has served China and Vietnam as part of an integrally conceived system, subject to continual adjustment, playing an important role in each country's economic achievements, with a high correlation among indicators, although FDI cannot be considered a panacea for development.

Foreign Direct Investment in Cuba

In the early 1990s, Cuba faced a serious economic crisis that gave rise to a reform period characterized as a process of adjustment, management of the crisis, and opening to the international economy. The first efforts sought to create a foreign opening to acquire, as quickly as possible, the external resources that had been reduced to minimal levels by the loss of Cuba's integration with the economies of the ex-socialist countries. Solving the problems linked to external financing of the Cuban economy became a major challenge because of Cuba's inability to generate the levels of internal savings needed for growth and development. The most important aspects of the economic opening to the outside world were the promotion and acceptance of foreign capital investment, the restructuring of foreign trade, and the accelerated development of international tourism.

The Cuban government began to analyze how foreign investment could benefit the country without compromising Cuba's resources or its sovereignty. To achieve satisfactory results would require a complicated set of decisions. The conclusion reached was that the most practical avenue for obtaining the necessary financial resources (and, hence, the technology that would enable Cuba to make its products and services competitive) was foreign direct investment. FDI thus began to play a significant role in financing Cuban development. The process of opening to foreign capital initially focused on solving practical problems in Cuban economic growth. Among these was the need to diversify exports in both quality and quantity, improve the acquisition of raw materials, secure capital, enter new markets, and introduce modern management practices.

The legislation governing FDI in Cuba, still in effect, is Law 77 of 1995 and Resolution 5290 of the Executive Committee of the Council of Ministers. Although there have been some modifications to adjust to current conditions, the reasons for attracting business with foreign entities remain the same. The goal is to:

1. Complement domestic efforts to reach high levels of economic and technological development in the sectors and regions the nation has prioritized.

2. Seek new export markets, competitive technologies, and financing, particularly over the long term.

3. Promote projects that would contribute to the National Import Substitution Program, stimulate domestic production, develop industrial activity, and stimulate exports.

4. Adapt these efforts to changing world conditions and to Cuba's concrete needs at specific moments in its development.

As an incentive to investment, Cuba continues to offer initial guarantees, although this process has not unfolded without difficulties and missteps, as indicated by the number of partners who have ended their contracts with Cuba. Arrangements vary according to the length of the association, the economic sector in which it occurs, and the foreign country involved. The investment incentives that Cuba offers are in the areas of tax-free repatriation of dividends, capping taxes at 30% on profits and 25% on payroll, and additional incentives that depend on the nature of the business, its size, and its degree of activity. Cuba emphasizes bilateral relations and has signed a total of sixty-two agreements for the reciprocal promotion and protection of investments with seventy-one countries, and eleven agreements to avoid double taxation.

The incentives that Cuba began offering in the early 1990s still remain and its government has added others; these could be broadened if the U.S. blockade on Cuba were to be loosened to allow U.S. nationals to do business with Cuba. Experience has shown that many foreign businesses have left Cuba after merging with companies based in the United States. At the end of 2009, there were 307 foreign businesses operating in Cuba, 75% of them in the form of joint ventures (international economic associations); Figure 7.12 shows the operations by type of agreement, revealing a change from the initial period.

The number of international economic associations (joint ventures) has dropped, as can be seen in Figure 7.13, but that does not mean this mode of investment is in great decline; rather, it reflects internal rearrangements. While the number of joint ventures had been trending upward until 2002, it has declined because of a number of factors. Some enterprises failed to achieve agreed-upon objectives in their original contracts; for example, joint

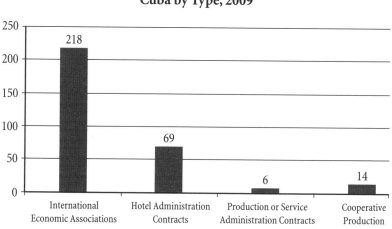

Figure 7.12. Total Foreign Direct Investment Businesses in Cuba by Type, 2009

Figure 7.13. Number of Joint Ventures with FDI in Cuba, 1990–2009

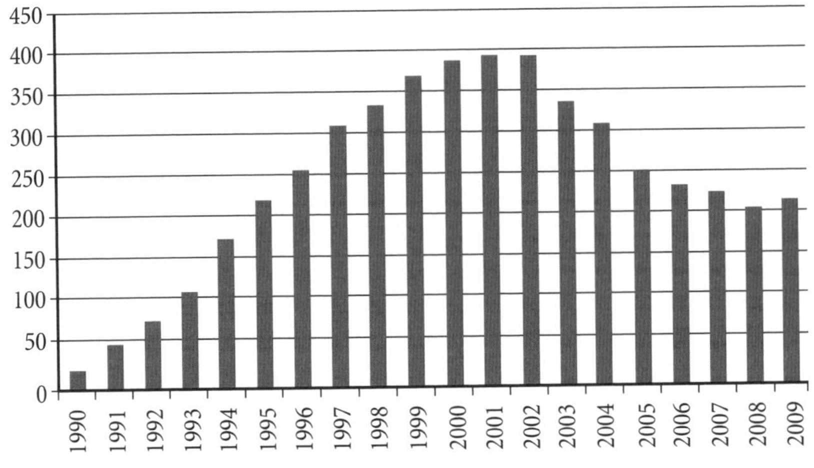

Source: Cuba, Ministry of Foreign Investment and Commerce.

ventures shifted their production to a product that was not in the original contract. In other cases, associations experienced losses in their balance sheets or failed to meet export targets stipulated in their contracts, which the Cuban government then did not renew. In addition, Cuba has shifted its strategy to prioritizing trade with specific foreign partners, such as Venezuela since 2006; these relationships create fewer economic associations.

As a result of the reorganization of joint ventures undertaken by the Cuban government in 2003, there has been an annual increase in approvals of new associations with foreign capital since 2005. This may indicate that the winds today are blowing more toward an increase in these kinds of businesses, while privileging select countries. Of the new joint ventures approved in 2007, sixteen were with the Bolivarian Republic of Venezuela, and most of those newly approved in 2008 and 2009 were also with that country. In general, Cuba's largest foreign partners are in Spain, Canada, Venezuela, and Italy. There are also many joint ventures with firms from other countries, but they are counted in the aggregate, not by individual country (see Figure 7.14).

The sectoral distribution of foreign firms has changed little, with the largest share still in the industrial sector (especially basic industry, within which mining and petroleum stand out), followed by tourism. Less investment is to be found in light industry, construction, transportation, food,

Figure 7.14. Number of Joint Ventures by Country, 2008

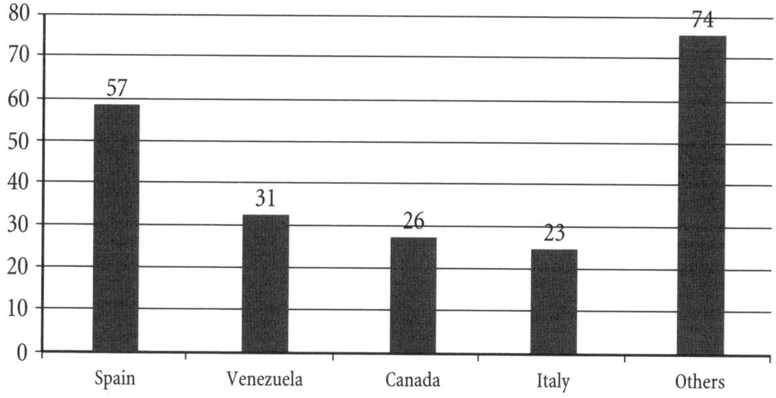

57 Spain
31 Venezuela
26 Canada
23 Italy
74 Others

Source: Cuba, Ministry of Foreign Investment and Commerce.

and telecommunications. The number of such ventures in high-value-added or high-tech areas is still minimal, with nine ventures based in the Polo Científico (a scientific research and development park). It should be noted that one of Cuba's most important assets is its human resources, and that the developing countries that have made the greatest strides in world commerce in recent decades have done so through the development of strong high- or medium-technology sectors.

Figure 7.15. Number of Joint Ventures by Sector, 2008

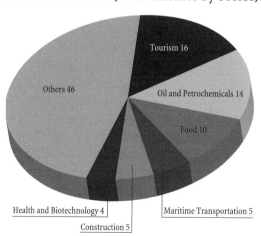

Tourism 16
Others 46
Oil and Petrochemicals 14
Food 10
Health and Biotechnology 4
Construction 5
Maritime Transportation 5

Source: Cuba, Ministry of Foreign Investment and Commerce.

As a result of the U.S. embargo, Cuba is subject to the impediments posed by a foreign law that restricts its access to FDI resources. Consequently, Cuba is rated a "risk country." Thus, whatever investment flows to Cuba acquires extra importance. Although a simple comparison of investment flows into Cuba with flows into other countries of the region can be of some analytic use, it will understate just how important FDI is for Cuba.

From 2004 on, the winnowing of cooperative production contracts, which had reached 441 at the end of 2003, accelerated; at the end of 2007, there were only seventeen such contracts, and fourteen in 2009. The causes of the decrease were the failure to obtain the expected results, whether financial or economic; the subjective assessments of firms and managers; and a change in the policy toward attracting such firms and how they were viewed as contributing to the future development of the Cuban economy. The remaining contracts are utilized in several areas, among them the Ministry of Transportation, Ministry of Basic Industry, Ministry of Food Industries, the Ministry of Metallurgical-Mechanical and Electronic Industries, and others. In addition to these fourteen cooperative production contracts, there were seven production or service administrative contracts and sixty-nine hotel administration contracts at the end of 2008.

Two decades after the renewed presence of foreign capital in Cuba, and despite the decline in the number of operating ventures involving such capital, existing ventures have matured with positive results. Joint ventures have steadily increased their total sales of goods and services, reaching nearly $5.3 billion in 2008 (see Figure 7.16), while their exports rose to $1.9 billion and direct income to the country totaled $1.07 billion, though decreasing in 2009. Thus, the government policy of rigorous selectivity in foreign investment is reflected in an annual drop in the number of joint ventures alongside continued growth in their main economic indicators. This suggests a few conclusions. First, the liquidated firms have not had significant enough size to affect the overall functioning of the economy. Second, the remaining firms have continually improved their efficiency and productivity and achieved high-volume economic outcomes. Third, among other factors, these foreign ventures have exercised more exacting control and budgeting in their operations and have thus been able to sustain positive results under what some would argue are not necessarily the most accommodating conditions for business operations. Finally, rising world prices for basic products have allowed improvement in the sales and exports of joint ventures operating in Cuba, such as nickel.

The degree of concentration of foreign enterprises operating in Cuba must also be stressed. No more than seven such operations represent more than 80% of sales, and thus of exports. The economic activities of these ventures

Figure 7.16. Joint-Venture Sales, Exports and Income Earnings, 1992–2009 (millions of dollars)

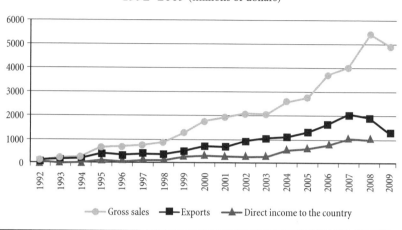

Source: Cuba, Ministry of Foreign Investment and Commerce.

are concentrated in nickel, tobacco and tobacco products, citrus fruit, tourism, and communications.

In a comparison of the average annual growth rate of these fundamental indicators for FDI to the economic indicators for the country as a whole, such as GDP, FDI figures are higher. This suggests very satisfactory results for FDI, and the real significance of these businesses must be recognized. In almost all the productive areas in which Cuba has shown its best production or export results, foreign capital is present in one form or another. This should point toward the potential for further developing such businesses, including in areas where the need is greatest or in the consumer sector. Comparison of the country's total exports of goods to the exports of economic associations involving foreign capital reveals that the latter have contributed a high and growing share (see Figure 7.17), above 50% in recent years.

Cuba has not renounced the attraction of FDI as part of its economic policy. It maintains a list of priortiy projects for investment. At this moment those priorities are[18]:

1. Tourism—construction projects to expand room capacities in the central and eastern regions and create extra-hotel infrastructure (such as new golf courses, marinas, and water parks).

2. Mining and petroleum—projects to explore for petroleum on spec, especially in the Gulf of Mexico Exclusive Zone, and exploit and develop serpentine minerals (saprolitic ores) and black and red nickel tailings.

Figure 7.17. Joint-Venture Exports in Relation to National Merchandise Exports, 1993–2009 (percent)

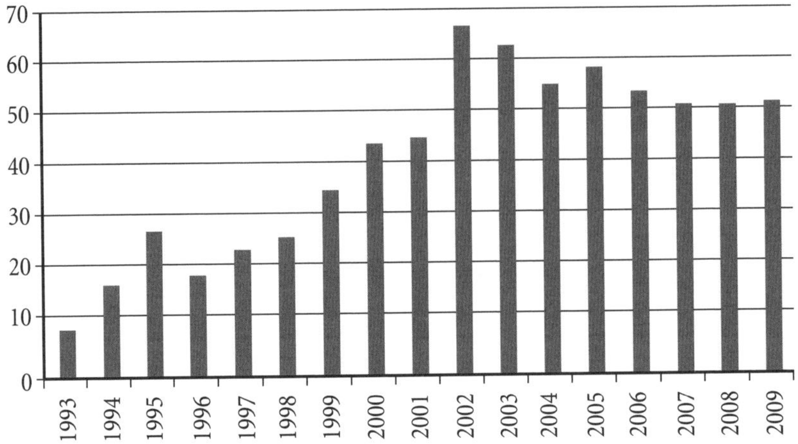

Source: Cuba, Ministry of Foreign Investment and Commerce.

3. Geological surveys and on-spec prospecting for mineral deposits, especially gold, copper, and zinc.

4. Infrastructure – construction projects to aid exploration for petroleum, nickel, and other mineral products, and highway and port development.

5. Agriculture – develop post-harvest collection, treatment, and distribution logistics; develop non-traditional sectors such as ecotourism and agrotourism.

6. Packaging industry – projects to stimulate production of packaging materials including aluminum containers, cardboard boxes, glass bottles and jars, and polyethylene and polypropylene packaging.

7. Renewable energy, including wind energy.

In the case of tourism, joint ventures operate some 5,500 rooms in fourteen hotels. There were sixty-five hotel administration contracts involving fourteen hotel groups, which account for 51% of total rooms. In addition to the fourteen joint-venture hotels, the wave of demand emanating from the sector's rapid development contributed to the creation of about seventy joint ventures in other sectors of the economy. The majority of these businesses, which support the tourist industry, arose in the areas of construction, food supply, beer and other beverages, bottled water, textiles and

Table 7.4. Hotel Rooms under Domestic and Foreign Administration in Cuba, 1990–2009

	Total	*With foreign administration contracts*		
Year	Rooms	Hotels	Rooms	%
1990	12,866	3	1,330	10
1995	24,233	29	8,424	35
1999	32,260	46	14,221	44
2001	37,225	53	17,420	47
2003	40,963	52	18,707	45
2004	41,050	54	19,124	48
2005	42,600	50	18,779	48
2006	43,500	52	19,326	44
2007	46,500	57	22,705	52
2008	48,000	62	24,167	50
2009	49,000	65	25,375	51

Source: Cuba, Ministry of Foreign Investment and Commerce.

perfume, air and ground transportation, agriculture, telephone communications, and air conditioning.

In terms of FDI trends for Cuba, it is likely that there will be a change in the tendency to reduce the number of joint ventures and the amount of foreign investment from some countries. The performance indicators for joint venture investments, especially those for sales, exports, and national income, will continue to rise thanks to the improvement in export prices.

The domestic products that have shown the greatest economic growth in recent years are associated with various types of arrangements with foreign capital. These include beverages, tobacco and tobacco products, nickel, petroleum, soaps and perfumes, and tourism. In addition, ventures have been initiated to begin the exploration and production of fuels; it is likely that these will remain popular in the Gulf of Mexico Special Zone. Hotel administration contracts will continue in order to develop that important sector.

The Cuban government's policy of according priority to selected partners does not exclude business arrangements with internationally prestigous companies that can offer technology and capital to develop consumer goods, whose production has lagged behind during the revival years of the nation's economy. Clearly, sufficient supply of these goods has been secured through their import in the short term, but in the long term, it would be advantageous to Cuba to develop its own capacity to produce these goods. For now, the key advantages of production ventures with foreign firms are job creation and fostering a new management culture.

The Treatment of FDI in China and Vietnam: Object Lessons for Cuba

Though there are important differences among Cuba, China, and Vietnam, the economic transformations or reforms undertaken in China and Vietnam occurred in conditions similar to those facing Cuba today. China and Vietnam made changes in socialist systems in their previously underdeveloped economies that had not managed to solve the problems of underdevelopment through centralized planning and the classic Eastern European socialist model. Further, the reforms in China and Vietnam were carried out by each country's respective Communist Party.

Major similarities observed in transformations in China and Vietnam:

1. Agricultural transformations played an important role, leading to increases in production and productivity.

2. Inefficient enterprises were eliminated or transformed through cooperativization, privatization, or association with foreign capital in search of international competitiveness.

3. The opening of the economy to various forms of property had a positive impact on economic growth.

4. Broader monetary-mercantile relations, especially the role of the market in the context of directed planning, led to a marked rise in economic growth and efficiency.

5. A significant external opening to large annual inflows of foreign capital increased exports.

6. As a result, the macroeconomic climate of these economies improved steadily as seen in the rise of annual average GDP growth rates, a sustained increase in international monetary reserves, and other indicators.

7. Individual consumption increased steadily through the granting of credits for consumption, higher salaries, and other incentives.

8. In both China and Vietnam, economic growth co-occurred with strong institutional reorganization.

9. In the case of Vietnam, rejoining international organization including the World Bank allowed access to important sources of credit.

10. The reforms in both China and Vietnam include deep transformations in other areas, especially in their financial systems.

11. There is a strong relationship between FDI and exports in China and Vietnam, and between exports and the growth of each country's international monetary reserves.

12. Foreign capital provided by the so-called overseas Chinese or Chinese communities in Hong Kong proved crucial, providing more than 70% of capital flows in some cases.

Similarities in foreign capital attractiveness to China and Vietnam:

1. They have adopted a variety of approaches and restrictions to attract foreign capital, but their decisions have been very pragmatic. For example, 70% of direct foreign investments in China are by just one hundred foreign companies.

2. Legislation governing direct foreign investment in China and Vietnam has been modified regularly as such companies have advanced.

3. Very favorable tax incentives steered foreign investment to particular geographic areas or economic sectors in need of economic stimulus.

4. Signficant results of foreign investment in China are evident in its foreign trade. In 2008, FDI accounted for 55% of total exports.

5. From a structural point of view, FDI's role among the sources of investment financing in China was that of a *complement to domestic financing sources.*

6. In China, the duration of association agreements with foreign capital was initially limited to ten-to-thirty years, but later extended to fifty-to-seventy.

7. Today, businesses with foreign investment have direct access to domestic and international markets, but in the initial phase there were "bridge companies" to facilitate ties with other entities within the country.

8. In China, companies with foreign capital participation hire their workers through a free labor market.

9. Foreign businesses that reinvest their earnings for at least five years receive 40% tax rebates, but they may obtain a full rebate of taxes levied on the portion that had been reinvested if they reinvest for at least five years to increase exports or introduce advanced technologies.

10. China offers many incentives to firms in agriculture or forestry, or those that locate operations in remote or underdeveloped regions. These incentives include tax holidays for the first five years when they show a profit.

11. There are also tax breaks or exemptions over various time periods for certain desired activities, especially in infrastructure such as port construction, or—in China—for access to cutting-edge technology.

12. In Vietnam, construction-operation-transfer contracts offer a way to attract large-scale capital, fundamentally for infrastructure construction.

13. The participation of Vietnamese living abroad is encouraged "as a contribution to national reconstruction."

14. Vietnam offers wide guarantees for foreign investors regarding repatriation of their shares of company profits, payments for technology transfer, and other services. Investors and foreign employers may buy housing while they are living in Vietnam.

15. The foreign investment sector now accounts for 37.2% of Vietnam's industrial production and 57.4% of its total exports.

In summary, these Asian experiences canprovide insights to Cuba on how to offer a larger role to, and increase the utilization of, foreign capital. Foreign financial resources are scarce and they are being attracted to Asian economies not only because of the benefits offered by each individual country, but also because Southeast Asia is the world's most dynamic area today and will be so in coming years.

In Cuba, current legislation and the Ministry of Foreign Investment and Commerce are not able to stimulate investment by themselves, if that direction were to be chosen. Cuban laws affecting foreign capital are broad and include elements that could attract a large flow of foreign capital, but there is no apparent intention on the government's part to make large-scale use of this possibility, at least not in the short run.

Judging on the basis of the Chinese and Vietnamese experiences, foreign direct investments are unlikely to be attracted without also developing domestic investment. Another point is that FDI increased in China and Vietnam only after domestic economic growth took off. In other words, this was a result of a comprehensive reform strategy, although it was very gradual.

The Asian experience shows that the rest of a country's institutions must also be aligned with the objective of attracting FDI, facilitating rather than obstructing the flow of such resources. In areas such as infrastructure, the recovery periods for invested capital are very long, which requires policies of tax exemption for specified periods or the presence of wholly owned foreign companies for a longer-than-average time period. The decisive roles played by foreign investment in Vietnam and China's advance toward economic development were authorized as part and parcel of integrated economic reform projects approved by the respective Communist Party Congresses of those countries. That is, they formed part of integrated national reforms.

Endnotes

1. Julio Díaz Vázquez and Eduardo Regalado, *China: El despertar del Dragón* (Havana: Editorial Ciencias Sociales, 2007).

2. United Nations Conference on Trade and Development (UNCTAD), "World Investment Report 2009: Transnational Corporations, Agricultural Production and Development" (New York: UNCTAD, 2009).

3. UNCTAD, 11.

4. Juan González, "China: Comercio exterior y crecimiento económico en el camino al mercado,"*Revista de Comercio Exterior de México* 46/12 (December 1996): 981–87.

5. World Bank, "Patterns of Foreign Direct Investment in China," 7.

6. Ministry of Commerce, People's Republic of China, "Invest in China," November, 2009. www.fdi.gov.cn.

7. Miriam Fernández, "Situación Actual y Perspectivas de la economía China y potencialidades de sus relaciones con América Latina y el Caribe" (Caracas: SELA, 1993).

8. Elvira Castro, "Sobre la reforma económica y la inversión extranjera en China," *Economía y Desarrollo* 118/2 (1995): 148–172 and "Beijing Informa," *Semanario Chino* 20, May 20, 1997, p. 23.

9. Spanish Economic and Commercial Office, Beijing, 2009.

10. Elvira Castro, "Sobre la reforma económica."

11. Yuming Chen, Commercial Office statement, Embassy of China in Santiago de Chile, 2005, and www.fdi.gov.cn.

12. Ibid.

13. P. A. Villezca Becerra, "Las reformas en China y su éxito económico: una breve descripción" in *Observatorio de la Economía y la Sociedad de China* 7 (June 2008). Full text available at http://www.eumed.net/rev/china/.

14. Elvira Castro and Magalys Macías, "El entorno económico y la inversión extranjera en Vietnam," *Economía y Desarrollo* 2 (1996): 148–172.

15. World Bank, *World Development Report 1996: From Plan to Market* (Washington, DC: World Bank, 1997).

16. Julián Coubert, "Voluntad con ojos rasgados," *Revista Bohemia* 19 (1987).

17. "La AIF en Acción en VietNam. Bases para un crecimiento sostenido," http://www.worldbank.org/ida.

18. Working papers published by Cuba's Ministry of Foreign Investment and Commerce and the presentation "Oportunidades de Negocios en Cuba," April 2008.

Commentary

Cuba and the Challenges of Globalization

Pedro Monreal González

Cuba could emerge as a developed economy within twenty-five years, and one of the catalysts for that transformation could be globalization. Globalization should not be viewed merely as the international context of development, nor should it be viewed exclusively as a source of challenges and obstacles to that process. Rather, it should be seen as a mechanism that creates opportunities for development. Making use of these opportunities could lead to extremely positive economic accomplishments characterized by a high level of value-creation based on increasingly complex technology, conditions that globalization imposes on contemporary development processes.

The predominance of radical changes in the economic system, the scarce margin for political error, and the fact that the global economy harshly penalizes slow rates of change should be factors of particular importance for Cuba. In order to develop within a context of globalization, therefore, Cuba would require an exceptional economic trajectory that very few governments have been able to manage successfully in the past fifty years. Does the Cuban state have the qualities needed to undertake such a trajectory, or can it acquire them? This question should occupy a central place in the country's economic and political discussion because it is at this level—and not at the level of specific policy measures or adaptations—where the keys to the country's progress can be found.

In a strict sense, the entity facing the challenges of globalization is not the Cuban economy but rather the Cuban state. Although a process with the characteristics just described must involve a complex framework of economic, political, and social actors of many types, the state (and not simply the government) has to be the main guarantor of the significant transformations in fundamental economic institutions and property relations needed for such national development. To put it another way, development must be seen as the state's principal function, and that public function must be carried out differently from how it has been up till now. This is not a matter of ideological preferences. Cuba's historical experience and its often-overlooked character as a small island economy leave no room for another course of action.

Exploring such a hypothesis—that globalization can offer a platform for Cuba's development—requires addressing two issues: first, whether such a supposition is even plausible (whether globalization could truly offer opportunities for Cuban development); second, the chances that such development would actually occur in that context.

The first topic implies an examination of the process of globalization itself, and the practical effects of such an examination on the concepts that must accompany an appropriate development strategy. The second, the probability that such development will take place, depends not only on the nature of globalization but more strongly on the local development model, economic system, and quality of institutions operating within that larger globalized framework. Thus the first examination explores mostly "exogenous" factors, while the second is more closely related to "endogenous" factors, or at least factors that are largely determined by "internal" activities dependent on state action.

Globalization as an Opportunity for Development

Globalization, of course, is a hotly debated issue that for some time has occupied a prominent place in academic and political discussion. My goal here is not a thorough study of this complex and multifaceted topic but rather a focus on three aspects that I believe are key to understanding Cuba's development prospects: a) an understanding of globalization as a recurring process of restructuring in the international economy that is constantly closing some spaces for international specialization while opening up others; b) the fact that globalization does not occupy the entire space of the world economy and, therefore, even if many processes of international respecialization occur as part of globalization, other activities operate within the interstices it leaves unoccupied; and c) the fact that being a small island economy conditions at least two of the Cuban economy's characteristics: one, that international specialization is not merely an option, and two, that the range of international specialization will always be relatively narrow.

As mentioned above, globalization is a phenomenon subject to many analyses. Therefore, the term has been defined in varying ways. In these pages, I emphasize the dimension of globalization as a restructuring of the world economy that affects all contemporary actors; the determinant elements of this process are both technological and political.

Contemporary development is a complex multidimensional procedure and so any attempt to unilaterally emphasize just one of its dimensions can weaken an analysis. Nonetheless, without underestimating the importance of frequently discussed dimensions of development (for instance, structural change, social justice, and sustainability), I want to highlight the dimension of development whereby a substantial part of a country's labor force acquires and exercises new technological skills. For more than two decades now, the primary requisite for development in this sense has been insertion into global value chains.

The development process in a globalized context is essentially equivalent to a competition to acquire the material and technological bases of contemporary production. This not the same as a simple notion of a country's "adaptive" insertion into the world economy. The main difference between developed and less developed countries today is not that the former possess a complete productive structure that includes all the fundamental productive activities in each of their phases, while the latter do not possess these. The essential difference today is in the degree of participation and relative position that each country has in the global production chains that make up the world economy, the control they exercise over these chains, and their prospects of being able to move up to the higher levels. Thus, one of the main analytical lessons to draw from examining a few cases of economic development in recent decades is that an absolutely necessary condition (although not a sufficient one) has been significant insertion of the country in the global economy.

The corollary, therefore, is that development in conditions of globalization demands renunciation of any notion of isolated or self-reliant development, and requires redefining the unit of analysis in development strategy. This does not mean, in any way, abandonment of national interests or the nation-state's active role in the development process. Nor does it mean giving up the most rigorous criticism of the prevailing international order. It does mean understanding that national interests are better served today if the nation-state recognizes the limits of any course of action based on the assumption that there is room to choose patterns of development with relative independence from, or underestimation of, the global economic dynamic. That is to say, the assumptions that in other historical periods could have justified notions of self-reliant development are not viable today. The state can and must continue to promote development but according to new and different premises.

Nonetheless, this corollary is frequently challenged, among other reasons, because globalization does not have universal reach nor is it a homogeneous process. There remain market segments, many geographical areas of the planet, and a considerable part of the world's population that—although they serve globalization, for instance, as reserves—are outside or only very tenuously inserted into the world economy and barely share in its benefits. These interstices within globalization can be of various sorts, some economic and some political. They have coped in various ways, one of which is the conscious design of economic survival tactics and sometimes development strategies constructed according to an interstitial approach. In fact, many countries have, in practice, put together dual economic models that seek partial and selective insertion in the world economy while simultaneously undertaking international projects of an interstitial nature. Since 2005, the Cuban state has gone this route, on the one hand encouraging processes of insertion in some global chains such as international tourism, while on the other hand expanding the export of professional services based on political arrangements, which I have elsewhere called the "Bolivarian Matrix"[1] (in particular, the complex special relationship with Venezuela) and that, in practice, occupy interstitial spaces. Available information does not allow a satisfactory analysis of this dual process. Therefore, despite some evidence as to rising incomes and a favorable change in Cuba's export profile, it cannot be affirmed that this dual model or its separate components (partial insertion in the world economy and interstitial activity) are leading the country toward development. As a result, there are not enough elements to uphold the superiority of such a dual model over arguments that the country's advance requires a more substantial connection to the world economic dynamic. As far as I know, there are no cases of economic development, or a successful approximation thereof, based on the dual model or purely interstitial prospects.

Finally, the design of a Cuban economic development strategy in the context of globalization requires a clear understanding of the particularities that stem from Cuba's situation as a small island economy. Paradoxically, until very recently the predominant concept of development in Cuba, which still has considerable influence, was that of industrialization through import substitution (ISI). In fact, such a concept is more appropriate for countries with large-scale economies than for a Caribbean island.[2]

Cuba is a typical "export economy." Until very recently, it specialized in producing a few commodities (such as sugar and nickel) or the equivalents of commodities (such as beach resort tourism) for the foreign market. As a result, a considerable share of national production was not directed to the internal market. Cuba's international specialization had two important dimensions: a) it was relatively narrow, and b) it was not very lucrative because it was limited to commodities. The growing role of Cuba's export of professional services (taking advantage of interstices within globalization) has modified that second characteristic. However, it has not significantly altered the fact that the range of international specialization of a small island economy must always be relatively narrow, as such specialization necessarily limits diversification of production and deprives the country of its own supply of capital goods, with the end result that internal savings do not automatically translate into investment. In such conditions, the country is structurally incapable of achieving a complete internal production cycle. The export sector serves as a "substitute sector" to acquire the missing internal production. As a result, exports rather than investment become the independent variable with respect to demand, which is exogenously created. This relatively small scale makes any broad process of import substitution extremely difficult. The development strategy of any small island country must take this principle into account.

The fact that Cuba is the largest island of the Caribbean could—under certain conditions—mitigate that restriction, but not eliminate it; neither can the export of professional services, though it has served to compensate for Cuba's structural weaknesses. Beyond arguments about the degree of stability of Cuba's export of professional services, it is clear that so far the compensation for structural weaknesses has been only partial. There is much less evidence to support the idea that the "Bolivarian Matrix" offers Cuba a chance to revive a process of ISI, based this time on taking advantage of a larger "concerted" economies of scale within that matrix.

Therefore, the new challenge facing Cuban economic planning also includes an old one. Along with the task of developing a sufficiently lucrative international specialization profile in the context of global value chains, we must recall the traditional challenge—often overlooked—that the characteristics of small island economy present for the process of re-specialization of a country like Cuba.

Development Strategy and Economic Reform

Because of the structural weaknesses limiting the production of capital goods in a small island economy like Cuba's, the country's development strategies must include both import substitution to diversify the national productive base, including some capital goods production, and also export substitution to replace the commodities of the past with more profitable exports derived from technological and knowledge inputs.

The concept of export substitution should not be confused with "export diversification." Cuba's route to development must involve export growth, but not just quantity. The issue is not simply to increase traditional exports and "diversify" the export bundle through the widening of export categories. The truly important achievement would be to increase (both absolutely and relatively) export lines based on technological inputs and intensive utilization of a trained workforce. That is, the key measure of diversification must be the degree to which such new technologically intensive exports constitute a growing share (and eventually the majority) of the total. In the country's total export structure, some elements must replace others.[3]

This double need for import and export substitution has been recognized in Cuba for some time; the development strategies implemented at various times and circumstances have included both components. The two types of programs must and can be complementary, but tensions frequently arise because the two compete for the same investment resources. For the past thirty years the central component of Cuban development was industrialization through import substitution (ISI), while export substitution has been a more recent and relatively smaller phenomenon.

Each development strategy—with its associated development pattern—is linked to a specific mode of international insertion. Or, to put it another way, each is linked to particular prospects for the country's international specialization. The dual strategy adopted in about 2005, in which modes of direct insertion in the global economy have coexisted with a specialization in professional services within the "Bolivarian Matrix," already manifests unmistakable signs of exhaustion. This weakening cannot be explained purely or mainly as a result of the global crisis of 2008–2009, although that has been an aggravating factor. Rather, the exhaustion of the strategy stems from the following problems:

a) It has become more and more difficult for export activities attached to the world economy to function as leading sectors in the national economic framework;

b) There are internal and external, political and economic limits to export substitution as conceived within the "Bolivarian Matrix";

c) The coordinated planning of industrial policy—or of an eventual "common" industrial policy in the "Bolivarian Matrix"—has been ineffective. The starting point for such planning would be to take advantage of complementarities and favor national-level coordination of capital-goods production to cover the needs of the participating countries.

To those issues may be added serious problems in three main areas: a) internal food production to reduce imports; b) internal market growth based on rising personal incomes to foster demand on which to base industrial upgrading and the creation of a capital-goods sector; and c) innovation to direct a growing share of the labor force toward acquiring and exercising greater technological and organizational skills, a process that should be organized in progressive steps, beginning in those sectors for which there is high internal demand, such as the production, processing, and distribution of food.

The exhaustion of the dual strategy referred to above has not given rise to a development strategy to replace it, which is a serious obstacle for national development. Yet even a development strategy and an international specialization linked to that older strategy would be of little benefit in the face of a dysfunctional economic system at work in the country.

The predominant view in Cuba seems to be that the solution to the country's economic problems—clearly a long and complex effort—can and should be the normal result of certain measures now generally accepted as necessary instruments of economic policy, which should be applied in "diligent" and gradual fashion. These include the creation of a single currency, modification of exchange rates, adjustment of salary scales, fiscal policies to reduce subsidies, price mechanisms, unique sectoral policies especially in agriculture, labor discipline, reorganization of public administration, and improvement of management techniques, among others.

The underlying notion is that the country's current economic system (in essence, a set of social relations) is adequate—although in need of certain adjustments—to carry out the fundamental economic functions needed to implement any "structural changes" that might be introduced.

However, the country's economic development—particularly in a globalized context—depends on certain key prerequisites, of which the most important is a system that can carry out the three basic functions that every economic system must guarantee:

a) The function of *economic calculus,* meaning precise measurement of economic results such that these measurements may have a corrective effect on economic activities. For instance, when price increases indicate that demand exceeds supply, an increase in production would follow.

b) The function of *stimulating* work.

c) The function of *economic innovation,* meaning permanent pressure to improve products and processes, and stimulate the capacity to turn challenges into opportunities and problems into solutions.

Any evaluation of Cuba's current economic system quickly reveals the existence of serious problems in each of these areas, but most especially in the third: innovation. As a rule, Cuban state enterprises (the predominant managerial structure in the country) have not undertaken economic innovation as a basic activity. That fact alone should be enough to indicate not only that the economic system has serious operational faults, but also that this particular form of organization has reached a dead end unless it is substantially transformed.

The economic system's institutions define the mechanisms of coordination, organization, property relations, and feedback within the economy. In order for the economic system in Cuba to fulfill its basic functions, a vast, deep, and integrated economic reform is thus required. This problem must be resolved before attempting to carry out other structural changes.

Cuba's economic problem is that its current economic system cannot serve as a departure point for development. The mechanisms that will lead to development cannot operate effectively in the current situation. Therefore, to remove an impediment to development, this departure point must be transformed by a substantive economic reform that precedes the rest of the changes.[4]

Evaluating Cuba's Options

The economic reforms that have taken place in Cuba since the early 1990s cannot be considered a solution to the formidable challenge of substantially modifying the country's economic output to achieve development in the midst of globalization. In fact, the dual strategy that has been adopted (partial insertion in global value chains and simultaneous exploitation of interstices within a globalized world economy) has quickly run out of steam. A replacement strategy is needed soon, for the global economy harshly penalizes slow rates of change.

For Cuba's open, small, island economy, a transformation of its economic structure oriented toward development must be carried out within a framework of restrictions that cannot be ignored, including the limitations imposed by the United States. Nonetheless, even with those restrictions in place, economic development is possible.

The most appropriate development strategy for Cuba in current conditions requires the adoption of a pattern of international specialization based on insertion into global value chains via export substitution to favor trajectories of growth in technological and organizational knowledge and training.

To be successful, the adoption of a development strategy in Cuba would require radical changes in policies, both in its international and internal spheres. Any opportunity to take advantage of Cuba's human capital within the framework of global value chains would be of little significance in the face of an economic system incapable of guaranteeing the basic functions that any such system must carry out.

The first action to be undertaken would be an economic reform—vast, deep, and integrated—to allow resolution of the country's key economic problems before trying to implement other structural changes, especially those related to changing the country's international specialization.

Endnotes

1. Pedro Monreal, "Cuban Development in the Bolivarian Matrix," *NACLA Report on the Americas,* 39/4 (Jan.–Feb. 2006): 22–26.

2. Pedro Monreal and Julio Carranza, *Dilemas de la globalización en el Caribe: Hacia una nueva agenda de desarrollo en Cuba* (Mexico: Siglo XXI Editores. 2004).

3. Pedro Monreal, ed., *Development Prospects in Cuba: Issues of an Agenda* (London: Institute of Latin American Studies, University of London, 2002).

4. Pedro Monreal, "El problema económico de Cuba," *Espacio Laical,* 3/14 (April–June 2008): 33–35.

Commentary

A View from the East: Trade, Investment, and Economic Reform

Regina Abrami

Knowing something of a country's organization of production, sources of capital, and system of pricing is important to understanding its growth model. In two important chapters, Omar Everleny Pérez Villanueva and Anicia García Alvarez describe Cuba's existing strategy. Of interest to both are the opportunities and challenges of reorienting Cuba's largely non-market-based growth model to one that might allow greater scope for non-state economic actors and market mechanisms.

Pérez Villanueva (chapter 7) focuses on the potential benefits of foreign direct investment, whereas García Alvarez (chapter 6) assesses recent agricultural reforms in Cuba. A shared argument for outward-oriented economic reform, with no shift in the political system, links these chapters together. Chapter 7 reflects on the same processes as they occurred in China and Vietnam. Each has pursued a successful course of economic liberalization under single party rule. Now lasting over several decades, their earliest stages of economic transformation certainly ran contrary to conventional wisdom regarding the need for institutional transparency as a means to economic growth.

Today, China and Vietnam are open economies, with close economic ties to the United States. They are also members of the World Trade Organization, having emerged as key links in global agricultural and manufacturing supply chains. How they got to this position has been the subject of many book length studies. It is worth noting that domestic economic reforms were well under way in both places years prior to each country's WTO accession. Each country's government, in other words, laid the foundation for out-side economic actors to seek closer engagement. They did so by set-ting out the parameters of preferred direct investment, while liberating domestic labor in various ways. Insistence on technol-ogy transfer through joint venture or licensing also meant that the potential for improving labor productivity underpinned much of what was happening from the earliest days of outward-oriented development. For foreign investors, this relationship was made attractive through preferential tariffs and consistent demonstra-tion of the productive potential of each country's workforce.

With the benefit of hindsight, we can set these actions and their consequences against proposals now being made by the above authors. To what extent, the question seems, is it reasonable to think of outward-oriented growth as Cuba's development panacea?

In his chapter, Pérez Villanueva focuses on the potential for pos-itive spillover effects through foreign direct investment. He directs most of his effort toward a description of market-based incentives. These include preferential tariffs, labor costs, and other forms to explain the ongoing draw of foreign direct investment to Vietnam and China. Combined with policies that situate these investments in specific zones, and under terms which facilitate technology transfer in key economic sectors, the author offers a positive case for Cuba's greater openness.

In other ways, however, China and Vietnam pose something of challenge. Weak protection of intellectual property rights, corrup-tion, restrictions on earnings repatriation, and joint-venture part-ner lift-outs of competitive assets and loss of competitiveness also resulted, damaging no small number of foreign investors. While large firms, such as Microsoft, absorbed these losses in China with an eye on the long term, others folded and went home. Given this, a deeper look into the persistent basis of foreign direct investment in these places is important to gauge its relevance to Cuba.

First, there is the remarkable Chinese diaspora. Besides its con-siderable size in terms of net worth and reach throughout East and Southeast Asia, these individuals proved willing to hedge China's uncertain business environment, and to an extent Vietnam's as well, through heavy reliance on social networks more than law. In Viet-nam, similar to Cuba, more recent memories of political loss had made the Vietnamese diaspora far more cautious to re-engage with their homeland. Today we are seeing a change, but it came largely in the wake of rather strong signals from the Vietnamese government that it welcomed its diaspora home, and with promises to protect them and their investments.

Second, there is the role of geography. Bluntly put, Vietnam and China have the luck of being in a good neighborhood. At each stage of their economic reform, they were able to fit within existing regional supply chains, more or less continuing the "flying geese" pattern which underpinned the rise of two prior generations of newly industrialized states in East and Southeast Asia. Foreign investors now speak of a "China plus One [Vietnam]" strategy, which has allowed them to hedge rising costs in China through transfer of lower value-added operations. The boom in garment and footwear manufacturing in Vietnam is one example of this pattern's unfolding.

Third, there is the United States, which offered China a degree of tolerance with regard to its pace and direction of economic liberalization that Vietnam has never known. Similar to Cuba today, it was isolated and blocked off from this large market until the mid-1990s. The tripling of foreign direct investment to Vietnam after its 2007 accession to the WTO also suggests on-going trepidation with its domestic institutions for investor protection.

For Cuba, then, the lesson is clear: domestic reforms are a necessary but insufficient condition for outward-oriented growth. Its current mix of foreign direct investment, including the tepid embrace of Cuba's diaspora and ongoing challenges facing trade normalization with the United States and other neighbors, may frustrate the promise of spillover effects. Outward-oriented development, after all, must depend not only on supply but also on demand from global markets. This leads naturally to the question of whether agriculture instead might be Cuba's economic engine, and well ahead of industry.

In her chapter, García Alvarez sets out to answer this question, focusing on a range of agricultural reforms under way and their potential to sustain economic growth. These include a reorganization of agricultural production, the introduction of new technologies, access to foreign currency self-financing, and ultimately to global markets. As she notes, the leading driver behind these changes was Cuba's growing dependency on food imports and its worsening balance of payments. A similar story can be told of Vietnam in the 1980s. Here too, price distortions between official state purchasing channels and informal farmers' markets made clear that increasing domestic productivity depended on closing this gap.

Early agricultural reforms in Vietnam and China aimed to do so through increases in official state purchasing prices and the introduction of contract-based farming. In no time, farmers' markets and state distribution networks were filled with an increasing volume and range of foodstuffs. At the same time, how these agricultural reforms contributed to each country's outward-oriented growth strategy differed substantially. Fiscal policy was a critical factor. China's sub-provincial governments were expected to self-finance. Vietnam's sub-provincial governments benefited from inter-provincial fiscal transfers, possibly tempering grassroots self-help efforts that might have jolted the countryside out of its low level of development. The industrial transformation of rural China, in turn, never really happened on similar scale or range in Vietnam.

The broader comparative story thus remains one of two distinct roads to rural-based outward-oriented growth. Rural China became a manufacturing base for the world. Industrial inputs of the kind suggested in García Alvarez's chapter also improved agricultural efficiency and production, with positive overall effects on China's balance of payments. A more visible link between agricultural production and outward-oriented growth, however, can be seen best in Vietnam.

Within three years of its shift to household-based production, Vietnam went from being a net importer of rice to the world's second largest supplier. Vietnamese cashews, pepper, and other agro-commodities also top the lists of several global supply chains. The story of coffee cultivation also offers a cautious lesson on unfettered direct engagement between farmers and the global economy. In this case, rapid demand for low-grade coffee sparked Vietnamese households to intensify production of this crop in the 1990s, with disastrous consequences once global prices dropped. The Vietnamese government subsequently aided households in crop diversification, but earlier intervention might have prevented the crisis.

In this, Cuba has something to learn from newly empowered local and national growers associations in China and Vietnam. Mirroring counterparts in places such as the United States and New Zealand, these associations are geared explicitly to protect the economic interests of farmers. More important perhaps has been government recognition that organized interests, even when privately operated, ultimately may serve the broader political and economic interests of the nation. As Cuba embarks on its own path, its leadership will as well have to think of what organizational rights it might allow to ensure the productivity and protection of its citizens as they "go out," to borrow a Chinese phrase, and seek closer, more direct global economic engagements.

Commentary

The Cuban Advantage

Sergio Silva-Castañeda

For Latin Americans born during the second half of the 20th century, underdevelopment seems to be almost second nature. We were born in underdeveloped countries and quickly accepted the idea that we were unlikely to see our countries escape that status during our lifetimes. Still, Pedro Monreal starts his comment with a brave statement: Cuba could be a developed country by 2036, and globalization offers an adequate platform for such a radical transformation. Although I suspect that most Latin Americans would react with skepticism to that idea, it is important to keep in mind that historical evidence suggests that such an outcome is possible, although certainly it is not an easy achievement.

Following Pedro Monreal's provocative statement, it is hard to avoid the question: what would a developed Cuba look like? One way to start sketching an answer to that question is to compare the trajectory of the Cuban GDP per capita with what has happened in some other countries. Three countries come to mind: the United States, which has for a long time been the benchmark against which Latin American development has been measured; Spain, which for more than a century shared the backwardness of its former colonies but now, despite its current economic troubles, is considered part of the developed world; and Mexico, Cuba's struggling travel-companion, which has also failed to build a fully developed economy, even if it has come closer than Cuba to meeting that goal, at least in terms of GDP per capita. Figure 1 shows the comparative trajectories of Cuba and these countries. We see that most of the gap between Cuba and the United States was already there by 1929, but, in the case of Mexico and Spain, the gap opened in the late 20th century. At the end of that century, Cuba stopped falling behind and even recovered some ground.

Still, if Cuba is to be a developed country by 2036, stopping the fall won't be enough. Cuba needs to catch up, and this brings us to a new question: would it be possible for Cuba to close the gap with either Spain or Mexico in the following couple of decades? It is possible, but it would be challenging. To catch up with Mexico, Spain, or the United States, Cuba would need to grow its GDP per capita by 3.04%, 5.4% or 7.16% per annum respectively, assuming zero GDP per capita growth for those countries. If we assume 1% growth per annum in Mexico, Spain and the United States, then Cuba can only catch up by growing at rates of 4.08%, 6.46% and 8.24% respectively. According to the World Bank, Cuban GDP per capita grew around 6.1% average per annum between 1999 and 2009.[1] That means that even considering very low rates of economic growth for Mexico, Spain, and the United States, at its current level of economic growth Cuba can aspire to catch up with Mexico, but in Monreal's time frame not with the other two. Although catching up with Mexico in terms of income would be an important achievement, especially if Cuba is able to get to those levels of GDP per capita without the accompanying levels of inequality present in Mexico, it is hard to imagine Mexico being considered a developed country by then if the Mexican GDP per capita were to grow only at 1% per year for the following 25 years. Most likely, Cuba needs to grow at higher rates.

This is not good news, but let's keep in mind that there have been experiences of countries catching up with the developed world in relatively brief periods of time. Certain countries have grown for sustained periods of time at rates higher than current Cuban rates. For instance, if we take Spain`s 1959 Plan of Economic Stabilization as the beginning of that country's take-off and its 1986 admittance to the European Community as the Spanish graduation, we could argue that it took only 26 years for Spain to cross the aisle and be considered a developed economy. During those 25 years, the Spanish GDP per capita grew at a rate of almost 7% per year. The experiences of Singapore, Taiwan, South Korea, and, of course, China, should also allow us to keep the door open for a Cuban comeback.[2] But none of those late 20th century experiences of rapid economic convergence with the developed world can be explained without taking into account a successful integration into global markets. It

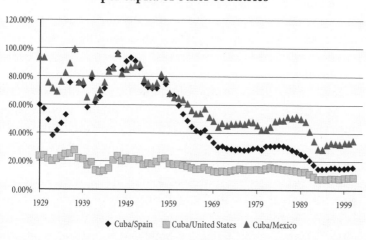

Figure 1. Cuban GDP per capita as percentage of GDP per capita of other countries

◆ Cuba/Spain   ▨ Cuba/United States   ▲ Cuba/Mexico

Data Source: Maddison, Angus, *The World Economy: Historical Statistics,* OECD, 2003.

is not impossible for Cuba to be developed in 25 years, but it is hard to imagine that scenario without a deeper and successful integration into global markets.

As in any Latin American economy, the debate in Cuba regarding integration into international markets as the path to sustainable economic growth was resolved a long time ago. In a complete report detailing the status of the Cuban economy in 2000, the UN-ECLAC already stated that "the reconstruction of the Cuban economy could hardly be isolated, as in the past, from foreign market forces in which it is already immersed."[3] Of course, the most difficult question is still on the table: how to integrate the Cuban economy into global markets? In answering this question, we must realize that Cuba, as a consequence of its well-known internal and external restrictions, has followed a path clearly different from many of its Latin American and Caribbean neighbors. The articles by Pedro Monreal and Pavel Vidal Alejandro offer an interesting picture of the challenges and possibilities that the Cuban path to globalization is facing.

Pedro Monreal's piece makes it clear that the needed Cuban integration should be based not on the export of traditional commodities like sugar or nickel, but on a process of export substitution favoring knowledge-intensive sectors that are assumed to be more profitable. Of course, it is not only a matter of deciding which sectors are more profitable, but also of assessing in what sectors Cuba is, at least potentially, competitive. To identify those sectors is already complicated, but Cuban integration faces another complication barely covered in Monreal's paper: politics clearly has a deep effect over Cuban economic possibilities on at least two fronts. In one of these cases, the effect is positive but limited; in the other, it is negative and hard to substitute. Let me comment on the latter. Monreal argues that even under the "limitations imposed by the United States" economic development is feasible. But when we think of countries that were able to overcome underdevelopment through a successful integration into global markets, none did so without having access to what still is the biggest market in the world. Remember that the Spanish take-off had as a prerequisite the creation of a political alliance with the United States, with obvious economic consequences, particularly for Spain. Can Cuba become successfully integrated without resolving its conflicted relationship with the United States? It seems hard to believe. If the answer were yes, as Monreal believes, an explanation of the mechanisms and markets involved in the Cuban alternative path would make his argument stronger. Monreal is also skeptical, and not without reason, of the sustainability of the "Bolivarian Matrix," which he describes as an "interstice within globalization." Although such agreements are insufficient, I do not think that Cuba should assume that the "export of professional services" is incompatible with a successful integration. More than an interstice within globalization, the Bolivarian Matrix seems to be a creative method Cuba has used to acquire Bolivian gas and Venezuelan oil, accessing them through its political agreements. In the end, for both cases, any process of commercial integration (even if simply an increment in the exchange of goods and services between two states) always includes a political element.

Pavel Vidal Alejandro offers another component of the challenge that the Cuban economy faces in a globalized economy: external financial shocks. As he shows, the current monetary and exchange strategy appears to be inadequate for the challenges that the international economy might impose. Although the Cuban state has, at least for now, been able to control inflation, the mechanisms used to achieve such goals have created other distortions, such as reducing the profitability of the agricultural sector and contributing to the crisis in the banking sector. Worse still, it does not seem credible that inflation is under control. Cuba's only success on this front—if it may be said to have had any at all—is not to control inflation but to defer it. Eventually the exchange rate will need to be adjusted, making it impossible for agricultural producers to keep producing unless prices are unfrozen, to give just one example. According to Vidal Alejandro, the monetary challenge for the Cuban state is how to deal with the "renewed inflationary pressures" that will follow. If these problems remain unresolved, it will be difficult to achieve the goal of development in 25 years through commercial integration. Even with access to important international markets, it is difficult for any nation to achieve sustainable growth without long-term monetary stability. If Cuba is to catch up in the following decades, this part of its economy will require major work.

The integration of Cuba into international markets, an important prerequisite to its goal of development in 25 years, still faces many obstacles. But Cuba has a sort of "Gerschenkronian advantage."[4] While many countries that embraced liberalization earlier (such as Mexico or Spain) are struggling to find their place in the global economy, Cuba has the opportunity to start from scratch, knowing that complete financial deregulation or strictly equilibrated public finances might not be the only pathways toward development. Cuba has the opportunity to start reforming its economic and political institutions, bearing in mind that "A thin layer of international rules that leaves substantial room for maneuver by national governments is a better globalization"[5] and knowing that the pace and rhythm of the integration should be dictated by practical reason and not by ideological determinants.

Endnotes

1. See World Bank, Cuba at a Glance, available at http://devdata.worldbank.org/AAG/cub_aag.pdf. Accessed July 18, 2011.
2. Spanish growth rates calculated with data from: Alan Heston, Robert Summers and Bettina Aten, Penn World Table Version 7.0, Center for International Comparisons of Production, Income and Prices at the University of Pennsylvania, May 2011.

3. United Nations, Economic Commission for Latin America and the Caribbean, *La Economía Cubana: Reformas Estructurales y Desempeño en los Noventa,* 2nd ed. (Stockholm: Styrelsen för internationellt utvecklingssamarbete, and Mexico, D.F.:Fondo de Cultura Económica, 2000), p. 21.

4. Gerschenkronian simply in the sense of an "advantage to backwardness."

5. Dani Rodrik, *The Globalization Paradox: Democracy and the Future of the World Economy* (New York: W. W. Norton, 2011), p. xix.

PART

III

Ensuring Equity and Social Mobility

Introductory Note

The Social Mobility Perspective and Its Usefulness for the Analysis of Inequality and Social Policy in Cuba

Mayra Espina Prieto

As a complement to the preceding texts and placed in dialog with them, the third part of this book deals with important aspects of the social problems facing contemporary Cuba by analyzing recent processes of social mobility. These processes were generated by the crisis and reforms of the 1990s, whose effects (influenced as well by later events) can still be felt today, especially that of widening inequality.

The choice of a social-mobility analytic perspective to study inequality and equity in today's Cuba is not haphazard. Within Latin American social science, the study of social mobility is being reinvigorated as a sub-specialty of the sociology of inequality, which allows for overcoming the structuralist and objectivist tradition of that field through dynamic and inter-related examination of the micro and macro connections and subjective dimensions shaping the structures of stratification. Mobility analysis also reveals the influence of macro constraints and social policy on the fates of individuals and families and, at the same time, the transformative effect of daily micro-practices.

Social mobility research also has an important contribution to make for understanding the impact of social policies. Observation of tendencies toward mobility within different social groups allows us to distinguish whether certain policies create equitable and sustained opportunities for upward mobility for all social strata.

In the sociological tradition, social mobility is defined as the process of individual or collective vertical displacement, upward or downward, within the hierarchy of a given society at a given historical moment. The usefulness of this categorization lies in its revealing which social groups and individuals, under what conditions, may rise in the established socioeconomic hierarchy of a specific society, and which ones are more likely to experience downward movement or run up against so-called "mobility barriers," in the sense that they lack the necessary initial conditions to make use of available opportunities for improving their status.

Social mobility is a "normal" and systematic process, but obviously it is more intense during times of change (economic, political, social) and when the bases of macro-social structures change (such as the social division of labor, the economic structure, and state-market relations). These upheavals can be expected to affect the economic and work trajectories of individuals and groups.

A study commissioned by CEPAL to assess the state of the art of such analyses in Latin America reports that the subject received early attention in the work of Gino Germani[1] and Solari and Labbens,[2] carried out in the 1950s and 1960s under strong influence of the structural-functionalist paradigm.[3] One of the region's most noteworthy contributions was a CEPAL study about occupational transformation and the social crisis of Latin America in the 1980s, based on data from population censuses of 1960, 1970, and 1980.[4] This study called attention to this cause of mobility and its complementarity with the analysis of individual displacement.

Other studies introduced the notion of "expectations of mobility" and, therefore, of a "double mobility deficit." This deficit has an objective aspect "that has been expressed in downward social mobility measurable in terms of the structural growth of lower-quality jobs, the growth of poverty, and greater concentration of income" and a subjective aspect that includes "frustrated expectations of future mobility with a rhythm similar to what had been experienced for two or more generations until the very recent past." The patterns of mobility that characterize each historical period are here interpreted as part of the logic of social evolution in both the structural sphere and the subjective one.[5]

Thus, a way of studying and interpreting mobility as part of the structures of inequality began to take root, superseding a dichotomous vision, which had diametrically separated objective and subjective dimensions. However, in the 1990s studies of mobility and stratification, in all of their varieties, suffered a retreat. This retreat has been attributed to the reorientation of the region's social sciences toward problems of poverty.

The resurgence of interest in mobility studies appears to be linked to the goal of broadening and diversifying approaches to poverty. One intention is to break down the dichotomy between the poor and the non-poor by "proposing the idea of vulnerable configurations (those susceptible to downward social mobility or quite unlikely to improve their condition)." Another is to overcome the explanation of poverty that relies exclusively on ownership of material resources. A new approach incorporates the notion of social assets, which are defined as the variety of resources a family possesses that it can use to maintain or improve its welfare. Such assets include income and accumulated tangible capital, but also non-material dimensions such as social networks, practical access to goods and services offered by the market or the state, levels of human capital the family can count on, and the family's capacity to make strategic plans.[6]

Applying Amartya Sen's[7] idea that individuals' and groups' potential for improved welfare depends on many personal and social characteristics that affect social mobility (ability to change socioeconomic position), some analysts have proposed the use of social mobility studies as a means toward deeper evaluation of the impacts of social policies on equity. These studies reveal the micro-stage on which changes in macrostructures play out, and they present a matrix of conditions that allow people to seize opportunities for upward mobility (or avoid downward mobility). Thus they help to identify which groups can make use of such opportunities and which groups experience the greatest limitations to doing so. In turn, this allows a reading of the currents of displacement unleashed by social policies, from the perspective of a concern for equity.[8]

Although the methodology is still lacking for including mobility as part of the toolkit used to design policies and to measure their impacts on equity, the issue has been outlined according to the following points:

- Mobility studies serve as a tool for considering the formulation of social policies, especially those related to reducing inequality and poverty or to promoting equity, because they broaden the notion of poverty beyond a definition purely in terms of income.[9]

- Mobility widens the questions that may be raised about poverty and inequality and how to affect them. It locates poverty and inequality in terms of processes, dynamics, and mechanisms that reproduce social stratification where, retrospectively, macro-scale and micro-scale factors can be linked.[10]

- It offers policy-makers a fuller social picture of why certain social groups maintain a given relative socioeconomic position over time, compared to others that display new facets and change and improve their positions. It explains the factors that determine how given groups escape poverty or stay trapped within its grasp.[11]

- From a policy-oriented perspective, similar to what has occurred in many studies of social exclusion, mobility allows a dynamic, process-based, and historical understanding of the mechanisms that generate, maintain, and aggravate poverty and inequality.[12]

- Mobility studies help to solve one of the greatest difficulties of targeted or affirmative-action policies, which is how to improve the identification of the target populations (the at-risk and vulnerable groups) and, within these, to recognize those whose disadvantaged situation is structural—that is, not conjunctural or temporary, but a long-term impossibility to achieve a minimum level of welfare, reproduced and transmitted over generations, which cannot be overcome without public action.[13]

- Social mobility describes what groups, under what conditions, and carrying out what actions may improve their socio-structural positions; what groups may reach new, advantageous positions under the influence of an economic or social policy; and what groups are falling or stuck in the least favorable positions. It offers a dynamic perspective on equity by observing the process of upward or downward socio-structural movement inter- and intra-generationally and the changes in this process over time.[14]

In contemporary Cuban society, the circumstances of crisis and reform, increased social inequality, and the growth of groups living in poverty during and since the 1990s, as well as the need to strengthen ties between the output of social sciences and the design of policy, suggest the importance of studying mobility as one dimension of inequality. As long as the country lacks a methodological tradition of this type of study because it relies on conjectural and non-systematic studies, it needs to collaborate with other institutions to achieve progress in this field.

This need pushed the David Rockefeller Center for Latin American Studies and the Center for Psychological and Sociological Studies to join forces to promote exchanges among well-known scholars in this field, holding the first international workshop on "Equity and Social Mobility: Theory and Methods." The first session was held in Brasilia in January 2007, cosponsored by DRCLAS and the United Nations International Poverty Centre (IPC). Specialists from Bolivia, Brazil, Cuba, South Africa, and United States participated. In their initial call[15] the organizers stated:

> Ensuring more equitable development outcomes continues to be a central concern for developing countries in all regions—and certainly in Latin America and the Caribbean. This need has become even more pressing as evidence emerges suggesting that neither developmental approaches adopted in the 1960s and 1970s, nor the "structural adjustment" reforms of subsequent decades, have been effective strategies

for increasing well-being evenly across society and reducing extreme disadvantages for the poorest and most vulnerable groups. Many developing countries, particularly in Latin America, continue to face high inequality. Consequently, there is growing consensus on the need to balance economic growth with equity and social justice concerns. Policies to address the development challenges countries are facing can be informed by the analysis of the different social and economic dimensions of the development process of countries as well as by the insights that can be provided by discussions of country cases as part of a comparison exercise.

For the Cuban participants, the most important result of this initial workshop was learning about methods to analyze macro-structural dimensions and the mechanisms of mobility, especially as these relate to social policies and the real capacity of such policies to overcome poverty and ruptures in historical patterns of equity. They also gained greater understanding of space, habitat, and region as dimensions of equity and public policies to promote it.

A second workshop with the same title, goals, and organizers took place in Rio de Janeiro in June 2009. This workshop examined facets of recent mobility process in Cuba, Mexico, Brazil, and Puerto Rico. For Cuba, the topics were macro and micro elements of mobility generated by the economic reforms of the 1990s and changes in social policy as well as ties between race and mobility and the role of region and habitat; for Mexico, inter-generational occupational mobility among young people in rural areas benefiting from the *Programa Oportunidades,* and processes of social stratification in Monterrey; for Brazil, perceptions of inequality, discrimination, and social mobility among black professionals, inter-generational income mobility and the persistence of income gaps between blacks and whites, the effects on mobility of conditional transfer programs such as *Bolsa Familia,* and spatial discrimination in Rio de Janeiro; and for Puerto Rico, issues of occupational stratification and the degree of upward mobility created by industrialization processes.

The spectrum of aspects and cases examined in this second workshop allowed advances in three directions. 1) Corroborating the usefulness of mobility analysis in evaluating social policies and their effects on social equity by showing the limitations of broadly focused policies on changing the socio-structural position of their target population beyond certain immediate benefits. 2) Understanding the importance of local settings in the expression of inequality and as key spaces to design and implement more narrowly focused policies. 3) Agreeing on the need to construct a methodological focus adequate to the heterogeneity and multiplicity of the processes of social mobility and the factors that influence them. Such a focus has to overcome the traditional dichotomies of macro/micro, society/individual, structure/agent, and objective/subjective to approach a multidimensional vision of the enmeshed planes and scales. The following chart is a synthetic representation of the progress thus far to create such an integrated perspective.

The optimal methodology would cover this entire schema using micro, meso, and macro evidence gathered in a single research process, with a common logic uniting them, and would describe and explain mobility that occurs in specific societies and socio-historical circumstances. This sort of research is not always practical because of the time and resources required. However, the schema sketched above has another very significant use, which is to allow undertaking partial studies that concentrate on particular planes, dimensions, or actors selected for some specific purpose while locating them in their larger context. Similarly, the schema contributes to inferential readings of related studies that, while carried out for other purposes, can be reinterpreted according to their contextualized position in the planes and dimensions of the model.

The chapters following this introductory section synthesize research results[16] inspired by the integrated approach, which were discussed in the above-mentioned workshops. Although lack of resources, time, and access to statistical information prevented the total use of the integrated approach, the research identified how the Cuban economic reforms put into practice in the 1990s affected the shape of pathways for upward and downward social mobility, as well as how such mobility was perceived. The research also highlights breaches in the previous state of equity in Cuban society and, based on these findings, proposes changes in social policy.

Findings about changes in economic structure and social policy generated by the reforms and the routes of mobility opened by these changes combine with the findings of a qualitative study that examined 111 mobility case histories between the years 1990 and 2008 in a particularly interesting way. The cases were selected according to the following criteria: they should illustrate upward and downward mobility experienced over the period 1990–2008, present a broad spectrum of the social stratification that typified the era of the crisis and reforms, and display regional diversity.

We interviewed people in more or less polar (advantaged or disadvantaged) socioeconomic situations whose condition stemmed from upward or downward mobility experienced during the reform period (1990–present).

Integrated Approach to the Study of Social Mobility

I. Contextual analysis

Processes or mechanisms of mobility (opening or closing channels of movement)	A. Economic policies and activities. B. Social policy. C. Demographic processes. D. Migration. E. Individual and family assets and capital.

II. Planes of mobility

Macro-social plane	Structural mobility (movement at the societal scale, upward or downward movement resulting from change in the economic-occupational structure, degree of social stratification).
Meso-social plane (plane of social inter-subjectivity)	Life styles, ways of thinking, prevailing perceptions linked to existing social stratification. Expectations about mobility within different social groups that shape their members' aspirations and life strategies.
Micro-social plane	Individual and/or family trajectories. Movement that changes socioeconomic status (income, access to material and spiritual well-being, possession of tangible and intangible assets). Individual and family strategies and expectations about mobility. Perceived mobility (inter-generational and intra-generational). Self-perception of success and upward mobility, or frustration of mobility expectations. Human and social capital of the family unit. Social networks.
Spatial position	Country/city and urban/rural differences. Habitat quality for different social groups. Regions with different development levels.
Temporal positions	Intra-generational movement. Inter-generational movement.

III. Effects of mobility

On equity	Overcoming or maintaining equity gaps (by class, gender, race, region, generations, ethnicity, etc.). Opportunities and obstacles due to social origins.

Thus, it was not our intention to prove that economic changes caused upward or downward mobility; we assume that to be the case. Our aim is to understand the key elements of that mobility when it does occur, compare the main characteristics of typical cases of upward and downward movement, and reflect on the consequences of those forms and degrees of mobility. Our goal has been to produce a first approximation about questions that statistics and quantitative research on Cuba's changing social structure cannot answer, such as the perception of mobility (i.e., the perceived change), the presence or absence of family strategies for achieving mobility, the criteria defining "upward" or "downward," and the implications of social networks. The study has also contributed to refining the profiles of advantaged and disadvantaged positions in contemporary Cuban society.

When compared to the general outline of the Cuban population, the sample matches the overall distribution by occupational groups, property sectors, and skin color. It overrepresents women, people with higher education, and residents of Havana City; it also lacks cases of mobility toward the agricultural sector, which limits its descriptive-explanatory scope. Nonetheless, the opportunity to compare the findings from statistical evidence with those from the interviews served as a means of triangulation and mutual corroboration of the limits, as well as the possible projections of the conclusions we reached. Obviously our goal was not statistical representativeness, but rather qualitative variety of enough breadth to serve as an exploratory study and as the basis for subsequent in-depth follow-up.

The study identified two historical moments: a point of departure that reflects the country's social structure at the end of the 1980s, and a point of arrival that showed the sample members' new social positions as of the 2000s. Comparing these two profiles and the implied social structures, and abstracting the intermediate period, fundamental changes could be identified. This comparison was based on dimensions that were both significant for their value in describing change in social stratification and observable from available published Cuban statistics.

The data do not always come from the same years because the research team could not always find available and public statistical information for the same precise moments. This did not, however, keep us from reaching conclusions about the changing routes of social mobility, given that the data were always from within two clearly distinguishable eras: those immediately before and after the crisis and reforms.

The first of the next two chapters addresses the macro context of social mobility, describing the most salient changes in two of the mechanisms of mobility that the reforms changed the most: economic policy and social policy. It also contains references to how the new routes of mobility affected social equity as well as to some micro elements. The last chapter centers on regional and habitat issues. In Cuba, this dimension has become a key element in shaping inequality and poverty but it also features good prospects for modernization and intensification of policies to promote social equity.

Endnotes

1. G. Germani, *La sociología científica* (Mexico, D.F.: IIS-UNAM, 1962).
2. A. Solari and J. Labbens, "Movilidad social en Montevideo," *Boletim do Centro Latino-Americano de Pesquisas em Ciencias Sociais* 4 (1961): 349–376.
3. Carlos Filgueira, "La actualidad de las viejas temáticas: sobre los estudios de clase, estratificación y movilidad social en América Latina," *Serie Políticas Sociales* 51 (Santiago: CEPAL, 2001): 1–51.
4. CEPAL, *Transformación ocupacional y crisis en América Latina* (Santiago: United Nations, 1989).
5. B. Kliksberg, ed., *¿Cómo enfrentar la pobreza? Estrategias y experiencias organizacionales innovadoras* (Buenos Aires: PNUD-CLAD-Grupo Editor Latinoamericano, 1989).
6. Filgueira, "La actualidad de las viejas temáticas."
7. A. Sen, *Development as Freedom* (New York: Knopf, 1999).
8. Vicente Espinoza, *La movilidad ocupacional en el Conosur. Acerca de las raíces estructurales de la desigualdad social* (Santiago: Instituto de Estudios Avanzados, 2002). Available at htpp/wwwasesoriaparaeldesarrollo.cl/secciones/documentos/movilidad_ocupacional_en_el_conosur.pdf.
9. E. Gacitúa-Marió et al., "Una evaluación de la exclusión social y de la movilidad social en Brasil," in *Exclusión social y movilidad en Brasil*, ed. E. Gacitúa-Marió and M. Woolock (Brasilia: IPEA-World Bank, 2005).
10. Ibid.
11. Ibid.
12. S. Schwartzman and E. Reis, "Pobreza y exclusión," in *Exclusión social y movilidad en Brasil*, ed. E. Gacitúa-Marió and M. Woolock (Brasilia: IPEA-World Bank, 2005).
13. R. Bonelli and A.Veiga, "Pobreza, movilidad y exclusión social en Brasil," in *Exclusión social y movilidad en Brasil*, ed. E. Gacitúa-Marió and M. Woolock.
14. Espinoza, *La movilidad ocupacional en el Cono Sur.*
15. Available at http://www.undp-povertycentre.org/ems/papers/concept_paper.pdf.
16. M. Espina, et al., "El análisis de la movilidad socia: Propuesta de una perspectiva metodológica integrada y caracterización del caso cubano" (Havana: Fondos del CIPS, 2009, research report).

8

Structural Change and Routes of Social Mobility in Today's Cuba: Patterns, Profiles, and Subjectivities

Mayra Espina Prieto and Viviana Togores González

In the early 1990s, changes in the global context deprived the U.S.-embargoed Cuban economy of its major commercial ties and foreign support. These changes were the disappearance of the socialist bloc in Europe, the end of the bipolar world balance of power, and the emergence of the United States as the sole superpower. Combined with the exhaustion of the domestic development model of the Cuban socialist regime, these events created an economic crisis of considerable magnitude in Cuba and highlighted the need for reforms to manage this crisis.[1] The crisis and reforms, in turn, undermined many of the daily life practices that had maintained the prevalent standard of living and the satisfaction of basic household needs, thus unleashing a process that would reshape the social structure and generate growing inequality.

We begin with the assumption that the crisis and reforms should be understood as processes of change in the constraints and facilitators of social mobility at work in socialist Cuba. The increased importance of mercantile mechanisms in the distribution of, and access to, material and spiritual goods and services began to generate a new differentiation in opportunities for upward mobility, with the logical effect of widening equity gaps that surged in the early 1990s and have continued to grow since then.

In addition to the introductory section, the next three parts of the chapter analyze the changes that have occurred as a result of the crisis sparked by the collapse of Cuba's trade with the socialist bloc and the reforms that were subsequently introduced. In these sections we review the transformations that have been generated in the macrosocial sphere (modifications in economic context and social policy, tendencies in social mobility, and resulting gaps in equity), drawing on government statistics and secondary data published in related studies. The fourth section examines microsocial and subjective dimensions of mobility (for example, pathways of ascent and decline, perceptions of success and of equality of opportunity, etc.) based on a qualitative study of 111 case histories undertaken by the authors. These cases of mobility illustrate a wide range of upward and downward trajectories under the influence of the changes generated by the crisis and reforms.

Analysis of Context: Reforms in Economic Strategy and Changes in Social Policy

The reforms of the Cuban economy in the early 1990s exemplify a relatively abrupt and accelerated adjustment of structural constraints resulting from a change in economic models within a given system, specifically a transition from a state-centered form of socialism toward a mixed or multi-actor form.[2] The new economic model opened important spaces for non-state actors to generate products, services, jobs, and income. The sum total of actions that implied discernible changes in the system's operating principles and changes in structural constraints has extended from 1990 until today, although most of the reform measures were implemented between 1993 and 1995. To understand how the reforms instituted in the early 1990s brought socio-structural reconfiguration, we review the key economic and social policy changes that directly affected the context and mechanisms of social mobility.[3]

1. Opening to foreign capital and growth of joint ventures involving state enterprises and foreign private capital.

2. Reorganization of land ownership: conversion of state farms into cooperatives and grants of usufruct rights to small parcels for household farming.

3. Broadened opportunities for self-employment by individuals or micro-enterprises (mostly household ones) in selected and limited activities (food service and room renting, for example).

4. Creation of farmers' markets for the sale of agricultural and animal products at supply-and-demand prices.

5. Establishment of a market in artisanal and light manufacturing products with freely fluctuating prices. Institution of currency exchanges and of personal foreign-currency savings accounts. Circulation of two currencies, one convertible (CUC) to international currencies and one (Cuban national peso) for purely domestic usage.

6. Restructuring and shrinking of the state administrative apparatus.

7. Reinforcement of a development model that emphasizes export diversification and import substitution.

8. Priority for key sectors that earn foreign exchange or solve strategic problems (including tourism, biotechnology, pharmaceuticals, oil exploration and production, and metallurgy).

9. Expansion of the tertiary (service) sector of the economy.

10. Constitutional reforms to redefine the role of socialist property, limiting it to the area of fundamental means of production and eliminating the previous irreversibility of socialist property status.

11. Legalization of the receipt of remittances and the holding of foreign currencies.

In addition, new measures have been introduced since 2007 to stimulate change consistent with the earlier reforms introduced in the early 1990s. These initiatives extend some aspects of the post-1993 transformations, especially those emphasizing a form of socialism with multiple economic actors—a goal of the original reforms that was insufficiently implemented and at times reversed.[4]

The measures may be grouped into four categories that (a) reactivate productive capacities and the social recognition of work; (b) restructure farm production to give a greater role to small farms and to local and municipal decision-making regarding the types and quantities of crops and the allocation of resources; (c) reorganize and shrink the state bureaucratic and administrative apparatus; and (d) provide greater support for disadvantaged groups by increasing pensions and social assistance programs.

Growth in the service sector has played an important role, as may be seen in Table 8.1. Between 1989 and 2006, 21.1% of employed persons shifted sectors. Workers flow toward the tertiary (service) and primary (including agriculture and mining) sectors to the detriment of the secondary (manufacturing) sector.

Table 8.1. GDP Structure by Sectors (%), 1989 and 2006

GDP	1989	2006
Total	100	100
Primary	10.4	4.7
Secondary	34.0	19.5
Tertiary	55.6	75.8

Source: Authors' calculations based on Oficina Nacional de Estadísticas (ONE), *Anuario Estadístico de Cuba,* and Comité Estatal de Estadísticas (CEE), *Anuario Estadístico de Cuba* (Havana: ONE, various years).

As shown in Figure 8.1, the drop in employment that characterized the early 1990s reversed starting in 1996, and since then there has been a sustained growth in employment. Thus, the labor force has recovered its importance as a factor in socio-structural location, social integration, and differentiation and stratification.

Changes in social policies were enacted in two stages. First, the state's strategy focused on creating conditions for economic recovery and mitigating the social costs of the crisis. The changes in employment and income policies included a reduction of state jobs; the growth of self-employment and other non-state opportunities for earning income; the linkage of salaries to individual and collective production results; the payment of salaries in foreign currency for specific occupations and activities; salary increases for selected activities that generate foreign currency or play priority social roles (health, education, science and internal order); guarantees of protection for employees of closed-down or restructured economic units; legalization of remittances and decriminalization of foreign currency ownership; creation of a public community network of subsidized food for low-income people; priority for education and health within public services to optimize resource use.

Figure 8.1. Employment and Unemployment, 1989–2007

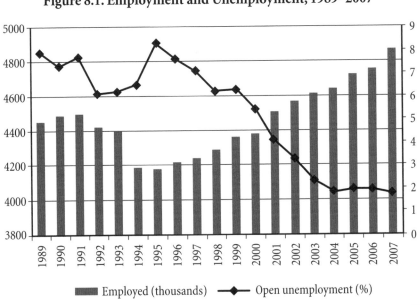

Employed (thousands)   ◆ Open unemployment (%)

Source: Constructed by authors on the basis of Comisión Económica para América Latina y el Caribe (CEPAL), *La economía cubana. Reformas estructurales y desempeño en los noventa* (Mexico City: Fondo de Cultura Económica, 2000), and ONE, *Anuario estadístico de Cuba*, various years.

During the second stage, beginning toward the end of the 1990s and continuing in the early 2000s, the state resumed a proactive role in actions related to social investment. New social programs were introduced to modernize and restore public services, especially in health and education, and to focus attention on special needs and vulnerable sectors.[5] Local social policy was also strengthened through the Program for Integrated Community Work, which placed a broad network of social workers in communities. Pensions and salaries in selected occupational groups were increased; housing construction through both state programs and private mechanisms expanded.

Even in the 1990s, in crisis conditions and in the midst of economic reforms, Cuba's social public spending as a share of gross domestic product (GDP) remained at about 20%, matched in Latin America only by Uruguay and Brazil.[6] Toward the end of the 1990s and beginning of the 2000s, average spending on health and education represented more than 47% of social spending (with the remainder spent on Social Security). These decisions highlighted the emphasis on prevention and social consumption, rather than market or autonomous individual consumption. Although the crisis of the 1990s affected the quality of public services and required a shift of a considerable proportion of household income for market consumption, there was no drop in social coverage and public service spending began to recover.

From the early stages of economic reform until the most recent changes, there has been a marked alteration of structural constraints and in the mechanisms of mobility, including the following:

1. A broadening of non-state income and employment sources (social mobility toward the non-state sector plus the reemergence of an urban petite bourgeoisie).

2. The emergence of new opportunities to increase income and material well-being, which are select and available only to some groups (not all groups have equal qualifications, resources, information, or access to the new advantageous opportunities).

3. Growth of the market as the venue to earn income and of monetary income as the means to determine and create living conditions. This income-consumption model established new patterns of social differentiation. The widening range of incomes within the population became one of the most important elements of differentiation over this period.

4. Expansion in service activities, favoring occupations that require more education and training.

5. A marked increase in access to higher education to ascend career ladders through the acquisition of higher skills.

6. A partial return to the land as more of the labor force turns to farming.

7. Vertical upward and downward movement as some types of economic activity decline and others emerge.

8. Currents of downward mobility linked to drops in personal or household income, impoverishment, and deterioration in living conditions and surroundings.

Macrostructural Mobility

In the macrosocial sphere, these changes in the mechanisms of mobility have been reflected in modifications of the structures of stratification, showing new patterns of social ascent and descent. This is especially true for social structures defined by forms of property ownership, sectors of economic activity, occupational categories, educational levels, and incomes.

Perhaps the most drastic change generated by the reforms is the growth in employment linked to non-state forms of property, in contrast to the absolute and hegemonic centrality of the state in shaping the social structure in previous periods. See the official data in Table 8.2, which groups in the "self-employed" category only those workers formally registered as such, with licenses to operate their productive or service activity privately. It is hard to quantify unregistered workers in the informal economy, although the expansion of that sector in Cuba is evident and empirically observable.[7]

Another phenomenon not reflected in official statistics is the formation of micro- and small private enterprises. Until recently, Cuban regulations restricted private businesses from hiring employees beyond those who were household members. The observations carried out in the course of our research confirmed the existence of activities that functioned as microenterprises already. There is a hierarchy for the employer-owner and his/her wage workers and sometimes apprentices, with corresponding income differences, especially in car repair workshops, construction projects, home repair, and furniture making.

A new mechanism of social mobility stems from the reorganization of farm production. State farms have been divided and turned into cooperatives. Small-scale farming and the sale of farm production to consumers have increased.

Table 8.2. Employment Structure by Forms of Property (%), 1988 and 2006

Employment area	1988[a]	2006	Difference 2006/1988
1.Total employed	100.0	100.0	
1.1 In state entities	94.0	78.5	−15.5
Of these:			
1.1.1 State enterprises	–	3.7	3.7
1.2 In non-state entities			
Of these:	6.0	21.5	15.5
1.2.1 Joint ventures	–	0.7	0.7
1.2.2 Cooperatives	1.8	6.2	4.4
1.2.3 Private non-foreign			
of which:	4.2	14.7	10.5
1.2.3.1 Self-employed and urban small proprietors	1.1	3.5	2.4
1.2.3.2 Private peasants (small farm owners or private producers on state land)	3.1	10.8	7.7
1.2.4 Subsidiaries of foreign companies, and non-profit NGOs (Cuban)	–	0.3	0.3

[a] Data from Ministerio de Economía y Planificación.

Source: Calculated by the authors on the basis of data ONE, *Anuario Estadístico de Cuba* (Havana: ONE, 1998 and 2020).

Table 8.3. Agricultural Land Area by Form of Property (%), 1990–2002

	1990	1992	1996	2002
State	75.0	75.2	33.0	34.7
Non-state	25.0	24.8	67.0	65.3
Peasant	25.0	24.8	25.0	26.1
Cooperative	11.0	10.2	11.0	9.0
Private	14.0	14.6	14.0	17.1
UBPC (Basic Units of Cooperative Production)	–	–	42.0	39.2

Source: Data supplied by the National Association of Agricultural Producers (ANAP).

At the same time, the "tertiarization" of the economy substantially changed the profile of occupations by activity sector. The movement into the service sector has become a significant path of mobility (see Table 8.4).

The combined effects of "tertiarization," increased access to higher education, and growth of the tourism, science, and technology sectors are evident in the greater share of the workforce employed within the occupational

Table 8.4. Employment Structure by Activity Sector (%), 1989 and 2006

Sector	1989	2006	Difference 2006/1989
Total	100	100	
Primary	12.2	20.5	8.3
Secondary	38.8	17.7	−21.1
Tertiary	49.0	61.8	12.8

Source: Authors' calculations based on ONE, *Anuario Estadístico de Cuba* and CEE, *Anuario Estadístico de Cuba* (Havana: ONE, various years).

categories of service workers, managerial/leadership posts, and professional/technical employees.[8] Fewer people entered the workforce as industrial and clerical workers, one of the most representative labor categories before the reforms (see Table 8.5).

Table 8.5. Employment Structure by Occupational Category (%), 1990 and 2005

	1990	2005	Difference
Total	100.0	100.0	
Manual workers (skilled and unskilled)	51.4	37.3	−14.1
Professional/technical	22.1	25.5	3.4
Clerical workers	6.3	5.4	−0.9
Service workers	13.6	23.5	9.9
Leaders and managers	6.6	8.3	1.7

Source: L. Núñez, "Categorías ocupacionales y movilidad social," in *El análisis de la movilidad social. Propuesta de una perspectiva metodológica integrada y caracterización del caso cubano. Informe de Investigación* (Havana: Centro de Investigaciones Psicológicas y Sociológicas, 2009).

The differentiation between these occupational categories has exerted upward pressure, fostering the growth of jobs that demand higher qualifications. There has been over a 5% growth in job opportunities in higher-qualification occupations between 1990 and 2005 (see Table 8.6). Within the categories in these tables, managerial/leadership jobs outstrip the remaining categories requiring lower shares of intellectual work as pathways of mobility (see Table 8.7). Moreover, improvement in educational level appears to be one of the best pathways for upward mobility, with a palpable impact on the employment structure (see Table 8.8).

Table 8.6. Employees Ranked by Occupational Categories, 1990 and 2005

	1990	2005	Difference
Total	**100**	**100**	
Employed in positions where intellectual work predominates (high and mid-level skill levels)	28.67	33.81	5.14
Employed in positions with a combination of intellectual and physical work (medium-low skill levels)	6.31	5.40	−0.91
Employed in positions where physical work predominates (medium-low and low skill levels)	65.02	60.79	−4.23

Source: L. Núñez, "Categorías ocupacionales y movilidad social," in *El análisis de la movilidad social. Propuesta de una perspectiva metodológica integrada y caracterización del caso cubano. Informe de Investigación* (Havana: Centro de Investigaciones Psicológicas y Sociológicas, 2009).

Table 8.7. Occupational Structure by Managers vs. Workers, 1988 and 2006*

	1988 %	2006 %	Difference 1988/2006
TOTAL	100.0	100.0	
Workers in non-managerial occupations*	93.2	92.3	−0.9
Leaders and managers	6.8	7.7	0.9

* The sum of manual, clerical, service, and technical/professional categories.

Source: Authors' calculations based on ONE, *Anuario Estadístico de Cuba* (Havana: ONE, various years) and CEE, *Anuario Estadístico de Cuba* (Havana: ONE, various years).

Table 8.8. Structure by Employees' Educational Level (%), 1986 and 2005

	1986	2005	Difference 2005/1986
Total employees	100.0	100.0	
Elementary school	24.0	10.7	-13.3
Junior high	38.0	29.8	-8.2
High school (vocational or college preparatory)	29.0	45.6	16.6
University	9.0	13.9	4.9

Source: Authors' calculations based on ONE, *Anuario Estadístico de Cuba* and CEE, *Anuario Estadístico de Cuba* (Havana: ONE, various years).

An essential component in this kind of analysis of macrostructural mobility would also look at changes in the structure of income groups and determine how these mobility pathways modified income levels. Unfortunately, this information is not available in published national statistics, and therefore we use an alternative method to explore this question. As a result of the socialist transition, income was less concentrated between 1959 and 1989. Monetary wages generated only limited social inequality and there was significant secondary redistribution outside the market. At that time, income was not a way to differentiate between groups because state employment dominated the labor market and the spread between state salaries was small.[9]

As a result of the crisis and the reforms undertaken in the 1990s, the distribution of income began to change. There has been a greater concentration of income and a change in the number of income sources, with a decrease in the state sector of the economy, which lost ground to the private, cooperative, and joint venture sectors. The receipt of remittances as a supplemental source of household income is also noteworthy. The Gini coefficient calculated for the early 2000s rose to 0.38, in contrast to its level of 0.24 in the 1980s, demonstrating growing levels of income inequality.[10]

In the first half of the 1990s decade, salaries dropped by 15.6%, lowering the population's total income.[11] In contrast to the pre-1990 period, the market became an important source of income generation and money income began to play a greater role in determining and creating living conditions.

In a second period, between 1994 and 2005, income sources diversified still further, and earnings began to recover. These higher earnings were associated with the changes in the labor market structure linking jobs to particular property sectors. Non-state employment increased in both agriculture and other areas. Nominal incomes in the private and cooperative sectors grew by 251%.[12]

This increase was made possible by broader opportunities for self-employment and a reduction in the level of goods and services distributed by the state. The rise of an important non-state economy improved the position of private service providers, producers, and private intermediaries.

At the same time, since the late 1990s, measures have been taken to raise pensions and salaries of state workers in selected occupations (teachers and professors, police, scientists, and healthcare personnel, among others). In 2005, median monthly salaries of all workers averaged 330 pesos versus 203 in 1996 or 284 in 2004.[13] The Ministry of Labor resolution 28 of 2006 set the minimum wage at 225 pesos a month, increased the minimum pension from 65 to 164 pesos, and raised social assistance grants from 62 to 122 pesos.

However, the effect of such salary and pension increases remained limited by the high prices of many products that are essential to meet essential needs. The price of a basic market basket of food was calculated at 156 pesos per person per month in 1998. The earned income from salaries in that year was below the cost of the market basket for at least 23.75% of the population (see Table 8.9).

Table 8.9. Salary Income Ranges of Employed People, 1998, in Cuban Pesos

Income range	<100	100–149	150–199	200–249	250–299	300–349	350–399	400–449	≥450
% of population in that range	3.47	20.28	24.63	17.45	15.51	10.08	4.08	1.96	1.47

Source: Boris Nerey, "El modelo de desarrollo y estado de bienestar en Cuba," Master's Thesis (Universidad de La Habana, 2000).

Another study completed in 2006 included other necessities for daily life (such as clothing and shoes, personal hygiene products, home cleaning products, and basic services) in addition to food. It confirmed that a gap remained between salaries and the cost of a basic market basket.[14] The monthly cost of the consumption basket was estimated to vary between 312.50 and 330.54 pesos per person, while the minimum salary that year was 225 and the median was 387.[15] The same result is evident from the share of the urban population living in poverty (as calculated based on income and unsatisfied basic needs), which rose from 6.3% in 1988 to 20% in 2004.[16] In contrast to the 1980s, the post-reform structuring of exclusive distribution mechanisms is affecting the degree to which basic needs are met.

Among income sources other than work, of key importance are the remittances from abroad, which affect not only the individual recipients but the monetary resources of the country as a whole. Since individual holding of foreign currencies was decriminalized in 1993, and despite restrictions imposed by the U.S. government, remittances have played a growing role in the economy and for the population. As Figure 8.2 shows, they have become the country's third largest source of foreign exchange earnings, exceeded only by exports and by net income from tourism. For households, they have unquestionably allowed for higher consumption of goods and services by recipients.

Given the characteristics of the Cuban economy, remittances provide a flow of foreign currency of which the state captures almost the entirety through foreign currency stores and the CADECA network of currency exchange booths.[17] Such channels for the capture and redistribution of foreign currency increase the impact that remittances have on the stratification of consumption and standards of living.

Studies have estimated the effect of remittances on household consumption and on overall consumption in the economy. In the case of households, previous consumption levels matter more than current economic growth; the effect of remittances allows households to double their consumption. [18] For imports (one of the determining elements of consumption in Cuba), the inertial factor of the previous year's imports is more important than current economic growth, and this effect is slightly greater when remittances are considered. Thus, recipients of foreign currency, via remittances or other means, have important advantages compared to those who do not possess any source of income in foreign currency or its equivalent in convertible pesos (CUC).

The total value of remittances reaching Cuba cannot be calculated with precision because most of these funds do not arrive in the country by way of bank transfers. Estimates vary not only because of "informational difficulties associated with estimating the phenomenon . . . but also the use of

Figure 8.2. Foreign Currency Earnings in the Cuban economy, 1994–2000

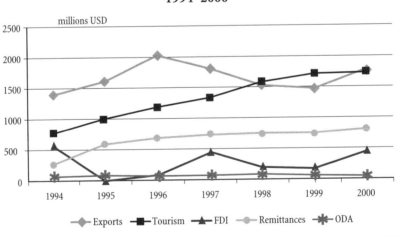

Key: In millions of U.S. dollars. Exports, tourism, foreign direct investment, remittances, development assistance.

Source: Jorge Mario Sánchez Egozcue, "Remesas y Consumo en Cuba." Mimeo 2006. Based on data compiled from ONE, FDI (Foreign Direct Investment) data reported by ECLAC and other indicators from the World Bank's World Development Indicators and The Economist Intelligence Unit.

differing assumptions, which are not always clearly stated."[19] Therefore the trends in other indicators—such as the share of foreign currency in private hands, or the volume of transactions of currency exchanges and consumption in foreign currency stores (TRD)[20]—are taken as indicators of the upward trend in remittances. According to estimates by CEPAL, remittances reached a total of about $3 billion between 1989 and 1996.[21] More recently, researchers have estimated possible annual totals, with results ranging from $300 million to $1.1 billion.

Other sources of foreign currency income include the tips received from providing services to foreign tourists or Cubans in state-owned enterprises or in establishments operated by the self-employed. These sources of foreign currency earnings combined with those from remittances have increased the purchasing power of select groups and also contributed to the growth, recirculation, and redistribution of these resources to the rest of the economy.

In sum, there is a powerful process of mobility in income groups, characterized by the widening and dispersion-polarization of these groups, rapid downward movement by some population segments (perhaps 40% of the total, including at least 14% of the urban population that experiences periods of impoverishment), and the ascent of other segments by various means of income diversification.

Tables 8.10 and 8.11 summarize the characteristics of mobility. These data testify that Cuba is undergoing an accelerated process of socio-structural recomposition. The trajectories underscore that actors have strong capacities to understand new situations and shape their strategies. The leading openers of pathways to upward mobility are linked to non-state property, diversification of sources of income, the "tertiarization" of the economy, and higher levels of education.

Table 8.10. Structural Mobility Balances[22] by Selected Dimensions, 1988–2006

Dimensions	Balances
Forms of property	15.5
Activity sectors	21.1
Occupational categories	15.0
Access to managerial jobs	0.9
Workers' educational levels	21.5

Source: ONE, *Anuario Estadístico de Cuba* (Havana: ONE, 1989 and 2007).

Table 8.11. Main Sending and Receiving Sectors, by Selected Dimensions of
Structural Mobility, for 1989–2006

Dimension	Receiver	Sender
Form of property	Private sector	State sector
Activity sector	Tertiary	Secondary
Occupational category	Service workers	Manual workers
Access to managerial jobs	Leaders and managers	Workers in non-managerial occupations
Workers' educational levels	High school	Elementary

Given the general aging of the Cuban population and therefore of the labor force, it is to be expected that the changes observed in social mobility, in both sending and receiving groups, would have different expressions in different age cohorts, and that retirement followed by possible re-insertion in the labor force would play a role. While it has not been possible to obtain this data at the national level, the case studies we will examine later indicate that retirement by state workers is a strategy to seek employment in the private sector, while young people prefer mobility pathways leading toward tourism and joint venture sectors.

Effect on Equity

Are there equal opportunities for social mobility in terms of parity among the results achieved by different groups? How do social mechanisms affect these changes? These questions are difficult to answer because available social statistics on a variety of events often do not differentiate their results by social groups, making it hard to assess specific impacts on disadvantaged groups. Nonetheless, an analysis based on a combined set of data sources suggests that the most widespread gaps in equity of opportunity are related to gender, race, and geography/habitat. In this section, we focus on gender and race; the next chapter in this book will examine the inequalities related to geography and habitat in depth.

The gaps in equity according to gender are evident in two imbalances in the socio-structural position of women: their overrepresentation among Cubans living in poverty and their marked underrepresentation in managerial positions relative to their share of total employment and specifically in occupations requiring advanced qualifications. Various quantitative and qualitative studies on women's poverty are associated especially with early childbearing, female-headed families, and single motherhood, circumstances that in turn associate with women leaving school and lacking conditions that would allow them to work and generate sufficient income.[23]

In the early 2000s, women represented only 30% of all persons employed in managerial and leadership positions in the national economy, 28% of the legislators, and 14% of members of the Council of State.[24] The higher up in the hierarchies of leadership and management one looks, the fewer women are to be found. This distribution is particularly asymmetrical in the production sectors, where women are almost entirely excluded.[25]

The relatively low presence of women in managerial-leadership jobs cannot be explained by lack of qualifications, because women make up more than 60% of the professional workforce and of the workers with higher and secondary education levels. The pattern of women facing entry barriers to managerial-leadership posts while being a majority of professionals was already present in the 1980s and 1990s; it has become more marked in the 2000s (see Table 8.12).

Table 8.12. Occupational Structure by Occupational Categories and Gender, 2001 and 2006 (%)

Year	2001		2006	
	Total	Women	Total	Women
Total	100	36.0	100	37.2
Manual workers	100	15.4	100	16.5
Professional/technical	100	64.7	100	60.0
Clerical workers	100	86.0	100	62.3
Service workers	100	50.0	100	40.4
Leaders and managers	100	31.2	100	29.4

Source: Authors' calculations based on ONE, *Anuario Estadístico de Cuba* (Havana, 2008).

There is also a lower rate of participation by women in sectors where employment is highly coveted because of the potential to earn higher income, such as tourism. In this sector, only 36.6% of the workforce is female and those who are employed are overrepresented in posts that are non-managerial or require fewer qualifications.[26] The tourism industry is organized in such a way that the structures of the social division of labor and the organization of political participation reserve certain positions for women and bar them from jobs that involve entrepreneurial decision-making and high-level strategies.

With regard to race, despite the real positive impact on overcoming racial inequalities made by universalizing and integrationist social policy makers, socioeconomic disadvantages based on skin color have been reproduced nonetheless. The difficulties and obstacles stem from the asymmetrical starting points from which different groups attempt to transform equality of opportunities into equality of results. The outcomes are the persistence and widening of structurally-based racial inequalities and the survival of stereotypes and prejudices that affect non-white groups.

Examination of the 2002 census data demonstrates various sorts of differences associated with skin color.[27] Non-white persons are overrepresented in the unemployed population and among those living in housing units classified as barely acceptable or bad. They are underrepresented among leaders and managers, office employees, professionals, scientists, and intellectuals, as well as among those who are self-employed, whose incomes tend to be higher than those for the equivalent occupations in the state sector. Non-white persons are also underrepresented among those who hold university degrees.

Other research from the 1990s and 2000s complements the census data, revealing other facets of race equity gaps. Correlations show up between income and living standards and race. White workers predominate in sectors with a higher concentration of economically advantageous jobs (such as tourism and joint ventures) and, conversely, there is a predominance of blacks and mixed-race people in the traditional industry and construction sectors. Whites tend to be better represented in high-qualification jobs in areas of the economy that have been revitalized by the reforms, and the proportion of white leaders and managers increases the higher one climbs in the managerial-leadership hierarchy. Remittances tend to flow in greater proportion to the white population. The black and mestizo population are overrepresented among those in the worst housing and environmental conditions.[28]

Similarly, out of 13,031 students who entered Cuban universities by passing entrance exams in 2004, 68% were white, 9% black, and 23% mestizo.[29] The relation of higher education access and skin color had already been identified in the previous decade, when the overrepresentation of white students was explained in terms of historical and accumulated factors. White families more frequently had economic and cultural conditions that allowed their youth to keep studying, without compelling the students to generate income at an early age. White youth could count on family help in their homework assignments, enjoy material conditions adequate for studying at home, and rely on a family tradition of higher education. A study of poverty in the city of Havana, defined in terms of unsatisfied basic needs, also found an overrepresentation of blacks and mixed race individuals in socioeconomically disadvantaged situations.[30]

Aspects of Mobility in the Micro-Sphere

Our case histories of upward and downward mobility are an exploratory effort to reveal some facets of the mobility process that are excluded from statistics and quantitative estimates, which could in turn serve as a basis for further study at a later stage. In this section, we summarize some of the findings from these 111 case studies.

• Perceptions of success and upward mobility.

Studies carried out in the 1980s found a consolidation "of the subjective pattern of ascent based on qualifications and access to intellectual work," in which positions such as doctor, engineer, university professor, and others were regarded as the summit of the pyramid of stratification, with little reference to the income generated by these professions.[31] This can be explained by two factors. On the one hand, the salary scale in effect at that time offered a relatively direct connection between qualifications and living standards because its main criterion was work complexity, as measured basically by education and other qualification requirements. On the other hand—in the context of 0.24 Gini coefficient, a 6.6% poverty rate, social policies offering universal access to services in health and education, and the small role played by the market in providing access to goods and services—income differences did not produce much differentiation in the society, which is why they had lost importance as a referent for upward mobility.

The cases we studied suggest that there has been a change in perception, and a new subjective pattern of mobility has emerged since 1990. Higher income has become central to the perception of upward mobility and more important than all other elements of social status. As a result, the occupations at the top of the pyramid are associated with jobs in tourism, self-employment (whether legal or illegal), employment in joint ventures or foreign firms, managerial jobs, and jobs that offer opportunities for foreign travel and the associated additional income. Although a university diploma retains symbolic value, securing high incomes is a more significant mobilizing force for household and individual strategies than the old criterion of value attributed to work complexity.

• Upward and downward mobility pathways, and associated resources.

Combining the mobility tendencies observed in the macro-sphere with the findings from the case studies illuminates the most common pathways of economic ascent in terms of jobs and living conditions. Based on the case studies, we conclude that the shifts that have brought relatively better economic situations are those leading from the state sector to the foreign capital sector (representatives and high-skilled employees of foreign firms and agencies) or to joint ventures (managers, professional, and service workers); those from lower to higher-skill jobs or from non-managerial to managerial ones within the state sector; and those from the state sector to small-scale private production or private provision of urban services.

Table 8.13. Common upward mobility pathways, 1989–present

Points of departure (emitting groups)	Points of arrival (receiving groups)
State sector	Private urban sector (petite bourgeoisie) Foreign capital sector
Secondary (industrial) sector	Tertiary (service) sector
Manual workers	Service workers and self-employed
Professional-technical	Managerial
Clerical	Professional-technical
Professionals and managers in the state sector	Professionals and managers in the joint venture and foreign capital sector

For those entering the foreign capital sector of the economy, the decisive prerequisites, according to the histories of those who have reached these new position in a firm or agency, combine high qualifications with connections or networks that inform these prospective workers about options and offer recommendations and contacts to ease entrance into this new sector. Because qualifications alone are not sufficient, social networks have proven to be decisive. Social origins are also important, favoring children and close relatives of people with the necessary connections—professional relationships with leaders-managers or with people occupying influential positions in foreign firms or agencies, joint ventures, or the state agencies that channel hiring for such jobs. Thus, individuals who come from families of intellectual or managerial-leadership origins have an advantage in access to these higher-paying jobs.

For those who secure a job in the joint-venture sphere of the economy, qualifications, experience, and connections are crucial. However, their economic advantage does not derive from higher earnings as much as from other incentives attached to the new position, such as use of a company car, a gasoline ration, trips abroad, and relationships that help to resolve various household needs.

For those who have moved toward urban small-scale production, the key resources are having a home with the necessary conditions, a car or a skill in high demand, and some start-up capital either in the form of savings, loans, remittances sent for this purpose, or the ability to extract state supplies to produce services or goods for private sale. In some instances, the subjects' incomes have reached such heights, and their relations have expanded to such an extent, that they even own businesses abroad (as coproprietors/investors in restaurants). Similarly but in the other direction, in some cases remittances from abroad serve as contributions to a family business in Cuba, especially when renting rooms or apartments.

The mobility pathway toward the urban private sector is seen to offer the most relative freedom for individual and household choices, despite the legal restrictions surrounding self-employment.[32] The case histories of those who followed this pathway contain frequent stories of breaking rules, which the entrepreneurs view as incompatible with the business operations normal to the economic activities in question—a component that statistical data do not capture. One illustrative case is that of a former state worker who currently works in the state tourism sector as the illegal private salaried subcontractor to a formal employee. This individual sells a variety of individual illegal services to foreigners whom s/he meets in the tourism establishment, a state-run food-service institution that functions in practice as a private business.

Another example of this strategy of upward socioeconomic mobility and the informal networks that weave together participation in the state sector, the private sector, the informal economy, illegality, and the market is what we shall call the "soft ice cream case." A state food service worker in a town in the central part of the country runs the soft ice cream machine in a local cafeteria and also sells ice cream at private parties and private restaurants (whether legal or not). S/he buys the necessary raw materials illegally from the state distribution system and uses the machine from her normal job to make the product. With these actions s/he has put together a considerable sum to buy, also illegally, some land to rent out and a small boat s/he uses to fish for recreation and also to sell the catch. This individual has one of the highest per capita monthly incomes of the cases in our study; the subject's ultimate goal is to amass enough capital to leave the country. Similarly, an agricultural worker uses the state's resources to offer private services of cattle insemination to individual private peasants and thus earns a high income.

These cases reveal a tangled relationship of state and non-state involvement of subjects who, strictly speaking, have no formal or legal tie to the non-state property sector but whose main or sole source of income is generated thanks to their ties with an economic sector that is either private or parallel to the state sector, and who act within a network of well-structured, stable, and systematic economic relationships that link the state and private spheres. They also demonstrate how it has become commonplace for illegal practices to be justified as a means to obtain high incomes.

In addition, upward mobility and improvement of economic conditions depend to a great extent on the situation of the household as a unit, and on its members' cooperation in developing common social mobility strategies and sharing multiple resources and tasks. These strategies may involve a mix of employment in a formal state job and a private activity, or the emigration of one member of the family, among other possibilities. Strategies based on a combination of options seem to be the most effective, given that any single option for generating income appears insecure and insufficient.

In the case histories, downward mobility occurs when a person shifts from stable employment to unemployment, receives social assistance grants, or gets temporary employment in the private sector (for example, as domestic worker or temporary farm worker) as well as continues to work in low-paid state sector jobs. These pathways appear to be associated with three circumstances that sometimes occur together: loss of ability to work (due to ill health or to the need to care for children or elderly relatives), absence of household resources to put to use in the market, and low educational level.

• Perceptions of mobility, equal opportunity, and success factors.

When asked about their current personal and household situations relative to their parents and their own situations in the 1980s, the subjects' answers differ markedly, depending on whether they experienced upward mobility or find themselves in disadvantaged positions.

The upward-mobile individuals offer an optimistic narrative, feel they are better off than their parents, and will further improve their situations. However, several among them report facing serious obstacles and having doubts about their ability to maintain the status they have achieved. They express feelings of uncertainty and frustration about future mobility. Several subjects explain this uncertainty in terms of the difficult world economic situation and its effects on Cuba, but there is a consensus that current Cuban strategies do not give enough weight to individual and household welfare.

Most persons in relatively disadvantaged situations believe that their situations are as bad as or worse than those of their parents. This perception tends to be accompanied by a sensation of a being stuck, frozen in time, or trapped in an unalterable fate, all reinforced by the crisis and reforms. All of these subjects refer to a disadvantaged situation experienced and transmitted by more than one generation, especially in terms of specific assets that they lack (housing, money, goods, connections, relatives abroad), which they perceive as the things that make a difference in current Cuban society.

Education still holds symbolic value, although it is no longer an assured avenue for upward mobility. The respondents still self-assess their positions in both economic and material aspects (although the latter are seen as the most important) but also note advances in education and training. Such advances allow many of these subjects to see progress in relation to their parents' lives, which to some extent compensates for frustrations about mobility and the sense of being economically worse off.

Nearly all the subjects, regardless of which direction of mobility they have traversed—including those we could view as the "winners" from the reforms—share a negative perception, a sense of loss, when they compare current Cuban society to that of the 1980s. They point to increased social inequality in general and particularly inequality of opportunities to improve living standards, to weakened social justice, and insecurity and uncertainty about meeting basic needs.

This widespread vision that Cuban society in the 1980s was in various ways better than it is today is largely due to two features of that decade. First, the 1980s were characterized by greater assurance that the population's basic needs would be met and by greater coverage of social policies. Second, in that decade the distribution of goods and services guaranteed by the state in free or subsidized form had a stronger effect on living standards than did markets and individual or household incomes. Almost all subjects perceive today's distribution of opportunities to improve socioeconomic status as being unjust. They note that such opportunities can only be utilized by those who have "connections or a lot of money." This perception forms one of the bases for legitimizing in their mind fraudulent, illegal, or under-handed behavior.

Equality as a social value remains present in the collective viewpoint, although those who have managed to rise in an economic terms speak of the need for "personal and household development" outside of obligatory egalitarianism. Those in disadvantaged positions offer negative comments about gaps in equity and the growth of socioeconomic inequality, but these do not add up to a perception of inequality as generalized injustice. Rather, the widespread feeling seems to be that "whom God anoints, St. Peter blesses," as one interviewee put it.

Economic success is attributed to the "ability to make use of what one has," referring particularly to resources such as education and training, housing, useful skills, money, and networks of influence. A change from the 1980s is the appearance of new, conscious strategies for upward mobility, such as movement out of the state sector, retirement in order to move into non-state activities, marriage to foreigners, emigration of one member of the household, moonlighting by one or several family members, sale of a variety of products, use of state property for private business or at least as a source of raw material and other resources for private activity, and use of contacts to get access to good jobs or outright buying one's way in.

Those in unfavorable conditions report turning to religion for getting through difficult life circumstances and envisioning future improvement, in the sense of "God will provide." Some people, despite severe economic limitations, mentioned future plans to *hacerse el santo*, to become initiates in the faith called Regla Osha; others belong to non-Catholic Christian faiths. A religious component, however, is not limited to subjects in unfavorable situations. More successful subjects may likewise attribute their upward mobility to personal effort and "help from God and the saints."

• Mobility and equity.

As already stated, this examination of mobility case studies is exploratory and qualitative and does not meet statistical standards for a representative sample that would justify generalized conclusions about the Cuban population as a whole. Nonetheless, triangulating the case history findings with the analysis of census data and the findings reported in other research studies that have documented equity gaps, we see that the individual upward and downward trajectories documented in our research match the overall pattern of advantages and disadvantages in these other data sources.

Men, white people, young people, subjects whose education level is medium or higher, and persons from better-educated families have a higher probability to be in advantageous positions. In addition, those with individual or household resources including skills, relationships, goods that can be put to use to produce saleable services and products, social networks that provide important information to make efficient labor market decisions, and contacts with influence to facilitate access to advantageous posts are also more likely to succeed. In contrast, disadvantaged positions tend to be associated with women, non-whites, low educational levels, and a lack of resources. These factors also combine with cross-generational transmission of disadvantages.

Conclusions

At present, distinct social groups are emerging at the national and local level in Cuba. This dynamic is leading to a greater density of the social fabric, the growth of new intergroup networks and connections, increased social innovation, increased inequality, and the possible appearance of conflicts and differentiation of interests. These changes include both formal and planned macrostructural phenomena (reform measures) as well as informal microstructural processes (life strategies, daily practices, social networks, and interactions in shared community spaces).

From a social mobility perspective, the crisis and the reforms changed the mechanisms that had functioned in earlier periods of the Cuban socialist transition, which were centered on state employment and systematic and widely majoritarian social structures. The result has been an accelerated process of social mobility based fundamentally on changes in the organization of property, changes in the sources and sizes of incomes, the "tertiarization" of the economy, and rising educational levels. This dynamic has affected the entire social structure.

The service sector (particularly tourism services, food services, and professional services), managerial and professional occupations, non-state sectors of the economy (self-employment, urban petite bourgeoisie, joint ventures and foreign capital), and other emerging sectors have become the most important pathways to gain income, goods, and services. The state sector, industry, and manual labor occupations have been the principal points of exit.

The economic and social policies of the reforms were able to mitigate the damage from the crisis by strengthening the social safety net and opening new avenues of upward mobility. However, these opportunities are narrow and selective. Upward mobility relies on a combination of factors such as education and training, tangible and intangible household resources, remittances, and social networks or connections that provide timely information, recommendations, contacts, and privileges to ease access to advantageous positions. The narrowness and selectivity of the channels of upward social mobility tend to reproduce and strengthen old equity gaps by gender, race, and social origins, as well as differentiation by geography. The real importance of social networks in certain upward mobility pathways remains to be corroborated, but it would suggest a seriously anti-egalitarian trend that affects access to opportunity and whose effect generates privileges and undercuts equity-based policies.

Our study shows that women, blacks, and mixed-race people are at a disadvantage when they seek to advance themselves because they have fewer resources of the kind listed above. Also, though to a still unknown degree, these disadvantages tend to be transmitted generationally, putting these groups at a further disadvantage. As a result, each group's initial conditions and cumulative resources have more weight in determining their unequal access to good living conditions. Moreover, these factors are linked to and reinforced by the persistence of a patriarchal and racially prejudiced culture.

The subjective responses of respondents and their practices suggest the emergence of a notion of individualized upward mobility linked to the economic and material realms. In addition, among those who have risen up the social ladder, we find that upward mobility was a goal of the household. As part of medium and even-long term perspectives, some household strategies included the emigration of members. This pattern also confirms that a de-territorialization of the household unit and its practices is taking place. At the same time, we observe that the public still believes in an ideal social model that combines a protective distribution of basic necessities (food, shelter, health, education, work, safety, and social assistance) as a universal right for all, along with a competitive sphere in which a higher level of welfare rewards some individuals based on their personal merits, within a generally egalitarian environment.

The purpose of our research was to revive and deepen the quality of social mobility studies in Cuban social science so they could be useful for the analysis and elaboration of social policy. Thus we conclude with two recommendations that should improve the quality of social policies.

First, we recommend a practice of cooperation between academic institutions and decision-makers to include mobility studies within the design and evaluation of social policy.

- Mobility goals should be a part of social programs. Among their medium- and long-term objectives, social programs should state their expected effects on the macrostructures of stratification and the expected changes in the socioeconomic status of their beneficiaries.

- Mobility patterns should be mapped as part of the diagnostics used to design policies and assess their effects.

- Mobility measurements should be included in the household and other surveys used to fine-tune policies and programs.

- Classifications that distinguish between social groups should be included in the statistical compilations and censuses about dimensions such as income, health equity, education, housing and environment.

- A program of social mobility research should be carried out from an integral perspective. It should also seek to strengthen qualitative research and research on the subjective perceptions of social processes by individuals, which would allow for a deeper understanding of the microsocial sphere of mobility and the points of view of the targeted beneficiaries of social policies.

Second, we recommend that social policy-makers should consider the recursive interrelation of the following four factors that tend to reinforce and widen equity gaps, and thus direct their efforts to have an impact on these processes.

1. Households face different and asymmetrical conditions in terms of initial conditions. For those with reduced resources, significant barriers and obstacles exist which prevent some households from taking advantage of existing (albeit equal) opportunities. This translates into barriers to upward mobility for disadvantaged groups and inequality in results.

2. The overabundance of homogenizing instruments and lack of targets in social policies, which limits their capacity to reduce the effect of different starting points for social groups.

3. The limited economic sustainability of the social project and the lack of sufficient material resources.

4. The comparative advantages of some geographical locations over others.

These factors, in turn, suggest four linked directions for practical action in social policy:

1. Supply resources at the micro-level. Consider the household as a target for social policy. Change social spending priorities to give more attention to the combined dimensions of housing-environment-work-income.

2. Use targeting tools and strengthen access to universal social policies for disadvantaged groups, especially in the housing-environment-work-income resource poor areas. Increase the skills of disadvantaged groups.

3. Recover the economic sustainability of social policy. Alongside development policies on the national level (which cannot be addressed in this essay[33]), the analysis of social mobility reveals the importance of simultaneous actions to generate opportunities at the micro-level, and broaden practical avenues to generate employment and incomes through the expansion of micro- and small businesses with various types of property ownership through cooperatives and through self-employment. This implies further changes in the regulatory structure and the creation of a flexible legal environment with more room in decision-making for local governments (municipal and provincial), and an overhauled tax policy.

4. Decentralize policy geographically. Offer more of a leading role to local governments and units and to the sphere of community practices with

a high level of self-management, in what might be called a geographically based, affirmative-action universal policy. Undertake priority interventions in depressed areas that tend to display a pernicious condition of equity gaps, appropriation of space, and social disadvantage. This does not mean replacing universal policies with targeted strategies, but rather allowing the two types of policies to complement each other.

Endnotes

1. See Pedro Monreal González, "La globalización y los dilemas de las trayectorias económicas de Cuba," *Temas* 30 (2002): 4–17. Among indicators of the severity of this crisis are the loss of foreign trade relations and preferential prices for sugar exports; the fall of the value of exports of goods by 33.5% from the 1990 total; the loss of preferential access to oil supplies, energy transmission, and industrial inputs (annual oil supply fell from around thirteen million tons to approximately six million); a drop of more than 40% in gross domestic product, or 43.1% per capita; a 30% drop in industrial productive capacity utilization; an estimated drop of 80% in import capacity between 1989 and 1992; a reduction of total consumption by a cumulative total of 28.2% and of gross domestic investment by over 25%; accelerated growth of monetary liquidity (6.125 million pesos in circulation not backed by the supply of products in 1991); a cumulative drop in labor productivity of more than 39%; a decrease in social consumption by 980 million pesos between 1985 and 1991; a decrease in personal consumption of 15% between 1989 and 1990, concentrated in food, transportation, industrial goods, and domestic fuels. See Comisión Económica para América Latina y el Caribe (CEPAL), *La economía cubana. Reformas estructurales y desempeño en los noventa* (Mexico City: Fondo de Cultura Económica, 2000), and Adriano García Hernández, Esperanza Alvarez Salgado, José Somoza Cabrera, Nancy Quiñones Chang, Isis Mañalich Gálvez, and Carlos Fernández de Bulnes, *Política industrial, reconversión productiva y competitividad. La experiencia cubana de los noventa* (Havana: Fundación Friedrich Hebert-Instituto Nacional de Investigaciones Económicas, 2003).
2. Juan Valdés Paz identifies four models of socialism put into practice in Cuba in terms of the relation between state and market: 1959–61, *non-capitalist development path*; 1961–1975, *national or autonomous socialist model*; mid-1970s–1989, *international socialist model* (similar to those put in practice in Eastern Europe); and 1990-present, *mixed socialist model* (state and non-state economic actors share import production functions, and state and market mechanisms combine in the distribution of goods and services).
3. Extensive analysis can be found in Julio Carranza, "La crisis: un diagnóstico. Los retos de la economía cubana," in *Cuba: apertura y reforma económica Perfil de un debate*, ed. Bert Hoffmann (Caracas: Nueva Sociedad, 1995), and García Hernández et al., *Política industrial, reconversión productiva y competitividad.*

4. Some characteristics of this new period are articulated in Raúl Castro's speech of July 26, 2007, his speeches after February 24, 2008, and his closing speech to the Sixth Plenum of the Cuban Communist Party in April of 2008.

5. In this new period of social policy, education has become even more of a factor in mobility and a tool to break the chains that reproduce social disadvantage. Therefore, many education reforms are in progress, including a program for Integral Attention to the Child in primary education, including a class size of no more than twenty students per teacher; a program to train more elementary school teachers to meet the growing demand; an audiovisual program to use televised classes, improve the quality of teaching, widen its content and guarantee its homogeneity for all students; a program to universalize computer education; a program to train more art teachers to enhance recognition of artistic talent and teach art at the primary and secondary level; dropout recovery programs to reincorporate former students by offering them opportunities to access higher education; and a program to decentralize higher education by creating university branches in all municipalities, teaching many subjects through distance-learning. The dropout recovery and decentralization programs create conditions for broader access without meritocratic requirements.

6. Viviana Togores González, "Una mirada al gasto social en Cuba a partir de la crisis de los 90," in *Seguridad social en Cuba Diagnósticos, retos y perspectivas*, ed. Lothar Witte (Caracas: Nueva Sociedad, 2003), and Comisión Económica para América Latina y el Caribe (CEPAL), *Panorama Social* (Santiago: CEPAL, 1994).

7. Regarding self-employment and its possible undercount, see Lilia Núñez,"Más allá del cuentapropismo en Cuba," *Temas* 11 (1997): 41–50; Viviana Togores González," El trabajo por cuenta propia. Desarrollo y peculiaridades en la economía cubana" (Havana: Fondos bibliográficos del Centro de Estudios de la Economía Cubana, 1996), and "Consideraciones sobre el Sector Informal de la economía. Un estudio de su comportamiento en Cuba" (Havana: Fondos del Centro de Estudios de la Economía Cubana, 1997).

8. This analysis is based on changes in the employment structure by occupational categories. See also Lilia Nuñez, "Categorías ocupacionales y movilidad social" in *El análisis de la movilidad social. Propuesta de una perspectiva metodológica integrada y caracterización del caso cubano, Informe de Investigación* (Havana: Centro de Investigaciones Psicológicas y Sociológicas, 2009).

9. Boris Nerey and N. Birsmart, "Estructura social y estructura salarial en Cuba. Encuentros y desencuentros" (Mimeo, 1999).

10. L. Añé, "La reforma económica y la economía familiar en Cuba," in *Reforma económica y cambio social en América Latina y el Caribe*, ed. Mauricio de Miranda (Cali: T/M Ediciones, 2000).

11. Julio Carranza, Pedro M. Monreal González, and Luis Gutiérrez Urdaneta, *Cuba, la reestructuración de la economía : una propuesta para el debate* (Caracas, Venezuela: Editorial Nueva Sociedad. Fundación Friedrich Ebert, Oficina para el Caribe, 1997).

12. Viviana Togores González, "Cuba: efectos sociales de la crisis y el ajuste económico de los 90," *Boletín del Centro de Estudios de la Economía Cubana* (Havana: CEEC, 1998).

13. Oficina Nacional de Estadísticas, *Anuario Estadístico de Cuba* (Havana, 2008).

14. Anicia García and B. Anaya, "Política Social en Cuba, nuevo enfoque y programas recientes" (Havana: Center for the Study of the Cuban Economy, 2006).

15. Oficina Nacional de Estadísticas, *Anuario Estadístico de Cuba* (Havana, 2008).

16. Angela Ferriol, "Política social y desarrollo. Una aproximación global," in *Política social y reformas estructurales: Cuba a principios del siglo XXI*, ed. Elena Álvarez and Jorge Mattar (Mexico City: CEPAL-INIE-PNUD, 2004).

17. An economy in which the state is the driving force of economic processes, based on central planning, with priority for social guarantees, and with markets functioning under regulated prices and subsidized products. Other characteristics, however, are a dual currency and market segmentation.

18. Jorge Mario Sánchez Egozcue, "Remesas y Consumo en Cuba" (Havana: Universidad de La Habana, Mimeo, 2006).

19. Pedro Monreal González, "Migraciones y remesas familiares: Veinte hipótesis sobre el caso de Cuba," *Economía y Desarrollo* 134 (2003): 89–124.

20. *Tiendas de recaudación de divisas:* "Shops for the collection of foreign currency."

21. Comisión Económica para América Latina y el Caribe (CEPAL), *La economía cubana. Reformas estructurales y desempeño en los noventa* (Santiago: CEPAL, 1997).

22. The "mobility balance" (*saldo de movilidad*) is the sum of the percentage gains of the groups that increased within each analyzed dimension. This table includes the balances calculated on the basis of Tables 8.2 (groups by forms of property), 8.4 (economic activity sectors), 8.5 (occupational categories), 8.7 (managerial or non-managerial occupations), and 8.8 (educational levels).

23. Regarding poverty and its profiles, see also Ferriol, "Política social y desarrollo"; Maria del Carmen Zabala, "Los estudios cualitativos de la pobreza en Cuba," in *Paper presented at the Taller XX Aniversario del Centro de Investigaciones Psicológicas y Sociológicas* (Havana: CIPS, 2003); Mayra Paula Espina Prieto, *Políticas de atención a la pobreza y la desigualdad. Examinando el rol del Estado en la experiencia cubana* (Buenos Aires: CLACSO-CROP, 2008); and Rodrigo Espina Prieto and Pablo Rodríguez, "Raza y desigualdad en la Cuba actual," *Temas* 45 (2006).

24. M. Álvarez Suárez, "Mujer y poder en Cuba," in *Cuba: Construyendo Futuro*, ed. Mayra Espina Prieto, Manuel Monereo Pérez, Miguel Riera and Juan Valdés Paz (Madrid: El Viejo Topo, 2000).

25. D. Echevarría, "Mujer Empleo y Dirección en Cuba: Algo más que estadísticas." Paper presented at the celebration of "15 años del Centro de Estudios de la Economía Cubana," Center for the Study of the Cuban Economy, 2004.

26. Álvarez Suárez, "Mujer y poder en Cuba," in *Cuba: Construyendo Futuro*, ed. Mayra Espina Prieto et al.

27. Oficina Nacional de Estadísticas (ONE), *Censo de Población y Vivienda* (Havana: ONE, 2006).

28. Rodrigo Espina Prieto and Pablo Rodríguez, "Raza y desigualdad en la Cuba actual," *Temas* 45 (2006): 44–54.

29. According to the census of 2002, Cuba's population by skin color is white at 65.05%, black at 10.08%, and mixed at 24.86%. See also ONE, *Censo de Población y Vivienda*.

30. L. Añé, Ángela Ferriol, and Maribel Ramos, "Reforma económica y Población en riesgo de Ciudad de la Habana," Summary Research Report (Havana: INIE, 2004).

31. Mayra Espina Prieto, "Reajuste y movilidad social en Cuba," *Cuadernos Sociológicos* 2 (2003): 19–43.

32. The legal standards regulating self-employment in Cuba restrict it to a purely individual form. With the exception of small private restaurants and some other cases, the rules generally prohibit hiring any additional labor force or creating micro- or small businesses or cooperatives. Moreover, the self-employed lack access to a wholesale market in products and raw materials that would allow them to lower their costs.

33. Consideration of the relationship between economics and social policy lies outside the scope of this analysis, but it is indispensable for policy recommendations. See Carranza, Monreal González, and Gutiérrez Urdaneta, *Cuba, la reestructuración de la economía: una propuesta para el debate*; Espina Prieto, *Políticas de atención a la pobreza y la desigualdad*; and Monreal González, "La globalización y los dilemas de las trayectorias económicas de Cuba."

9

Geography and Habitat: Dimensions of Equity and Social Mobility in Cuba

Lucy Martín Posada and Lilia Núñez Moreno

Scholars and government officials in Latin America have lately begun to pay attention to all the forms of inadequate living conditions and surroundings, housing insecurity, and social segregation that many households in the region face.[1] In designing development policies and programs, the correct spatial scale is particularly important because it can show internal differences within large national aggregates, revealing smaller and less complex units with which to work. For those involved in planning, applying, and evaluating equity policies, it is essential to understand processes of social exclusion and differences in access to economic, cultural, and political resources or to opportunities for better living conditions.

Policy recommendations for promoting equity should be based on an understanding of its multidimensional nature and the advantages and disadvantages of the effects of differential accumulation on different groups. We must examine how the changes in opportunities may be reinforcing the differentiating effects in the social structure. The Latin American approach to analyzing poverty offers interesting avenues for understanding how public policies interact with the production of poverty, with a sharp focus on the emergence or consolidation of a set of practices and mechanisms that weaken citizen participation, and on processes of intergenerational transmission and reproduction of political exclusion that can impoverish the less powerful social groups.[2]

From the perspective of development, geography has a dual role as a source and recipient of inequality.[3] It is a regulator of opportunity for various population groups because of the differential access to opportunities for housing, work, income, education, etc. of those who live in diverse places. Thus, even in the presence of strong proactive policies to promote greater geographic social justice, the differences in well-being among population groups living in different areas can persist and even grow in consonance with each area's level of insertion in the logic of development, especially in conditions of crisis and high levels of decentralization.

Selection processes occur in two different spheres. One is the set of choices that individuals make and the other is the institutionalized social selection related to public policy and processes that impoverish or enrich groups possessing unequal access to power. The borders between the individual and the institutional spheres are not easily identified, yet clearly the actions of certain groups are more effective and there are systematic differences in income, education, etc., that persist through intergenerational reproduction.[4] A similar process in the opposite direction occurs with those groups in a situation of relative disadvantage. To alter this reproduction of inequalities would require active policies to promote equal opportunities and also differentiated policies to favor the more socially disadvantaged groups in order to close the widening equity gaps in the interest of greater social justice.

Some groups remain in disadvantaged or excluded positions even in the presence of active policies to promote equity and social justice; this is a subject of great interest to researchers of inequality. Its study requires attention to household-level practices based on the study of coping strategies and how these are situated within a larger economic structure determined by public interventions. Formal and informal mechanisms combine to mobilize individual and collective resources and networks with the aim of increasing the satisfaction of social needs in the most efficient manner.

Cuba is burdened by the enormous difficulty of eradicating the economic, cultural, material, and symbolic imprint of a colonial experience and the limitations imposed by its insertion into a global economy as a country with limited natural resources and subject to an intense embargo. Yet it is also crucial to focus on the country's planning of its development process, noting its insufficient attention to a concept of sustainability and self-development driven by local socioeconomic actors.

In this chapter, we describe the most important effects of social policy on social mobility and equity in the 1990s and early 2000s, as measured along two main axes that reveal differences in development in Cuba: geography and habitat. We work with information gathered from our own research and also from that of other scholars from a wide array of Cuban institutions. We then construct an up-to-date diagnostic of the equity gaps in spatial terms and present a set of policy recommendations directed at them. Our premise is based on the understanding that the persistence of social disadvantage and social mobility barriers affecting certain social groups requires special attention in both the research and social policy spheres.

An Assessment of Geography and Social Mobility from an Equity Perspective

In discussions of equity and spatial factors, we emphasize the role of geographical location in the reproduction and generational transmission of social advantages and disadvantages, producing accumulated differentials between social groups. Different localities have comparative and competitive advantages and these generate substantial differences between population groups. These differences may be observed in the formation of new social strata and development agents, in their degree of insertion into the labor market, in their access to material well-being, and in life strategies and subjective components.

We analyze the variation in development among Cuban provinces and between urban and rural areas. These units of analysis are representative of the distinct types of complex economic and social networks and ties that exist in Cuba. Under the current political-administrative divisions, the provinces are the disaggregated statistical category best-suited to illustrate the island's socio-structural dynamics. Although most studies have directed limited attention to the impact of rural-urban dichotomies on the processes of inequality and social mobility in Cuba, we believe that the study of these dynamics is critical because of the central role that the agricultural transformations undertaken in recent decades have played for the development strategies of rural areas.

Cuban socioeconomic policies have sought to address the marked geographic inequalities which the revolution inherited through planning and the distribution of the available resources toward greater proportionality at the provincial level and through universal and unitary social policy coverage, including the provision of a broad range of social services in rural areas and backward provinces. Over the last five decades, educational, public health, and social service structures were expanded in various regions and these investments contributed to an evident narrowing of gaps between provinces and between rural and urban areas, as well as an improvement in housing quality for the Cuban population. The widening of equal opportunity for all social groups and the concomitant upward mobility of the most disadvantaged groups—the poor, women, peasants, other rural inhabitants, and those living in the eastern end of the island—fostered the incorporation of a great many people into modern sectors of the economy and the political system. Just as economic growth is not distributed homogeneously, the structure of opportunities that determines social equity also reveals important geographic differences. In this context of many types of inequalities, social policy is stronger to the extent that it recognizes such disparities and remains sufficiently malleable to avoid social exclusion.

Recent studies of current trends in structural mobility in Cuba show that access to opportunities varies for different urban and rural social groups (in terms of gender, schooling, and occupational level) (see Table 9.1).[5] At the same time, a strong effort has been made to equalize the opportunities for citizens living in different geographical areas and to broaden access to housing and basic services, including the supply of water and electricity, among others.

Nevertheless, rural areas are still characterized by a shrinking population due to migration, a greater concentration of people with low levels of education and training, and the lowest relative levels of access to electricity and potable water, among other social disadvantages. Processes of fragmentation

Table 9.1. Selected Indicators for 1985, by Province

Province	Investments per capita (pesos per inhabitant)	Index of employment (employed persons as a share of working-age population, %)	Average monthly salary (pesos per worker)	School attendance (among those 6–14 years old), %	Infant mortality (per thousand live births)	Maternal mortality (per 100,000)
Pinar del Río	505	51	177	97.5	14.9	17.3
La Habana	698	66	192	99.2	15.2	9.9
C. Habana	577	70	197	98.1	14.0	36.6
Matanzas	691	62	187	97.8	14.5	21.2
Villa Clara	403	52	185	98.8	15.3	8.3
Cienfuegos	1152	66	200	97.6	17.0	32.6
S. Spíritus	551	50	186	97.1	18.6	46.8
C. Ávila	537	56	187	97.8	15.4	49.1
Camagüey	615	56	185	98.7	15.7	31.3
Las Tunas	659	50	183	97.2	21.9	10.4
Holguín	950	44	189	95.3	16.9	42.1
Granma	359	43	173	98.2	19.0	31.0
S. de Cuba	451	45	178	97.6	16.4	39.7
Guantánamo	433	40	175	98.8	18.9	26.7
Isla de la J.	744	75	185	99.9	23.7	48.4

Source: Elier Méndez and Carmen Lloret in "Desarrollo Humano en Cuba y América Latina" (Universidad Central de las Villas, 2006). Published by Eumed.net.

and polarization of social structures are under way. Groups of highly successful producers with evident material well-being, especially in the western part of the country, and those involved in raising diverse crops and livestock with access to important markets, coexist with other clearly disadvantaged groups, most notably people living in the eastern part of the country and farmers growing crops such as coffee, who have not been able to enter such market spaces adequately and whose situation is precarious. Unequal structures of opportunities for population groups across geographical areas stem from material conditions, environmental or natural resource endowments, human resource qualifications, traditions and customs, levels of development of economic structures, and the functioning of relationships and networks.

In Cuba, there is a general tendency toward the strengthening of the peasantry, especially private farmers, which has helped them to avoid impoverishment. This is the result of state policies and the ingenuity of these farmers to take effective advantage of opportunities in a context of universal-equity policies (see Table 9.2). Nevertheless, the rural areas remain at a relative disadvantage. Agriculture remains unable to meet the population's food needs and nutritional requirements. Cuba has a high dependence on food imports. Yet at the local level there are considerable reserves of resources and capacities that could allow for better solutions to the problems that now plague the Cuban food production, and there are new approaches to rural development that increasingly recognize the value of communities and nascent local agriculture. It is therefore vital to reorganize the development of rural areas with a more integrated vision of development.

Table 9.2. Indicators of Urban-Rural Development[6]

	Up to 1990		2000s	
	urban	rural	urban	rural
% population	(1990)73.9	(1990)26.1	(2008)75.3	(2008)24.7
% population with access to potable water	(1990)83.6	(1990)77.8	(2004)98.2	(2004)87.3
% population with access to sewage services	(1990)96.1	(1990)68.2	(2004)97.9	(2004)86.2
% population with access to electricity	(1981)98.7	(1981)45.6	(2002)99.5	(2002)85.5

Source: Anuarios Estadísticos 1989, 2004 and 2008; Censo de Población y Viviendas 1981 and 2002; and Oficina Nacional de Estadísticas (ONE).

One criticism leveled at socialist planning is precisely that its geographic vision has subordinated regional and local economies and societies to centrally defined goals without managing to adjust these goals adequately in conformity with local interests and peculiarities. The predominant viewpoint of policymakers involved in Cuban socioeconomic planning sees local territories as replicas of national logics and minimizes the role of local societies and actors and their potential for self-transformation. Moreover, decisions about where to locate new investment should take markets and competitiveness into account to a greater extent than had been the case before the collapse of trade with the Soviet bloc. These considerations may represent tradeoffs, as policy-makers may be dissuaded from their goals of reducing inequalities.

A useful tool to illustrate the differences associated with differing localities in Cuba is the Geographic Human Development Index (*Índice de Desarrollo Humano Territorial*, or IDHT) developed by the *Centro de Investigaciones de la Economía Mundial* (CIEM) and the United Nations Development Program (UNDP). This index is based on provincial socioeconomic performance across selected indicators; it has been measured in 1996, 1999 and 2003. The eastern provinces, Camagüey, and Pinar del Río occupy the most disadvantaged positions.

Table 9.3. Geographic Human Development Index in Cuba

	1996*	1999	2003
Ciudad de La Habana	0.7278	0.9331	0.9427
Cienfuegos	0.7203	0.8525	0.8389
La Habana	0.6748	0.8365	0.8289
Ciego de Avila	0.6249	0.8213	0.8205
Matanzas	0.6796	0.8352	0.8122
Sancti Spíritus	0.6492	0.8179	0.7995
Villa Clara	0.6856	0.7915	0.7914
Las Tunas	0.4348	0.7671	0.7746
Pinar del Río	0.5382	0.7763	0.7745
Camagüey	0.4641	0.7813	0.7737
Holguín	0.4932	0.7867	0.7572
Santiago de Cuba	0.5194	0.7612	0.7466
Guantánamo	0.4661	0.7304	0.7329
Granma	0.3724	0.7122	0.7209

* The procedures of the first study differ from those used in the other two; quantitative comparisons are possible only between the latter two.

Source: Martínez (1997) and (2000); López (2004).

Figure 9.1. Cuban Provinces by HDI Levels

Key: Alto = high; Medio = middle; Bajo = low.

Source: Constructed by the authors based on 2003 measurements of provincial HDI.

Relative to 1999, most areas show a drop in the level of development in 2003 (see Table 9.3). The poles are represented by Havana City and the eastern province of Granma, with a widening of the gap between them, even though Granma has been one of the provinces with the most development in recent years. Based on provincial values for the latest HDI measurements, the provinces can be grouped in three categories:[7] Advanced level (greater than 0.80): Havana City, Havana Province, Matanzas, Cienfuegos, and Ciego de Avila; Mid level (between 0.76 and 0.80): Pinar del Río, Sancti Spíritus, Villa Clara, Camagüey, Las Tunas, and Holguín; and Low level (0.75 and below): Granma, Santiago de Cuba, and Guantánamo.

The dimensions that most strongly account for the inequality among provinces are the volume of investments and economic activity and living conditions measured by access to housing, potable water and electricity. At the same time, perhaps as a particular trait of the Cuban development model, inequality coexists with a high degree of homogeneity in a group of basic indicators of human welfare, such as school attendance rates, life expectancy at birth, infant mortality, and maternal mortality. In addition, equity is further reflected in the fact that the achievements in various spheres of human development are not concentrated in particular provinces.[8]

Inspired by the general UNDP methodology, various Cuban universities have developed and applied similar methods to calculate indices for provinces and municipalities based on available data (the universities of Las Villas, Cienfuegos, and Las Tunas, among others). These research efforts have put the achievements and opportunities of the residents of various geographical areas on the map of inequality research.

Our review of the studies undertaken since the early 1990s from a geographic perspective allowed us to identify the characteristics of social re-stratification. These studies confirm that locality has become an important marker of inequality. The following summary, as well as the policy recommendations we will outline later in this chapter, are based on the findings of specialists from well-known institutions in Cuba. Research indicates that there is:

- Uneven geographic expression of recent favorable economic policy changes.[9]

- A positive linear relationship between population and economic activity, evidenced by the population growth experienced in areas where various economic sectors have revived.[10]

- Widening inequality between and within provinces and municipalities.[11]

- Disequilibrium of socioeconomic processes within provinces, and the accentuation of inter-municipal disparities by the dismantling of some economic sectors (the sugar industry) and the strengthening of others (tourism).[12]

- Weakened policies aimed at diminishing regional disparities, along with the rise of territory-based comparative advantages that promote social inequalities according to place and geography.[13]

- Migratory processes spurred by the contraction of public investment, contributing to a surge in the share of the population residing in the nation's capital.[14]

- Differentiation within municipalities marked by a concentration of dwellers in unhealthy tenements and districts (even in the most "luminous" municipalities).[15]

- Reproduction of particularly poor living conditions in the outskirts of the capital city, where residents who have migrated from rural areas concentrate.[16]

- Persistence of disadvantaged conditions for the Eastern provinces, Camagüey, and Pinar del Río, all with the lowest HDIs.[17]

- Correlation between the most rural areas and those with lowest HDI (eastern provinces and Pinar del Río).[18]

- Policies oriented, even in moments of crisis, toward greater geographic equity in social indicators.[19]

- Strong trends toward greater heterogeneity of local actors and societies. Formation of four broad, geographic socio-structural typologies:
  mixed-state, private, farmers' cooperatives, and state-private foreign.[20]

- Tendency of rural areas to continue to show lower levels of development and greater levels of deterioration in living conditions in terms
  of technical infrastructure, hygienic-sanitary conditions, availability
  of services, cultural and recreational options, housing, and transportation conditions.[21]

- Diversification of groups linked to agriculture, which accentu-
  ates socio-structural heterogeneity and the complexity of ongoing
  transformations.[22]

- Differential socioeconomic gains for some producers, most particularly individual private peasants. Fewer opportunities for cooperative
  members or agricultural wage workers to improve their economic
  situations.[23]

- Sectoral differentiation in response to economic incentives, provoking
  significant movement from mountains and coffee farms to other more
  attractive areas and sectors.[24]

- Weakening of rural culture and identity because urban culture is
  overvalued and the educational system is not adapted to rural
  particularities.[25]

- Limited opportunities for initiating and nurturing local development
  or for the effective promotion of the local population's interests.[26]

The differentiating effects of social structures have been reinforced by
the structuring of opportunities in the new economy, in particular, the cir-
cular relationship between structural conditions and individual practices.
The analysis of individual trajectories[27] points to the emergence of a disparate pattern of opportunities for social groups born in different provinces,
which causes greater population movement out of the eastern provinces.
Thus the western provinces have a greater role as the end-points of migration, while province-of-birth and social extraction act as markers of
inequality in terms of the type of economic integration that individuals
achieve. Personal strategies of upward mobility emerge; people leave old
jobs for new ones in more advantaged sectors or economic spaces, or move
to provinces with a higher level of development, or partner with people in
more advantageous social positions.

The following excerpts from our interviews illustrate some of these
mobility strategies:

"Ha, ha, ha, who doesn't want to live in the capital? . . . When I graduated, I didn't like what I was assigned to do for social service, which was to be an engineer in a tobacco cooperative. So then I got another gig in a discotheque and in a nightclub in Pinar, but that's a whole different thing, we really had no prospects there, and by then we had the baby girl and we didn't want her growing up without some better kind of social development, cultural development, you know what I mean? . . . and, what can I say, a school friend found me a job and we decided to come here . . . the most important factors in people's economic success are their personal initiative and their social contacts." (Male, 35, agronomic engineer, hotel bartender, from Pinar del Río, now living in Havana, of working class background.)

"My parents were always looking to improve their conditions, so they moved to Havana when my father, who was a military pilot, was given a house there . . . now I live apart from my parents, in my own place, since I got married four years ago." [Since she finished high school, she has worked at various posts, first in a government office,[28] then in an auto-body shop, then as a teacher's aide in a school, and as secretary to a provincial court] . . . *"each time just for a little while, because I really never lasted very long in any job."* [Now she is a housewife, and her husband, a foreign sailor, gives her a thousand dollars a month.]

"I have an advantageous position, economically very good. I don't lack for anything, in general I live better than my parents because I have fewer worries and more income." (Female, 27, white, high school education, no formal employment, from Las Tunas, now living in Havana, from a professional family background.)

Other trajectories have been less successful, such as that of a woman who worked for twenty years at a Maternity Hospital and lives with her husband, a kiln operator in a brick factory, and their thirteen-year-old son, a student in the eighth grade. Her main income comes from her job:

"My husband sometimes borrows his father's car to take a little trip, which is how we've gotten the electric fan and some clothes for our kid . . . I'm better off than my parents and other relatives, because I have a profession, a job, and some accomplishments." (Female, 34, black, high school education, works in a blood bank, born and raised in Cienfuegos, of working class background.)

In sum, the factors that affect social advantages to a greater or lesser extent in present-day Cuba include social background, place of origin, and personal behavior, which are in turn largely conditioned by one's social and cultural resources, education, training, networks, and social interactions. The interviewees' assessments of their personal upward or downward mobility reveal a more judgmental and critical attitude from those groups that at face value have a more advantageous position, who are from more highly developed geographical areas and from social strata not linked to agriculture. Furthermore, our results suggest that the crisis and reforms have produced geographically differentiated effects on inequality. Negative impacts tend to be concentrated in the eastern region and in rural areas, deepening historical disadvantages.

Changes in Habitats and Mobility: The Impact on Social Equity Policy

Every country struggles with the challenge of the problems surrounding the variety of habitats where its citizens reside. The relationship between habitat, equity, mobility, and social policy is a central node of analysis of social transformations and the effectiveness of such transformations. Access to housing constitutes an essential good required for each family for a decent life and to develop its members' human capacities. Although for some time housing problems were not prioritized in policy or in academic discussion, they are again coming to the fore in debates about poverty and social exclusion. Residential exclusion is one form of social exclusion that becomes a source of social disadvantage.[29]

Studies of poverty customarily associate social deterioration with inadequate housing, pointing to insufficiencies in material conditions, availability of services, and security of tenure.[30] From an equity perspective, access to adequate housing (or access to the means to get it) is a right, an essential element of human welfare at the level of daily life. Lack of such access is a major symptom of inequality or exclusion. Among the most easily visible expressions of social inequality are the differences in housing patterns among groups, evident in residential practices and associated social relations. Movement toward better housing conditions can signify changes in individual trajectories.

Since 1976, international bodies have put forward a new approach to housing. They have stopped viewing it as a "product," linked to an interpretation of housing as mere shelter, and started to regard it as a "process."[31] This new view includes physical access, adequate security, and proximity to sources of employment and basic services, in short, decent living conditions, the meaning of which varies for countries according to cultural, economic, social, and environmental factors.[32] This represents a shift from a simple material concept to a more diverse and interconnected analytical framework: "An understanding of habitat implicitly involves a connection between the physical and the imaginary, irreducible and inseparable, including both the home and its surroundings, stretching from near to far, all within a complex notion of habitat."[33]

This reinterpretation of the notion of housing broadens it to mean a space appropriate to human life, available at a reasonable cost and with access to services, to which one can retreat in isolation if one so desires, and which constitutes an area of both individual and collective identity and recognition. Such a space is "a symbolic referent of human existence, involving economic, political, social, esthetic, and cultural dimensions."[34] Thus, habitat is the space occupied by an individual, a group, or a human community beyond the physical area where they reproduce their biological needs. It is the context in which the social organism approaches its natural and cultural potential; it constitutes a support and condition for human development. This integral notion of housing (or home or habitat) includes physical configuration of the infrastructure (its dimensions and space), and external infrastructure that supports the residence with fundamental services, environmental quality, and access to participatory spaces. It may also include elements of residents' subjectivity such as perceptions of satisfaction that would offer evidence to be used in the evaluation of housing policies.

The degree of adequacy of housing can be used to measure the residents' relative social position and explain their trajectory. Upward or downward mobility is equivalent to improvement or lack thereof in habitat, depending on the opportunities that social policies offer to achieve decent living conditions, whether these policies are universal ones or are directed toward specific groups.

In Cuba, habitat is essential to equity and a marker of inequality. Yet despite public housing and the national government's commitment to guarantee access to housing, deficiencies in habitat form part of the profile of poverty and social vulnerability in Cuba.[35] Within the Cuban social project, housing has been regarded as a social good, and the goal of housing policy has been for every family to reside in an adequate home. In the housing area, the strategy of equitable social development has been expressed as "achieving a better balance in urban development by prioritizing secondary cities and improving living and working conditions in rural and mountain areas while fostering better rural-urban integration."[36] This understanding has shaped efforts toward equality.

In Cuba, unlike in many other countries, housing policy upholds the principle of personal property, provided that housing cannot be converted into a means of personal enrichment. The intent has been to eliminate private property from the real estate sector. In terms of social justice, this implies access to housing for all families and limits on segregation and spatial polarization among different social groups. Over the past twenty years, the achievements of various Cuban programs derive from this social policy model.

Table 9.4. Summary of Housing Indicators, 1970–2002

Indicators	1970	1981	2002
Persons per housing unit	4.49	4.2	3.1
Type of unit	(%)	(%)	(%)
House	63.5	66.9	74.6
Apartment	9.9	14.8	17.9
Other	26.7	18.3	7.5
Water supply			
By pipes within the unit	45.5	52.7	76.2
Outside the unit	21.2	21.5	23.8
Other	33.3	25.8	–
Bathtub or shower			
Within the unit	46.6	49.2	87.5
Outside the unit	53.0	46.1	12.5
None	0.4	4.7	–
Toilet facilities			
Flush toilet within the unit	36.3	45.2	59.7
Outside the unit (flush toilet or latrine)	45.7	45.9	31.7
None	18.1	8.9	8.6
Cooking facilities			
Exclusively for use of the unit	88.3	93.6	99.5
Common to several units	11.3	0.7	0.5
None	0.4	5.7	–
Lighting methods			
Electricity (of all sorts, including alternative energy)	70.7	82.9	95.5
Kerosene lamps	28.9	16.9	4.4
Other	0.4	0.2	0.05
Coverage by sewage service[*]			
Total served	–	94.7	94.2
Sewer piping	–	38.2	38.4
Septic tanks, pits, or latrines	–	56.5	55.8

Sources: Authors' calculations based on Censo de Población y Viviendas 1970, 1981, and 2002.
[*]*Source:* Anuario Estadístico de Cuba 2003, % of population rather than units.

Over these years, too, there has been a rising tendency to use such indicators of housing and habitability, as compared with those chosen by CEPAL, to characterize the adequacy of urban housing conditions and their recent evolution in Latin America.[37] This tendency demonstrates tangible progress in the housing conditions of the Cuban population (see Table 9.4).

The effects of the Cuban housing policy are also evident by provinces. A comparison of data from the censuses of 1970, 1981, and 2002 shows improvements in living conditions measured by the reductions in several measures of overcrowding across Cuban provinces (see Table 9.5). Although the results do not correlate directly with provincial HDI, the eastern provinces still exhibit less favorable parameters in these variables, coinciding with their low HDI indices and calling attention to various levels of provincial differentiation in housing.

Table 9.5. Housing Conditions by Province, 1981 and 2002

Provinces	Persons per unit		Persons per room (all rooms included)		Persons per bedroom	
	2002	1981	2002	1981	2002	1981
CUBA	3.2	4.1	0.8	1.0	1.3	2.1
Pinar del Río (low HDI)	3.2	4.5	0.8	1.0	1.4	2.1
Havana Province (medium HDI)	3.2	4.3	0.8	0.9	1.3	2.0
City of Havana (high HDI)	3.2	3.6	0.8	1.1	1.4	2.0
Matanzas (medium HDI)	3.2	4.2	0.8	1.0	1.3	2.0
Villa Clara (low HDI)	3.2	4.3	0.7	0.9	1.3	2.0
Cienfuegos (high HDI)	3.1	4.3	0.8	1.0	1.3	2.1
Sancti Spíritus (medium HDI)	3.2	4.5	0.7	0.9	1.3	2.0
Ciego de Ávila (medium HDI)	3.1	4.1	0.8	1.0	1.3	2.1
Camagüey (low HDI)	3.2	4.1	0.8	1.0	1.3	2.0
Las Tunas (low HDI)	3.1	4.2	0.8	1.0	1.3	2.2
Holguín (low HDI)	3.1	4.2	0.8	1.1	1.3	2.1
Granma (low HDI)	3.1	4.2	0.8	1.1	1.3	2.3
Santiago de Cuba (low HDI)	3.3	4.1	0.9	1.2	1.4	2.3
Guantánamo (low HDI)	3.4	4.1	0.9	1.2	1.4	2.2
Isle of Youth (medium HDI)	3.4	4.1	0.9	1.1	1.4	2.0

Source: Censos de Población y Viviendas 1981 and 2002.

The characteristics of the housing stock have also improved (see Table 9.6). Although we lack information disaggregated at the provincial level, regional disparities are to be expected. The 2002 census revealed that houses with palm-bark or palm-board walls, earthen floors, and palm-thatch roofs can still be found outside the City of Havana—these are houses of minimal quality similar to those in the sixteenth century.[38]

As Espina and Togores explained in Chapter 8 of this volume, the 1990s ushered in a new era in the social composition of Cuban society at the

Table 9.6. Characteristics of the Housing Stock, 1999 and 2007

	1999	2007
Total	100%	100%
Good	52.8	59.5
Fair and poor	47.2	40.5
Of these, can be demolished	8.6	4.3
Of these, can be rehabilitated	–	14.0

Source: Authors' calculations based on INV 1999, "Situación del fondo de viviendas," and René Lozano, "Programa de viviendas, urbanizaciones y tecnologías," paper presented at the workshop-seminar "Reflexiones sobre la vivienda en Cuba." Fondos del INV, Havana, 2007, cited in Gazmuri 2009:63.

national, provincial, and local levels. In the current period, there is a tension between continuity and rupture; while some components remained the same, others have been transformed, and new socioeconomic groups have emerged in accord with the economic strategy that the country has adopted.

The income distribution of the Cuban population in the 1990s shows differences in access to consumption goods and in the standards of living for different groups, including access to better housing conditions. For many reasons, in spite of housing policies, the government has not been able to solve existing problems in this area. One factor that helps to explain this unmet target is the continuing gap that remains between strategic goals and housing administration policies.

Moreover, habitat is one of the spheres where the greatest social differences are expressed.[39] Documents outlining the direction of the country's environmental policy (such as the 2011–15 Outline of a New Environmental Strategy) list major environmental problems such as the deterioration in hygienic-sanitary conditions in populated areas and point to the deteriorated condition of the housing stock as a major factor that provokes adverse environmental impacts in both urban and rural areas. Studies dealing with the country's housing and habitat published since the late 1990s include official reports, essays, articles, and research results that draw on a wide range of methodological strategies: quantitative, qualitative, national scope, and local scope.[40] Some authors also comment on the scarcity and unreliability of data and indicators related to housing. These works display near unanimity in policy recommendations for housing and its surrounding environment (projections of housing policy; models of habitat development; legal approaches; material resources; construction technologies, design, and execution; human and financial resources). Table 9.7 summarizes the contrasts identified between strategic aspirations and concrete outcomes.

Table 9.7. Summary of Policy Analyses on Habitat

Strategic principles

- Housing policy formulated according to basic principles of equity with a leading role by the state, without a housing market, with the permanent central goal of improving the population's living conditions.
- Political will and commitment to respond to housing needs. Universal policy of broad social coverage to create equal opportunities for access to housing. High percentage of home ownership.
- Centralized model of housing production and management. Model of fully socially-provided housing coverage on a national level. Prevalence of an egalitarian concept of equal housing for all based on an idea of "typical" buildings.
- Carrying out some local housing efforts with grassroots participation.
- City planning measures to avoid spatial segregation, in search of a high degree of social integration in cities.
- Development of strategies to reduce the housing deficit, such as construction brigades of workers from state enterprises, with training, materials, and equipment supplied by the state.
- Broadening opportunities for varied social actors to build housing.
- Legislation intended to eradicate the real estate market and the concept of housing as a mercantile good, making the state the lead actor in construction, production, and distribution of housing units, so as to avoid reproduction of housing stratification.
- Regulations govern internal migration from other provinces to the capital city, and living conditions in the capital's most crowded boroughs.
- A centralized conception of how to produce and distribute material resources.
- Studies of the relationship between types of habitat, environmental conditions, and their influence on differential health patterns within the population; strong impacts on the quality of life through health.
- Proposals to use quick and low-cost technologies.
- Policy to repopulate rural areas, in response to a need for agricultural labor force.
- Accumulation of broad human and institutional capital. Availability of highly qualified workforce. Introduction of novel practices such as "community architects" to advise and strengthen self-building by residents.
- Openness to international cooperation in the housing sphere.

Current situation

- Limited conception of housing policies, still poorly integrated. In the formulation of solutions to the housing problem, lack of attention to issues at the micro level: economic, social, and environmental sustainability; the role of families and their diversity in the development of a new understanding of their needs; synergistic integration of local institutions, disciplines, and actors; or similarities and differences at the provincial level.
- Rigid housing strategies, not well adapted to the socioeconomic conditions of each stage of the country's development.
- Insufficient implementation of the housing construction model; does not take local particularities into account. Infrequent use made of successful local experiences.
- State-designed and constructed housing with low quality in terms of temperature control or visual and acoustic qualities, all of which influence quality of life and health.
- Ugly, monotonous developments, lifeless and poorly constructed, lacking in urban amenities, with resulting rejection by a part of the population.
- Low-quality plans and projects that generate low self-esteem and little sense of ownership among residents.
- Implementation of programs prioritized by central state administration entities, which have reproduced sectoral isolation, such as the creation of neighborhoods whose residents come from a single economic sector (doctors, scientists, tourism employees, armed forces personnel, high officials, employees of food programs).
- Loss of construction brigades' initial design, mission, and goals, which did not succeed in solving the problem of insufficient housing construction.
- Inequality between private and public space in terms of their functional and esthetic levels, corresponding to the needs and means of different social groups.
- Disequilibrium in the legal system because of inflexible and segmented visions that have prevented local adaptations.
- Legislation removed from reality and distanced from needs, limited to codifying rights and increasing duties so as to contain the accumulated housing deficit. Laws restricting the process of creating and managing housing, focused on what is not allowed.
- Proliferation of illegal settlements in the boroughs on the outskirts of the capital, with poor living conditions.
- Growth of underground speculation in housing and corrupt acquisition of housing.

Table 9.7. Summary of Policy Analyses on Habitat (continued)

Current situation (continued)

- Material poverty has weighed heavily on the housing sector. Total dependence on non-local resources.
- Predominant "constructivist" and "technologist" outlook centered on "quantity" absent integrated technological approaches. Rejects traditional technologies, favors importing technologies from other sources.
- Failure to develop a diversified and proactive construction materials industry at the local level.
- Uncritical country-wide application of a uniform housing design to both large cities and small ones and to both urban and rural areas.
- Undervalues socio-cultural variables. Transgresses cultural identity in the building of rural housing.
- Low levels of integration in the design of urban projects; fails to include public space (parks, services, or green areas to improve residential atmosphere). Less-than-optimal land use choices.
- Failure to take advantage of the potential of qualified human resources. Defunding of resources because of lack of stimuli and loss of technical authority.
- Low priority for housing in the state budget.
- Absence of financial administration by local government, and lack of authority to promote or choose between habitat investments. Absence of functional or credit-providing connection between local government and national banks.
- Underuse of possible sources of financing, too few relationships between different actors and institutional integration of research, construction, and development of international cooperation.

The interviews we carried out to examine the relationship between social mobility and housing at the micro level show that our interviewees can be seen to act as proprietors regardless of the condition of the housing unit or their position as head of household or family member.[41] This results from the housing policies implemented on a wide scale, in universal fashion, and for all population groups in the early years of the Cuban revolutionary process. Home property ownership is more widespread in Cuba than in other Latin American countries.[42] For our interviewees, the housing unit is a symbol of well-being and an income-generating resource; those with homes in good condition, many acquired through inheritance, often rent out rooms to obtain foreign currency earnings.

Only a few of our interviewees were rent-paying non-owners, even though this situation is quite common in Cuba. There are legal procedures to rent housing; the regulations to do so in domestic currency are much more flexible than those for renting to foreigners. Also not uncommon is the illegal renting of rooms for both short and long periods, even exceeding the three months allowed by law in the case of foreigners. The most common home renters are single people or families that would like to live independently and are in advantageous economic conditions because they receive foreign currency income that allows them to pay rent above officially established levels.

Our interviews also corroborated a positive correlation between housing quality and economic status; subjects living in "fair" or "poor" conditions were always nuclear families in unfavorable economic situations. Thus, our findings are consistent with those of a recently concluded study on poor Cuban families, which found that these households were characterized by bad living conditions in terms of type of housing unit, state of repair, living space, overcrowding, availability of domestic appliances, and hygienic-sanitary conditions.[43] In addition, those of our interviewees who worked on home improvements in recent years corresponded to those who had experienced upward mobility during that time. In these cases, once the family began to obtain income in foreign currency or experienced a substantial rise in income in general, its members almost immediately improved their homes or even moved "to a better neighborhood."

Interviewees whose housing situations had improved arrived at these situations in various ways but always thanks to an improved economic situation:

My situation now is much better than it was in the '80s. Now we have regular income and live well. Sure, it means working day and night, because when you're your own boss, you have to devote all twenty-four hours to whatever it is you do. The house I've had for sixteen years had been just a couple of poorly built rooms, but on a big lot. I fixed it up, and seven years ago I rebuilt it entirely. Now it has five bedrooms, living room, dining room, kitchen, two big patios (one that's ours, for the business, and another to rent) and a porch. We have air conditioners in every bedroom, a computer, an electric stove, etc." (Male, 56, white, self-employed, Havana.)

Since I joined the workforce I've always been in managerial positions, from shift supervisor in a laboratory or head of supply for a tourist facility to municipal director of commerce and restaurants. I don't have any other strategy to raise my income outside of my formal job, though I've always wished to have my own business. The house I live in belongs to my

wife, who acquired it in 2000. We've made some improvements, expand-
ing the kitchen, subdividing the living room to add another bedroom,
and in general the house has been totally restored. We have two refriger-
ators, a phone line and a cell phone, computers, a washing machine, two
air conditioners and cleaning service. I have a bank account, and a car
that belongs to my wife but I pay most of the cost of maintaining it.
(Male, 40, white, Havana.)

We've got problems and scarcities but we live better than in the '80s. It
hasn't been easy, but from our work we get what we need to live and help
out our old folks. We divide our time between our jobs and the Jehovah's
Witnesses. I've had several occupations: biology teacher, merchant
marine, and musician alongside my wife—right now we're working in
restaurants and hotels in Old Havana as a guitar duo. My house is five
years old, it's got four bedrooms (one for guests), living room, dining
room, kitchen, a big patio, a porch. It's got a good supply of appliances,
including air conditioners in each bedroom, microwaves in the kitchen,
etc. (Male, 44, mixed-race, Havana.)

From the viewpoint of equity, a set of factors directly threaten the fulfillment of the principles that have distinguished Cuba's social policies in the
realm of housing. If these disparities are not adequately confronted, they
could give rise to the reemergence of social fragmentation and residential
segregation. Among the most significant factors are:

- Economic inequalities in access to housing and habitat.[44]
- Excessive state centralization in housing construction.[45]
- Deficient design quality and execution in state housing, which generates low self-esteem and little sense of ownership among residents.[46]
- Limited vision of habitat, which fails to see it as a space offering productive opportunities (job creation, renting, small and medium-sized
  businesses, and other income-generating activities).[47]
- Impossibility of choosing among housing alternatives, or "socialist
  resignation."[48]
- Absence of a culture of coexistence to link the new urban complexes
  to the existing ones; thus there is a new generation of segregation and
  spatial inequality.[49]
- Socio-economic differences in families' ability to take on maintenance
  and conservation of older buildings.[50]

- Re-emergence of spontaneous settlements, which re-create unhealthy neighborhoods largely as a result of domestic migration.[51]
- Prolongation of stays in "transitory shelters," which has given rise to rootlessness, lack of self-esteem, rejection and social conflicts among many people.[52]
- Lack of technical assistance to do-it-yourself builders, which increases the esthetic gap between "popular" and "cultured" architecture.[53]
- Lack of housing integration because of the establishment of neighborhoods for specific sectors: doctors, teachers, scientists, etc.[54]
- Inadequate laws, giving rise to the rise of black market in real estate, and speculation and corruption in the production and distribution of housing.[55]
- Disconnection within urban areas due to deficient public transport and a street network that limits exchange and communication among neighborhoods.[56]

The accumulated housing deficit followed by the economic crisis of the 1990s (characterized by a contraction of construction and a re-stratification of Cuban society) intensified the serious disequilibrium between the housing supply and families' or individuals' opportunities to satisfy their housing needs. Thus housing became a powerful element of social differentiation in terms of possession of a housing unit and the differences in housing and habitat quality. The results were a spontaneous redistribution of living space, a proliferation of illegal construction reflecting income inequalities, differences in access to consumption goods among social groups, and the emergence of an informal and illegal market in real estate, which exists parallel to the governmental housing system and sometimes in contradiction with it.

After 1959, the Cuban government designed housing policies based on new ethical and human principles. Their major thrust was to increase the number of housing units built by the state and improve the living conditions of the poorest population sectors through eradication of evictions, elimination of unhealthy slums, and reductions in rents. The model was seen as unitary and appropriate for application throughout the country. It was therefore poorly structured in terms of focus and process, and it did not sufficiently take disparate social, geographical, sectoral, architectural, or subjective particularities into account. Thus, a largely inflexible paradigm has been implemented with little room left to incorporate alternative solutions. At the same, the results achieved in terms of habitat quality for the whole population during the early revolutionary period were part of an ambitious and transformational Cuban social policy model. Indeed, considering the gaps and difficulties of fully covering housing needs, the Cuban development model committed to equality and social justice represents an alternative to the hegemonic visions predominant in most of the countries of the region.

Policy solutions are now needed to foster greater degrees of creativity and integration as well as to recognize the country's geographic heterogeneity and its varied potential for housing and habitat development. Research has a role in generating policy prescriptions; the studies carried out in this area have led to a set of practical suggestions to confront problems of equity in the spatial realm. These proposals advance a more totalizing concept of development, including the capacity to combine local experience, initiative, autonomy, and self-financing coherently with central state planning. They include the following suggestions:

- *Improvement of the development planning process*, which includes:

  - A greater role for local communities and greater recognition of local practices in development planning;

  - More dynamic grassroots participation with a greater role for self-management and participation of local actors;

  - Incorporation of a "planning from below" approach, which would not be in conflict with central planning;

  - Make the model of housing construction and management more flexible, decentralized, diverse, and based on economic, social, and environmental viability;

  - Establish an investment policy to favor the provinces and areas from which most people are emigrating;

  - Consider geographic socio-structural differences when designing national economic and social policies. Identify local social actors when evaluating the advantages and limitations of each region;

  - Accord a greater role to the family when designing housing and habitat policy, recognizing their diversity, plurality, and changed needs under current conditions;

  - Improve available data to map living conditions in different geographical areas; and,

  - Revise legal regulations related to housing to facilitate the best use of resources.

- *Improvement of municipal administration*, as expressed through:

  - A leading role for local government in strategic regional development projects that require horizontal coordination of interests, financial administration, and resources;
  - Locating production processes in municipalities to give local governments a share of the earnings and better ensure that spillovers are generated to the surrounding area;
  - Gradual eradication of poor housing and living conditions;
  - Plan for production chains that stem from the industrialization of agricultural and livestock production in appropriate geographical areas;
  - New tools to develop municipal initiatives to reverse the accumulated disequilibria in provincial development and migration flows;
  - Evaluation and replication of successful experiences that achieve a proper balance among quality, utility, economy, and beauty in solving housing and habitat problems; and,
  - Expanding and integrating the system for financing housing to complement the state's role without eliminating it.

- *Strengthening the ties between agriculture and rural development*, as exemplified by:

  - A closer relationship among local political bodies (local government and other institutions) and farming activities, so as to strengthen the ties between different kinds of production in a given geographical area and form a more effective linkage of agriculture with development strategies;[57]
  - Fostering the patrimony and cultural identity of rural communities;
  - A scientific and creative renovation of educational curriculum to make room for discovery and the empowerment of community patrimony and its actors;
  - Strengthening the cooperative as the basic unit of the Cuban entrepreneurial-economic agricultural system;
  - Shaping a central structure for the cooperative sector to represent its interests, define its overall strategies, and implement them to guarantee its ability to interface with the state and other actors;
  - Managing and regulating agricultural and livestock activity to allow social actors in rural areas to make best use of property on a sustainable basis and acquire organization and management skills;

- Establishing a market for inputs and services that are needed by producers; and,

- Programs of community action to give women greater participation and greater visibility and recognition of their contributions to society.

These recommendations contribute to a strategic conception committed to social equity and sustainable development; a leading role for local areas; a strengthening of the productive dimension; government actors; community self-management; and local institutions with a democratic profile as a basis for small-scale development processes. Local communities and housing and living conditions stand out as spaces in which both inequality and solidarity may be expressed, where social policies can have concrete effects, and the role of local actors may be developed and strengthened. Likewise, daily micro-practices can affect social change, in interaction with other processes at the macro level.

Conclusion

Research on social mobility is a multidimensional undertaking. In this chapter, we have shed light on finding ways to formulate and implement more proactive social policies for dealing with inequalities. We now summarize our findings about the relationship of geography, habitat, and equity:

- Geography and habitat are markers of inequality; it is possible to include geographical and household differences in national development strategies.

- Economic variables can help to outline the contours of geographic inequality.

- The conditions of greatest social disadvantage are concentrated in Cuba's eastern region and in rural areas.

- There is a geographic segmentation of social classes.

- The province of birth and social origin of an individual are markers of a person's place in society and opportunities for upward mobility.

- There are favorable conditions for promoting endogenous local development that include the high level of organization and development of Cuban society, the abundant cultural capital, and the country's commitment to an essentially humane project.

- Although social policies have enabled access to adequate housing and habitat for all social groups, persons from areas of less development (provinces with lower HDI) or from a social background linked to agricultural activity or to manual labor do not have the most advantageous housing conditions.

- There is an association between the improvement in one's housing quality and one's socioeconomic conditions.
- Housing plays a central role in social mobility:
  - as a concrete expression and fundamental goal of strategies for upward socioeconomic trajectories (increasing income by acquiring and/or improving housing units, contents, and neighborhood);
  - as a resource whose possession is linked to upward mobility (it may generate income through renting rooms and other spaces, or through other economic activities in the home); and
  - as a symbol or sign or upward movement.
- A subjective pattern related to perceptions about personal mobility pathways and intergenerational mobility has developed, and it reflects a more judgmental vision from people in more developed regions and from non-agricultural social backgrounds.

A national effort has favored broad and sustained processes of social integration at a macro level. However, in some places individuals are still unable to fulfill their potential, and the conditions persist that prevent an adequate integration of these people into the nation's social framework. During an economic crisis, this problem becomes aggravated. Our study of individual mobility pathways shows that these patterns are being reinforced and that Cuba's eastern and rural areas are more disadvantaged. The trajectories of individuals also point to a tension between the processes of equity and social justice and those of domestic migration.

The inclusion of geographical and habitat concerns in research, planning, and policy development requires a deeper understanding of differences, particularities (geographic, natural and human resource, cultural, and historical), potentials, and actors at the local level. It also requires, therefore, strengthening local participation and organization in order to solve problems at this level. Even a focused approach from central state entities cannot cover the complexity of the processes of geographic socio-structural diversification and the local contrasts that have been stimulated by the Cuban crisis and reforms.

Endnotes

1. See the current challenges as identified by the Foro Regional de Ministros y Autoridades Máximas del Sector de la Vivienda y el Urbanismo (MINURVI). Ricardo Jordán, and Daniela Simioni, eds., *Gestión urbana para el desarrollo sostenible en América Latina y el Caribe* (Santiago: CEPAL, 2003).

2. See also Ray Pahl, "Market Success and Social Cohesion," *International Journal of Urban and Regional Research* 25/4 (2001): 879–83; Juan Fernando Terán, *Las quimeras y sus caminos: La gobernanza del agua y sus dispositivos para la producción de pobreza rural en los Andes ecuatorianos* (Buenos Aires: CLACSO, 2007).

3. Luisa Iñiguez and Omar Everleny Pérez, eds., *Heterogeneidad social en la Cuba actual,* Centro de Estudios de Salud y Bienestar Humano, Universidad de La Habana (Havana: 2004).

4. Raúl Atria, *Estructura ocupacional, estructura social y clases sociales* (CEPAL, Serie Políticas Sociales 96, 2004).

5. See also "Equidad y movilidad social en el contexto de las transformaciones agrarias de los años noventa en Cuba" and "La vivienda en Cuba desde la perspectiva de la movilidad social," both studies prepared by the authors of this chapter for the 2007 international seminar "Equity and Social Mobility: Theory and Methodology with Applications in Bolivia, Brazil, Cuba and South Africa," held in Brazil.

6. The available statistics for both rural and urban areas do not permit the use of additional indicators nor of more up-to-date information, and they require the use of differing years in the table.

7. The groupings were constructed through segmentation according to HDI values (excluding the City of Havana because of its marked differentiation from the rest of the group) into three HDI levels (high, medium, and low). If the City of Havana had been included, it would have been the only province in the high-level group, while Holguín, Las Tunas, Camagüey, Villa Clara, and Pinar del Río would all have been included in the low-level group.

8. Cándido López, "Desarrollo Humano Territorial en Cuba: Metodología para su evaluación y resultados," *Economía y Desarrollo* (2004): 127–149.

9. Iñiguez and Pérez, eds., *Heterogeneidad social en la Cuba actual*; Francisco Becerra, "Evolución del desarrollo socioeconómico a escala territorial: El caso de la provincia de Cienfuegos," *Economía y Desarrollo* (2004); Luisa Iñiguez and Mariana Ravenet, "Heterogeneidad territorial y desarrollo local. Reflexiones sobre el contexto cubano," in *Desarrollo local en Cuba* (Havana: Editora Academia, 2006); López, "Desarrollo Humano Territorial en Cuba: Metodología para su evaluación y resultados"; Lucy Martín, Mayra Espina Prieto, and Lilia Nuñez, "Expresiones Territoriales del Proceso de Reestratificación, Informe de Investigación" (Havana: CIPS, 1999); and Blanca Morejón, "Características Diferenciales de los migrantes internos en Cuba," *Novedades en Población, CEDEM* 3/6 (2007): 26–44.

10. Iñiguez and Ravenet, "Heterogeneidad territorial y desarrollo local. Reflexiones sobre el contexto cubano"; and Morejón, "Características Diferenciales de los migrantes internos en Cuba."

11. Iñiguez and Pérez, eds., *Heterogeneidad social en la Cuba actual*; Iñiguez and Ravenet, "Heterogeneidad territorial y desarrollo local. Reflexiones sobre el contexto cubano"; López, "Desarrollo Humano Territorial en Cuba: Metodología

para su evaluación y resultados"; Becerra, "Evolución del desarrollo socioeconómico a escala territorial: El caso de la provincia de Cienfuegos"; and Elier Méndez, and Carmen Lloret, "Estudios del Desarrollo Humano en la provincia de Villa Clara (1990–1999)" (Villa Clara: Universidad de Villa Clara, 2004).

12. Becerra, "Evolución del desarrollo socioeconómico a escala territorial: El caso de la provincia de Cienfuegos," and Luisa Iñiguez. "Desigualdades espaciales en Cuba: Entre herencias y emergencias," in *Heterogeneidad social en la Cuba actual*, edited by Luisa Iñiguez and Omar Everleny Pérez (Havana: Centro de Estudios de Salud y Bienestar Humano, Universidad de La Habana, 2004).

13. Iñiguez, "Desigualdades espaciales en Cuba: Entre herencias y emergencias"; Morejón, "Características Diferenciales de los migrantes internos en Cuba"; Mayra Espina Prieto, Lucy Martín, and Lilia Nuñez. "Heterogenización y desigualdades en la ciudad. Diagnóstico y perspectivas, Informe de Investigación" (Havana: CIPS, 2000); Instituto de Planificación Física, "Diagnóstico de asentamientos de la Franja de Base" (Havana: Instituto de Planificación Física, 1998); Pablo Fernández Domínguez "El sector agropecuario en Cuba: evolución y perspectivas," in *Cuba: el sector agropecuario y las políticas agrícolas ante los nuevos retos*, ed. INIE-MEP-ASDI-Universidad de la República Oriental del Uruguay (Montevideo: INIE-MEP-ASDI-Universidad de la República Oriental del Uruguay, 2002); Alodia Alonso. "Desigualdades territoriales y Desarrollo Local. Consideraciones para Cuba," *Economía y Desarrollo* (2004): 150–168; Carmen León, "Desarrollo Local, una alternativa en tiempos de globalización" (Havana: Dpto. Desarrollo Económico, Facultad de Economía, Universidad de la Habana, 2005); Carlos García Pleyán, "Estrategia y territorio. Reflexiones sobre algunos temas clave en la planificación territorial," *Cuba: Investigaciones Económicas*, 1 (Havana: Instituto Nacional de Investigaciones Económicas INIE, 1997): 121–134; and Morejón, "Características Diferenciales de los migrantes internos en Cuba."

14. Morejón, "Características Diferenciales de los migrantes internos en Cuba."

15. Iñiguez and Pérez, eds., *Heterogeneidad social en la Cuba actual*; Iñiguez, "Desigualdades espaciales en Cuba: Entre herencias y emergencias"; Pablo Rodríguez, and Rodrigo Espina Prieto, "Pobreza, marginalidad o exclusión?: un estudio sobre el barrio Alturas del Mirador, Informe Preliminar de Investigación" (Havana: Centro de Antropología, 2004).

16. Rodríguez and Espina Prieto, "Pobreza, marginalidad o exclusión? un estudio sobre el barrio Alturas del Mirador, Informe Preliminar de Investigación"; Iñiguez and Pérez, eds., *Heterogeneidad social en la Cuba actual*.

17. Centro de Investigaciones de la Economía Mundial (CIEM), *Investigación sobre Desarrollo Humano en Cuba 1996* (Havana: Editorial Caguayo, 1997); Centro de Investigaciones de la Economía Mundial, *Investigación sobre Desarrollo Humano en Cuba 1999* (Havana: Editorial Caguayo, 2000); Centro de Investigaciones de la Economía Mundial, *Investigación sobre Ciencia, Tecnología y Desarrollo Humano en Cuba 2003* (Havana: Editorial Caguayo, 2004); López, "Desarrollo

Humano Territorial en Cuba: Metodología para su evaluación y resultados"; and Méndez and Lloret, "Estudios del Desarrollo Humano en la provincia de Villa Clara (1990–1999)."

18. Ibid.

19. López, "Desarrollo Humano Territorial en Cuba: Metodología para su evaluación y resultados."

20. Martín, Espina Prieto, and Nuñez, "Expresiones Territoriales del Proceso de Reestratificación, Informe de Investigación."

21. Instituto de Planificación Física, "Diagnóstico de asentamientos de la Franja de Base"; Ada Guzón, and Dávalos Roberto. "Asentamientos poblacionales: una visión necesaria para el desarrollo," in *Ciudad y cambio social en los 90s*, ed. Roberto Dávalos and Aymara Hernández (Havana: Universidad de La Habana, 2004); and Lucy Martín, "Equidad y movilidad social en el contexto de las transformaciones agrarias de los años noventa en Cuba, Working Paper 07/08–02," in *Working Paper Series*, edited by Harvard University David Rockefeller Center for Latin American Studies (Cambridge: David Rockefeller Center for Latin American Studies, Harvard University, 2008).

22. Iñiguez and Pérez, eds., *Heterogeneidad social en la Cuba actual*; Martín, "Equidad y movilidad social en el contexto de las transformaciones agrarias de los años noventa en Cuba, Working Paper 07/08–02"; María de los Ángeles Arias, "Nuevos productores usufructuarios: hacia un estudio de su estructura interna. Cambios fundamentales de las estructura interna de los obreros agrícolas después del triunfo de la revolución. La clase obrera agrícola en la región oriental" (Tesis doctorado. Universidad Pedagógica de Holguín, 1999); Niurka Pérez, Ernel González and Miriam García, "Transformaciones en el agro cubano durante la década de los años 90" (Havana: Universidad de La Habana, 2006); Víctor Figueroa, "La reforma de la tenencia de la tierra en Cuba y formación de un modelo mixto de economía agraria" (Las Villas: Ediciones Universidad Central de Las Villas, March–April 1995); Víctor Figueroa, "Reforma y ajustes al modelo económico cubano en los años 90" (Mimeo, 1997); and Rebeca González, "Estudios rurales en la provincia de Camagüey. Experiencias a nivel local" (Camagüey: Centro de Investigaciones de Medio Ambiente de Camagüey. Instituto de Geografía Tropical, 2002).

23. Santiago Alemán et al. "El cooperativismo en la reforma económica cubana" (Villa Clara: Escuela provincial del Partido, 2005); Armando Nova González, "Las Unidades de Producción Cooperativas y Las Granjas cañeras 1993–2000" (Havana: Centro de Estudios de la Economía Cubana CEEC, Universidad de La Habana, 2001); Armando Nova González, "El cooperativismo. Línea de desarrollo en la agricultura cubana" (Havana: Centro de Estudios de la Economía Cubana CEEC, Universidad de La Habana, 2004); and, Armando Nova González, "Nuevas formas de organización agrícola," *IPS-Cuba* www.cubaalamano.net, 2009.

24. Yisel Herrera, "El campesinado y la política social en el territorio montañoso de Cienfuegos. Un acercamiento desde la perspectiva sociológica" (Havana:

Diplomado Sociedad Cubana, Centro de Investigaciones Psicológicas y Sociológicas, 2009); and Yenisei Machado, "La gestión del conocimiento científico/tradicional en el perfeccionamiento del sistema agroproductivo de la comunidad montañosa de Crucesitas" (Havana: Diplomado Sociedad Cubana, Centro de Investigaciones Psicológicas y Sociológicas, 2009).

25. Fernando Agüero, "Sociedad y comunidad rural" (Cienfuegos: Universidad de Cienfuegos, 2000); and Fernando Agüero, "La educación ambiental en la zona montañosa: experiencias, resultados y retos" (Cienfuegos: Universidad de Cienfuegos, 2004).

26. Mayra Espina Prieto, Viviana Togores González, Lucy Martín, and Lilia Nuñez, "Equidad y movilidad social en Cuba. Impactos del reajuste estructural, Informe de Investigación" (Havana: CIPS, 2009), and "Los estudios sobre heterogeneidad social y desigualdades en Cuba hoy. Síntesis de diagnósticos, problemas y propuestas para la promoción de equidad, Informe de Investigación" (Havana: CIPS, 2010); Dania González, "La vivienda es algo más que un objeto a construir," *Revista Temas* 58 (2009): 32–39; Carmen León, "Desarrollo Local, una alternativa en tiempos de globalización" (Havana: Dpto. Desarrollo Económico, Facultad de Economía, Universidad de la Habana, 2005); Juan Valdés, "Notas sobre el modelo agrario cubano en los 90," in Niurka Pérez et al., *Participación y formas organizativas de la agricultura* (Havana: Universidad de la Habana, 2000); and Alonso, "Desigualdades territoriales y Desarrollo Local. Consideraciones para Cuba."

27. This study of mobility trajectories was part of the project called "Equidad y movilidad social en Cuba. Impactos del reajuste estructural," carried out by CIPS in 2009. See the introductory essay to this section of the book.

28. OFICODA, the Oficina de Registro de Consumidores.

29. See also Cedric Pugh, "The Theory and Practice of Housing Sector Development for Developing Countries, 1950–99," *Housing Studies* 16/4 (2001): 399–423; Alex Marsh and David Mullins, "The Social Exclusion Perspective and Housing Studies: Origins, Applications and Limitations," *Housing Studies* 13/6 (1998): 749–59; and Chris Paris, "International Perspectives on Planning and Affordable Housing," *Housing Studies* 22/1 (2007): 1–9.

30. CEPAL studies have been very important in the quantification of housing situations.

31. Carlos Pisoni, "Hábitat y pobreza: otra mirada sobre las políticas de vivienda," *Observatorio Social* 12 (2003): 30–32.

32. Selma Díaz, text presented at Taller de la *Revista Temas*, "La ciudad social" (Havana, 2006).

33. Programa de las Naciones Unidas para los Asentamientos Humanos -UN Hábitat y el Centro de Estudios de la Construcción y el Desarrollo Urbano- Regional, Programa de las Naciones Unidas para el Desarrollo, "Hábitat Cuadernos, Hábitat y Desarrollo Humano Colombia" (Bogota: PNUD, 2004), has helped us shape and sharpen our analysis.

34. Ibid.

35. See also Maria del Carmen Zabala, *Familia y Pobreza en Cuba. Estudio de casos* (Havana: Publicaciones Acuario, Centro Felix Varela, 2010).

36. Salvador Gomila, *Informe Nacional de Cuba para Hábitat II* (Havana, 1996). http://habitat.aq.upm.es/iah/ponenc/a008.htm

37. Joan MacDonald, "Pobreza y precariedad del hábitat en ciudades de América Latina y el Caribe," *CEPAL Serie Manuales* 38 (2004).

38. According to Mario Coyula, the 2002 census reported "138,035 houses with wooden walls . . . 35, 944 with palm-bark (*yagua*) or palm-board walls, 61,146 with earthen floors, and 76,716 covered by palm-leaf roofs." See his Mario Cowley Coyula, "El derecho a la vivienda: una meta elusiva," *Temas* 58 (2009): 21–31.

39. Espina Prieto, Martín, and Nuñez, "Heterogenización y desigualdades en la ciudad. Diagnóstico y perspectivas, Informe de Investigación."

40. Espina Prieto et al., "Los estudios sobre heterogeneidad social y desigualdades en Cuba hoy. Síntesis de diagnósticos, problemas y propuestas para la promoción de equidad, Informe de Investigación."

41. Espina Prieto et al., "Equidad y movilidad social en Cuba. Impactos del reajuste estructural, Informe de Investigación."

42. According to the CEPAL *Anuario* for 2005, the percentages of housing units occupied by proprietors were smaller. In 2002, they were: Brazil, 74.6%; Chile, 72.5%; Costa Rica, 71.6%; Dominican Republic, 62.3%; Mexico, 75.3%; Panama, 68.3%; and Paraguay, 79.3%, in 2001, Argentina, 74.9%; Bolivia, 66.8%; Honduras, 76.9%.

43. Zabala, *Familia y Pobreza en Cuba. Estudio de casos.*

44. Rafael Betancourt. "Más allá de la guanaja echada: alternativas para el financiamiento de la vivienda," *Temas* 58 (2009): 73–80; Coyula, "El derecho a la vivienda: una meta elusiva"; Espina Prieto et al., "Equidad y movilidad social en Cuba. Impactos del reajuste estructural, Informe de Investigación"; Patricia Gazmuri, "Reflexiones sobre algunas peculiaridades del crecimiento poblacional en relación con la familia y la demanda de viviendas," Ponencia presentada al Taller XX Aniversario del CIPS (Havana, 2004); and Madeline Menendez, "Habitar el Centro Histórico. Privilegio y responsabilidad," *Temas* 58 (2009): 65–72.

45. Miguel Coyula, "¿Un lugar dónde vivir o un lugar para vivir?" Temas 58 (2009): 40–49; Coyula, "El derecho a la vivienda: una meta elusiva"; Gazmuri, "Reflexiones sobre algunas peculiaridades del crecimiento poblacional en relación con la familia y la demanda de viviendas"; José Fernando Martinera, "Producción de eco materiales para construcción de vivienda de interés social como vía de descentralización," in *Desarrollo local en Cuba* (Havana: Editora Academia, 2006); Rosendo Mesías, "Apuntes pensando el problema de la vivienda desde el municipio," in *Desarrollo local en Cuba*; and Pedro Vázquez, "De recursos y discursos en la vivienda cubana," *Temas* 58 (2009): 50–57.

46. Coyula, "El derecho a la vivienda: una meta elusiva"; Centro de Salud en la Vivienda de Cuba, *Informe Bienal del 2000–2002* (Havana, 2003); A. Atienza,

"La vivienda en Cuba," in *Política Social y Reformas Estructurales: Cuba a principios del siglo XXI* (Mexico D.F.: CEPAL-PNUD-INIE, 2004); and González, "La vivienda es algo más que un objeto a construir."

47. Coyula, "El derecho a la vivienda: una meta elusiva"; Alberto Aliena, "Hábitat: su gestión social desde una perspectiva integral y multinivel. Ponencia Simposio Centro de Investigaciones Psicológicas y Sociológicas (Havana, 2009); and Espina Prieto et al., "Equidad y movilidad social en Cuba. Impactos del reajuste estructural, Informe de Investigación."

48. This definition was used by Carlos Rafael Rodríguez. Cited in Coyula, "El derecho a la vivienda: una meta elusiva."

49. Ibid; Alberto Aliena, "Hábitat: su gestión social desde una perspectiva integral y multinivel"; and Coyula, "¿Un lugar dónde vivir o un lugar para vivir?"

50. Coyula, "El derecho a la vivienda: una meta elusiva"; Patricia Gazmuri, "Reflexiones sobre algunas peculiaridades del crecimiento poblacional en relación con la familia y la demanda de viviendas"; Instituto Nacional de la Vivienda. *Estudio sobre la situación de los barrios y focos insalubres* (Havana, 2002) and Instituto Nacional de la Vivienda, *Cuarto Taller sobre Las Estrategias de Viviendas* (Havana, 2004).

51. Coyula, "¿Un lugar dónde vivir o un lugar para vivir?"; Menendez, "Habitar el Centro Histórico. Privilegio y responsabilidad "; and Instituto Nacional de la Vivienda, *Cuarto Taller sobre Las Estrategias de Vivienda.*

52. Coyula, "¿Un lugar dónde vivir o un lugar para vivir?"; Gazmuri, "Reflexiones sobre algunas peculiaridades del crecimiento poblacional en relación con la familia y la demanda de viviendas"; and Instituto Nacional de la Vivienda, *Cuarto Taller sobre Las Estrategias de Viviendas.*

53. Ibid; Vázquez, "De recursos y discursos en la vivienda cubana"; Mesías, "Apuntes pensando el problema de la vivienda desde el municipio."

54. Coyula, "El derecho a la vivienda: una meta elusiva"; González, "La vivienda es algo más que un objeto a construir."

55. Coyula, "¿Un lugar dónde vivir o un lugar para vivir?"; Vázquez, "De recursos y discursos en la vivienda cubana."

56. Coyula, "El derecho a la vivienda: una meta elusiva"; Espina Prieto et al., "Los estudios sobre heterogeneidad social y desigualdades en Cuba hoy. Síntesis de diagnósticos, problemas y propuestas para la promoción de equidad, Informe de Investigación"; Aliena, "Hábitat: su gestión social desde una perspectiva integral y multinivel"; and García Pleyán, "Estrategia y territorio. Reflexiones sobre algunos temas clave en la planificación territorial."

57. This requires awareness of the variety of forms of agriculture, technologies employed, social actors, and subjective perceptions as well as consideration of such other local resources as knowledge, other kinds of production, and markets.

Commentary

Is Cuba Becoming More Latin American?

Elisa Reis and Graziella Moraes Dias da Silva

The study of social mobility and stratification has a deep-seated tradition in sociology. The empirical investigations of the subject that took place in the mid-twentieth century in England and in the United States were part and parcel of the canon of the discipline. Some of these studies became classics and still appear in course syllabi on the subject.[1]

As early as the 1960s, scholars already sought to assess the fluidity of social structures in Latin America.[2] The major concern of such studies was to look into the prospects for broadening the chances of democratic improvements in the region. The assumption was that modernization and economic growth would expand the opportunities for upward mobility, thus overcoming inequalities and opening space for a fluid social structure. Indeed, the structural processes taking place at the time contributed to lend credibility to such a premise. That is, usually the mere migration from rural to urban areas brought income improvements and better access to public goods—even though migrants got very little of both.

Most of these early studies assumed that low mobility was typical of backward societies marked by rigidity of traditional stratification patterns. Modernization plus industrialization was supposed naturally to offer dynamic social stratification structures. As a corollary, mobility would bring along more equality. The postwar economic growth in non-central areas frustrated the expectations of trickle-down effects, however, and suggested the worth of investigating the potential of specific processes and policies to affect stratification.

In particular, economic growth had little effect on equality in Latin American countries. Even if most countries experienced strong structural mobility—pushed especially by rural-to-urban migration—inequality rates remained among the highest in the world. Thus, for example, Brazil's already unequal social structure became even more so after the so-called economic miracle of the late seventies. The country's Gini coefficient of income inequality jumped from 0.5 in 1960 to 0.59 in 1980—among the highest in the world.[3]

The frustrated expectations of trickle-down effects gave birth to efforts to design policies that aimed to change distribution patterns. The focus was on social policies as possible correctives to market mechanisms that generated or perpetuated persistent inequalities. The broad interest in the prospects for equal opportunity led as well to a more focused concern with the possibilities for reducing social inequality. Social mobility studies contributed to a clearer understanding of the persistence of these inequality rates, and provided a more dynamic approach to the issue.

Building on pioneer studies such as those by Pastore and Nelson do Valle e Silva, recent sociological researchers of social mobility in Latin America have stressed that inequality and social mobility are not mutually exclusive in the region.[4] These studies indicate that not only class stratification but also race, ethnicity, and gender remain significant variables to explain social mobility.[5] Most studies suggest that high mobility rates were the result of structural mobility, a predominance of low-range (or horizontal) mobility paths, and high elite closure (i.e., no downward mobility). Such processes resulted in stratification patterns characterized by significant fluidity, but restricted to the lowest levels of the social pyramid, therefore preserving the features that account for the persistence of a rigid hierarchy. As suggested by Torche, the Latin American stratification regimes highlight the importance of looking beyond the degree of mobility and analyzing carefully its pattern.[6]

From the 1990s onwards, Latin America experienced strong market liberalization and, as predictable, the resulting changes affected distribution patterns in the region. Relying on data from the U.N. Economic Commission for Latin America and the Caribbean (ECLAC) for eight Latin American countries, Portes and Hoffmann analyzed class stratification in the region during the 1990s.[7] They identified four major trends: a decline in public employment; a shrinkage in formal employment; the rise of a segment of petty entrepreneurs; and the expansion or stabilization of the informal sector that had been declining in previous decades. The authors take both the decline in public employment and the rise of petty entrepreneurs as indications of growing instability and insecurity for much of the Latin American population. They also call attention to the decline in real wages (with the exception of Chile), increasing inequality rates,[8] and the continuation of elite cohesion (elite defined as the 10% richest in each of the countries under study) with a high share of resources. Looking at the 1998 regional Gini coefficient of 0.52, they indicate that, excluding the richest ten percent, the index would drop to 0.36—a value close to that of the United States at that time.

These studies signaled promising new ways of looking at issues that have long concerned analysts of Latin America. However, research on mobility and stratification traditionally had not included Cuba, which was frequently presented as an exceptional case where social policies succeeded in creating equality. As Michael Woolcock put it, cases of growth without development abound in the international debate but Cuba was a rare case of development without growth. Cuba was seemingly able to achieve great social indicators without economic growth while avoiding market mechanisms.[9]

Since the 1990s, however, the crisis of the socialist model and the incipient process of liberalization have challenged the sustainability of the older Cuban model. As Espina Prieto and Togores González point out, in the past few decades the Gini index of inequality rose substantially in that country, from 0.24 in the 1980s to 0.38 in the early 2000s. Is the rise of inequality a sign that Cuba's stratification regime is becoming more similar to that of the rest of Latin America? That is a hard question to answer at this point. Yet the Cuban case presents us with an interesting opportunity to investigate both the implication of deep-seated distribution patterns typical of a planned economy, and the consequences of recent market mechanisms.

By relying on social mobility data, the studies presented here avoid the assumption that Cuba is departing from a firm commitment to equality. The narratives presented in chapters 8 and 9 stress unequal starting points and aim to understand inequality as a dynamic rather than a static feature of society. Such efforts are even more relevant because of the lack of available data to analyze mobility in Cuba. Even though we cannot yet generalize, the analysis that Espina Prieto and Togores González provide allows for a better understanding of patterns of mobility, along the lines suggested by Torche.[10] In particular, three of the issues raised in the chapters point to a fruitful research agenda for stratification studies in Cuba.

First, the transition from a mobility structure shaped by central coordination to the new structure that is influenced by market mechanisms opens a good opportunity to compare the shortcomings and potentialities of these two distinct strategies to affect distribution patterns. The change in policy orientation can already inform us about altered perceptions of mobility, as Espina Prieto and Togores González's chapter indicates. They point out that although mobility had been perceived earlier as an issue of education and as an asset distributed through social policies, nowadays it is largely seen as a matter of economic entrepreneurship, that is to say, a market asset. It will be interesting to follow up on the impact of this transformation on shaping people's strategies of mobility as well as on the appearance of the overall stratification structure.

Second, by stressing the importance of geography, Martín and Núñez show that targeting policies do not necessarily compromise universality of scope. As they convincingly argue, to overcome historical unequal development processes it is essential to focus on rural versus urban differences. They also indicate that former state control of internal migration probably had unintended consequences in maintaining, perhaps even deepening, Cuban social inequalities.

Finally, the focus on housing calls attention to the importance of wealth disparities in explaining social mobility differences. As the authors point out, the differences in access to housing and the asset differentials for investing in home renovation seem to be key elements in providing routes for mobility and economic entrepreneurship. That property differences have become so central in a country that has invested so much in property redistribution raises the issue of its relevance for social mobility in general.

The portraits that these two chapters present indicate that social mobility patterns in Cuba have significant similarities with those discussed in the literature regarding other Latin American countries.

In our view, elite positions seem to have been preserved in Cuba, despite 40 years of strict political engineering, in a process similar to that described in studies for other countries in the region.[11] Race and gender inequalities also seem to persist, despite the widespread implementation of universal policies.[12] Finally, the growth in informal labor, even under strong state surveillance, might lead to labor precariousness with the same perverse consequences that it has produced in other Latin American countries. In short, as put by Barberia et al., Cuba might be exceptional in its experience but its dilemmas have become very similar to those of the region.[13]

Endnotes

1. Seminal works include John H. Goldthorpe, Catriona Llewellyn, and Clive Payne, *Social Mobility and Class Structure in Modern Britain* (Oxford: Clarendon Press, 1980), and Seymour Martin Lipset and Reinhard Bendix, *Social Mobility in Industrial Society* (Berkeley: University of California Press, 1959), on the United States.
2. Archibald O. Haller, Donald B. Holsinger, and Helcio Ulhôa Saraiva, "Variation in Occupational Prestige Hierarchies: Brazilian Data," *American Sociological Review* 77/5 (1972): 941–56 and Seymour Martin Lipset and Aldo Solari, *Elites in Latin America* (New York: Oxford University Press, 1967).
3. Based on the National Household Survey (PNAD/IBGE) as reported by Maria Cristina Cacciamali, "Mudanças estruturais recentes: uma comparação entre os países industrializados e aqueles em desenvolvimento," *Revista Brasileira de Economia* 45/2 (1991).
4. José Pastore, *Desigualdade e mobildade social no Brasil* (São Paulo: T.A. Queiroz Editor, 1979) and Nelson do Valle Silva, "White-Non-white Income Differentials: Brazil" (Doctoral thesis, Michigan, 1979).
5. Marcia Lima, "Serviço de 'branco,' serviço de 'preto': um estudo sobre cor e trabalho no Brasil urbano" (Rio de Janeiro: Universidade Federal do Rio de Janeiro, 2001); Maria Celi Scalon, *Mobilidade social no Brasil: padrões e tendências* (Rio de Janeiro: Editora Revan: IUPERJ, Universidade Candido Mendes, 1999); Carlos Antonio Costa Ribeiro, "Classe, Raca, e Mobilidade Social no Brasil," *Dados* 49/4 (2006): 833–73.
6. Florencia Torche, "Unequal but Fluid: Social Mobility in Chile in Comparative Perspective," *American Sociological Review* 70 (2005): 422–55.
7. Alejandro Portes and Kelly Hoffman, "Latin American Class Structures: Their Composition and Change during the Neoliberal Era," *Latin American Research Review* 38/1 (2003): 41–82.

8. Recent trends in Brazilian inequality, however, challenge this interpretation. Since the 2000s, the Brazilian GINI coefficient has actually declined while real wages increased. However, it is also questionable whether market liberalization progressed there as much as in other Latin American countries, despite some significant privatization of state firms in the pre-Lula era.

9. As cited in Lorena Guadalupe Barberia, Xavier de Souza Briggs, and Miren Uriarte, "The End of Egalitarianism? Economic Inequality and the Future of Social Policy in Cuba," in *The Cuban Economy at the Start of the Twenty-First Century*, ed. Jorge I. Dominguez, Omar Everleny Pérez and Lorena Guadalupe Barberia, 297–319 (Cambridge: DRCLAS, Harvard University Press, 2004).

10. Torche, "Unequal but Fluid: Social Mobility in Chile in Comparative Perspective."

11. Scalon, *Mobilidade social no Brasil : padrões e tendências*; Torche, "Unequal but Fluid: Social Mobility in Chile in Comparative Perspective."

12. Mark Q. Sawyer, *Racial Politics in Post-Revolutionary Cuba* (New York: Cambridge University Press, 2006).

13. Barberia, Briggs, and Uriarte, "The End of Egalitarianism? Economic Inequality and the Future of Social Policy in Cuba."

Acknowledgments

We are grateful for the generous support from the Ford Foundation that has enabled the David Rockefeller Center for Latin American Studies at Harvard University (DRCLAS) to develop an active scholarly collaboration with Cuban academics. Early versions of several chapters in this volume were written by Cuban scholars who visited Harvard on short-term research visits as part of the Center's Cuban Studies Program with grant support from the Foundation. In addition, the Ford Foundation supported the "Social Mobility and Equity in Latin America: Policies, Theory and Methodology" workshop, jointly organized by the Cuban Studies Program at DRCLAS, Cuba's Centro de Investigaciones Psicológicas y Sociológicas (CIPS), and the United Nations Development Program's Centre for Inclusive Growth, held in Rio de Janeiro in June 2009. The Foundation also supported two workshops on the Cuban economy held in 2009 and 2010 in Havana and Cambridge, Massachusetts. The discussions at these meetings improved the chapters in this book.

We are also indebted to the University of Havana's Center for the Study of the Cuban Economy (CEEC) and the Cuban Ministry of Science, Technology and the Environment's Centro de Investigaciones Psicológicas y Sociológicas (CIPS). Both institutions have been at the forefront of advancing applied social science research in Cuba. Each significantly contributes to the valuable scholarship focused on how to understand the development challenges confronting Cuba.

The editors also thank the reviewers of this volume whose comments greatly improved the final product, June Erlick and Anita Safran for their careful editorial assistance in the final stages of the manuscript preparation, Dick Cluster and Andy Klatt for their excellent translations of the Spanish chapters into English, Lena Bae for research assistance, and Kathleen Hoover, Yadira Rivera, Maximiliano Mauriz, and Linda Rodriguez for administrative support.

Editors and Contributors

Regina Abrami is a Senior Fellow at Harvard Business School and Faculty Chair of the Immersion Experience Program (IXP), a field-based learning opportunity allowing MBA students to apply leading ideas in management theory to real world situations. She is also on the executive committee of Harvard University's Fairbank Center for Chinese Studies and a Faculty Associate of the Weatherhead Center for International Affairs. Her primary area of expertise is comparative political economy. Her current research is focused in three areas: the politics of industrial strategy; the impact of historical institutional differences on political economic development; and doing business in emerging markets, focusing especially on China and Vietnam where she has lived and conducted research for many years.

Lorena Barberia is a Program Associate at the David Rockefeller Center for Latin American Studies at Harvard University. With Jorge I. Domínguez and Rafael M. Hernández, she is author and co-editor of *Debating U.S.-Cuban Relations: Shall We Play Ball?* (Routledge, 2011) and with Jorge I. Domínguez and Omar Everleny Pérez Villanueva, she co-edited *The Cuban Economy at the Start of the Twenty-First Century* (Harvard University Press and David Rockefeller Center for Latin American Studies, 2004). Previously, she worked in Ecuador and Panama as a junior economist and on research projects at the Harvard Institute for International Development that focused on developing and transition economies.

Jorge I. Domínguez is the Antonio Madero Professor for the Study of Mexico and Vice Provost for International Affairs at Harvard University. He is the author of *Cuba: Order and Revolution* (1978) and *To Make a World Safe for Revolution* (1989), both from Harvard University Press; and, from Editorial Colibrí, *Cuba hoy: Analizando su pasado, imaginando su futuro* (2006), and *La política exterior de Cuba (1962–2009)* (2009). With Rafael M. Hernández, and Lorena G. Barberia, he co-edited *Debating U.S.-Cuban Relations: Shall We Play Ball?* (Routledge, 2011). With Rafael M. Hernández, he co-edited *U.S.-Cuban Relations in the 1990s* (Westview Press, 1989). With Omar Everleny Pérez Villanueva and Lorena Barberia, he co-edited *The Cuban Economy at the Start of the Twenty-First Century* (Harvard University Press and David Rockefeller Center for Latin American Studies, 2004). He is a past president of the Latin American Studies Association.

Mayra Espina Prieto is a program officer for the Swiss Agency for Development and Cooperation (COSUDE) in Havana. Prior to joining COSUDE, she was a researcher at the Centro de Investigaciones Psicológicas y Sociológicas (CIPS). She is also an Adjunct Professor at the University of Havana's Department of Sociology, past president of the National Commission for Enlace MOST/UNESCO in Cuba and a member of the editorial board of *Temas* and *Cuadernos Sociológicos*. Her research focuses on social structure, social mobility inequality and social policy. She is the author of *Políticas de Atención a la Pobreza y la Desigualdad: Examinando el Rol del Estado en la Experiencia Cubana* (CLACSO-CROP, 2008) and *Desarrollo, Desigualdad y Políticas Sociales* (Centro Félix Varela, 2010).

Anicia García Álvarez is a professor in the Economics Department at the University of Havana. Most recently, she served as the Director of the Center for the Study of the Cuban Economy (Centro de Estudios de la Economía Cubana) for six years. Her research focuses on the competitiveness of Cuban industry and agriculture, agricultural markets, economic policies and their impact on agricultural exports. Prior to joining the CEEC, she was an economist at the National Institute for Economic Research, a think-tank of the Ministry of Economics and Planning. In 2010, she was a visiting researcher at the David Rockefeller Center for Latin American Studies at Harvard University.

Lucy Martín is a researcher at the Centro de Investigaciones Psicológicas y Sociológicas (CIPS), in its Department of Social Structure and Inequalities specializing in the study of Cuban agrarian society. Trained as a sociologist, she has focused on project evaluation and, in particular, the impact of participatory and self-transformation processes on policy design and implementation. She has participated in more than 20 research projects on Cuban society and in national and international events. She has published articles in books and magazines both in Cuba and abroad and taught courses for undergraduate and graduate students.

Pedro Monreal González is an economist and author. He currently serves as Program Specialist for the Human and Social Sciences at the United Nations Educational, Scientific and Cultural Organization (UNESCO) for the Caribbean in Kingston, Jamaica. He has been a university professor and senior researcher with 28 years of broad international practice in education and research in the field of development studies, with a focus on Latin America, the Caribbean, and Cuba, and he has been a panelist and invited speaker to events in the United States, Europe and Latin America. Monreal is an author of books and articles published in various languages and was awarded the International Prize "Caribbean Thought" in Economics in 2003, for his work, *Dilemas de la globalización en el Caribe: Hacia una nueva agenda de desarrollo en Cuba* (Siglo XXI, 2004), co-written with Julio Carranza.

Graziella Moraes Dias da Silva is Assistant Professor of Sociology at the Federal University of Rio de Janeiro (UFRJ) and a research affiliate of the Interdisciplinary Center for Inequality Studies (NIED) in Brazil. Her doctoral research was aimed at studying the experiences and perceptions of black professionals in Brazil and South Africa. Her current research projects include a comparison of elites' attitudes about poverty and inequality in Brazil, South Africa and Uruguay, a survey on ethnic and race relation in Latin America (with Edward Telles from Princeton University and Marcelo Paixão from UFRJ), and a study about the development of the NGO sector in Brazil (a partnership of NIED, the Brazilian Institute for Applied Economic Research/IPEA, and the Brazilian Center for Planning/Cebrap).

Armando Nova González is a Professor in the Economics Department and researcher at the Center for the Study of the Cuban Economy (Centro de Estudios de la Economía Cubana) at the University of Havana. A specialist in Cuban agricultural economics with a doctoral degree in economics from the University of Havana, Professor Nova Gonzalez has held posts at the Citrus Group of the Ministry of Agriculture, the Central Planning Board, and the National Economy Research Institute. He is President of the Scientific Council of the CEEC, vice-president of the National Tribunal for Applied Economics, a board charged with doctoral thesis examinations, and a member of the Advisory Group to the Ministry of Sugar. He is author of several articles and chapters and three books, *Aspectos Económicos de los Cítricos en Cuba* (Editorial Científico Técnico del Ministerio de Cultura, 1984), *Teoría y Práctica de la Economía Agropecuaria*, vols. I and II (Ediciones Universitarias, 1989), and *La Agricultura Cubana 1959–2005, Evolución y trayectoria* (Editorial Ciencias Sociales del Ministerio de Cultura, 2006). In 2010, he was a visiting researcher at the David Rockefeller Center for Latin American Studies at Harvard University.

Lilia Núñez Moreno is a researcher at the Centro de Investigaciones Psicológicas y Sociológicas (CIPS). She has worked as a sociologist on social structures and inequalities since 1978 and has also taught courses at the University of Havana on related topics. In addition, she has worked on impact evaluation studies focused on measuring the socio-environmental impact for the Centro de Gestión e Inspección Ambiental (CICA) and as an adviser to a group that focuses on the inclusion of social aspects in the study of the environment in the Ministry of Science, Technology, and the Environment's environmental agency.

Omar Everleny Pérez Villanueva is a professor in the Centro de Estudios de la Economía Cubana at the University of Havana. He most recently edited *Cincuenta años de la Economía Cubana* (Editorial Ciencias Sociales, 2011), a retrospective volume on the Cuban economy. With Armando Nova González and Pavel Alejandro Vidal, he edited *Miradas a la Economía Cubana*, vols. *I* and *II* (Editorial Caminos, 2010). With Jorge I. Domínguez and Lorena G. Barberia, he edited *The Cuban Economy at the Start of the Twenty-First Century* (Harvard University Press, David Rockefeller Center for Latin American Studies, 2004). His earlier books include *La realidad de lo imposible: La salud pública en Cuba*, with Miguel Figueras (Editorial Ciencias Sociales, 1998). He has also served as an adviser to the Government of the City of Havana, a visiting professor at the Institut des Hautes Etudes de l'Amérique Latine (IHEAL) at the Université Sorbonne Nouvelle, and a visiting researcher at the Institute of Developing Economies, Japan External Trade Organization (IDE-JETRO) in Japan. He was a visiting researcher at the David Rockefeller Center for Latin American Studies at Harvard University in 2004 and 2010.

Dwight H. Perkins is the Harold Hitchings Burbank Research Professor of Political Economy at Harvard University, past Director of the Harvard University Asia Center, past chairman of the Department of Economics, 1977–1980, and former Director of the Harvard Institute for International Development (HIID), 1980–1995. He has authored or edited twelve books and over one hundred articles on economic history and economic development, with special references to the economies of China, Korea, Vietnam, and other nations of East and Southeast Asia. His most recent books include *Innovative East Asia: The Future of Growth* (with Shahid Yusuf and others) (Oxford University Press 2003) and *Industrialization and the State: The Changing Role of Government in Taiwan's Economy, 1945–1998* (with Chen Kuo Hsu and Li-Min Hsueh) (Harvard University Press, 2001).

Elisa Reis is a Professor of Sociology and Political Science at the Federal University of Rio de Janeiro (UFRJ) and a member of the Executive Committee of the International Sociology Association. She chairs the Interdisciplinary Research Network on Inequality (NIED) supported by the Excellence Networks Program (PRONEX) of the Brazilian Ministry for Science and Technology. She has published extensively in Brazil and abroad and is on the editorial boards of several national and international periodicals. Her research activities have covered theoretical and empirical issues. She is currently working on two research projects focusing on nation-states between globalization and localism, and on research on state, civil society, and market initiatives to reduce social inequalities.

Dani Rodrik is the Rafiq Hariri Professor of International Political Economy at the John F. Kennedy School of Government, Harvard University. He has published widely in the areas of international economics, economic development, and political economy: What constitutes good economic policy and why some governments are better than others in adopting it are the central questions he seeks to answer in his research. He is the author of *Has Globalization Gone Too Far?* (Institute for International Economics, 1997) and *The Globalization Paradox* (Norton, 2011).

Sergio Silva-Castañeda is a College Fellow in History and Senior Fellow for the Mexico and Central America Program at DRCLAS. A native of Mexico City, he studied economics at CIDE in Mexico and received a Ph.D. in Latin American History at Harvard. His dissertation topic was economic development under authoritarian rule, focusing on the cases of Mexico and Spain in the 20th century. He has taught in Mexico for the ITESM-CCM and has worked for the UN-ECLAC and the Mexican think tank CIDAC. He has taught courses on many different topics (from statistics to Colonial Latin America) in Mexico and at Harvard University.

Viviana Togores González is a researcher at the Centro de Investigaciones Psicológicas y Sociológicas (CIPS), in its Department of the Social Structure and Inequalities. Previously, she was an assistant professor in the Department of Economics and a researcher at the Centro de Estudios de la Economía Cubana (CEEC) of the University of Havana. Her research focuses on poverty, the informal sector, labor markets, cooperatives, and the development of small and medium enterprises in Cuba.

Pavel Vidal Alejandro is an assistant professor in the Centro de Estudios de la Economía Cubana (CEEC) at the University of Havana. He worked as an analyst in the Monetary Policy Division of the Central Bank of Cuba for seven years (1999–2006) and was head of the Econometric Models Group. His fields of specialization are monetary policy and time-series econometric models. He has been professor of macroeconomics and econometrics and visiting scholar at universities and central banks in Latin America and Europe. In 2010, he was a visiting researcher at the David Rockefeller Center for Latin American Studies at Harvard University.